Police Conduct, Complaints & Efficiency

Police Conduct, Complaints & Efficiency

Fraser Sampson
& Niran de Silva

Consultant Editor:
John Bowers QC

 Blackstone Press

Published by
Blackstone Press Limited
Aldine Place
London
W12 8AA
United Kingdom

Sales enquiries and orders
Telephone +44-(0)-20-8740-2277
Facsimile +44-(0)-20-8743-2292
e-mail: sales@blackstone.demon.co.uk
website: www.blackstonepress.com

ISBN 1-84174-123-X
© F. Sampson, N. de Silva, J. Bowers, 2001
First published 2001

British Library Cataloguing in Publication Data
A catalogue record for this book is available from the British Library

Typeset in 10/11pt Plantin by Style Photosetting Ltd, Mayfield, East Sussex
Printed and bound in Great Britain by Antony Rowe Limited,
Chippenham and Reading

CONTENTS

FOREWORD

This very detailed work considers the whole question of police officers' 'employment' status on their appointment to the office of 'constable'. The police are not 'employees' in the normal sense and do not enjoy many of the rights of other workers, such as the right to strike.

The authors explore the constitutional position of the police in the context of the new human rights legislation in Britain, dealing in detail with police efficiency, misconduct and the whole question of complaints against the police.

Rarely a week passes without new criticisms of police conduct and calls for 'independent investigation' of police actions. Indeed this was one of the recommendations arising out of the groundbreaking and influential report of Sir William Macpherson into the murder of black teenager, Stephen Lawrence.

This very readable volume is an essential tool for the practitioner in the police service, for lawyers dealing with questions of police conduct, and those simply required to understand this 'minefield' of employment law, and related regulations governing the police.

As a 'one-stop shop', it brings under one cover a reference guide in which I would have delighted, during my 35 years of policing both on the frontline and as a senior officer investigating complaints against the police.

I commend the work for its detail and its clarity.

The Lord Mackenzie of Framwellgate OBE LL.B (Hons)

PREFACE

The work of the police attracts a phenomenal amount of interest. A glance at the TV listings on any given day will testify to the peculiar and perennial appeal of policing as a spectator sport. As well as, or perhaps because of, this public fascination, the police receive their fair share of attention from other quarters — from editors and journalists, social scientists and politicians. And also, of course, from lawyers. As a result there have been many books about the police: about what they do and how they do it, what they should do, and what you can do about it if they don't.

However engaging and dramatic their work, police officers are still a part of the general workforce — a part that, in England and Wales, exceeds 120,000 personnel. In common with other sizeable sectors of the workforce, there are many self-evident reasons why police officers should be trained, supervised and managed in a coherent and effective manner. The nature of their duties, together with their legal status, however, puts police officers into an unconventional class of 'worker', requiring unconventional structures and mechanisms within the field of their employment. As public office holders enjoying considerable powers and privileges, the police should be accountable and responsible; as workers within complex organisations, they should receive appropriate treatment from those who employ and deploy them; and as men and women they should receive an appropriate level of protection for their own individual rights. The legal infrastructure through which it is sought to achieve a proper balance between these overlapping areas has grown considerably over recent years, culminating in the collection of new statutory regulations introduced in 1999.

When we sat down some two years ago, it was our aim to produce a book that would be of use to all who, for whatever reason, become involved in the realities of police conduct, complaints and efficiency. Our intention was to create a practical guide that would help such people navigate their way through the many legal and procedural provisions that surround the more prosiac but pragmatic issues of policing. What follows has been produced with that aim in mind.

The authors would like to thank Fiona Barton, barrister, for her helpful suggestions on the draft of this work.

Fraser Sampson
Niran de Silva
John Bowers QC
April 2001

TABLE OF CASES

TABLE OF STATUTES

TABLE OF STATUTORY INSTRUMENTS

INTRODUCTION

One measure of a true democracy is the accountability of those who police it. The accountability of the police in England and Wales has probably never been greater, both organisationally and on an individual basis. Many factors have contributed to this situation including a number of well-publicised inquiries and investigations, recent legislation and, most importantly, some determined efforts by the police service itself to improve the quality of service it provides.

Legislation such as the Police and Criminal Evidence Act 1984 and the Human Rights Act 1998 has placed significant restraints and checks upon the operational activities of the police. This and other legislation, together with the general supervision of the courts, has increased the accountability of the police in terms of what they may lawfully do. But that in itself is not enough. Police accountability in its broadest sense must not only be concerned with what the police do, but also with *how* they do it. This introduces issues of performance management and employee relations — as well as further legal considerations.

Before the service can improve standards of performance, tackle inappropriate conduct and promote professionalism in its widest forms, there must be, among other things, a clear framework that supports and enables those objectives. Although there have been rigorous legal mechanisms governing the recording and investigation of complaints against individual officers, along with regulations addressing matters of police discipline for over 40 years, the structure for managing performance and conduct within the police service of England and Wales has been less than clear — and, arguably, less than effective. Mechanisms that have become *de rigeur* for employers and employees in other industry sectors have not existed for the police service.

In 1999 the government introduced a number of statutory instruments in an attempt to provide the police service with a new legal and procedural framework for managing poor performance, discipline and complaints.

Although this framework drew upon some existing processes, it introduced a number of new concepts and a number of new roles; it also brought with it new rights and protections for individual police officers. Responsibility for supervising the various stages within this new framework has spread to all levels of police and civilian managers, many of whom will never have been involved in such processes before. To help chief officers and those under their command, the Home Office issued guidelines detailing the intended purposes behind the statutory provisions and aiding interpretation of the various Regulations. Nevertheless, the new framework is particularly complex and its responsibilities onerous. If it is to succeed, the framework must be understood by all those who become involved in its machinery, principally:

- police officers
- police supervisors and managers
- senior officers
- staff associations and representatives
- complainants
- panel members
- police authorities

and, of course, legal practitioners and advisers to all of the above.

Though the framework is still very much in its infancy, there are already plans to revise further the infrastructure surrounding complaints against the police. The purpose of this book is to provide a practical guide to all whose work brings them into contact with matters of police conduct, complaints and efficiency. It approaches each part of the various processes on a step-by-step basis, looking at the relevant legislation, against the background of overarching legal considerations such as the Human Rights Act 1998. The book is intended as an aid to help practitioners, advisers, 'friends' and panel members navigate their way through the many legal and procedural issues raised by this important development in police accountability.

But before doing so, it is perhaps worth remembering that police accountability does not mean police infallibility. Police officers and those who direct their activities will still get things wrong and no amount of legislation or regulation will change that. The real value of the new provisions can be found in their enabling framework which gives the police service robust mechanisms by which it can implement and maintain high professional standards — the same high standards which have been set by the majority of conscientious, committed and courageous officers for almost 200 years.

1   HUMAN RIGHTS

WHAT IS THE ACT?

The European Convention for the Protection of Human Rights and Fundamental Freedoms (the Convention) was adopted by the Council of Europe
in 1950, and came into force in 1953, for the purpose of protecting
individuals' rights against infringement by States.

The Convention has not so far been recognised as a direct source of law
by UK courts. It has, however, sometimes been used to resolve an ambiguity
in a statute; or as a guide in developing the common law when the common
law was uncertain.

The Human Rights Act 1998 (HRA 1998) in effect incorporates Convention rights further into UK law. The White Paper, *Rights Brought Home; the
Human Rights Bill* (October 1997), gave as the primary aims of this incorpora-
tion:

- to enable Convention rights to be enforced in the UK;
- to save time and money;
- to enable alleged breaches of rights in the UK to be decided by UK courts
  and tribunals;
- to increase the influence of UK judges on European case law; and
- to ensure closer scrutiny of human rights implications of new legislation.

The HRA 1998, which came for most purposes into force on 2 October
2000, has three main principles: that in interpreting legislation the UK courts
should have regard to the European Convention on Human Rights; that
public authorities can be sued if they violate the Convention rights; and that
the courts may grant declarations of incompatibility if statutes are in breach
of the Convention.

Interpreting legislation

Under the HRA 1998, s.3, all courts and tribunals in determining questions which arise in connection with a Convention right must *take into account* judgments of the European Court of Human Rights, so far as relevant and so far as it is possible to do so.

This goes beyond using the Convention as a way of resolving ambiguity in legislation; courts will simply not be bound by previous interpretations of existing legislation even by higher courts, a point made explicitly in the White Paper, if they are incompatible with the Convention. This rule of statutory interpretation applies whenever the legislation was enacted. As Lester and Pannick put it at para. 2.3.2 of their book on *Human Rights Law and Practice* (Butterworths, 2000): 'the role of the court is not (as in traditional statutory interpretation) to find the true meaning of the provision but to find (if possible) the meaning which best accords with Convention rights'.

Public authorities

Under the HRA 1998, ss. 6 to 8, all public authorities including the police must act in compliance with the Convention. Indeed, s. 6(1) provides that it is 'unlawful for a public authority to act in a way which is incompatible with a Convention right'. It is a defence, however, to show that the public authority was prevented from acting in accordance with the Convention as the result of UK primary legislation (s. 6(2)). If the legislation requiring the public authority to act in a particular way is subordinate legislation, the court may strike it down as invalid. An example might be where there is a statutory requirement to pass on information, as under the Vehicle Excise and Registration Act 1994 and that requirement is enforced by the police or the DVLA. If an individual successfully claimed that such a requirement unnecessarily infringed his/her Convention right to privacy (Article 8), the actions of the police and the DVLA (as 'public authorities') may well be protected by s. 6(2). The proper remedy in such a case would be to seek a declaration from a higher court that the legislation concerned was in fact incompatible with the Convention.

If a public authority acts in a way which is inconsistent with Convention rights, then a claim for a declaration, damages or an injunction will lie against it. The police are clearly public authorities.

Claims by victims

Under the HRA 1998, s. 7(1), a victim of unlawful acts by such a public authority may:

- bring proceedings against the public authority in the appropriate court; or
- rely on the Convention right in any legal proceedings.

The applicant must, in order to be able to mount a claim, be a victim of the act in question (s. 7(3)). 'Victim' is, however, narrowly defined in Article 34 of the Convention to which express reference is made in s. 7(7) of the Act. In deciding whether a person counts as a 'victim' the court may take into account the importance of the issue at stake in the proceedings and the presence or absence of any other responsible challenger of the conduct in question. This is a narrower test than that used in judicial review applications. These requirements are found in the case law from the European Court of Human Rights and principally mean that the person must show that he/she is (a) directly affected, or (b) at risk of being directly affected, by the act/omission complained of. There is no need for the person to have actually been affected by the act/omission, as long as the person can show a real risk of their being directly affected by it in the future.

There is clearly no role for 'public defenders' of human rights to be recognised (*Klass* v *Germany* (1978) 2 EHRR 214) in Strasbourg jurisprudence. Instead, the applicant must satisfy the European Court that he/she is actually and directly affected by the act or omission he/she wishes to complain about (*Klass*). The European Court has, however, accepted that 'a law may by itself violate the rights of the individual if the individual is directly affected by the law in the absence of any specific measure of implementation' (*Marckx* v *Belgium* (1979) 2 EHRR 330).

Remedies

Under the HRA 1998, s. 8(1), a court which finds that an act of a public authority is unlawful may grant such relief or remedy 'within its jurisdiction' as it considers just and appropriate. However, damages may be awarded only by a court which can award damages or order payment of compensation in civil proceedings (s. 8(2)), and damages are only to be awarded if they are necessary in order to afford just satisfaction to the victim (s. 8(3)).

Time limits

Claims may be brought within one year from the date when the act complained of took place or such longer period from the date on which the act complained was done if the court or tribunal considers it just and equitable to extend time. This is, however, subject to any rule imposing stricter time limits in relation to particular proceedings, e.g. judicial review (HRA 1998, s. 4(5)).

Striking a balance

Some of the Convention's provisions are absolute, that is, they do not permit any infringement under any circumstances. An example would be the right to freedom from torture under Article 3. Other rights are often limited or restricted in some way, such as the right to liberty under Article 5. Rights have to be limited if the 'democratic society' is going to work. If a person is lawfully arrested or detained, his/her right to liberty has been infringed but the Convention takes account of such situations and imposes limitations on that right. Similarly, there will be times when the freedom of an individual conflicts with the public interest, i.e. freedom of assembly (Article 11) and the maintenance of public order. These areas of potential conflict are of particular significance to the police and other law enforcement agencies.

In some cases, the rights of individuals may directly compete with one another. An example would be one person's right to freedom of expression (Article 10) and another person's right to respect for private and family life (Article 8). The potential for such rights to conflict, particularly in the areas of communications (see Chapter 3) and civil disputes (see Chapter 7) is painfully clear to most police officers — and will become more so now since the HRA 1998 has been operative.

What the Convention — and the European Court of Human Rights — sets out to do is to balance these rights against each other and against the needs of the democratic society within which they exist. For this reason, many of the Convention's Articles include any relevant limitations or exceptions. Although each is different, the approach of the European Court and the European Commission when interpreting their extent has been the same — applying the 'three tests'.

The three tests

Where the Convention gives individuals a particular right, any qualification or limitation on that right will be carefully defined and cautiously applied. Otherwise the effect of the Convention would be diluted by a series of 'get out' clauses or circumstances where the right could be easily overridden.

Generally, any limitations on a Convention right must be:

- prescribed by law;
- intended to achieve a legitimate objective;
- proportionate to the end that is intended to be achieved.

Each of these areas has a significant impact on the work of police officers and needs to be examined in turn.

The Convention as a living instrument

The Convention is also a 'living instrument which must be interpreted in the light of present-day conditions' (*Tyrer* v *United Kingdom* (1978) 2 EHRR 1). This means that its interpretation will develop alongside society without the need for older cases to be specifically overruled. If the acceptable standards within society become more tolerant (say, of consensual sexual activity or of behaviour in public), then the Convention should be interpreted and applied accordingly.

THE IMPACT ON POLICE CONDITIONS

As Lord Steyn said, 'A new legal order will come into existence when the Human Rights Act comes into effect' [1999] Public Law 55), and employment law will not be immune from this.

The Articles of the Convention which it can be predicted will have most importance in relation to police conduct and efficiency are:

- the right not to be subjected to inhuman or degrading treatment (Article 3);
- the right to a fair trial (Article 6);
- the right to respect for private and family life (Article 8);
- the right to freedom of thought, conscience and religion (Article 9);
- the right to freedom of expression (Article 10);
- the right to freedom of peaceful assembly and to freedom of association with others, including the right to form and to join trade unions (Article 11); and
- the right to enjoy the substantive rights and freedoms set forth in the Convention without discrimination (Article 14).

Before looking at these articles in detail, it is important to distinguish the different respects in which the HRA 1998 and the Convention may make an impact in police conduct law. They may be predicted to be as follows as against the police:

- by direct s. 6 HRA 1998 claims;
- in the interpretation of statutory provisions, in particular the exercise of discretion in discrimination claims;
- in the continued development of implied terms in the contract, especially that of mutual trust and confidence.

ARTICLE 3: INHUMAN OR DEGRADING TREATMENT

It has been held by the European Commission that causing mental anguish without any physical assault could be a violation of Article 3 (see *Denmark* v *Greece* (1969) 12 YB Eur Cony HR special Vol.). Oppressive interrogation techniques such as sleep deprivation, exposure to continuous loud noise and forcing suspects to adopt uncomfortable postures for prolonged lengths of time have been held to fall within the second and third categories of inhuman and degrading treatment (*Ireland* v *United Kingdom* (1978) 2 EHRR 25). In each case, it must be shown that the prohibited behaviour went beyond the 'minimum level of severity'. In determining whether the behaviour did go beyond that level, and under which particular category that behaviour falls, the courts will take into account factors such as the age, sex, state of health and general life experience of the victim.

ARTICLE 6: RIGHT TO A FAIR TRIAL

The Convention, Article 6 provides that:

> 1 *In the determination of his civil rights and obligations or of any criminal charge against him, everyone is entitled to a fair and public hearing within a reasonable time by an independent and impartial tribunal established by law.*

The basic requirements

The basic requirements of Article 6(1) in civil proceedings (which alone are considered here) are:

- a fair and public hearing;
- an independent and impartial tribunal;
- a trial within a reasonable period.
- a public judgment (although there are some exceptions to this); and
- a reasoned decision to be given.

It has been held that Article 6 applies to professional disciplinary proceedings (*Wickramsinghe* v *United Kingdom* [1998] EHRLR 338) and there is a strong argument for its provisions being applied to police disciplinary hearings. However, in a case arising from the denial of access to a solicitor during the conduct of a police disciplinary investigation the ECtHR has held that Article 6 does not apply — *Lee* v *United Kingdom* (2000) LTL 22 September 2000 (see Chapter 4).

Article 6 allows for the right to a public hearing to be restricted under certain circumstances but requires any judgment to be publicly pronounced. Article 6 has been interpreted as creating a requirement for 'equality of arms' in any civil or criminal proceedings (*Neumeister* v *Austria* (1968) 1 EHRR 91). Equality of arms requires that both parties be afforded the same opportunities to present their case and to cross-examine each other. Additionally, both parties should be given the opportunity to be legally represented.

Recruitment, employment and dismissal of public officials

Generally, disputes relating to the recruitment, employment and retirement of public servants have been held by the European Court of Human Rights to fall outside the scope of Article 6(1). There is also some jurisprudence excluding disputes about the recruitment, employment and dismissal of public officials, although as with much Strasbourg jurisprudence, the rationale and precise scope of the doctrine has not been clearly spelt out (e.g. *Neigel* v *France* [1997] EHRLR 424).

The prospect of an end to the uncertainty of when Article 6 would apply came in *Pellegrin* v *France* (application 28541/99) where the European Court held that a new functional criterion should be applied based on the nature of the employee's duties and responsibilities. In so doing, the European Court was giving an autonomous Convention meaning to the term 'civil service' irrespective of the domestic system of employment. The only disputes excluded from Article 6 were those raised by public servants whose duties typified the specific activities of the public service insofar as the public service was acting as the depository of public authority responsible for protecting the general interests of the State or other public authorities. The applicant in *Pellegrin* was recruited as a technical adviser to the Minister for the Economy, Planning and Trade which gave him considerable responsibilities in the field of the State's public finances, which was a sphere in which States exercised sovereign power. Thus Article 6(1) was not relevant. A clear example would be the armed forces or police. No disputes between administrative authorities and employees who occupied posts involving participation in the exercise of powers conferred by public law could use Article 6(1). The cases in the European Court of Human Rights suggests that police disciplinary proceedings are not covered by Article 6 (e.g. *X* v *UK* (1980) 21 DR 168; *Sygounis, Kotsisgournas* v *Greece* 78 —A DR 71). As already mentioned, the UK courts need only take account of these decisions and could extend the law further.

On the other hand, disputes concerning pensions all came within the ambit of Article 6(1) because, on retirement, employees broke the special bond existing between themselves and the authorities. An example of the latter in a police context is *Couez* v *France*, 24 August 1998 (unreported). The applicant, a police officer, had a heart attack during a cross-country race organised by his police force. He was refused his full salary whilst on sick leave on the ground that the injury did not occur in the performance of his duties. He was then transferred to an administrative position on the ground that he was permanently unfit for active police work. When he refused to transfer, he was compulsorily retired. The European Court of Human Rights acknowledged that 'at first sight' the applicant's claims appeared to relate to his career but it was willing to treat the claim as an essentially private dispute about the economic implications of the events which had occurred so that Article 6 was applicable.

ARTICLE 8: RIGHT TO RESPECT FOR PRIVATE AND FAMILY LIFE

The Convention, Article 8 provides that:

1   Everyone has the right to respect for his private and family life, his home and his correspondence.

2   There shall be no interference by a public authority with the exercise of this right except such as in accordance with the law and is necessary in a democratic society in the interests of national security, public safety or the economic well-being of the country, for the prevention of disorder or crime, for the protection of health and morals, or for the protection of the rights and freedoms of others.

This right includes respect for personal identity including sexual identity, moral or physical identity, sexual activities and personal relations. It is to be noted that the word used is 'respect', so that there is no absolute right to privacy as such. The right to respect for private life, however, clearly does not stop at the doors of the workplace.

Security measures

Security measures at work may fall within the scope of Article 8; thus a search of a lawyer's office was held to be in breach of the Article (*Niemietz* v *Germany* (1992) 16 EHRR 97). The European Court said that 'to interpret the words "private life" and "home" as excluding certain professional or business activities or premises would not be consonant with the essential object and purpose of Article 8'. In *Halford* v *United Kingdom* (1997) 24 EHRR 523 (the case involving Alison Halford, the Assistant Chief Constable of Merseyside Police) the then absence of domestic legislation dealing with an employer's right (or lack of right) to 'tap' telephone calls at work was found to be a breach of Article 8. In that case, the applicant (who was a senior police officer) had alleged that her office telephone was being tapped by her employers in order to obtain evidence to use in a sex discrimination claim which she had brought against them. The European Court held that to tap an office telephone was a *prima facie* breach of Article 8, unless the employer warned the employee that it was doing so.

In *Leander* v *Sweden* (1987) 9 EHRR 433, the European Court decided that storing information about a job applicant in a secret police register and releasing it to a prospective employer breached the right to respect for private life. This interference could, however, be justified as 'necessary in a democratic society' (the defence in Article 8(2)). Whether it did so in a particular case would depend on whether the action taken was proportionate to the risk posed. The use of such information for vetting candidates for posts which are *not* of importance for national security may be harder to justify.

Medical checks

The collection of medical data and the maintenance of medical records fall within the sphere of private life (*Chare nee Julien* v *France* App No. 14461/88 DR 141), and there may be interference when the employer collects highly sensitive health-related information about its employees. There was a potential breach in *MS* v *Sweden* (1999) 3 BHRC 248, 28 EHRR 313, where the applicant injured her back at work and claimed compensation under the Swedish Industrial Injury Insurance Act. The clinic which treated her disclosed her medical records in full to the Social Insurance Office without her permission. Whilst this was a potential breach, it was held to be proportionate in the pursuit of the legitimate aim of protecting the economic well-being of the country by ensuring that public funds were only allocated to deserving claimants. The European Court said that 'the domestic law must afford appropriate safeguards to prevent any such communication or disclosure of personal health data as may be inconsistent with the guarantees in Article 8'.

Failing to protect an individual from the unwanted advances of others, searching through an employee's office or directing employees as to where they can and cannot live would all potentially fall within the remit of Article 8, depending on the precise circumstances of the case.

ARTICLE 9: FREEDOM OF THOUGHT, CONSCIENCE AND RELIGION

The Convention, Article 9 provides that:

1 *Everyone has the right to freedom of thought, conscience and religion; this right includes freedom to change his religion or belief and freedom, either alone or in community with others and in public or private, to manifest his religion or belief, in worship, teaching, practice and observance.*

2 *Freedom to manifest one's religion or beliefs shall be subject only to such limitations as are prescribed by law and are necessary in a democratic society in the interests of public safety, for the protection of public order, health or morals, or for the protection of the rights and freedoms of others.*

Article 9 covers a wide scope of belief (beyond the purely religious) so that in *Arrowsmith* v *United Kingdom* (1980) 3 EHRR 218 at para. 69, the European Commission of Human Rights accepted that 'the attitude of pacifism may be seen as a belief protected by Article 9(1)'. A balance is struck between the needs of the religion and wider societal requirements including the concerns of employers which was most clearly articulated in *X* v *United Kingdom* (1984) 6 EHRR 558, where the European Commission stated that:

Article 9 primarily protects the sphere of personal beliefs and religious creeds . . . In addition, it protects acts which are intimately linked to these attitudes, such as acts of worship or devotion which are aspects of the practice of a religion or a belief in a generally recognised form. However in protecting this personal sphere, Article 9 of the Convention does not always guarantee the rights to behave in the public sphere in a way which is dictated by such a belief, for instance by refusing to pay certain taxes because part of the revenue so raised may be applied for military expenditure.

The Article clearly protects not only ideas which are favourably received but also expression which would be regarded as offensive to all or to a sector of the population. This is indeed when protection is most needed.

This is an important right, which has the potential to cover a variety of situations in the employment-related sphere. First, and most obviously, it presents employees of public authorities with a general entitlement to practise their religion and, more importantly, not to be disciplined or dismissed for doing so. This has the potential to go further than the protection afforded to employees (and prospective employees) by the Race Relations Act 1976, which protects individuals from discrimination on grounds of colour, race, ethnicity or national origin but *not* merely a religion or set of beliefs. Jews, Sikhs and gypsies have already been held to fall within the 1976 Act (*Mandla v Dowell Lee* [1983] 2 AC 548), but Rastafarians have been held to be a religious grouping only and not to fall within any of the prescribed categories. The same is probably true for Hindus and Muslims (*Walker v Hussain* [1996] IRLR 11). In a claim under Article 9, it is overwhelmingly likely that Rastafarians, as well as various denominations of Christianity and other world religions, will be able to claim protection.

Such guidance as exists from Strasbourg, however, does not suggest that Article 9 is a licence for employees to insist on time off to practise their religion during working time. For example, in *Ahmad v United Kingdom* (1982) 4 EHRR 126, a Muslim schoolteacher wanted to pray at his mosque for 45 minutes every Friday. The ILEA refused and relied on the contract of employment which clearly required him to work on Fridays. The European Court held that the ILEA's refusal did not infringe Article 9, since the employee had voluntarily accepted a teaching post which prevented his attendance at prayers (and had not complained, or requested time off, during his first six years at work). The European Court identified the issue as being whether, in relying on the contract of employment, the ILEA was arbitrarily disregarding the right to freedom of religion. To some extent this means that employers can contract out of their obligations under the Convention, provided they have good reason for doing so. Further, in *Knudsen v Norway* (1985) 42 DR 247, the European Commission said that Article 9 might apply where an individual is already employed but faces dismissal unless he changes his beliefs.

Secondly, Article 9 has implications for working on religious holidays and special days. However, in *Stedman v United Kingdom* [1997] EHRLR 545, the applicant was dismissed for refusing to work on Sundays in accordance with her religious belief. The European Commission rejected her claim, on the grounds that she was not dismissed because of her religious beliefs, but because she refused to work contractual hours. It did not consider at any length the point that her refusal to work contractual hours was *because* of her religious beliefs. A different result would have been reached in *Prais v EC Commission* [1976] ECR 1589 largely because of the less intrusive nature of the requirement to enjoy religious beliefs. The applicant, an orthodox Jewess, complained to the European Court of Justice (which itself must apply human rights principles) to the effect that the holding of exams on a Saturday in connection with a weekday job violated her rights under Article 9. Her case failed, but only because the date for the examination had already been fixed when she complained about it. Otherwise she would have succeeded.

The European Court has also emphasised that a balance must be struck between the religious views and the essential needs of the job, including the ethos of the organisation in which the applicant works. In *Kalac* v *Turkey* (1999) 27 EHRR 552, the application was brought to the European Court by a judge advocate in the air force with the rank of group captain who was the high command's director of legal affairs. He was compulsorily retired from that post because his 'conduct and attitude revealed that he had adopted unlawful fundamentalist opinions'. The principle of secularism was inherent in the Turkish armed forces and the European Court did not think that his rights were infringed.

ARTICLE 10: FREEDOM OF EXPRESSION

The Convention, Article 10 provides that:

> 1 *Everyone has the right to freedom of expression. This right shall include freedom to hold opinions and to receive and impart information and ideas without interference by public authority and regardless of frontiers. This Article shall not prevent States from requiring the licensing of broadcasting, television or cinema enterprises.*
> 2 *The exercise of these freedoms, since it carries with it duties and responsibilities, may be subject to such formalities, conditions, restrictions or penalties as are prescribed by law and are necessary in a democratic society, in the interests of national security, territorial integrity or public safety, for the prevention of disorder or crime, for the protection of health and morals, for the protection of the reputation or rights of others, for preventing the disclosure of information received in confidence, or for maintaining the authority and impartiality of the judiciary.*

In this respect, 'expression' covers words, pictures, images and actions intended to express an idea or to present information (*Stevens* v *United Kingdom* (1986) 46 DR). The exceptions to the right should be 'narrowly interpreted' and 'convincingly established'. Crucially, the right applies not only to ideas which are favourably received or regarded as inoffensive but those which 'offend, shock or disturb the State or any sector of the population. Such are the demands of pluralism, tolerance and broadmindedness.'

In the police employment sphere, the cases may be analysed broadly under the following heads:

- the right to political views and to manifest them;
- whistleblowing; and
- the operation of dress codes.

The right to political views and to manifest them

The crucial case for the exercise of political rights by employees is now *Vogt* v *Germany* (1995) 21 EHRR 205. Previous claims to speak out in respect of an officeholder of the State had been held not to be protected (*Glasenapp* v *Germany* (1987) 9 EHRR 25; *Kosiek* v *Germany* (1987) 9 EHRR 328).

Indeed, in *Glasenapp*, the European Court, holding that the applicant's rights had not been violated, said that in refusing her access to an office the public authority 'took account of her opinions and attitude merely in order to satisfy itself whether she possessed one of the necessary personal qualifications for the post'.

In *Kosiek*, Rolf Kosiek, a physics lecturer, was an active member of the extreme right-wing German National Democratic Party (NPD). It was a condition for appointment and for continued employment in the German civil service that he should abide by his obligation of loyalty and allegiance to the Constitution. He was dismissed because of the inconsistency between his political activities and writings and this duty of loyalty. The European Court held that the dismissal did not constitute an interference with the right to freedom of expression. Instead, it was held that Kosiek had been refused access to the civil service because he lacked one of the 'personal qualifications' for the post in question, namely the ability to give the requisite oath of loyalty.

Such an approach conflicts with the case law of the European Court which has recognised that sanctions imposed *after* publication can have a chilling effect and therefore interfere with freedom of expression. More recently, however, in the important case of *Vogt* v *Germany*, the European Court has sought to limit the application of the reasoning in *Kosiek* so that it would apply, at most, to conditions laid down for access to employment. Dorothea Vogt taught German and French at secondary school level. She was appointed as a permanent civil servant in February 1979 notwithstanding that the authorities were aware at that time that she was a member of the DKP (the German Communist Party). However, disciplinary proceedings were commenced against her in July 1982 on the grounds that she had failed to comply with her duty of political loyalty as a result of her activities with the DKP since August 1980. She was dismissed in October 1987 on the basis that by associating herself with the DKP she had betrayed the relationship of trust between herself and her employer. The majority of the European Court held that this indeed constituted interference with Ms Vogt's free speech rights as were protected by Article 10.

In any event, the gist of the decision in *Vogt* was a recognition that free speech rights are not given up when entering the workplace. A similar approach was taken by the Privy Council in *De Freitas* v *Ministry of Agriculture* (1998) 4 BHRC 563. Relying on *Vogt*, the Privy Council held that a provision in Bermuda and Antigua which prohibited civil servants from publishing information or expressions of opinion on matters of national or international controversy was unconstitutional due to the breach of free expression rights. The blanket restraint was held to be too wide, especially as it applied to all civil servants irrespective of how junior they might be.

The case of *Ahmed* v *United Kingdom* [1987] EHRLR 670 shows how the court reasons in such cases. This was an important challenge to the restriction on senior local government officers engaging in political activity set out in the Local Government (Political Restrictions) Regulations 1990. The first issue raised by the European Court was that the restriction was prescribed by law (although there was some uncertainty it was inevitable that such measures were couched in broad terms given that they were laying down rules of general application). It was in pursuance of one or more legitimate aims (that is, to protect rights of others, council members and electorate, to effective political democracy at the highest level); local government has long resided on the bond of trust between elected members and the permanent corps of local government officers who both advise them on policy and assume responsibility for implementation of policies adopted and this was necessary in a democratic society. The proper test to be applied was whether there was a pressing social need and States have a wide margin of appreciation in assessing whether such need exists. Thus the Regulations passed muster under Article 10. Similar restrictions for police are likely to be upheld in the same manner.

General restriction of freedom of speech

The nature of a particular employment may properly require some degree of restriction of freedom of speech. Thus in *Morissens* v *Belgium* (1988) 56 DR 127, the European Commission said that 'by entering the civil service [as a teacher] the applicant accepted certain restrictions on the exercise of her freedom of expression, as being inherent in her duties'. On the other hand, in *B* v *United Kingdom* (1985) 45 DR 41 the disciplining of an Aldermaston atomic weapons worker who criticised atomic weapons on a TV programme was found to be justified.

In *Rekvenyi* v *Hungary* (1999) 6 BHRC 556, the European Court considered a provision in the Hungarian constitution whereby members of the armed forces and police could not join any political party or engage in political activity. The Court recognised, especially in the light of Hungary's recent history, the legitimacy of the public being entitled to expect that 'in their dealings with the police they are entitled to be confronted with politically-neutral officers who are detached from the political fray'.

Whistleblowing

There may be some question as to whether the Public Interest Disclosure Act 1998 (which came into force 2 July 1999) is compatible with the Convention. It specifically excludes police officers from its ambit. 'Whistleblowing' is used to describe a worker who reports a matter of concern in relation to his/her current employer or employment. Only a limited number of disclosures are protected under the 1998 Act, and those disclosures must either be to designated persons or otherwise comply with strict requirements laid down in the Act. The right to freedom of expression of the worker derived from Article 10 may go further than this. Its extent depends on how the courts construe the limitation imposed by Article 8(2) that the right does not extend where the law (for example, the law of contract) prohibits such disclosure on the grounds that it may affect the reputation or rights of others (i.e. the employer).

In many cases where the restriction on freedom of expression relates to whistleblowing, it would appear likely that the restriction on expression could be said to be aimed at protecting the rights of employers. In *B* v *United Kingdom* (1985) 45 DR 41 a civil servant, who was also a local politician, participated in a television programme concerning safety at the atomic weapons research establishment at Aldermaston where he worked. The civil servant had been refused permission to speak on the programme and he received a severe reprimand which he challenged as being in breach of Article 10(1). The European Commission found that there was an interference with free expression but that this was justified in order to protect the rights of the employers. Similar reasoning would apply in most whistleblowing cases since an employee would rarely have permission to criticise the employer, albeit that in the particular circumstances protection of the employer's rights may not justify the interference. Indeed, interference need not even be for the purpose of protecting legally recognised rights. In *X* v *United Kingdom* (1979) 16 DR 101, the European Commission was prepared to accept that protecting fellow members of teaching staff from being offended by a colleague's evangelical posters and stickers fell within the meaning of 'protecting the rights of others'. Thus the European Commission was prepared to accept that there is a legitimate interest in protecting the rights of others not to be offended by speech.

Equally, where the employee is involved in raising concerns about the employer, the imposition of a sanction might be regarded as being effected on the basis of protecting the employer's reputation. In *Morissens* v *Belgium* (1988) 56 DR 127, a Belgian teacher was dismissed after she had sought to highlight discrimination against homosexuals by complaining on Belgian television that she was not appointed as a head teacher because she was gay. The European Commission held that the dismissal was in pursuance of the legitimate aim of the protection of the reputation of those whom she had implicitly suggested had refused to promote her on grounds of her homosexuality.

Even in cases which would not appear to fit neatly into any of the recognised categories of the legitimate aim set out in Article 10(2), such difficulties have been overcome by a flexible application of the legitimate aim test. In *Vogt*, for example, the insistence on political loyalty was imposed because, especially in the light of Germany's history in the last century, it was felt that there was a need for democracy to be able to defend itself and that the civil service was the guarantor of the German Constitution and democracy. On its face it is not apparent that defence of the constitution falls within any of the legitimate aims which can be pursued but the European Court appears to have accepted the German Government's assertion that the restriction was aimed at protecting national security, preventing disorder and protecting the rights of others.

In seeking to rely upon Article 10 to broaden the protection of the Public Interest Disclosure Act 1998, it will be in the interest of the whistleblower to emphasise that the matters raised are of public concern. In *Thorgeirson* v *Iceland* (1992) 14 EHRR 843 (a non-employment case), the applicant made claims of police brutality. The Icelandic Government contended in response for a distinction between political discussion in which freedom of expression should have full rein and 'discussion of other matters of public concern' in which expression could be restricted. This could have provided a severe constraint on the freedom of the whistleblower. However, the European court expressly rejected the proposition that the wide limits of acceptable criticism in political discussion do not apply equally to other matters of public concern. Equally, the margin of appreciation for the State in interfering with free expression was held to be correspondingly narrower in cases of political speech, and speech in relation to matters of public concern, than in other cases.

A similar approach was taken in *Barthold* v *Germany* (1985) 7 EHRR 383 where the applicant was quoted in a newspaper interview as being critical of the absence of emergency veterinary services at night. Proceedings were brought on the basis that this infringed professional guidelines restricting advertising. Injunctions were issued under Germany's competition laws restraining the applicant from reporting to the press (except in professional journals) the difficulties in relation to the night service and the problems experienced by his own practice. The European Court held that although this interference with expression was in pursuit of the legitimate aim of the protection of rights of other vets, it was not necessary in a democratic society. The newspaper article had sought to inform the public about the situation in respect of veterinary services at a time when new legislation was being considered. While the illustrations given by the applicant might have had the effect of publicising his own veterinary practice, the European Court considered that this was secondary to the raising of a matter of public concern. The European Court specifically expressed concern that if, as the German court had decided, an injunction could be imposed merely on the basis of an intention to act for a commercial motive, this could have a chilling effect in discouraging others from contributing to public debate. A ban on lawyers' advertising in Spain was upheld in *Casado Coca* v *Spain* (1994) 18 EHRR 1. Further, in *Jacubowski* v *Germany* (1995) 19 EHRR 64, the decision of a German court to enjoin a former editor publishing articles critical of his employers was upheld by the European Court on the basis of a wide margin of appreciation.

Where a whistleblower seeks to raise issues of concern as to the management of his employer, there may well be a question as to whether in the circumstances this raises issues of public concern. Some assistance in relation to this might be derived from the recent decision in *Fressoz and Roire* v *France* (case 29183/95), 21 January 1999, unreported. The weekly satirical newspaper *Le Canard Enchaine* published an article referring to salary increases awarded to Mr Jacques Calvet who was Peugeot's Chairman and Managing Director. The article was accompanied by extracts from Mr Calvet's tax assessments. The tax assessments could only have been obtained by virtue of disclosure in breach of confidence by a tax official, albeit that the identity of that tax official could not be identified. The journalist who reported the story and the editor of *Le Canard Enchaine* were convicted of handling the stolen photocopies. They then claimed that this was a breach of Article 10 of the Convention. In upholding this complaint, the European Court noted that the article related to a matter of public concern in that it was published during an industrial dispute at Peugeot over pay and showed that the Company Chairman had received large pay increases whilst opposing the employees' pay claims. The European Court rejected the argument advanced by the French Government that the disclosure of the remuneration of one person, even if he was the head of a major private company, did not contribute to debate on a matter of public interest and that the particular situation at Peugeot was too specific to be a matter of public interest.

Dress codes

The requirement by the employer of a certain dress code may raise issues under Article 10 (see *Burrett* v *Birmingham HA* [1994] IRLR 7). Some restrictions may be justified and proportionate. In *Kara* v *United Kingdom* [1999] EHRLR 232, for example, the European Commission dismissed an application from a bisexual male transvestite employed by the London Borough of Hackney as a Careers Adviser. He went to work in female clothing such as leggings, tights, halter-neck tops and a dress. His manager warned him not to do this as it was likely to break the Code of Conduct on 'appropriate clothing'. The European Commission held that this instruction was in accordance with law and a proportionate measure in pursuit of a lawful aim.

ARTICLE 11: FREEDOM OF ASSEMBLY AND ASSOCIATION

The Convention, Article 11 provides that:

> *1 Everyone has the right to freedom of peaceful assembly and to freedom of association with others, including the right to form and to join trade unions for the protection of his interests.*
>
> *2 No restrictions shall be placed on the exercise of these rights other than such as are prescribed by law and are necessary in a democratic society in the interests of national security or public safety, for the prevention of disorder or crime, for the protection of health and morals or for the protection of the rights and freedoms of others. This Article shall not prevent the imposition of lawful restrictions on the exercise of these rights by members of the armed forces, of the police or of the administration of the State.*

There are various respects in which Article 11 may give rights to workers, but the right to strike is the only right relevant to the police. There is no general right to strike guaranteed by the Convention. This was the clear conclusion reached by the European Court in *Schmidt and Dahlstrom* v *Sweden* (1976) 1 EHRR 632. This case concerned collective bargaining practices in Sweden. In the event that national pay negotiations continued beyond the date on which the annual pay increase was due to take effect, the normal practice was to give retroactive effect to the pay increase when it was finally agreed. However, it was a principle of the system that the members of any union which chose to strike during this period would automatically forfeit the right to benefit from this retroactive effect. The applicants in *Schmidt and Dahlstrom* claimed that this practice violated their rights under Article 11. However, the European Court found against them. It reasoned that the right to strike was not inherent in the right to freedom of association, and accordingly the State was free to restrict the right to strike as it saw fit.

ARTICLE 14: PROHIBITION OF DISCRIMINATION

The Convention, Article 14 provides that:

> *The enjoyment of the rights and freedoms set forth in this Convention shall be secured without discrimination on any ground such as sex, race, colour, language, religion, political or other opinion, national or social origin, association with a national minority, property, birth or other status.*

Article 14 is an unusual provision, narrower in some important respects than might be anticipated but wider in the statuses which are prohibited as grounds for discrimination than the national law. This Article does *not* prohibit discrimination by public bodies — rather, it prohibits public bodies from discriminating on the listed grounds (which includes the vague ground 'status') when complying with *other* Convention requirements. In that sense it is dependent on the other rights; there need be no breach of the Article but the allegation must come within the ambit of one of them. A key example of the operation of this aspect was *Abdulaziz* v *United Kingdom* (1985) 7 EHRR 471. The applicants were lawfully and permanently settled in the UK and complained because their husbands were refused permission to join them. It was held that there was no breach of Article 8 alone but there was a breach of Article 14 in conjunction with Article 8. Although it was legitimate to restrict admission of non-national spouses to the UK, it was not legitimate to distinguish between non-national spouses of males who were permitted entry and non-national spouses of females who were not.

The use of the words 'such as' and 'other status' indicates that the categories of prohibited discrimination are not closed; it includes sexual orientation, marital status, military status, status as trade union and imprisonment. Further, it covers a much wider range of subject areas than domestic law which is restricted to discrimination in employment, education and the provision of goods and services.

Unlike domestic law, discrimination under this Article can be justified by an 'objective and reasonable justification' for the differential treatment. This depends on the aim and effect of the measure; whether there is a reasonable relationship of proportionality between the means employed and the aims sought to be realised.

2 THE STATUS OF POLICE OFFICERS

INTRODUCTION

The law recognises various categories of worker. Whether a worker is classified as, for example, an employee, an apprentice, an independent contractor or a public-office holder will determine what rights and what duties he/she has in matters related to work.

STATUS OF POLICE OFFICERS AS PUBLIC SERVANTS

The status of police officers in the law is determined by the nature of their work. Although they are commonly described as servants of the Crown, the law draws a distinction between the service of a police officer and the service of an employee. As the duties of the former are considered to be in the realms of *public* service, a police officer generally has a wider discretion in carrying out his/her duties than an employee and is not considered to be subject to the control of the Crown or anyone else to the same extent as an employee is subject to the control of his/her employer. Note, however, that a police cadet is considered by the law to be neither an officer nor an employee: the role has a status peculiar to itself (*Wiltshire Police Authority* v *Wynn* [1980] ICR 649).

Thus, under the common law (the law originating from the early English communities and developed in the Royal Courts after the Norman Conquest) the Crown is not held responsible for the wrongful acts of a police officer in the way that an employer is for the wrongful acts of an employee. Similarly, in the case of *Attorney-General for New South Wales* v *Perpetual Trustee Co. Ltd* [1955] All ER 846, the Court ruled that the Crown could not bring a claim in respect of injuries to a constable in the same way that an employer could bring a claim in respect of injuries to one of its employees.

However, the House of Lords has recently held it to be at least arguable that the relationship between a police officer and his/her chief constable (or commissioner) produced duties that were analogous to those owed by an employer to an employee (*Waters* v *Metropolitan Police Commissioner* [2000] 1 WLR 1607). That relationship, together with the provisions of s. 88(1) of the Police Act 1996 (making chief constables liable for the torts of an officer under their direction or control) meant that a police officer could have a valid cause of action in negligence against the chief constable where that chief constable had failed to protect the officer against victimisation and harassment from fellow officers leading to injury.

THE STATUS OF POLICE OFFICERS UNDER STATUTE LAW

Statute law, in the form of enactments of Parliament, is generally regarded as supplementary to the common law. Whether or not a particular statute applies to police officers depends on the terms of the Act itself.

Statutes (or parts of statutes) whose application to the police is excluded

The Employment Rights Act 1996 (which consolidated a number of previous enactments) provides individuals with various rights relating to their employment. The 1996 Act also gives various rights to persons including police officers, in particular, the right to a written statement of terms, minimum notice of termination and redundancy payments.

However, a number of sections of the Employment Rights Act 1996 are excluded from application to 'employment under a contract of employment in police service' (s. 200). Accordingly, police officers do not have rights relating to:

- itemised pay statements (ss. 8–10);
- guarantee payments (ss. 28–35);
- protection from suffering detriment in matters relating to health and safety (s. 44);
- Sunday working (s. 45);
- acting as employee representatives for the purposes of consultation about redundancy (ss. 47, and 61–63);
- time off work (ss. 50–57);
- rights on suspension from work (ss. 64–70);
- maternity leave (ss. 71–85);
- written reasons for dismissal (ss. 92–93); and
- the right to return to work after childbirth (s. 137).

Most significantly, a police officer cannot bring a claim for unfair dismissal (ss. 94–134). Note that these exclusions used also to apply to prison officers (as a result of the decision in *Home Office* v *Robinson and the Prison Officers' Association* [1982] ICR 31) but they no longer do by statutory amendment.

The exclusions in the 1996 Act of unfair dismissal rights are somewhat qualified by s. 4 of the Police (Health and Safety) Act 1997 (inserting s. 134A into the Employment Rights Act 1996), which provides that police officers are treated as employees (and therefore have rights relating to unfair dismissal) for the purposes of dismissals on the grounds of health and safety (as defined by the 1996 Act).

An individual employed in the police service is also specifically excluded from all rights derived from:

- the Trade Union and Labour Relations (Consolidation) Act 1992 (for example, the right to consultation before redundancy and to freedom of access to employment); and
- the Disability Discrimination Act 1995.

Statutes which do apply to police officers

Police officers (including police cadets and special constables) are deemed to be employed by their Chief Constable (the chief officer of police) or by the relevant police authority for the purposes of:

- the Sex Discrimination Act 1975 (SDA 1975), s. 17;
- the Race Relations Act 1976 (RRA 1976), s. 16, s. 71.

The SDA 1975 and the RRA 1976 protect employees from three types of unlawful conduct: direct discrimination, indirect discrimination and victimisation.

Direct discrimination

Under the RRA 1976, a person directly discriminates against another if 'on racial grounds he treats that other less favourably than he treats or would treat other persons' (s. 1(1)(a)). 'Racial grounds' includes that person's colour, race, nationality, or ethnic or national origins (s. 3(1)). It is now settled that 'ethnic origins' is wider than 'national origins' and that an ethnic group may encompass religious, cultural and racial differences.

In *Mandla* v *Dowell Lee* [1983] 2 AC 548, Lord Fraser stated that there were two essential conditions for there to be an ethnic group for the purposes of the RRA 1976: a long and shared history and a cultural tradition (including family and social customs). In addition, he cited a number of other relevant characteristics, such as common language, religion or geographical origin. Thus Sikhs, Jews and Romany gypsies have been held to be ethnic groups whereas Rastafarians and Muslims have been held not to be (although action taken against, for example, Muslims such as the refusal to have time off for religious observance may constitute indirect discrimination against a particular racial group which has a large proportion of Muslim members such as Pakistanis or Bangladeshis — *J H Walker Ltd* v *Hussain* [1996] IRLR 11).

The SDA 1975 defines discrimination as less favourable treatment on the grounds of a person's gender (s. 1(1)(a)), marital status (s. 1(2)) or the fact that that person intends to or is undergoing gender reassignment (s. 2A(1)).

An example can be seen in *Chief Constable of West Yorkshire Police* v *A* [2000] IRLR 465, where a male-to-female transsexual was turned down for a police post on the grounds that she was still legally male and therefore could not lawfully search female suspects and prisoners beyond their outer garments. The applicant, who was born male but who then underwent gender reassignment surgery in adulthood, alleged sexual discrimination. The employment tribunal found in her favour and the Chief Constable appealed. The primary ground of appeal was that the applicant was not able to do the full range of duties expected of a constable, particularly in relation to the searching of individuals.

The Employment Appeal Tribunal considered the Sex Discrimination (Gender Reassignment) Regulations 1999 (SI 1999 No. 1102), which extended the 1976 Act to cover direct discrimination on the ground of gender reassignment. Section 7B(2)(a) of the Regulations allows an employer to rely on a Genuine Occupational Qualification (GOQ) where 'the job involves the holder of the job being liable to be called upon to perform an intimate physical search pursuant to statutory powers'.

However, the Tribunal held that the risks to the police in permitting the applicant as a transsexual to carry out the full range of police duties were so small that to deny her access to the office of constable would be 'wholly disproportionate' to the denial of the applicant's fundamental right to equal treatment. Section 7B(2)(a) of the regulations effectively imposed a ban on the recruitment of transsexuals to the police. Therefore, the Tribunal held, it offended Community law because it precluded the principle of *proportionality*: 'denying the applicant her fundamental right by reference to a form of searching which any police force can easily accommodate by calling upon another police officer to attend'. The Chief Constable's appeal was consequently dismissed.

In *James* v *Eastleigh Borough Council* [1990] IRLR 288, the House of Lords confirmed that discrimination occurs when, 'but for' her gender a woman would not have been treated less favourably than a man in similar circumstances. The 'but for' test applies equally to the RRA 1976. The complainant does not have to show that the employer's intention or motivation was to discriminate; it may have been an entirely benign motive but the effect may be to differentiate between persons on one of the prohibited grounds. Further, the person whom a complainant takes as a comparator (that is the person whom he/she alleges that he/she received less favourable treatment than) can either be a particular individual in similar circumstances or a hypothetical individual in similar circumstances. If it is a hypothetical person, the question for the tribunal is whether the complainant has been treated less favourably than another person would have been treated in similar circumstances.

Direct discrimination may also arise in the arrangements which an employer makes for determining who will be offered employment, in the terms in which employment is offered and in the refusal to offer that employment (SDA 1975, s. 6(1) and RRA 1976, s. 4(1)). Furthermore, under the SDA 1975, discrimination on the grounds of sexual orientation is unlawful (*MacDonald* v *Ministry of Defence* [2001] ILR 1).

Indirect discrimination

Under the RRA 1976, s. 1(1), a person *indirectly* discriminates against another if:

> *(b)   he applies to that other a requirement or condition which he applies or would apply equally to persons not of the same racial group as that other but—*
> *(i)   which is such that the proportion of persons of the same racial group as that other who can comply with it is considerably smaller than the proportion of persons not of that racial group who can comply with it; and*
> *(ii)   which he cannot show to be justifiable irrespective of the colour, race, nationality or ethnic or national origins of the person to whom it is applied; and*
> *(iii)   which is to the detriment of that other because he cannot comply with it.*

These provisions are mirrored in the SDA 1975 to protect women, men and married persons. Unmarried persons are not, however, protected from indirect discrimination (or indeed direct sex discrimination).

It is the potentially discriminatory *effect* of a requirement or condition applied to all which makes the conduct unlawful. The discriminatory effect (i.e. what proportion of the relevant group can comply with the requirement or condition as against the proportion of those outside the group who can comply) is measured by looking at the effect of the requirement or condition on a pool of workers in a similar situation to the complainant. The pool may be limited to the persons to whom the requirement or condition was in fact applied or may be a much wider group of workers (even the national labour force as a whole). Thus, in certain circumstances, complex statistical information may have to be assessed.

Cases of indirect sex discrimination commonly concern conditions of work (such as hours and shift patterns) which women find it hard to meet as a result of their child care responsibilities (see, for example, *London Underground* v *Edwards* [1998] IRLR 364) but any requirement or condition may be potentially subject to the test of indirect discrimination. In the case of *Greater Manchester Police Authority* v *Lea* [1990] IRLR 372, for example, Mr Lea applied for one of four vacancies as an operations room assistant with the police. He was shortlisted and selected as suitable by the interviewing officers. However, he was not appointed because he was in receipt of an occupational pension following compulsory medical retirement as a result of a road traffic accident. The police authority's policy was that in order to take account of the needs of the unemployed, those who were in receipt of occupational pensions or those who had accepted voluntary redundancy or early retirement as a general rule should not be considered for appointment. The authority was held to have discriminated against Mr Lea, and the Employment Appeal Tribunal said that it was not enough for it to be shown that the condition was imposed in pursuance of an intrinsically laudable and otherwise reasonable policy of helping the unemployed.

An example of indirect race discrimination by reference to area of appointment is *Hussein* v *Saints Complete House Furnishings* [1979] IRLR 337, in which the employer's rule that no applicant who lived in a city centre (broadly Liverpool 8) could be given a job (because there was a tendency for unemployed friends of employees to loiter in its shop) was held to be discriminatory where 50% of the population of Liverpool 8 was black or coloured compared to 2% of the population of Merseyside as a whole.

The key difference between direct and indirect discrimination is that what otherwise amounts to indirect discrimination (but not direct discrimination) may be justified by an employer. Where an employer seeks to justify an indirectly discriminatory requirement or condition, the justification for the requirement or condition will be balanced against the detriment to the individual in question. It is a question of fact for the tribunal whether a particular practice is justified.

Victimisation

Under the RRA 1976, s. 2, a person discriminates by way of victimisation against another if he/she treats that person less favourably than he/she treats or would treat another person in the same circumstances because the victimised person has done or intends to do any of the following:

(a)   brought proceedings against the discriminator or any other person under the RRA 1976;
(b)   given evidence or information in connection with proceedings brought under the RRA 1976 *by any person*;
(c)   done anything under or by reference to the RRA 1976 in relation to the discriminator or any other person;
(d)   made an allegation that the discriminator has committed an act which would amount to a contravention of the RRA 1976 (even if the allegation does not specify that there has been a contravention), for example, where an individual complains that the discriminator has racially abused him but does so without referring to the Act.

These provisions are mirrored in the SDA 1975, s. 4(1), by reference to claims of contravention of that Act, the Equal Pay Act 1970 and the Pensions Act 1995, ss. 62–65 (that is, claims for equality in occupational pension schemes). There is, however, a specific defence in the RRA 1976, s. 2(2) and the SDA 1975, s. 4(2) that victimisation cannot be claimed where the allegation made was false and not made in good faith. Therefore a complaint in bad faith (for example, one which is made for a collateral purpose other than a wish to complain of discrimination) which is based on false allegations will afford the complainant no protection and he/she can be dealt with without fear of having to defend a claim for victimisation.

The scope of protection against victimisation is illustrated by the decision of the Court of Appeal in *Waters v Metropolitan Police Commissioner* [1997] IRLR 589. In this case, Ms Waters alleged that she had been victimised (under s. 4(1)(d): allegation of contravention of the SDA 1975) following the making of a complaint of sexual assault by a colleague. As the assault was held not to amount to a contravention of the SDA 1975 (having taken place outside work (see below)), she was unable to bring herself within s. 4 and her complaint of victimisation failed. The case was considered in the House of Lords.

In the case of *Nagarajan* v *London Regional Transport* [1999] IRLR 572, the House of Lords (reversing the decision of the Court of Appeal), held that there was no need to show that the discriminator had a conscious motive connected to the RRA 1976: it was enough to show that the reason for the less favourable treatment (in that case, the unwillingness to employ Mr Nagarajan) was race, whether or not the discriminator was personally conscious of that. This brings the law on victimisation into line with the law on direct discrimination, where it has long been recognised that it is not necessary to show racial motivation to succeed in a claim for race discrimination.

An employer will generally be liable for the discriminatory acts of its employees and the chief constable for acts of his/her police officers. However, in proceedings brought under either the RRA 1976 or the SDA 1975, there is a defence available to an employer and the chief constable or other chief officer of police that it or he/she took such steps as were reasonably practicable to prevent the employee from doing the act or acts of that type (RRA 1976, s. 32 and SDA 1975, s. 41). An employer may rely on the fact that it complied strictly, for example, with its equal opportunities policy, its induction and training programmes, its disciplinary procedures and its conduct towards the discriminator to demonstrate that such reasonable steps were taken. It is important that equal opportunities policies be properly communicated and monitored if they are to provide an effective defence.

Discrimination and the police

As a result of the SDA 1975 and RRA 1976, police officers may bring claims for sex or race discrimination or victimisation relating to their work. Such a claim may be brought not only against the chief officer or police authority but also against the officer who is alleged to have committed the discriminatory act (see *AM* v *WC and SPV* (1999) 1 CR 1218). However, if the act of discrimination did not take place in the course of the employment of the officer who is alleged to have carried out the discrimination, the chief officer (or police authority) may not be liable.

Two cases illustrate the care which is needed in analysing whether the discriminatory act has taken place within the scope of the employment of the officer accused of discrimination. In the case of *Waters* v *Metropolitan Police Commissioner* [1997] IRLR 589, the allegation by Ms Waters was one of sexual assault by a male colleague. The Court of Appeal ruled that, as the alleged assault had taken place while both officers were off-duty, the Commissioner could not be held liable. The same principle would apply in claims for race discrimination. However, in the later case of *Chief Constable of Lincolnshire Police* v *Stubbs* [1999] IRLR 81, the Employment Appeal Tribunal found that the discriminating officer had acted in the course of his employment when he subjected a colleague to inappropriate sexual behaviour at a work party even though this was a private event which the chief constable had no role in organising. The Court noted, however, that the position might have been different had the discriminatory acts occurred during a chance meeting outside work. The case is at the outer end of the doctrine of imposed liability.

It should also be noted that the SDA 1975 provides that regulations made under the Police Act 1996, ss. 50–52, may treat female and male officers differently in relation to:

- height, uniform and equipment;
- pregnancy or childbirth; and
- pensions for special constables or police cadets.

On the issue of health and safety, the Police (Health and Safety) Act 1997, s. 1 (which inserts a new s. 51A into the Health and Safety at Work etc. Act 1974) provides that police officers are treated as employees for the purposes of Part I of the 1974 Act (which deals with an employee's rights in relation to health, safety, welfare and control of dangerous substances).

The Race Relations (Amendment) Act 2000 broadens greatly the scope of race discrimination law by making it unlawful for a public authority including the police to 'do any act which constitutes discrimination' (new s. 19B). Any public body must also 'promote equality of opportunity and good relations between persons of different racial groups' (new s. 71). The Secretary of State may impose particular duties on public bodies to ensure that they comply with these general duties (s. 71(2)). The Commission for Racial Equality (CRE) may serve a compliance notice in the event of failure to comply with such a duty (new s. 71D(1)), and in the event of non-compliance with it the CRE might apply to a county court requiring the person concerned to give any information required (s. 71E).

Statutes (or parts of statutes) whose application to police officers is excluded

Trade Union and Labour Relations (Consolidation) Act 1992
Disability Discrimination Act 1995
Employment Rights Act 1996 (ss. 8–10, 28–35, 44–45, 47, 50–57, 61–85, 92–134 except certain health and safety dismissals, s. 137)

Statutes (or parts of statutes) which do apply to police officers

Health and Safety at Work Act 1974 (Part I)
Sex Discrimination Act 1975
Race Relations Act 1976

Statutory liability for wrongful acts of police officers

Under the Police Act 1996, s. 88, the chief officer of police may be liable for the wrongful acts of police officers committed in the performance (or purported performance) of their duties (known as vicarious liability). For example, civil claims for negligence may be pursued against the chief officer as well as (or instead of) the officer alleged to have committed the wrongful act. However, one important limitation to this is when an officer negligently fails to identify and arrest a criminal where that failure results in his/her committing further offences.

Where a claim is being brought against a police officer or a chief constable for the negligent failure to identify and arrest a criminal where that failure results in his/her committing further offences, the ordinary rule, based on public policy considerations, is that the officer should not be liable (*Hill* v *Chief Constable of West Yorkshire* [1989] AC 53). However, in *Osman* v *UK* [1999] 1 FLR 193, it was held that this does not amount to a total immunity to the police and there may be other public interest considerations which may result in a claim being brought against an officer. In that case, the court held that the restriction on the applicants' ability to proceed in a claim against the police for negligence in the investigation of a crime was a disproportionate restriction on the right of access to a court and amounted to a violation of s. 6 of HRA 1998.

Common law liability for wrongful acts of police officers

A chief constable can also be vicariously liable for a breach of contract by a subordinate officer in his/her force (see *Savage* v *Chief Constable of Hampshire* [1997] 1 WLR 1061). This principle has recently been extended to agreements made by police officers with participating informants. Any agreement concluded between the officer and the informer in exchange for some consideration for the latter (usually a financial reward) may result in the creation of a legally binding contract. Moreover, the police officer may also owe the informant a duty of care. A breach of any contractual obligations or any duty of care may thereafter result in the chief officer being held vicariously liable. In a case brought against 10 chief constables by a participating informant who alleged that his identity had been revealed during interviews with suspects and at their subsequent trial (*Donnelly* v *The Chief Constable of Lincolnshire & Others* (2000) LTL 6 October 2000), the judge decided that he could not strike out the claim because of *Savage*, but that it was unlikely to succeed. (The recruitment and deployment of informers is now governed by the Regulation of Investigatory Powers Act 2000 — see *Blackstone's Police Manuals: Crime.*)

No right to strike

Police officers do not have the right to strike which is generally accorded to workers. Under the Police Act 1996, s. 91, withholding service is a breach of the police disciplinary regulations, and inducing a member of the police force to withhold his/her services is a criminal offence. Furthermore, although officers have the Police Federation, they are not allowed to join an ordinary trade union (unless they were a member of one before joining the force in which case they can retain their membership (s. 64)).

PROCEDURES IN RELATION TO CONDUCT, COMPLAINTS AND EFFICIENCY

There is a widely held view that, as police officers occupy a unique role within society, the highest possible standards of conduct should be demanded of them. Thus, when conducting their duties, in addition to being answerable to the criminal law, officers are answerable to a police disciplinary code.

Until the 1999 Regulations (see below) with which this book is largely concerned, police officers were subject to a disciplinary code and complaints procedure set out primarily in the Police Act 1967, the Police and Criminal Evidence Act 1984 and Regulations made under those Acts, in particular the Police (Discipline) Regulations 1985 which set out:

(a)   the disciplinary offences (e.g. disobedience, neglect of duty, drunkenness), which had to be proved beyond reasonable doubt;
(b)   the procedures for cases in which a police officer could be the subject of the following sanctions: dismissal, requirement to resign, demotion, reduction in pay, fine, reprimand and caution.

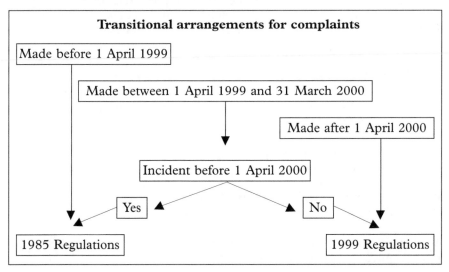

Constraints of the previous procedures

Many of those who operated the disciplinary procedures set out in the 1985 Regulations complained that these procedures were cumbersome, legalistic and unnecessarily lengthy. Furthermore, concerns were expressed, in particular by the Police Complaints Authority in its Triennial Review of 1991, about the high standard of proof required to secure the conviction of police officers for disciplinary offences. The Authority suggested that the standard of proof required for the conviction of officers for minor offences should be shifted from the criminal standard of 'beyond reasonable doubt', to the civil standard of 'the balance of probabilities'.

The Authority was also concerned about the rule against 'double jeopardy' in the Police and Criminal Evidence Act 1984, s. 104(1), whereby a member of a police force who was convicted or acquitted of a criminal offence could not be charged with a disciplinary offence which was in substance the same as the criminal offence.

Furthermore, the government and many chief officers were troubled by the lack of a procedure for dealing with an officer's unsatisfactory performance which was short of being a disciplinary offence, for example, lateness, poor appearance and failure to deal promptly with case papers.

THE NEW LEGISLATION

The foundation for the new procedures for police complaints and discipline was laid by the Police and Magistrates' Courts Act 1994 but the legislation is now set out within the Police Act 1996, which was a consolidating measure and introduced no new law itself. The 1996 Act also sets out legislation on other matters, in particular, on the organisation of the police force and on the liability of chief officers for the negligent acts of police officers committed in the line of duty.

The Police Act 1996

The Police Act 1996 sets out procedures relating to complaints against police officers. Those procedures can be divided into:

- dealing with the initial complaint;
- informal investigation;
- formal investigation;
- steps to be taken after investigation; and
- how the complaints procedure is reviewed.

In addition, the 1996 Act contains the enabling provisions which allowed the 1999 Regulations (see below) to be made.

Dealing with the initial complaint

The Police Act 1996 requires that, where a complaint by or on behalf of a member of the public is submitted to a chief officer, the chief officer should:

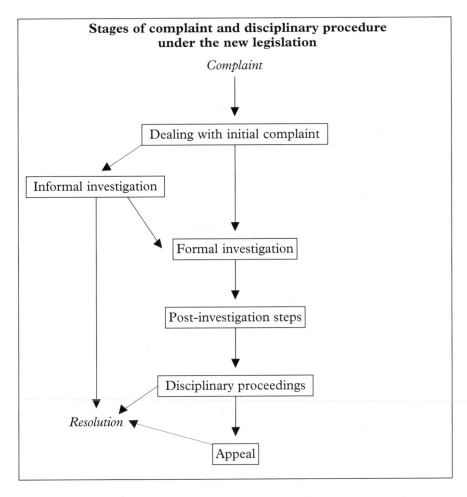

**Stages of complaint and disciplinary procedure
under the new legislation**

Complaint

Dealing with initial complaint

Informal investigation

Formal investigation

Post-investigation steps

Disciplinary proceedings

Resolution

Appeal

(a) take whatever steps appear to be necessary for the purposes of preserving evidence;

(b) determine who the appropriate authority is to deal with the complaint. For a complaint against an officer in the Metropolitan Police, the appropriate authority is the Commissioner, and for a complaint against an officer of any other force, the appropriate authority is the chief officer of that force. However, if the complaint is against an assistant chief constable or above, the appropriate authority is the police authority itself. (Sections 1 to 4 of the 1996 Act divide England and Wales into the relevant police areas which are listed in sch. 2 to the Act.);

(c) if the chief officer is not the appropriate authority, send details of the complaint to the relevant authority and inform the officer in question that this has been done;

(d)   if the chief officer is the appropriate authority, record the complaint and decide whether the complaint is suitable for informal resolution. The investigating officer must as soon as practicable inform the officer who is the subject of the complaint of the nature of the allegation. If the investigating officer delays until the conclusion of any criminal proceedings, this may entitle the officer who is the subject of the complaint to have the proceedings discontinued.

It should also be noted that, if the conduct complained of has already been the subject of criminal or disciplinary proceedings, the provisions of the 1996 Act which relate to the recording and investigation of complaints do not apply in respect of that conduct.

Informal resolution

The procedure in relation to informal complaints has not yet changed from the previous legislation (although the government has, at the time of writing, circulated some draft proposals in this area). Under the Police Act 1996, s. 69, a complaint is suitable for informal resolution only if the member of the public in question consents to it and the chief officer is satisfied that, if proved, the allegation would not lead to criminal or disciplinary proceedings. If attempts at informal resolution fail or if it appears that the complaint is not suitable for informal resolution, the chief officer should appoint an investigating officer to investigate the complaint formally.

Formal investigation

The investigation into the complaint is carried out by the investigating officer unless it is referred to the Police Complaints Authority. Under the Police Act 1996, s. 71, complaints alleging any of the following *must* be referred to the Authority for investigation:

- assault occasioning actual bodily harm;
- corruption (under the Prevention of Corruption Act 1906, s. 1);
- a serious arrestable offence within the meaning of the Police and Criminal Evidence Act 1984, s. 116;
- conduct resulting in the death or serious injury to some other person.

Any other complaint *may* be referred to the Authority. In addition, the Authority may itself require the submission of a complaint for its consideration. Furthermore, the chief officer may refer a matter to the Authority which is *not* the subject of a complaint if it appears that it ought to be referred by reason of its gravity or exceptional circumstances.

Post-investigation steps

Once the chief officer has received a report from the investigating officer or from the Police Complaints Authority, he/she must do the following:

- if he/she considers that a criminal offence has been committed, send a copy of the report to the Director of Public Prosecutions;
- if he/she does not consider that a criminal offence has been committed, in certain specified cases, he/she must send a signed memorandum to the Authority to that effect, stating whether disciplinary proceedings have been (or will be) brought and, if not, giving reasons;
- where a complaint was not supervised by the Authority, in certain specified cases, send a memorandum, a copy of the complaint (or record of it) and the report of the investigation.

If the memorandum states that the chief officer *will* bring proceedings, it is his/her duty to bring and proceed with them. If it states that he/she *has* brought proceedings, it is his/her duty to proceed with them.

Review of complaints procedure

Under s. 77 of the 1996 Act, police authorities and inspectors of constabulary must keep themselves informed of the workings of the complaints procedure. Under s. 79 of the 1996 Act, the Police Complaints Authority must submit an annual report on the workings of the complaints procedure to the Home Secretary and report any exceptional matters coming to its notice. At the time of writing the government has published a draft paper outlining a number of proposed changes to the police complaints system and, in particular, the 'independent' elements of complaint supervision.

The Police Act 1997

The Police Act 1997 made provision for the establishment of the National Crime Intelligence Service (NCIS) and the National Crime Squad (NCS), each with its own Service Authority whose duty it is to maintain the Service in question.

Sections 37 to 39 of the 1997 Act provide for the making of regulations for discipline and for complaints in relation to the conduct of members of the NCIS. Before the 1999 Regulations (see below) came into force, disciplinary regulations had been made in respect of complaints made by (or on behalf of) members of the service. These generally mirror the regulations in respect of complaints against the police under the Police and Criminal Evidence Act 1984.

Sections 81 to 83 of the 1997 Act make corresponding provisions for the conduct of members of the NCS.

THE 1999 REGULATIONS

The various 1999 Regulations make substantial changes to the manner in which complaints against police officers are dealt with. They were introduced under the Police Act 1996. The Police (Conduct) (Senior Officers) Regulations 1999 (SI 1999 No. 731) and the Police (Efficiency) Regulations 1999

(SI 1999 No. 732) were introduced under s. 50 of the 1996 Act. That section allows the government to make regulations about the administration and conditions of service of the police force. In particular, that section states that the regulations made shall establish or make provision for:

(a)   the establishment of procedures for cases in which a police officer may be dealt with by dismissal, the requirement to resign, demotion, reduction in pay, fine, reprimand or caution; and

(b)   securing that an officer holding a rank above that of superintendent shall be dealt with in any of those ways by the Commissioner of the Police for the Metropolis (for an officer who is a member of the Metropolitan Police) or by the relevant police authority (for any other officer).

The Police (Conduct) Regulations 1999 (SI 1999 No. 730) were introduced under ss. 50 and 84 of the 1996 Act, the latter section setting out what representation an officer should have at disciplinary and other proceedings. The Police Appeals Tribunal Rules 1999 (SI 1999, No. 818) were made under s. 85 of the 1996 Act which allows the government to make regulations as to the procedure on appeals to Police Appeals Tribunals.

FREEDOM OF INFORMATION ACT 2000

The Freedom of Information Act 2000 (FIA) gives individuals a general right of access to information held by public authorities. Police authorities and chief officers are listed in the Act as being within the definition of public authority (Schedule 1 Part V). Therefore they may be the subject of a legitimate request for information under the FIA. Such a request might be for information about matters relating to internal proceedings.

If a person makes a request for information from a police authority or chief officer, the authority/officer is under a duty to confirm or deny in writing whether or not it holds that information (s. 1(1)(a)), and, if it does hold it, to have that information communicated to him/her (s. 1(1)(b)). The FIA will, therefore, give internal proceedings a greater degree of transparency. If further information is needed in order to identify and locate the information requested (and the applicant is informed of this), the authority is not obliged to comply with subsection (1) unless it is supplied with that further information.

Information may, however, be exempt from the requirement to be provided if it is the subject of an absolute exemption (s. 2(1)(a)) or a qualified exemption, i.e. exempt on the basis that the public interest in maintaining the exemption outweighs the public interest in disclosing the information (s. 2(1)(b)). Examples of absolute grounds of exemption are the fact that the information is otherwise reasonably accessible to the applicant (s. 21), or that it relates to, for example, the Security Service (s. 23). Examples of qualified grounds of exemption are the safeguarding of national security (s. 24), and the likelihood of prejudicing the defence of the British Islands (s. 26). If there is a legitimate ground of exemption, the duty under s. 1(1)(a) to confirm or deny whether the authority holds the information does not arise.

3 POLICE EFFICIENCY

INTRODUCTION

Although there are procedures for dealing with allegations of *misconduct* levelled against police officers (see Chapter 4), there has been a lack of any formal internal structure by which police managers can address issues of perceived poor *performance*. The distinction here between conduct and performance is an important one and is discussed below. The formal system for recording and investigating complaints against police is generally inadequate and often inappropriate for tackling issues of performance management and it had been clear for some time that another, separate mechanism similar to those used by many private sector employers — and indeed, by police managers in relation to their civilian colleagues — was needed. Against this background, the government introduced new procedures to enable managers within the police service to tackle issues of poor performance, giving them an objective structure by which to evaluate and address any suspected failures to meet the required standard of performance by their police staff at an early stage.

These procedures are generally set out in the Police (Efficiency) Regulations 1999 (SI 1999 No. 732). The 1999 Regulations do not apply to:

- officers above the rank of superintendent;
- probationers;
- cadets; and
- non-warranted (civilian) staff,

each of which has its own specific procedures. For the provisions relating to officers seconded to 'central services' or working for service authorities such as the National Crime Squad, see Chapter 9. Cadets and probationers are also discussed in Chapter 9.

ACTION PLANNING

If there is to be any meaningful progress made by an officer during the period identified for performance monitoring, that performance must be supported and directed by an appropriate Action Plan.

Although action planning is becoming a regular feature of day-to-day management and many managers feel comfortable in their construction, there are several key features that are generally recognised as being essential to any effective Action Plan. These features have come to be known by the acronym 'SMARTER'.

S — Specific

If a person is expected to demonstrate skills or behaviour to another, he/she will need to have a clear understanding of just what it is that is required of him/her. This means that any desired behaviour or competency must be specified at the outset of the review period so that the officer concerned knows exactly what it is that is being measured.

Examples of specific objectives might be:

- to become competent in the use of a piece of equipment such as a roadside breathalyser;
- to become familiar with the correct sequence of documents/events in an internal administrative process;
- to conduct an operational briefing of a group of police officers;
- to attend and speak at a community forum.

This heading should deal with the 'what' part of the plan — What is the officer expected to do?

M — Measurable

The American management 'guru' Deming is often credited with the phrase 'if you can't measure it, you can't manage it'. Whether or not one subscribes to this view of performance management generally, it is clear that, in order to be able accurately to report back on an issue under review, there is a need to identify a measurable outcome in advance.

Workplace performance is notoriously difficult to measure accurately, particularly when subjective notions such as attitude are introduced. It is therefore advisable to avoid nebulous objectives that invite subjectivity such as 'to get along with colleagues' or 'to communicate views appropriately'. Qualifying expressions such as 'adequately' or 'properly' will also be difficult to measure at the end of a performance review. It is probably more constructive to identify the relevant competency from the force's internal rank/role description and to select the relevant descriptor(s) from it. The introduction of a new national competency framework (anticipated for April 2001) should greatly assist here.

Measures of performance may be quantitative (e.g. 'how many', 'how much' or 'how often') or qualitative ('how well' or 'how efficiently'). Quantitative measures can appear more attractive as they provide 'harder' data and are easier to evidence (e.g. 'how many HORT/1 forms did the officer issue to drivers of motor vehicles?'). They also provide an easy comparison with previous performance or the performance of peers. Such measures can be inappropriate, particularly where they relate to the use of discretionary powers by police officers (e.g. the number of people stopped and searched under the Police and Criminal Evidence Act 1984) where the measurement process itself becomes the sole reason for executing the power.

Peers, members of the community, managers and subordinates can all be useful sources of performance measurement data but the most important feature under this SMARTER heading is that the means of measurement is identified at the outset.

This heading should deal with the 'evidential' part of the plan — How will the officer and the reporting officer *know* whether there has been any improvement or not?

A — Achievable

If an objective is not achievable it is not an 'objective'; it is an unrealistic aspiration. Although there is much written about 'stretch goals' and 'striving for excellence' in high-performing organisations, any defensible and meaningful Action Plan needs to contain objectives that are realistically attainable by the officer concerned.

Achievability should be gauged in relation to:

- the time available;
- the knowledge and skills of the officer;
- the opportunities that will arise during the review period.

In addition to the practical considerations, officers undergoing a performance review might generally be expected to feel under some pressure — pressure which itself will affect their potential to perform effectively. There is little point in unduly adding to this pressure by imposing unrealistic objectives and deadlines. Moreover, in extreme cases, it might be suggested that the setting of unachievable targets is an abuse of authority by the reporting officer.

This heading should deal with the realistic nature of the plan — Can these things be done by:

- this officer,
- in this time frame,
- with these opportunities/resources?

R — Relevant

Another practical consideration is the relevance of the objectives to:

- the officer's overall performance; and
- the areas raised at previous stages of the process.

If the objectives and their measures are not relevant, why have they been set? Why should the officer achieve:

- these things,
- in this way,
- by this time?

This heading then deals with the 'why' part of the plan — Why is the officer expected to do this?

T — Timely

Timing is important as a feature of an Action Plan in several respects. First, there must actually be some finite time limit identified and agreed upon at the outset. Under the efficiency procedures this is in fact regulated by Home Office guidance (see Appendix 1).

Secondly, the amount of time allowed for demonstration of the required performance will impact upon the other headings set out above. Insufficient or unclear timescales may result in the plan being unspecific, unmeasurable and/or unachievable.

There are some aspects of performance where the collection of evidence of improvement will require a longer period than in others. This may be particularly relevant where there are several competency areas that need to be assessed.

Timing is also relevant to the Action Plan where a specific person is needed to assess and appraise the officer's performance, either for continuity (e.g. where the person is only available for limited periods) or where they have a specific and relevant role in the process (e.g. a crime manager or a supervisor from a specialist department).

This heading should deal with the 'when' part of the plan — When is the officer expected to do these things and when will the process be reviewed/ concluded?

E — Evaluated

The whole purpose of any Action Plan is to assess the extent to which there has been a change in relevant performance. This evaluative stage of the developmental cycle is even more important where the Action Plan forms part of a formal unsatisfactory performance process. The officer's performance must be evaluated against the relevant criteria set out in the Action Plan and within the agreed timescales.

This heading provides probably the most critical information, namely — How far has the officer's performance improved towards the required standard?

R — Recorded

Finally, every aspect of the action planning process must be accurately recorded. All stages of the process should be documented and updated as necessary. Once again this is of particular importance in unsatisfactory performance procedures as the need for evidence, both of what is expected of and ultimately achieved by the officer concerned is paramount.

This heading addresses the 'where' part of the process — Where is the relevant information to be found?

GRIEVANCE PROCEDURES

All police forces will have their own organisational grievance procedures. These will usually contain detailed instructions to members of the organisations — police officers and civilian staff — who are unhappy about the way in which they have been treated by colleagues and/or managers. Such grievance procedures are usually supported by equal opportunities policies, organisational values and 'mission statements'.

When dealing with matters set out in this book generally, but more so those within this chapter, it will be important to keep the various procedural mechanisms separate. Often the facts and evidence of the case may be relevant to two or more different aspects of internal organisational policy in addition to the legal processes being pursued. It is particularly important to identify the various deadlines and reporting levels/ranks and to separate the requirements of internal grievance processes from those set out in the relevant legislation addressed in this book.

Most grievance procedures follow various 'stages' (e.g. Stage 1, Stage 2 and so on) with each involving an interview/meeting. This can lead to some confusion as the Police (Efficiency) Regulations 1999 adopt a similar format but with an entirely different purpose. Adding to the potential for confusion, the Home Office Guidance document on the efficiency procedures makes reference to 'first and second stage' interviews (as opposed to 'first interview and second interview' which is the term used in the 1999 Regulations) and the sample forms in the appendix to that document follow the same terminology (see Appendix 1).

A WORD ABOUT COMPETENCE

What's the difference between a competence and a competency? This is a pertinent question which ought to be answerable by every manager, particularly those who are involved in implementing competency matrices such as those being introduced into the police service. While many people use these increasingly popular bits of jargon as if they were interchangeable, there is more to distinguish a competence from a competency than a carelessly inserted 'y'.

Far from being co-terminous, these two important features of measurement describe different aspects, or incremental stages of a person's performance and therefore have very different functions.

Competence

What is a competence? A competence can be seen as referring to the basic demonstration of an activity which is assessed with a 'yes' or 'no'; you are either competent or you are not. Such competences represent the first stage of performance measurement and can be grouped together to form a checklist against which a person's ability might be tested — a little like an MOT for a car. Successful completion in the workplace may allow a person to use a piece of equipment or to carry out particular tasks. In each case the person is showing simply that they are 'competent' in the execution of those activities.

Take, for example, assessing an officer's competence with the PR-24 baton. One aspect of the training in the baton's use might be to draw it from the user's weak side. If the officer succeeds in drawing the baton from their weak side, they have demonstrated *competence* in this area and that fact is recorded. The assessor does not award marks for artistic interpretation, but simply notes whether or not the officer did in fact draw the baton as required.

Competency

A *competency* on the other hand describes, not only *what* was done but also *how* it was done. It almost begs an adjective. How did the officer draw the baton? Purposefully, inconspicuously, nervously?

In terms of its complexity, competency represents the next stage in performance measurement. Being concerned with more than mere sufficiency, competencies reflect variation in levels of performance. They are therefore much more difficult to *define* and also to *measure*, two key principles in any meaningful assessment of performance. Clearly it is far easier to describe and evidence an officer's ability to draw a baton (competence) than to capture their capacity for innovation or their ability to deal with conflict (competency).

It can be seen then that competencies represent 'softer', more evanescent skills than hard yes/no competences, often requiring observation over a period of time. Softer still are critical notions such as loyalty, integrity and commitment. These features, at the next level of complexity, describe neither the competent demonstration of an activity, nor the way in which the activity is carried out. So what are they? Some commentators have suggested that they are best regarded as 'behaviours' which can be either morally or intellectually based. These behaviours — which relate closely to the values of an individual — would include such areas as loyalty and trustworthiness. Standing at the opposite extreme of the competence/behaviour spectrum, it may well be that they are incapable of being measured and evidenced with any great degree of reliability.

Does it matter?

As many forces begin to create competency matrices and pursue competence-based training, and as the Home Office prepares to launch a national competency matrix for the police service as a whole, this area is becoming increasingly relevant to police managers generally. In the area of performance measurement, improvement and the Police (Efficiency) Regulations processes it is even more so.

In order to design, deliver or decipher the results of exercises, courses, events and appraisals which purport to measure an individual's skills and abilities it is important to have a clear understanding of what it is that is being measured. It is also important to understand how far that activity or behaviour is measurable at all. Recruitment exercises, skills assessment, staff development and appraisal systems all need to reflect this reality in both their objectives and their methodology.

So yes, there is a difference between competence and competency which goes beyond the changing of one letter — just as there is with aptitude and attitude — and, yes, it does matter if accurate and reliable reports of performance measurement are to be achieved.

POLICE EFFICIENCY

Even under the new Code of Conduct for police officers (see Chapter 4) the focus is still on enforcement and punishment, with the process following a linear path from first report, through the investigative stages to ultimate sanction or disposal. In matters of perceived poor performance however, the process is designed to be cyclical, with the emphasis being on:

- the early identification of problems, followed by
- discussion and agreement on action and
- provision of an opportunity to improve, followed by
- a monitoring period, followed by
- a review of performance and further agreement and action as appropriate.

These notions of providing the under-performing officer with guidance, action plans and structured opportunities to improve are key features of this new process and can be found right up until after any formal inefficiency hearing has started. In other words, from the point of view of the officer concerned, it is rarely 'too late' to show a sufficient improvement. Clearly there needs to be an end to the process somewhere and that final stage may well involve sanctions but the general tenor of the process is ultimately intended to be *developmental*. As well as being apparent from the wording and provisions of the Police (Efficiency) Regulations 1999 themselves, this developmental nature of the procedures, together with the importance of managerial discretion, is echoed throughout the Home Office guidance to chief officers (see Appendix 1).

The Police (Efficiency) Regulations 1999

Unlike several of the other Regulations covered in this book, the Police (Efficiency) Regulations 1999 (SI 1999 No. 732) (see Appendix 2) have no equivalent predecessor. Made under the Police Act 1996, s. 50, the 1999 Regulations establish procedures for the management — and ultimately the punishment — of officers whose performance is felt to be unsatisfactory. In the majority of cases, general managerial discretion and appropriate words of guidance will probably suffice. In other cases, however, there may be a need to invoke the formal procedures set out below. The Regulations came into force on 1 April 1999.

Definitions

Most of the general terms used throughout the Police (Efficiency) Regulations 1999 can be found in reg. 3, the principal ones being:

- 'Countersigning officer' — a member of the police force concerned who has supervisory responsibility and who is senior in rank to the reporting officer. Given the comments on 'member concerned' below, the countersigning officer will be a police officer and will usually be an inspector or chief inspector.
- 'Interviewing officer' — the officer who conducts a 'first interview' (see reg. 4).
- 'Member concerned' — the member of a police force in respect of whom proceedings under these regulations are, or are proposed to be, taken. Although a key expression in the Regulations, 'member of a police force' is not itself defined. There is no definition in the parent Act (the Police Act 1996), but the use of the expression throughout both the Regulations and the Act (especially in s. 29 of the Act) would suggest that it can only refer to a sworn police constable (as it does in the Police Pensions Act 1976). This interpretation, which also finds support in the Home Office guidance to chief officers, is used throughout this book.
- 'Personnel officer' — a person employed under the Police Act 1996, s. 15 (a civilian) or a police officer who, in either case, has responsibility for personnel matters relating to members of the force to which the member concerned belongs.
- 'Reporting officer' — a member of the police force concerned who has the *immediate supervisory responsibility* for the member concerned. Given the discussion relating to 'member concerned' above, the reporting officer will also be a police officer. Unlike the countersigning officer, the reporting officer must have immediate supervisory responsibility for the officer whose performance is in question; it is not enough for an officer with general supervisory responsibility within the organisation to act as the reporting officer. For most practical purposes, the reporting officer is likely to be a sergeant or inspector.

- 'Senior manager' — the officer who is for the time being the supervisory officer of the countersigning officer. Although reg. 3 uses the expression 'officer' here, there is no requirement that the senior manager be a *police* officer. Given the rest of the definition, it is likely that the senior manager will, in many cases, be a chief inspector or superintendent. Where the member concerned is a superintendent, the 'senior manager' will be his/her supervising officer but again there is no stipulation that this must be a police officer and might, for instance, be an unsworn member of the force's command team.

First interview

The Police (Efficiency) Regulations 1999, reg. 4 provides that:

Where the reporting officer for a member of a police force is of the opinion that the performance of that member is unsatisfactory, he may require the member concerned to attend an interview (in these Regulations referred to as a first interview) to discuss the performance of the member concerned.

Practice Note

For 'reporting officer' (see above). Where the officer's immediate supervisor is a civilian member of staff, a police officer having supervisory responsibility for the 'member concerned' will need to be identified — although he/she will probably need to consult closely with the civilian supervisor.

The 1999 Regulations only require that the reporting officer be *of the opinion* that the performance of the officer concerned is unsatisfactory. However, single instances of poor performance would not generally be enough to invoke these Regulations and, as discussed in Chapter 2 above, the instigation of formal proceedings would not normally happen before much day-to-day supervisory discretion had been applied.

There are two features within the content of reg. 4 that reinforce the developmental tone of the efficiency procedures. The first is the purpose of the first interview which is to *discuss* the performance of the officer concerned. This makes it clear that, despite their name, the first and subsequent 'interviews' are not intended to be one-way cross-examinations or an adversarial presentation of facts. They are intended as an opportunity to discuss with the officer concerned those areas in which his/her performance is observed to be falling short and to agree some remedial action (as to which, see Chapter 3).

The second feature of reg. 4 that corroborates this developmental aspect of the process is the fact that the regulation does not impose an *obligation* on the reporting officer to order an interview; rather the decision to do so is left to his/her supervisory discretion. (There is an occasion where the discretion in requiring a first interview is removed under reg. 18 (see below)).

Although the 1999 Regulations do not say so, it would seem fair that, in assessing the 'performance' of the member concerned, nothing done before April 1999 is taken into account.

The source of the reporting officer's 'opinion' may be from internal observations and reports made by other people within the organisation, but it may also arise from members of the public. Although the procedures for performance improvement and the investigation of complaints (see Chapter 4) are quite separate, there may be cases where there is an overlap.

Arranging first interview

The Police (Efficiency) Regulations 1999, reg. 5 provides that:

> *(1)   If the reporting officer decides to require a member of a police force to attend a first interview, he shall—*
> *(a)   send a notice in writing to the member concerned—*
> *(i)   requiring him to attend, at a specified time and place, an interview with the reporting officer or, if the member concerned so requests, the countersigning officer;*
> *(ii)   stating the reasons why his performance is considered unsatisfactory;*
> *(iii)   informing him that he may seek advice from a representative of his staff association and be accompanied at the interview by a member of a police force selected by him; and*
> *(b)   send a copy of the notice to the countersigning officer.*
> *(2)   A member of a police force who receives a notice pursuant to paragraph (1) may, not later than 7 days (or such longer period as the reporting officer may permit when sending the notice under paragraph (1)(a)) after the date on which the notice was received by him, request by notice in writing that the interview be conducted by the countersigning officer; and if the member concerned so requests the interview shall be conducted by the countersigning officer.*

Practice Note

It is for the officer concerned to request that a countersigning officer conduct the interview. In the absence of such a request, the reporting officer will conduct the first interview.

The 'countersigning officer' will be a police officer and is the person having supervisory responsibility and who is senior in rank to the reporting officer (as to which, see reg. 4 above). In many cases the countersigning officer will be an inspector although the wording of reg. 5 does not require that officer to have any particular responsibility *for the officer concerned*. Again, if the relevant line manager for the member concerned is a civilian member of staff, the countersigning officer will probably have to liaise closely with him/her.

It is important to note that any superintendent or assistant chief constable/commander who attends or *is otherwise involved in* the first interview is barred from appearing on the panel of any later inefficiency hearing involving the member concerned (see below).

The 'first interview' will be with the reporting officer unless the officer concerned asks for it to be with the countersigning officer. There is, however, a general time limit on making that request (reg. 5(2)).

Unlike some of the other procedures in this chapter, there does not appear to be any restriction on the timing of the first interview.

The responsibility for sending out the notice containing the details set out at reg. 5(1)(a)(i) to (iii) falls to the reporting officer. The notice, which must be copied to the countersigning officer, must advise the officer concerned that he/she may seek advice from the relevant staff association representative *and* that he/she may select another officer (as opposed to an unsworn or civilian colleague) from *any* police force, to accompany him/her to the interview. This 'friend' is able to advise and assist the officer concerned, to speak on the officer's behalf and to produce witnesses and exhibits where appropriate. Frequently, the friend will be a representative from the officer's staff association such as the Police Federation or the Superintendents' Association.

The notice must also set out the *reasons* why the member's performance is considered to be unsatisfactory. Despite the developmental nature of the efficiency process, the effect of serving a notice under reg. 5 should not be underestimated. Although the requirement to attend a first interview should not come as a surprise to the officer concerned, the serving of a notice under reg. 5 may still have a considerable impact.

It will be important to record the timing of the decision to require a first interview, not least because there may be a suggestion later that the decision was only made in response to the officer concerned complaining of discriminatory behaviour against him/her. Unless such a record is available, the officer may claim that the instigation of the poor performance procedures amounted to 'victimisation' (as to which, see Chapter 2).

Procedure at first interview

The Police (Efficiency) Regulations 1999, reg. 6 provides that:

> *(1)   The following provisions of this regulation apply to the procedure to be followed at the first interview.*
> *(2)   The interviewing officer shall—*
> *(a)   explain to the member concerned the reasons why the reporting officer is of the opinion that the performance of that member is unsatisfactory; and*
> *(b)   provide the member concerned, or the member of a police force who has accompanied him to the interview, or both of them, with an opportunity to make representations in response.*

Practice Note

The 'interviewing officer' is the person conducting the first interview (reg. 3(1)) and could be either the reporting officer or the countersigning officer.

The interviewing officer is under an obligation to explain to the officer concerned the reasons *why* his/her performance has been unsatisfactory, and this reinforces the need for accurate and objective assessment and record keeping discussed in Chapter 3. Without clearly evidenced examples, the interviewing officer would find it difficult to explain his/her *own* opinion as to the officer's performance let alone the opinion of someone else (namely the reporting officer) as required here.

Having explained the reasons why the officer's performance is unsatisfactory, the interviewing officer must provide the member, his/her 'friend' *or both*, with an opportunity to make representations in response. This suggests that a reasonable amount of time must be allowed for the making of such representations.

Those representations must be 'considered' by the interviewing officer, not simply acknowledged or dismissed and the interviewing officer cannot simply impose some pre-drafted action plan or strategy for improvement. It may be that the interviewing officer should adjourn the first interview (under reg. 6(5)) in order fully to consider the officer's representation. Failure to give proper consideration to those representations may lead to the process being challenged on the grounds of natural justice (as to which, see Chapter 10).

Regulation 6 goes on to provide that:

> *(3)   If after considering any representations made in accordance with paragraph (2)(b), the interviewing officer is satisfied that the performance of the member concerned has been unsatisfactory, he shall—*
>
> *(a)   inform the member concerned in what respect his performance is considered unsatisfactory;*
>
> *(b)   warn the member concerned of any specific action which he is required to take to achieve an improvement in his performance; and*
>
> *(c)   warn the member concerned that, if a sufficient improvement is not made within such reasonable period as the interviewing officer shall specify, he may be required to attend a second interview in accordance with regulation 9.*
>
> *(4)   The interviewing officer may, if he considers it appropriate, recommend that the member concerned seek assistance in relation to any matter affecting his health or welfare.*
>
> *(5)   The interviewing officer may adjourn the interview to a specified later time or date if it appears to him necessary or expedient to do so.*

Practice Note

The interviewing officer, having so considered the representations made, must carry out the actions set out in reg. 6(3)(a) to (c), provided he/she is 'satisfied' that the officer's performance has been unsatisfactory. In so 'satisfying' himself/herself in this respect, the interviewing officer should be able to justify and explain how he/she arrived at that decision.

The expression 'warn' at reg. 6(3)(b) seems odd in this context, particularly when the word 'inform' is used at the next stage (see below), but the 'warning' is referred to again later in reg. 8 (as to which, see below). Whatever the terminology, the interviewing officer must tell the officer concerned what he/she must do to achieve an improvement in his/her performance. Under reg. 6(3)(c), the interviewing officer must specify a 'reasonable period' during which this improvement is to take place. This would appear to be normally no less than three, and probably no more than six months.

Regulation 6 makes specific provision for the situation where the officer's performance may have been affected by his/her *health or welfare* and these matters should be explored in an appropriate way. Most, if not all police forces have a welfare officer together with a policy for identifying and addressing such issues. Similarly, it may be that the officer concerned is experiencing some form of workplace harassment or bullying and again police forces will have clearly publicised policies and procedures for dealing with such matters. For the disciplinary offences of overbearing conduct and abuse of authority, see Chapter 4.

Regulation 6 says nothing about what must be done if the interviewing officer does *not* find the officer's performance to be unsatisfactory. Presumably the issue comes to a halt at this stage, although the reporting requirements under reg. 7 (see below) appear to apply irrespective of the outcome of the first interview.

The 1999 Regulations are also silent on the issue of recording this stage of the process. Given the importance of record keeping throughout the entire process, it would be inadvisable not to make a full note of any first interview irrespective of its outcome.

After first interview

The Police (Efficiency) Regulations 1999, reg. 7 provides that:

> *(1)   The interviewing officer shall, not later than 7 days after the date of the conclusion of the first interview—*
>
> *(a)   cause to be prepared a written record of the substance of the matters discussed at the interview; and*
>
> *(b)   send one copy or, where the member concerned was accompanied at the interview by a member of a police force selected by him, two copies of that record to the member concerned together with a notice in writing informing him that he may submit written comments, or indicate that he has no comment to make, not later than 7 days after the date on which the copy is received by him.*
>
> *(2)   Subject to paragraph (3), the member concerned shall be entitled to submit written comments in relation to the record of the interview to the interviewing officer not later than 7 days after the date on which the copy is received by him.*
>
> *(3)   The interviewing officer may, on the application of the member concerned, extend the period specified in paragraph (2) if he is satisfied that it is appropriate to do so.*

Practice Note

The written record need not be a verbatim account of all that took place at the first interview but it must summarise the 'substance' of the matters discussed including, it may be presumed, any representations made by the officer or any 'friend'. If the officer concerned does not agree with the record, he/she may raise this is the form of written comments submitted under reg. 7(2).

If the officer concerned was accompanied by a friend, two copies of the record must be sent *to the officer*. The requirement under reg. 7(1)(b), to *send* the member one or two copies of the record suggests that there is no need for personal service. The seven-day period for responding to the service of the documents begins when the copy of the record *is received by the officer*. This would mean that, if the officer were on annual leave or was otherwise unable to receive the posted documents at the place to which they were sent, he/she may not have 'received' them. If so, the time limit should not begin until he/she physically receives the documents. If the member concerned applies for the time period to be extended, the interviewing officer may do so if it seems appropriate. The interviewing officer cannot extend the time period of his/her own volition.

Any written comments received by the interviewing officer must be retained with the record of interview (reg. 7(5)). Records of any stage of the unsatisfactory performance procedures will be expunged from an officer's personal record after two years have elapsed since the last action was taken (or the last review/appeal was heard (see below)). This is similar to the corresponding provision for civilian employees under the ACAS Code of Practice (although there is no specific time limit set out in that Code).

Other copies

Regulation 7 goes on to provide that:

(4)   The interviewing officer shall send a copy of the record of the interview, and of any written comments of the member concerned, to—
   (a)   the senior manager;
   (b)   the personnel officer; and
   (c) (i)   if the interview was conducted by the reporting officer, the counter-signing officer; or
      (ii)   if the interview was conducted by the countersigning officer, the reporting officer.
(5)   If the interviewing officer receives any written comments under paragraph (2), he shall ensure that they are retained with the record of the interview.

Practice Note

'Senior manager' means the officer who is for the time being the supervisory officer of the countersigning officer (reg. 3(1)(a)). Although the 1999 Regulations do not specify that this person must be a 'member of a police force' — and therefore need not be a police officer — the senior manager will generally be a chief inspector or superintendent. Where the officer concerned is a superintendent, the 'senior manager' will be his/her supervising officer but again there is no stipulation that this must be a police officer (reg. 3(1)(b)).

'Personel officer' means a person employed under the Police Act 1996, s. 15 (a civilian) or a police officer who, in either case, has responsibility for personnel matters relating to members of the force to which the member concerned belongs (reg. 3(1)).

Second interview

The Police (Efficiency) Regulations 1999, reg. 8 provides that:

> *(1)   Where the reporting officer is of the opinion that a member of a police force who was warned under regulation 6(3)(b) that he was required to improve his performance has, at the end of the period specified by the interviewing officer under regulation 6(3)(c), failed to make a sufficient improvement in his performance, he may refer the case to the countersigning officer.*
>
> *(2)   Where a case is referred under paragraph (1), the countersigning officer may, after consulting with the personnel officer, require the member concerned to attend a further interview (in these Regulations referred to as a second interview) to discuss the performance of the member concerned.*

Practice Note

As with the first interview (see above), the expressed purpose of reg. 8 is to facilitate a *discussion* of the officer's performance and the comments made in the Practice Note under reg. 6 (see above) are equally applicable here. Similarly, it is not mandatory for the reporting officer to refer the case back to the countersigning officer if the officer concerned has failed to make sufficient improvement. Regulation 8(1) says that he/she *may* do so (although, if there has been no improvement, it is difficult to see what else the reporting officer might usefully do).

All that is necessary in order to make such a referral is that the reporting officer *is of the opinion* that there has been insufficient improvement in the member's performance. This broadly drafted requirement gives the reporting officer a considerable degree of latitude but again the importance of general supervisory discretion (and accurate record keeping) should perhaps be reinforced here. Such a referral can only be made at the end of the specified period.

Although the process is started by the reporting officer, the decision to hold a second interview will be made by the countersigning officer. Once again, there is no requirement to hold such an interview and the wording of reg. 8(2) is permissive rather than mandatory. What *is* mandatory however is that, in reaching his/her decision, the countersigning officer consult with the personnel officer (as defined above) and it would be good practice for a detailed note of that consultation to be kept.

Regulation 9 provides that:

> *If the countersigning officer decides to require a member of a police force to attend a second interview, he shall—*

    (a)   send a notice in writing to the member concerned—
       (i)   requiring him to attend, at a specified time and place, an interview with the countersigning officer and the personnel officer;
       (ii)   stating the reasons why his performance is considered unsatisfactory and that further action will be considered in the light of the interview; and
       (iii)   informing him that he may seek advice from a representative of his staff association and be accompanied at the interview by a member of a police force selected by him; and
    (b)   send a copy of the notice to the reporting officer, the senior manager and the personnel officer.

Practice Note

Once the decision is reached by the countersigning officer to hold a second interview, the responsibility to comply with the requirements of reg. 9 falls to him/her.

Again the notice must set out the *reasons* why the officer's performance is considered unsatisfactory. It is critical, therefore, that any incidents evidencing the officer's continued poor performance are well documented and accurately recorded. The countersigning officer must remind the officer of his/her entitlement to consult the relevant staff association and to be accompanied by a 'friend' (police officer).

It is important to note that any superintendent or assistant chief constable/ commander who attends *or is otherwise involved in* the second interview is barred from appearing on the panel of any later inefficiency hearing involving the officer concerned (see below).

Regulation 10 provides that:

    (1)   The following provisions of this Regulation shall apply to the procedure to be followed at a second interview.
    (2)   The interview shall be conducted by the countersigning officer and the personnel officer.
    (3)   The countersigning officer shall—
    (a)   explain to the member concerned the reasons why the reporting officer is of the opinion that the member concerned has failed to make a sufficient improvement in his performance or, as the case may be, that his performance is unsatisfactory and the conditions specified in regulation 8(2) are satisfied; and
    (b)   provide the member concerned, or the member of a police force who has accompanied him to the interview, or both of them, with an opportunity to make representations in response.

Practice Note

The personnel officer (as defined above) must take part in the second interview although it is clear from reg. 10(3) that the countersigning officer takes the lead in running the proceedings. The countersigning officer must explain the grounds for the second interview and must provide the opportunity for the officer, his/her 'friend' *or both* to make representations in response. The explanation should be given in a clear, unambiguous way that the officer understands. Given this requirement and the fact that the explanation is an account of someone else's opinion (namely that of the reporting officer), it may be appropriate for the countersigning officer to have a prepared document for this purpose.

As with the first interview (see above) there will be an option of 'no further action', in which case any note of the procedure followed will be expunged from the officer's personal record after two years have elapsed.

Regulation 10(4) goes on to provide that:

(4) If after considering any representations made under paragraph (3), the countersigning officer is satisfied that the performance of the member concerned has been unsatisfactory during the period specified by the interviewing officer under regulation 6(3)(c) or, as the case may be, the period specified in regulation 8(2), he shall—

(a) inform the member concerned in what respect his performance is considered unsatisfactory;

(b) warn the member concerned that he is required to improve his performance in any such respect;

(c) inform the member concerned of any specific action which he is required to take to achieve such an improvement; and

(d) warn the member concerned that, if a sufficient improvement is not made within such reasonable period as the countersigning officer shall specify, he may be required to attend an inefficiency hearing at which the officers conducting the hearing will have the power, if appropriate, to require the member concerned to resign from the force or to order reduction in rank.

(5) The countersigning officer may adjourn the interview to a specified later time or date if it appears to him necessary or expedient to do so.

Practice Note

Once again, the representations made under reg. 10(3)(b) must have been *considered* by the countersigning officer (and presumably, though it does not say so, the personnel officer). As with the first interview (as to which, see above) it may be appropriate to adjourn the interview (under reg. 10(5)) for proper consideration to be given to any representations.

The officer concerned must be:

- told of any specific action that he/she is required to take to achieve the necessary improvement in performance;
- warned at this stage that failure to achieve sufficient improvement by the set date *may* result in a further hearing; and
- warned that such a hearing would have the power to require the member to resign or to reduce him/her in rank.

The warning will also contain a timescale for improvement which, as with the first interview, will not normally be less than three or more than six months from the time of the interview. (For guidance in action planning in general, see above.)

The wording of reg. 10(4) suggests that only those performance issues that have been specified at reg. 10(4)(a) can be the subject of a required action plan for improvement under reg. 10(4)(c). This would mean that any action plan would need to be very specific to the issues raised by the reporting officer and could not simply target the generic competencies of the officer's rank or role.

The countersigning officer may adjourn the second interview to a later time or a later date if it appears necessary or expedient to do so (reg. 10(5)).

After second interview

The Police (Efficiency) Regulations 1999, reg. 11 provides that:

> *(1)   The countersigning officer shall, not later than 7 days after the conclusion of the second interview—*
> *(a)   in consultation with the personnel officer, prepare a written record of the substance of the matters discussed during the interview; and*
> *(b)   send one copy or, where the member concerned was accompanied at the interview by a member of a police force selected by him, two copies of that record to the member concerned together with a notice in writing—*
> *(i)   if a warning was given under regulation 10(4), confirming the terms of that warning; and*
> *(ii)   informing him that he may submit written comments, or indicate that he has no such comments, not later than 7 days after the date on which the copy is received by him.*
> *(2)   Subject to paragraph (3), the member concerned shall be entitled to submit written comments in relation to the record of the interview to the countersigning officer not later than 7 days after the date on which it was received by him.*
> *(3)   The countersigning officer may, on the application of the member concerned, extend the period specified in paragraph (2) if he is satisfied that it is appropriate to do so.*
> *(4)   If the countersigning officer receives any written comments under paragraph (2), he shall ensure that they are retained with the record of the interview.*
> *(5)   The countersigning officer shall send a copy of the record of the interview, and of any written comments by the member concerned, to the reporting officer, the personnel officer and the senior manager.*

Practice Note

The written record must be prepared *in consultation with* the personnel officer. The 1999 Regulations appear to require a summary of the substance rather than a verbatim account of what took place. The record must be accompanied by a written notice confirming the 'warning' if one was given under reg. 10(4). As the requirement refers to a singular warning (there are in fact *two* warnings under reg. 10(4)), that warning seems to be the one given in relation to the consequences of failing to improve (i.e. the warning at reg. 10(4)(d)). In practice, such a warning may only be given twice within a period of two years before resulting in a hearing.

Once again, as with the first interview (as to which, see above), there are requirements relating to the sending of copies to the relevant people concerned, together with the notice of opportunity to submit written comments within seven days. There are also similar requirements in relation to the retention of written responses and the countersigning officer may, on the application of the officer concerned, extend the seven-day deadline. The trigger for the seven-day deadline is the *receipt* of the record by the officer concerned, highlighting once more the need for accurate record keeping.

Assessment of performance

The Police (Efficiency) Regulations 1999, reg. 12 provides that:

> *(1)   Not later than 14 days after the date on which the period specified under regulation 10(4)(d) ends—*
> *(a)   the countersigning officer shall, in consultation with the reporting officer, assess the performance of the member concerned during that period; and*
> *(b)   the countersigning officer shall inform the member concerned in writing whether the reporting officer and the countersigning officer are of the opinion that there has been a sufficient improvement in performance during that period.*
> *(2)   If the countersigning officer is of the opinion that there has been an insufficient improvement, the member concerned shall also, within the period of 14 days mentioned in paragraph (1), be informed in writing that he may be required to attend, at a time (being not sooner than 21 days, but not later than 56 days, after the date on which the notification under this paragraph is received by him) to be notified separately, a hearing (in these Regulations referred to as an inefficiency hearing) to consider his performance.*
> *(3)   The countersigning officer shall refer any case in which the member concerned has been informed in accordance with paragraph (2) to the senior manager, who shall, if he thinks it appropriate to do so, direct that an inefficiency hearing be arranged under regulation 13.*

Practice Note

The countersigning officer, *in consultation with* the reporting officer, must assess the performance of the officer concerned and this must be done no later than 14 days after the period set out in the warning under reg. 10(4)(d). The assessment must relate to the officer's performance *during that period*. Following this assessment, the countersigning officer must inform the officer in writing whether or not he/she considers that there has been a sufficient improvement in the officer's performance.

It will be important to be able to demonstrate a number of elements over this critical assessment period and it is suggested that the principal ones will be:

- *Objectivity* in the way in which the officer's performance was observed, assessed and recorded.
- *Reasonableness* in respect of any specific tasks or duties that were presented to the officer concerned, particularly in relation to his/her peers or predecessors.
- *Realistic expectations* of the officer concerned given the expectations that would ordinarily be made of someone sharing his/her level of experience and knowledge.

If both the reporting officer and the countersigning officer agree that there *has* been a sufficient improvement, however, there is no specific requirement as to when the officer must be so informed. Given the requirement at reg. 12(2) — to inform the officer within the 14-day period that he/she may have to attend an inefficiency hearing — it would seem that, if the officer has not heard anything from the countersigning officer within 14 days of the assessment period ending, he/she can assume that there must have been, sufficient improvement in his/her performance.

The wording of reg. 12(2) suggests that if the countersigning officer alone feels that there has not been a sufficient improvement (irrespective of the reporting officer's view), he/she must refer the case to the 'senior manager' (as defined above) who then has the discretion whether to direct that an inefficiency hearing be held. As with the other stages of the process so far, this next element is *discretionary* and there is no compulsion on the senior manager to direct that a hearing be held.

Inefficiency hearing

The Police (Efficiency) Regulations 1999, reg. 13 provides that:

> *(1)   The personnel officer shall, not less than 21 days before the date fixed for the hearing, send a notice in writing to the member concerned—*
> *(a)   requiring him to attend an inefficiency hearing at a specified time and place;*
> *(b)   stating the reasons why his performance is considered unsatisfactory;*
> *(c)   informing him that he may be represented at the hearing—*
> *(i)   either by counsel or a solicitor; or*
> *(ii)   by a member of a police force selected by him; and*
> *(d)   warning him of the powers under regulation 17 which are available to the officers conducting the inefficiency hearing in the event that they find that the performance of the member concerned has been unsatisfactory.*

(2)   If the member concerned wishes to call any witnesses other than the person representing him at the inefficiency hearing, he shall, not later than seven days before the hearing, give notice in writing to the personnel officer of the names and addresses of those witnesses.

(3)   In paragraph (2), the reference to the hearing includes a reference to any hearing under regulation 15; and in relation to such a hearing the period within which notice is to be given under that paragraph shall be such period as the chairman of the hearing may direct when he postpones or, as the case may be, adjourns the hearing.

Practice Note

The responsibility for sending out the relevant notice here falls to the personnel officer. Such a notice must be *sent* — though not necessarily received — not less than 21 days before the proposed date of the hearing. Why these regulations use this expression and the Police (Conduct) Regulations 1999 (see Chapter 4) use the phrase '21 days in advance' is unclear. Equally lacking in clarity is why the above regulation refers to the 'time and place' of the proposed hearing, while the Police (Conduct) Regulations 1999 use a more complete reference which includes the 'time, *date* and place'.

The notice will advise the member that he/she may be represented at the hearing by a solicitor/counsel *or* a police officer and the officer concerned must elect which. This right emanates from the Police Act 1996, s. 84, which provides that an officer (of the rank of superintendent or below) may not be dismissed, required to resign or reduced in rank as a result of a hearing unless he/she has been given an opportunity to elect to be legally represented.

If the officer concerned wants to call *any* witnesses, he/she must give the personnel officer (as defined above) their names and addresses. This is a different requirement from that which applies in cases of misconduct (as to which, see Chapter 4) where the officer concerned need only give notification of those witnesses whose attendance he/she wishes the countersigning officer to secure. Notification under reg. 13 must be lodged no less than seven days before the hearing, not the date *originally fixed* for the hearing and therefore the cut-off time for such notification moves with any change in the date of the hearing. Regulation 13(3) goes on to make provision for those occasions where the chair of the hearing orders an adjournment or postponement.

The requirement under reg. 13(2) is important as only those witnesses that are mentioned in the member's notification are *entitled* (under reg. 14(7)) to give evidence at the hearing (though the chair may admit them under his/her discretion even if they were not specified above).

Regulation 14 provides that:

(1)   The inefficiency hearing shall be conducted by three officers appointed by the chief officer of police one of whom shall—

(a)   where the member concerned is a member of a police force maintained under section 2 of the 1996 Act, be a member of such a police force holding the rank of assistant chief constable;

(b)   where the member concerned is a member of the metropolitan police force, be a member of that police force holding the rank of commander; and

(c)   where the member concerned is a member of the City of London police force, be an assistant commissioner or a member of that police force holding the rank of commander,

(referred to in these Regulations as the chairman of the inefficiency hearing).

(2)   The chairman and any assessor assisting him under paragraph (3) shall be a person who has neither attended nor otherwise been involved with the first interview or the second interview held in relation to the member concerned.

(3)   The chairman shall be assisted by two assessors who shall be—

(a)   in a case falling within paragraph (1)(a) or (c)—

(i)   where the member concerned is of the rank of superintendent, members of a police force other than the police force concerned who hold the rank of assistant chief constable or commander in the metropolitan police force, and

(ii)   where the member concerned is below the rank of superintendent, members of a police force who hold the rank of superintendent; and

(b)   in a case falling within paragraph (1)(b)—

(i)   where the member concerned is of the rank of superintendent, members of the metropolitan police force who hold the rank of commander, and

(ii)   where the member concerned is below the rank of superintendent, members of the metropolitan police force who hold the rank of superintendent.

Practice Note

The inefficiency hearing will be conducted by three officers, one of whom will be (reg. 14):

- in the case of a provincial police force — an assistant chief constable;
- in the case of the Metropolitan Police — a commander in that force;
- in the case of the City of London Police — a commander in that force.

This officer will chair the hearing (reg. 14(1)).

The other two officers (termed 'assessors') will usually be superintendents appointed without further qualification or restriction (subject to the rule under reg. 14(2)). However, the following provisions are made in respect of the specified officers:

- Where the officer concerned is a Metropolitan Police officer, the superintendents will be Metropolitan Police officers (reg. 14(3)(b)).
- Where the officer concerned is a superintendent, the hearing will comprise two assistant chief constables from outside the officer's own force, together with an assistant chief constable from the officer's own force who will chair the hearing.
- Where the officer concerned is a Metropolitan Police superintendent, the hearing will be chaired by a commander from the officer's own area with two commanders from another area/other areas.

- Where the officer is concerned is a City of London Police superintendent, the hearing will be chaired by a City of London Police commander or the assistant commissioner, with two assistant chief constables or Metropolitan Police commanders.

In any case, the chair and any of the officers assisting him/her must not have attended or otherwise been involved with the first or second interview held in relation to the officer concerned (reg. 14(2)).

Regulation 14 goes on to provide that:

> *(4)   As soon as the chief officer of police has appointed the chairman, the personnel officer shall arrange for a copy of any document—*
>> *(a)   which was available to the interviewing officer in relation to the first interview;*
>> *(b)   which was available to the countersigning officer in relation to the second interview; or*
>> *(c)   which was prepared or submitted under regulation 11, 12 or 13,*
> *to be made available to the chairman; and a copy of any such document shall be sent to the member concerned.*
> *(5)   Subject to the provisions of this regulation, the procedure at the inefficiency hearing shall be such as the chairman may determine.*
> *(6)   The inefficiency hearing shall be held in private unless the chairman, with the consent of the member concerned, decides otherwise.*
> *(7)   The chairman shall afford the member concerned an opportunity to make representations in relation to the matters referred to in the notice sent under regulation 13(1) and to call any witness in respect of whom notice has been given under regulation 13(2).*
> *(8)   A verbatim record of the proceedings at the inefficiency hearing shall be taken and, if the member concerned so requests within the time limit for any appeal and after he has lodged notice of appeal in accordance with rules made under section 85 of the 1996 Act, a transcript of the record or a copy thereof shall be supplied to him by the chairman.*
> *(9)   Subject to regulation 15(1), if the member concerned does not attend the inefficiency hearing or at any adjournment thereof, the hearing may be proceeded with and concluded in his absence if it appears to the chairman just and proper to do so.*
> *(10)   Where, owing to the absence of the member concerned, it is not possible to comply with the whole or any part of the procedure described in this regulation or regulation 15, the case may be proceeded with as if that procedure had been complied with.*

Practice Note

The personnel officer must collate copies of any documents which were available to the interviewing officer and the countersigning officer at the first and second interview respectively and also copies of any document prepared or submitted under regs 11 to 13. The personnel officer must arrange to make these copies available to the chair of the hearing *as soon as one has been appointed*. These copies must also be sent to the officer concerned, although there does not appear to be a specific time limit on this requirement.

Subject to the other provisions in reg. 14, the chair will determine the procedure to be followed at the inefficiency hearing (reg. 14(5)). As such, the chair might decide the 'batting order' for the respective parties and may call witnesses to the proceedings. This apparently wide discretion will, however, also be subject to the general principles of natural justice.

The inefficiency hearing will be held in private but may be in public *if both the chair and the member concerned agree* (reg. 14(6)).

The officer concerned must be given the opportunity to make representations in relation to the matters referred to in the notice sent out by the personnel officer under reg. 13 (reg. 14(7)). A further effect of reg. 14(7) is that the officer concerned is *entitled* to call any witnesses that he/she named in the notification to the personnel officer under reg. 13(2). There may be good reasons why the officer failed to include details of potential witnesses in the reg. 13(2) notification and it would seem that the general discretion given to the chair under reg. 14(5) would allow for other witnesses not previously named to be called.

Unlike the procedure to be followed at the first and second interview stages, a verbatim record must be made of the proceedings (reg. 14(8)).

Regulation 14(9) and (10) makes provision for those cases where the officer concerned is absent from the hearing. These provisions (and those under reg. 15 below) are included in order to address the situation where the officer concerned attempts to frustrate the proceedings by failing or refusing to attend the hearing after one has been arranged.

Postponement and adjournment

The Police (Efficiency) Regulations 1999, reg. 15 provides that:

> *(1)   If the member concerned intimates to the chairman that he will be unable to attend the inefficiency hearing, or in the absence of such intimation does not attend the hearing, and the chairman is satisfied that a good reason for such non-attendance is given by, or on behalf of, the member concerned, he shall postpone, or as the case may be adjourn, the hearing.*
>
> *(2)   The chairman may also adjourn the inefficiency hearing if, having given the member concerned the opportunity of making representations under regulation 14(7), he considers it appropriate to allow a further period for assessment of the performance of the member concerned.*
>
> *(3)   Where the chairman adjourns the inefficiency hearing for the purposes of paragraph (2), he shall—*
>
> *(a)   specify a period (not exceeding 3 months) during which the reporting officer and the countersigning officer shall assess the performance of the member concerned;*
>
> *(b)   fix a date on which the hearing shall resume; and*

(c)   require the member concerned to attend on that date at a specified place.

(4)   Not later than 14 days after the date on which the period for further assessment specified by the chairman under paragraph (3)(a) ends—

(a)   the reporting officer and the countersigning officer shall prepare a report containing their assessment of the performance of the member concerned during that period; and

(b)   the countersigning officer shall send the report to the chairman of the inefficiency hearing and a copy of the report to the member concerned.

(5)   At the continuation of the inefficiency hearing the chairman shall afford the member concerned an opportunity to make representations in relation to the matters referred to in the report mentioned in paragraph (4) and to call any witnesses in respect of whom notice was given under regulation 13(2).

(6)   Where at the time the report mentioned in paragraph (4) is sent under paragraph (4)(b) the chairman of the inefficiency hearing is absent, incapacitated or suspended from duty and it is likely that his absence, incapacity or suspension will continue for a period of more than 28 days, the chief officer of police shall arrange for another member of a police force, being a person who would have been eligible for appointment as chairman of the inefficiency hearing under regulation 14(1) and (2) in relation to the hearing in question, to carry out in relation to the member concerned the functions of the chairman of the inefficiency hearing specified in paragraph (5) and in regulations 16 and 17.

(7)   The chairman of an inefficiency hearing may adjourn the hearing to a specified later time or date if it appears to him necessary or expedient to do so.

Practice Note

Unless the officer concerned:

- 'intimates' to the chair that he/she will be *unable* to attend, or
- does not attend the hearing but gives reason that satisfy the chair as being a 'good reason',

the hearing may continue in his/her absence.

'Intimation' suggests a fairly loose standard of communication that might even be satisfied by inference from the officer's behaviour, although the requirement that such intimation be made to the chair implies that some direct form of communication is required.

Regulation 15(1) clearly envisages the situation where an officer is in some way prevented from attending as opposed to simply making a conscious decision not to attend the hearing or forgetting/neglecting to do so. If the circumstances in reg. 15(1) apply, the chair *must* postpone or adjourn the hearing.

Ill health

Home Office guidance (see Appendix 1, annex J) suggests that the provisions of the Police Regulations 1995 (SI 1995 No. 215), reg. 35, relating to absence from duty owing to sickness, do not apply to attendance at an inefficiency hearing. Therefore, an officer who is on sick leave may still appear at such a hearing. Nevertheless, if the state of the officer's health means that he/she is incapacitated to the extent that attendance at the hearing is not possible, the hearing is likely to be postponed (under reg. 15(1)).

It is unlikely that such postponement would continue indefinitely. Guidance from the Home Office to chief officers points out that the unsatisfactory performance procedures should not prevent or delay the retirement of an officer who, in the circumstances, would normally have been retired on medical grounds.

Discretionary adjournment

In addition to the general discretionary power to adjourn the proceedings under reg. 15(7), the chair may adjourn or postpone the hearing in a number of specified circumstances.

The chair of the hearing may adjourn the proceedings if, *having heard the representations from the officer concerned*, he/she considers it appropriate to allow a further period for assessment of the officer's performance. Therefore, even after the hearing has begun, the officer concerned may still be given the opportunity to address his/her shortcomings, once again reinforcing the developmental nature of these proceedings.

Any further period under this regulation must not exceed three months (reg. 15(3)). The time and date for the resumed hearing must be fixed by the chair and, within 14 days of the end of that period, the reporting officer and countersigning officer will prepare a report containing an assessment of the officer's performance over that time (reg. 15(3)).

When the hearing resumes, the officer concerned will be allowed to make representations on the matters referred to *in that latest report* and may call any of the original witnesses set out in the notification under reg. 13(2).

Regulation 15(6) makes provision for the absence, incapacity or even the suspension of the chair of the inefficiency hearing and imposes a requirement on the chief officer to arrange for a suitably qualified substitute to take over the resumed hearing if the absence, incapacity or suspension of the original chair is expected to continue for more than 28 days.

The finding

The Police (Efficiency) Regulations 1999, reg. 16 provides that:

> *(1)   Subject to paragraph (2), at the conclusion of the inefficiency hearing, the officers conducting the hearing shall reach a decision whether the performance of the member concerned—*
> *(a)   in the period referred to in regulation 10(4)(d); or*
> *(b)   where the hearing was adjourned under regulation 15(2), over the whole of the period comprising the period referred to in regulation 10(4)(d) and*

the further period specified by the chairman under regulation 15(3)(a), has been satisfactory or not.

(2)   The chairman may, at the conclusion of the hearing defer reaching a decision until a later time or date if it appears necessary or expedient to do so.

(3)   The decision of the officers conducting the hearing shall state the finding and, where they have found that the performance of the member concerned has not been satisfactory, their reasons as well as any sanction which they impose under regulation 17.

(4)   The chairman shall record the decision in writing, and shall, not later than three days after the finding is stated under paragraph (3), send a copy of it to—

> *(a)   the member concerned;*
> *(b)   the senior manager; and*
> *(c)   the personnel officer;*

and the copy sent to the member concerned shall be accompanied by a notice in writing informing him of his right to request a review under regulation 19.

(5)   Any decision of the officers conducting the hearing under this regulation or regulation 17 shall be based on a simple majority, but shall not indicate whether it was taken unanimously or by a majority.

Practice Note

Unless the chair decides to defer the decision under reg. 16(2), the officers conducting the hearing must reach a conclusion as to whether the officer's performance in the relevant period has been satisfactory or not. That decision — or a decision under reg. 17 (see below) — need not be unanimous and may be based on a simple majority but this will not be indicated in the finding (reg. 16(5)). This appears to give the officers an equal say in the judgment with no special 'casting' vote being held by the chair.

Their decision must state their finding and, if the officer's performance is found not to have been satisfactory, the decision must give reasons. Once again, the drafting of such a reasoned finding will be very important and the chair may wish to adjourn (under reg. 15(7)) to take advice before stating/ recording any finding. The record of the decision must be sent to the relevant parties no later than three days *after the finding is stated.* The copy sent to the member must also be accompanied by a notice in relation to the officer's right to ask for a review under reg. 19 (see below).

It is important to record the date on which the written decision is *received* by the officer concerned as this will determine the earliest date from which a requirement to resign under reg. 17 can come into operation. It also determines the timescale for requesting a review under reg. 19 (see Chapter 6).

The decision of the hearing must state the relevant sanction to be imposed. Although it is not explicit in the 1999 Regulations, there may of course be a finding that the officer's performance has been satisfactory in which case there will be no further action and the records relating to the alleged poor performance will be removed from the officer's personal file.

Sanctions

The Police (Efficiency) Regulations 1999, reg. 17 provides that:

> *(1)   If the officers conducting the inefficiency hearing make a finding that the performance of the member concerned during the relevant period has been unsatisfactory, they may—*
>
> *(a)   require the member concerned to resign from the force either one month after the date on which a copy of the decision sent under regulation 16(4) is received by him or on such later date as may be specified;*
>
> *(b)   order reduction in his rank with immediate effect and issue a written warning to the member concerned that unless a sufficient improvement in his performance is made within such period as the chairman shall specify, he may, following consideration of his performance during that period in accordance with regulation 18, be required to attend a first interview in respect of that performance; or*
>
> *(c)   issue such a written warning as is mentioned in sub-paragraph (b).*
>
> *(2)   Where the sanction under paragraph (1)(a) is imposed and where the member concerned has not resigned from the force in accordance with the requirement, then the effect of the decision shall be to dismiss the member concerned from the force as from the time referred to in that paragraph.*

Practice Note

Any requirement for the officer to resign cannot take effect before one month after the notice of the finding *was received* by the member. It may, however, take effect at some later date. If the officer has not resigned as required by the specified date, he/she will automatically be dismissed as of that date (reg. 17(2)).

Any reduction in rank must take effect 'immediately', that is immediately the finding is made as opposed to its being sent to, or received by, the officer concerned. The effect of this finding will not be held up or deferred by any review or appeal process.

In accordance with the developmental and ongoing nature of this process, a reduction in rank must be accompanied by a warning that a sufficient improvement is still required with a specified period. This indicates that the process is by no means over and that, under reg. 18 (see below), further reports as to the officer's performance will be assessed.

A similar procedure involving a written warning followed by a further report is available as a third sanction without any reduction in rank.

Any sanction imposed under reg. 17 is to be expunged after two years if that period was free from any such sanction (see the Police Regulations 1995, reg. 17).

At the time of writing there was no provision requiring an officer reduced in rank to 're-qualify'. Therefore an officer who has passed the relevant qualifying examinations to the rank of sergeant or inspector (under the Police

Promotion Regulations 1996 (SI 1996 No. 1685)) retains his/her qualification and will be eligible for promotion in the future.

Further period of assessment

The Police (Efficiency) Regulations 1999, reg. 18 provides that:

    (1)   This regulation applies where the member concerned has been given a written warning under paragraph (1)(b) or (c) of regulation 17.
    (2)   Not later than 14 days after the end of the period specified in the warning the reporting officer shall—
        (a)   assess the performance of the member concerned during that period;
        (b)   cause to be prepared a report on the performance; and
        (c)   send a copy of the report to the member concerned.
    (3)   Where the report prepared under paragraph (2)(b) concludes that the performance of the member concerned has been satisfactory during the period specified in the warning, no further action shall be taken in respect of that performance during that period.
    (4)   Where the report prepared under paragraph (2)(b) concludes that, in the opinion of the reporting officer, the performance of the member concerned has been unsatisfactory during that period, the reporting officer shall request the member concerned to attend a first interview in accordance with regulation 4; and these Regulations shall have effect for the purposes of the performance of the member concerned during that period as if he had been invited to a first interview under regulation 4.

Practice Note

It falls to the reporting officer to make any further assessment and subsequent report under reg. 18.

Unlike the other stages in the process, this next stage makes specific provision for occasions where the officer's performance is found to have been satisfactory. In such cases there is to be no further action in respect of *that* performance during *that* period. This does not necessarily mean that there can be no further action in relation to any performance during any other stage of the whole process. If the 'reporting officer' is of the opinion that the officer's performance during this most recent assessment period has been unsatisfactory, the reporting officer *must* request a 'first interview' and the whole cycle begins again. Unlike the original 'first interview' (see above), the wording of reg. 18 does not leave the request of the 'first interview' to the reporting officer's discretion.

KEY STAGES: EFFICIENCY PROCEDURE

What	Who	How	When
Notice of first interview	Reporting officer (police officer)	Written notice given to officer concerned	When decision made after forming opinion that performance is unsatisfactory
Response to notice of first interview requesting countersigning officer to conduct	Officer concerned	Written notice sent to countersigning officer	Not later than seven days after receipt of notice (unless reporting officer permits longer period)
First interview	Interviewing officer (police officer)	Following requirements of reg. 6	Time and place specified in notice of first interview
Record of first interview	Interviewing officer	• Prepare written summary of substance of matters discussed • Send copy to officer concerned (two copies if officer was accompanied by friend) plus notice inviting written/no comment • Send copy of record and any written comments to senior manager, personnel officer and either countersigning or reporting officer (whichever did not conduct interview)	Not later than seven days after conclusion of first interview

What	Who	How	When
Notice of second interview	Countersigning officer (police officer)	Written notice to officer concerned	When decision made after consulting with personnel officer that interview required
Second interview	Countersigning officer (police officer) with personnel officer	Follow requirements of reg. 10	Time and place specified in notice of second interview
Record of second interview	Countersigning officer (police officer)	• Prepare written summary of substance of matters discussed (in consultation with personnel officer) • Send copy to officer concerned (two copies if officer was accompanied by friend) • Notice of any warning given under reg. 10(4) and inviting written/no comment • Send copy of record and any written comments to senior manager, personnel officer, reporting officer.	Not later than seven days after conclusion of second interview

What	Who	How	When
Assessment of performance during relevant period	Countersign-ing officer (police officer)	• In consultation with reporting officer • Inform officer concerned in writing whether or not countersigning officer and reporting officer are of opinion that there has been sufficient improvement • If not, inform officer concerned in writing of possible requirement to attend inefficiency hearing and refer case to senior manager	Not later than 14 days after end of period specified in reg. 10(4)(d)
Notice of inefficiency hearing	Personnel officer	Following direction by senior manager, send notice to officer concerned including warning regarding sanctions	Not less than 21 days before date fixed for hearing
Notification of witnesses	Officer concerned	Send written notice in response to reg. 13(2) notice of names and addresses of witnesses to personnel officer	Not later than seven days before the hearing (or period directed by chair of hearing in the event of postponement or adjournment)

What	Who	How	When
Appointment of chair and assessors	Chief officer (police officer)	Three officers appointed under requirements of reg. 14 (e.g. one assistant chief constable/commander and two superintendents)	Before hearing (and in time to allow arrangement and copying of documents below)
Arrangement of documents	Personnel officer	• Arrange for all documents mentioned in reg. 14 to be made available to chair of hearing • Send copies to officer concerned	As soon as chair is appointed
Reach decision as to whether officer's performance was satisfactory or not	Officers conducting hearing (police officers)	By simple majority but without stating ratio of votes	By conclusion of hearing (or deferred period if appropriate)
State decision of hearing	Chair (police officer)	Record decision in writing stating finding and reasons	Conclusion of hearing
Copy of decision	Chair (police officer)	Send written copy of decision to: • senior manager • personnel officer Send written copy of decision plus notice regarding right to review to officer concerned	Not later than three days after finding is stated (above)

What	Who	How	When
Impose sanction if appropriate	Officers conducting hearing (police officers)	By simple majority but: • without stating ratio of votes • impose relevant sanction in accordance with provision of reg. 17	After making finding that the officer's performance was unsatisfactory
Further assessment of officer's performance	Personnel officer	Where hearing gave a written warning under reg. 17, comply with requirements of reg. 18	Not later than 14 days after the end of the period specified in the warning

4 POLICE MISCONDUCT

INTRODUCTION

In addition to performance management, it is also an important supervisory and managerial function to be alert to the way in which individuals conduct themselves. As with issues of performance (see Chapter 3), a great deal of supervisory and managerial discretion is called for in dealing with information concerning the conduct of individual officers. The exercise of supervisory and managerial discretion is generally a matter for local and organisational policy. Any such policy relating to the alleged misconduct of police officers is, however, subject to the legislative provisions discussed in this chapter.

Who?

The new legislative provisions relating to allegations of misconduct can be found in the Police (Conduct) Regulations 1999 (SI 1999 No. 730) (see Appendix 3). These Regulations apply to all police officers other than those above superintendent and, subject to the provisions below, revoke the previous Police (Discipline) Regulations 1985 (SI 1985 No. 518) and their respective amendments. As well as setting out the procedures to be followed in cases of alleged misconduct, the 1999 Regulations also introduce a new Code of Conduct which replaces the former Discipline Code (see below).

In very serious cases involving criminal offences, the 1999 Regulations have been modified to allow expedition in disposing of the case. The modified Regulations are set out at the end of this chapter.

For the provisions relating to officers on secondment to 'central services' or working for service authorities such as the National Crime Squad, see Chapter 9. In general terms, a seconded officer is only subject to NCS and NCIS Regulations if a complaint is made. If there is no complaint but there is an allegation or report, the officer must complete the secondment and be made the subject of disciplinary proceedings under the Police (Conduct) Regulations 1999.

When?

The Police (Conduct) Regulations 1999 came into force on 1 April 1999. Where a report, complaint or allegation has been received in respect of conduct that occurred or began *before 1 April 1999,* the 1999 Regulations will not apply and the former 1985 Regulations will apply (reg. 2(2)). If the report, complaint or allegation in respect of conduct that occurred or began before 1 April 1999 is *received on or after 1 April 2000,* the conduct will be treated as if it had occurred or begun after 1 April 1999 (reg. 2(3)). In other words, where the conduct reported or complained of took place before the starting date of the 1999 Regulations, the former Regulations will apply unless that report or complaint was itself received on/after 1 April 2000.

The Code of Conduct is discussed below. On many occasions involving an alleged breach of the Code there is likely to be some overlap between the various heads. In some more serious cases there is also likely to be some overlap with substantive criminal offences.

THE CODE OF CONDUCT

The Police (Conduct) Regulations 1999, sch. 1 provides that:

1. Honesty and integrity
It is of paramount importance that the public has faith in the honesty and integrity of police officers. Officers should therefore be open and truthful in their dealings; avoid being improperly beholden to any person or institution; and discharge their duties with integrity.

Practice Note

Placed at the top of the list of requirements that are made of police officers, this rule stresses the 'paramount' importance of its content. Although the initial focus is on securing the *faith* of the public (a very subjective concept), the actual requirements imposed under rule 1 are:

- openness and veracity in all matters;
- avoiding being *improperly* indebted to individuals/organisations; and
- discharging duties with integrity.

In some roles (e.g. undercover operations, authorised test purchases etc.) police officers are not only required to hide the truth but are trained to do so. Although no saving is made under rule 1 for such occasions, those increasingly common duties should be regarded as a legitimate and limited suspension of the general requirement for openness and honesty.

In relation to the second requirement there is also a provision under the Police Regulations 1995 (SI 1995 No. 215) Schedule 2 (see Appendix 13) requiring police officers properly to discharge any lawful debts.

2. Fairness and impartiality
Police officers have a particular responsibility to act with fairness and impartiality in all their dealings with the public and their colleagues.

Practice Note

This rule specifically extends the officer's responsibilities to both the general public and his/her colleagues. All police forces will have a published grievance procedure for use in cases where a member of the organisation feels that they have been treated unfairly and such policies will be directly relevant to any internal conduct alleged to have breached this rule.

Police officers are also under a number of statutory duties not to discriminate against others (e.g. under the SDA 1975 and RRA 1976 (see Chapter 2) etc.).

Individual actions by police officers can also attract vicarious liability for discrimination to their respective chief officers and this can happen even where the conduct concerned was off duty.

In the leading case of *Chief Constable of Lincolnshire Police* v *Stubbs* [1999] IRLR 81, some acts of sexual harassment took place at social occasions organised by officers over which the chief constable had no control either as to access or what occurred during the course of the events. The Employment Appeal Tribunal, however, stressed that they were 'social gatherings involving officers from work either immediately after work or an organised leaving party', and emphasised that it would have been different if the acts 'occurred during a chance meeting . . . at a supermarket for example'. It was a matter for the employment tribunal to decide which side of the narrow borderline each case fell.

3.   Politeness and tolerance
Officers should treat members of the public and colleagues with courtesy and respect, avoiding abusive or deriding attitudes or behaviour. In particular, officers must avoid: favouritism of an individual or group; all forms of harassment, victimisation or unreasonable discrimination; and overbearing conduct to a colleague, particularly to one junior in rank or service.

Practice Note

Again, this rule specifically mentions both the general public and the officer's colleagues, indicating a clear internal and external focus. Even when lawfully executing their powers of enforcement, police officers are under an obligation to be respectful and courteous.

'Attitudes' are notoriously difficult to identify let alone prove and are often defined largely by the relative perspective of the individual.

'Deriding' would include mocking and ridiculing another person.

Police officers must *avoid* favouritism and harassment; this wording suggests more than simple abstention and includes taking steps to distance oneself from the proscribed behaviour. This rule covers behaviour that might be reported as 'bullying' and, again, all police forces will have grievance policies and procedures that may be relevant here. In extreme cases, the provisions of the Protection from Harassment Act 1997 may also be relevant. For example:

Offence — Harassment — Protection from Harassment Act 1997, ss. 1 and 2
Triable summarily. Six months' imprisonment and/or a fine.
(*Arrestable offence*)

Offence — Racially Aggravated — Crime and Disorder Act 1998, s. 32(1)(a)
Triable either way. Two years' imprisonment and/or a fine on indictment; six months' imprisonment and/or fine summarily.
(*Arrestable offence*)

The Protection from Harassment Act 1997, ss. 1 and 2 provide that:

1.—(1)   A person must not pursue a course of conduct—
(a)   which amounts to harassment of another, and
(b)   which he knows or ought to know amounts to harassment of the other.
(2)   For the purposes of this section, the person whose course of conduct is in question ought to know that it amounts to harassment of another if a reasonable person in possession of the same information would think the course of conduct amounted to harassment of the other.
2.—(1)   A person who pursues a course of conduct in breach of section 1 is guilty of an offence.

Offence — Putting People in Fear of Violence — Protection from Harassment Act 1997, s. 4
Triable either way. Five years' imprisonment and/or a fine on indictment; six months' imprisonment and/or a fine summarily.
(*Arrestable offence*)

Offence — Racially Aggravated — Crime and Disorder Act 1998, s. 32(1)(b)
Triable either way. Seven years' imprisonment and/or a fine on indictment; six months' imprisonment and/or a fine summarily.
(*Arrestable offence*)

The Protection from Harassment Act 1997, s. 4 provides that:

(1)   A person whose course of conduct causes another to fear, on at least two occasions, that violence will be used against him is guilty of an offence if he knows or ought to know that his course of conduct will cause the other so to fear on each of those occasions.
(2)   For the purposes of this section, the person whose course of conduct is in question ought to know that it will cause another to fear that violence will be used against him on any occasion if a reasonable person in possession of the same information would think the course of conduct would cause the other so to fear on that occasion.

This rule overlaps to an extent with rule 2 in relation to discrimination, but any discrimination must be 'unreasonable' before it will breach rule 3.

Managers, supervisors and senior police constables ought to take particular note of this rule which prohibits overbearing conduct with specific reference being made to rank and seniority. As with 'attitudes' above, there are difficulties in identifying and proving overbearing conduct. This is another slightly subjective concept and it will usually be necessary to look at the setting within which the conduct occurred. Some operational situations (e.g. where there is an immediate risk to life or public order) may call for a more forceful and robust approach to the issuing of orders than would be the case in a purely administrative environment. 'Conduct' would include words and communications (e.g. memoranda and e-mails).

4. Use of force and abuse of authority
Officers must never knowingly use more force than is reasonable, nor should they abuse their authority.

Practice Note

This rule overlaps with rule 3 on overbearing conduct and consists of two elements:

- *knowingly* using more force than is reasonably necessary; and
- abusing one's authority.

The use of force is also subject to the European Convention on Human Rights (see Chapter 1) and the Criminal Law Act 1967. Section 3(1) of the 1967 Act provides that:

> *A person may use such force as is reasonable in the circumstances in the prevention of crime, or in effecting or assisting in the lawful arrest of offenders or suspected offenders or of persons unlawfully at large.*

Although it does not make specific provision for *internal* matters, rule 4 would clearly apply to any abuse of authority within a police force (e.g. between a manager or senior officer and a junior colleague) as well as to the external application of statutory and common law police powers.

5. Performance of duties
Officers should be conscientious and diligent in the performance of their duties. Officers should attend work promptly when rostered for duty. If absent through sickness or injury, they should avoid activities likely to retard their return to duty.

Practice Note

In addition to requiring the diligent and conscientious performance of all their duties, this rule imposes a duty on officers while on sick leave to refrain from any physical activity that is *likely* to retard their return to duty. There is no stipulation that the retarded return to work is *to full operational* duties and therefore even an activity that impedes an officer's returning to 'light' or 'special' duties may be caught under this rule.

6. Lawful orders

The police service is a disciplined body. Unless there is good and sufficient cause to do otherwise, officers must obey all lawful orders and abide by the provisions of Police Regulations. Officers should support their colleagues in the execution of their lawful duties, and oppose any improper behaviour, reporting it where appropriate.

Practice Note

This rule makes allowance for disobedience to orders where there is good and sufficient cause. Whether there was such good and sufficient cause will be a question of fact for the relevant hearing to determine.

For the 'Police Regulations' referred to, see the Police Regulations 1995 (Appendix 13).

Rule 6 imposes a requirement to support colleagues in the execution of their lawful duties and therefore may be breached by omission as well as by a positive act. It also obliges police officers to *oppose* improper behaviour and to report it where 'appropriate' and, again, an omission may attract liability for breaching the rule. In deciding whether it is appropriate to report a particular incident, the discretion of the officer(s) concerned will be relevant (as to which, see note (b) to the Code of Conduct below). Where the incident itself discloses a potential contravention of the Code it is very likely that there would be a duty to report the incident under rule 6.

Police are excluded from the 'whistleblowing' provisions in the Public Interest Disclosure Act 1998 but in the House of Commons debates on the matter the Home Secretary indicated that officers would be given equivalent protection by regulation (*Hansard HC cols 1143–4, 24.4.98*). At the time of writing, no such provision had been made.

7. Confidentiality

Information which comes into the possession of the police should be treated as confidential. It should not be used for personal benefit and nor should it be divulged to other parties except in the proper course of police duty. Similarly, officers should respect, as confidential, information about force policy and operations unless authorised to disclose it in the course of their duties.

Practice Note

There are further, wide-ranging restrictions and duties in relation to dealing with information imposed by the Data Protection Act 1998 (see P. Carey, *Blackstone's Guide to the Data Protection Act 1998*, Blackstone Press, 1998).

There is a need for considerable care to be taken when police officers are providing information to public forums and when dealing with the media. In addition to possible implications under the Data Protection Act 1998 and rule 7 above, the improper disclosure of some personal data (e.g. the name and address of a suspected paedophile) may also have significant consequences under the European Convention on Human Rights (as to which, see Chapter 1).

Information that is presented to police officers taking the national promotion examinations is treated as being subject to rule 7 and candidates are served with written notice warning them of the consequences of disclosing that information once they have taken the examination.

8. Criminal offences
Officers must report any proceedings for a criminal offence taken against them. Conviction of a criminal offence may of itself result in further action being taken.

Practice Note

The requirement to report criminal 'proceedings' would not appear to include an arrest or alternative methods of resolution such as the fixed penalty procedure under the Road Traffic Offenders Act 1988.

It does not require police officers to report criminal proceedings taken against spouses or members of their family.

Although many of the new paragraphs had a corresponding 'offence' under the former discipline code, there is not an exact overlap. For a table showing what went where, see below. The former offence of being an accessory to a disciplinary offence has gone, but such conduct is probably now subsumed under paras 6 and 12 of the Code of Conduct. The former protection against double jeopardy has gone. The rule (under the now repealed s. 104 of the Police and Criminal Evidence Act 1984 (see the Police Act 1996, sch. 9, part II)) provided that, where an officer had been convicted or acquitted of a criminal offence, he/she would not be liable to be charged with a general disciplinary offence which was in substance the same as the criminal offence.

9. Property
Officers must exercise reasonable care to prevent loss or damage to property (excluding their own personal property but including police property).

Practice Note

This rule imposes an objective standard of care in relation to property. Although its provisions do not extend to the officer's personal property, it does apply to police property.

Failure to take reasonable care of someone else's property may also give rise to a civil action against the police and may have implications under the European Convention on Human Rights (as to which, see Chapter 1).

10. Sobriety
Whilst on duty officers must be sober. Officers should not consume alcohol when on duty unless specifically authorised to do so or it becomes necessary for the proper discharge of police duty.

Practice Note

The requirement in relation to sobriety while on duty is absolute. No allowance is made for the nature of any specific duty. Allowance *is* made for the *consumption of alcohol* (but not drunkenness) on duty provided:

- the officer has been specifically authorised to do so; or
- it *becomes necessary* for the proper discharge of police duty.

The wording of the second point suggests a response to an unforeseen development. Where there is a reasonable anticipation of the need to consume alcohol while on duty, it would be in an officer's best interests to obtain the relevant *specific* authority first.

In relation to 'sobriety', many supervisory and managerial ranks are now required to provide 'on call' cover whereby, although not 'on duty' in the strict sense, these officers must be available to be called out to provide the relevant level of managerial cover should the operational need arise. Home Office guidance suggests that, where *superintendents* are under such an obligation to be on call, they will be classed as being 'on duty' for the duration of that period. They will not, however, be 'on duty' by reason only of their general 24-hour responsibility for their own area of command or department. The situation in relation to other ranks (such as detective inspectors) is unclear although there would seem to be a strong argument that it is the officer's fitness to perform any formally anticipated duties that matters here rather than their substantive rank within the organisation. The Home Office guidance further provides that any officer who is *unexpectedly* called out for duty should be able, at no risk of discredit, to say that he/she has had too much to drink, a provision that appears to reinforce the distinction between an unscheduled call out and the formal provision of 'on call' cover for an area or sphere of operations.

For the restrictions on police officers being on licensed premises, see Chapter 11.

11. Appearance
Unless on duties which dictate otherwise, officers should always be well turned out, clean and tidy whilst on duty in uniform or in plain clothes.

Practice Note

Provision is made for those duties requiring a lesser standard of dress (e.g. plain clothes operations). Otherwise, rule 11 applies to both uniform and plain clothes alike. No mention is made about the *appropriateness* of an officer's dress, nor of the suitability of the clothing that he/she wears. There may be some human rights considerations here since dress has been seen in some cases as an aspect of freedom of expression.

Rule 11 does not extend to the wearing of jewellery such as earrings or nose studs. However, these issues may fall under rule 12 below.

12. General conduct
Whether on or off duty, police officers should not behave in a way which is likely to bring discredit upon the police service.

Practice Note

This is general 'catch-all' provision. It extends to 'behaviour' while off-duty although this may be restricted by the European Convention on Human Rights in so far as there is a right to respect for private life. It is qualified by note (c) to the Code of Conduct (see below).

It would seem that this rule could be contravened by a failure to act as well as by a positive action by the officer concerned. For the more serious cases involving the acts and omissions of police officers generally, see Chapter 11.

Notes to rule 12
(a)   *The primary duties of those who hold the office of constable are the protection of life and property, the preservation of the Queen's peace, and the prevention and detection of criminal offences. To fulfil these duties they are granted extraordinary powers; the public and the police service therefore have the right to expect the highest standards of conduct from them.*

(b)   *This Code sets out the principles which guide police officers' conduct. It does not seek to restrict officers' discretion: rather it aims to define the parameters of conduct within which that discretion should be exercised However, it is important to note that any breach of the principles in this Code may result in action being taken by the organisation, which, in serious cases, could involve dismissal.*

(c)   *This Code applies to the conduct of police officers in all ranks whilst on duty, or whilst off duty if the conduct is serious enough to indicate that an officer is not fit to be a police officer. It will be applied in a reasonable and objective manner. Due regard will be paid to the degree of negligence or deliberate fault and to the nature and circumstances of an officer's conduct. Where off duty conduct is in question, this will be measured against the generally accepted standards of the day.*

Practice Note

The notes at the end of the Code indicate that, although police officers are under a continuing duty to observe certain minimum standards of behaviour even while off duty, any misbehaviour away from work will have to be shown to be serious enough to suggest that the person is not fit to be a police officer. In assessing this conduct, regard will be had to the 'standards of the day' and this concept (which is similar to the approach of the Strasboug court under the European Convention on Human Rights) will change over time.

What went where

The 'Discipline Code'		The New 'Code of Conduct'
1.	Discreditable conduct	General conduct
2.	Misconduct towards a member of a police force	Politeness and tolerance. Fairness and impartiality
3.	Disobedience to orders	Lawful orders
4.	Neglect of duty	Performance of duties
5.	Falsehood or prevarication	Honesty and integrity
6.	Improper disclosure of information	Confidentiality
7.	Corrupt or improper practice	Honesty and integrity
8.	Abuse of authority	Use of force and abuse of authority
9.	Racially discriminatory behaviour	Politeness and tolerance. Fairness and impartiality
10.	Neglect of health	Performance of duties
11.	Improper dress or untidiness	Appearance
12.	Damage to police property	Property
13.	Drunkenness	Sobriety
14.	Drinking on duty or soliciting drink	Sobriety
15.	Entering licensed premises	General conduct
16.	Criminal conduct	Criminal offences

THE POLICE (CONDUCT) REGULATIONS 1999

Suspension

The Police (Conduct) Regulations 1999, reg. 5 provides that:

(1)   Where there has been a report, complaint or allegation which indicates that the conduct of a member of a police force does not meet the appropriate standard the chief officer of the force concerned may suspend the member

concerned from membership of the force and from his office of constable whether or not the matter has been investigated.

(2)   The chief officer concerned may exercise the power to suspend the member concerned under this regulation at any time from the time of the receipt of the report, complaint or allegation until—

(a)   the supervising officer decides not to refer the case to a hearing,

(b)   the notification of a finding that the conduct of the member concerned did not fail to meet the appropriate standard,

(c)   the time limit under regulation 34 for giving notice of intention to seek a review has expired, or

(d)   any review under regulation 35 has been completed.

(3)   Where the member concerned is suspended under this regulation, he shall be suspended until there occurs any of the events mentioned in paragraph (2)(a) to (d), or until the chief officer decides he shall cease to be suspended, whichever first occurs.

(4)   Where the member concerned who is suspended is required to resign under regulation 31, he shall remain suspended during the period of his notice.

(5)   The chief officer concerned may delegate his powers under this regulation to an officer of at least the rank of assistant chief constable or, where the member concerned is a member of the City of London or metropolitan police force, to an officer of at least the rank of commander.

Practice Note

Many of the terms used within the 1999 Regulations are defined under reg. 4(1).

'Complaint' has the same meaning, as a complaint under the Police Act 1996, s. 65, i.e.:

. . . a complaint about the conduct of a member of a police force which is submitted—

(a)   by a member of the public, or

(b)   on behalf of a member of the public and with his written consent.

Home Office guidance (see Appendix 1) provides that complaints from members of the public can only be received from people who are well informed about the facts of the alleged incident. Therefore it would be difficult to accept and investigate a 'complaint' from an anonymous source.

Not every allegation of misconduct will amount to a 'complaint', particularly where the source of the allegation is internal. However, where there has been a 'complaint' so defined, the provisions under the 1996 Act will apply and, as with allegations of unsatisfactory performance, there will be occasions where there is some overlap. The distinction is of fundamental practical effect on the Regulations to be used, especially for NCS and NCIS officers.

'Appropriate standard' means the standard set out in the Code of Conduct (see above).

'Member concerned' means the officer in relation to whose conduct there has been a report, complaint or allegation.

The 'supervising officer' is the person appointed under reg. 7 (see below) to supervise the investigation of the case.

For an explanation of regs 34 and 35 which relate to the review procedure, see Chapter 6.

The power to suspend an officer appears to be very wide and applies whether or not the matter has been investigated (reg. 5(1)). Such a power must, however, be exercised in accordance with the general principles of law, including human rights where relevant, and will be subject to judicial review. The power under reg. 5 may be delegated to an assistant chief constable or, in the case of Metropolitan Police or City of London Police officers, to a commander (reg. 5(5)).

The general effect of suspension is that the member is no longer a 'member' of his/her force for most purposes, and ceases to enjoy the powers and privileges of the office of constable. Given the wording of reg. 5, it may be necessary for any suspension notice to specify that the officer concerned is suspended from both membership of his/her own force *and* from the office of constable. This will make it absolutely clear that the officer is not simply suspended from his/her own employing organisation, but is temporarily removed from the general public office of constable (as to which, see Chapters 2 and 3) preventing transfer between police forces. However, the effect of reg. 4 of the Police Regulations 1995 (see Appendix 13) is that the officer will still be treated as a member of his/her force for the purposes of those Regulations (which cover the key conditions of service).

A further effect of suspension is that the officer will not, under the rules of the Police Promotion Examinations Board, be able to sit the qualifying examination(s) for promotion unless his/her chief officer expressly authorises it.

Generally, an officer who is suspended will continue to receive full pay unless his/her whereabouts are unknown or where he/she is in custody following conviction. Suspension should not be imposed or taken as an indication of guilt. Any removal or reduction of pay or allowances might be seen as a punitive measure and, as such, may not sit appropriately alongside an impartial and fair investigation.

The power to suspend *may* be exercised at any time from the receipt of the allegation up until any of the circumstances set out at reg. 5(2)(a) to (d) *or* until the chief officer decides otherwise, whichever occurs first. Therefore, although a chief officer may end the member's suspension *before* any of the circumstances set out at reg. 5(2)(a) to (d), he/she may not extend the suspension beyond the time when the first of those things occurs.

If a suspended officer is ultimately required to resign under reg. 31 (see below), he/she will remain suspended during his/her period of notice (reg. 5(4)).

Outstanding criminal proceedings

The Police (Conduct) Regulations 1999, reg. 6 provides that:

Where there are criminal proceedings outstanding against the member concerned, proceedings under these Regulations, other than exercise of the power to suspend under regulation 5, shall not take place unless the chief officer concerned believes that in the exceptional circumstances of the case it would be appropriate for them to do so.

Practice Note

Although as a general rule disciplinary proceedings other than suspension will not be brought against an officer while there are any outstanding criminal proceedings against him/her, reg. 6 leaves it open to the chief officer to do so. That discretionary power to institute disciplinary proceedings is limited to 'exceptional circumstances' where the chief officer *believes* it to be appropriate, though there is no further requirement for that belief to be a 'reasonable' one. It would, however, be a rare case where it would be fair to proceed while a serious criminal charge was pending.

Investigation procedure

Supervising officer

The Police (Conduct) Regulations 1999, reg. 7 provides that:

(1)   Subject to paragraph (2), where a report, complaint or allegation is received by the chief officer which indicates that the conduct of a member of a police force did not meet the appropriate standard, the case may be referred by him to an officer, who shall satisfy the conditions in paragraph (3), to supervise the investigation of the case.
(2)   . . .
(3)   The supervising officer shall be—
  (a)   at least one rank above that of the member concerned;
  (b)   of at least the rank of superintendent;
  (c)   a member of the same force as the member concerned; and
  (d)   not an interested party.

Practice Note

It is not mandatory that a case be referred to a supervisory officer, although the subsequent appointment of a person to investigate the complaint is made by that supervising officer.

Regulation 7(1) does not apply where the case arises from a complaint the investigation of which *must* be supervised by the Police Complaints Authority (see Chapter 5).

The supervising officer must meet all of the criteria set out at reg. 7(3)(a) to (d).

The 'supervising officer' is not the same as the 'investigating officer' (see below).

An 'interested party' is 'a witness or any person involved in the conduct which is the subject of the case or who otherwise has a direct interest in the case' (reg. 4(1)).

Investigating officer

The Police (Conduct) Regulations 1999, reg. 8 provides that:

> *(1)   The supervising officer may appoint an investigating officer to investigate the case.*
> *(2)   The investigating officer shall be—*
> *(a)   a member of the same police force as the member concerned or, if at the request of the supervising officer the chief officer of some other force agrees to provide an investigating officer, a member of that other force;*
> *(b)   of at least the rank of inspector or, if the member concerned is a superintendent, of at least the rank of assistant chief constable or, if the investigating officer is a member of the City of London or metropolitan police force, of at least the rank of commander;*
> *(c)   of at least the same rank as the member concerned; and*
> *(d)   not an interested party.*
> *(3)   The provisions of this regulation are without prejudice to the powers of the Authority with regard to the approval of the investigating officer under section 72(3)(a) and (b) of the 1996 Act in a case where the Authority are required, or have determined, to supervise the investigation of a complaint or other matter under that section.*

Practice Note

The investigating officer must meet all the criteria set out at reg. 8(2)(a) to (d).

Unlike the supervising officer (above), he/she may be from a different force from the officer concerned (if requested in accordance with reg. 8(2)(a)) and must be at least of inspector rank. If the member concerned is a superintendent then the investigating officer must be of at least assistant chief constable/commander rank. Although reg. 7 does not specifically require it, it is likely that in cases where the investigating officer is a senior officer, the 'supervising officer' would also be of ACPO rank.

The provisions of reg. 8 are without prejudice to the powers of the Police Complaints Authority to make requirements in relation to the appointment of investigating officers (reg. 8(3)).

The Police Act 1996, s. 72 provides that:

> *(3)   Where an investigation is to be supervised by the Authority, they may require—*
> *(a)   that no appointment is made under section 68(3) or 69(5) unless they have given notice to the appropriate authority that they approve the person whom that authority propose to appoint, or*

(b)   if such an appointment has already been made and the Authority are not satisfied with the person apponted, that—

(i)   the appropriate authority, as soon as is reasonably practicable, select another member of a police force and notify the Authority that it proposes to appoint him, and

(ii)   the appointment is not made unless the Authority give notice to the appropriate authority that they approve that person.

Notice of investigation

The Police (Conduct) Regulations 1999, reg. 9 provides that:

The investigating officer shall as soon as is practicable (without prejudicing his or any other investigation of the matter) cause the member concerned to be given written notice—

(a)   that there is to be an investigation into the case;

(b)   of the nature of the report, complaint or allegation;

(c)   informing him that he is not obliged to say anything concerning the matter, but that he may, if he so desires, make a written or oral statement concerning the matter to the investigating officer or to the chief officer concerned;

(d)   informing him that if he makes such a statement it may be used in any subsequent proceedings under these Regulations;

(e)   informing him that he has the right to seek advice from his staff association, and

(f)   informing him that he has the right to be accompanied by a member of a police force, who shall not be an interested party, to any meeting, interview or hearing.

Practice Note

The written notice must be given 'as soon as is practicable'. 'Practicable' has been accepted as meaning 'possible to be accomplished with known means or resources' (see *Adsett* v *K & L Steelfounders* [1953] 1 All ER 97). The giving of such a notice must not, however, be to the prejudice of the investigation of the matter — whether by the investigating officer or someone else — so there may be some justifiable delay in the provision of a reg. 9 notice.

The wording 'cause to be given' — as opposed to 'sent' — suggests that, unlike some of the requirements relating to poor performance (see Chapter 3), personal service is required.

The making of a statement in response to the receipt of a reg. 9 notice may have significant implications for the member concerned and serious consideration ought to be given to exercising the right to consult with a staff association representative.

Where an officer is to be interviewed for a *purely disciplinary* matter, he/she has no free-standing right to access to a lawyer, even if being interviewed under caution (*Lee* v *United Kingdom* (2000) LTL 22 September 2000). Such matters have been held by the ECtHR not to amount to a 'criminal charge' for the purposes of Article 6 in a case where the officer is not at risk of the deprivation of his/her liberty or a fine. Clearly in most cases where there is the possibility of a conduct hearing there will also be a risk of a fine and the matter may be arguable on this point. However, where there is a joint criminal and internal disciplinary investigation, Article 6 will apply as it does to any other criminal investigation. In relation to disciplinary investigations, the government proposes to allow adverse inferences to be drawn from an officer's silence by extending the scope of s. 34 of the Criminal Justice and Public Order Act 1994 to police conduct proceedings (see clause 124 of the Criminal Justice and Police Bill which had not, at the time of writing, received Royal Assent).

Investigating officer's report

The Police (Conduct) Regulations 1999, reg. 10 provides that:

(1) At the end of his investigation the investigating officer shall submit a written report on the case to the supervising officer and, if the Authority are supervising the investigation, also to the Authority.

(2) If at any time during his investigation it appears to the investigating officer that the case is one in respect of which the conditions specified in Part I of Schedule 2 are likely to be satisfied, he shall, whether or not the investigation is at an end, submit to the supervising officer—

(a) a statement of his belief that the case may be one to which regulation 39 applies and the grounds for that belief; and

(b) a written report on the case so far as it has then been investigated.

Practice Note

If the investigation is being supervised by the Police Complaints Authority (see below), the investigating officer must submit two reports: one to the supervising officer and one to the Authority.

If it appears to the investigating officer that the case is a 'special case' as provided for under reg. 39 (i.e. involving a serious allegation of an imprisonable offence; see below), the investigating officer must submit a report stating his/her belief and setting out the current position of the investigation. Given the seriousness of 'special cases', this report would probably need to be submitted immediately and reg. 10(2) makes it clear that the report does not need to be delayed until the end of the investigation.

Regulation 11 provides that:

(1) Subject to paragraphs (2) and (3), on receipt of the investigating officer's report the supervising officer may refer the case to a hearing.

(2) Where—

(a)   the chief officer has a duty to proceed under section 75(7) or 76(2) or (5) of the 1996 Act; or

(b)   the member concerned has received two written warnings about his conduct within the previous twelve months and has in a statement made under regulation 9 admitted that his conduct failed to meet the appropriate standard, the supervising officer shall refer the case to a hearing.

Practice Note

On receiving the report from the investigating officer, the supervising officer *may* refer the case to a hearing. Alternatively, he/she may decide not to refer the case and, where that happens, no reference to the case is to be made on the member's personal record (reg. 11(4); see below).

If the case comes under reg. 11(2)(a) or (b), the supervising officer *must* refer the case to a hearing (unless it is likely to be a 'special case').

The duties referred to at reg. 11(2)(a) (under s. 75(7) or 76(2) or (5) of the Police Act 1996) relate to the notification to, and supervision by, the Police Complaints Authority. The Police Act 1996, s. 75 provides that:

(7)   Where a chief officer has sent the Authority a memorandum under subsection (4) or (5), he shall—

(a)   if the memorandum states that he proposes to bring disciplinary proceedings, bring and proceed with them, and

(b)   if the memorandum states that he has brought such proceedings, proceed with them.

The Police Act 1996, s. 76 provides that:

(2)   Where a chief officer has brought disciplinary proceedings in accordance with a recommendation under subsection (1), he shall proceed with them.

. . .

(5)   Subject to subsection (6), it shall be the duty of a chief officer to comply with such a direction.

The circumstances at reg. 11(2)(b) require that the member has received two written warnings about his/her conduct in the last 12 months *and* that he/she has made a statement under reg. 9 (see above) that his/her conduct failed to meet the required standard. It would seem that the written warnings must relate to the officer's *conduct* and not simply his/her *performance* (as to which, see Chapter 3).

Regulation 11 goes on to provide that:

(3)   Where the supervising officer, on receipt of a report submitted by the investigating officer under paragraph (2) of regulation 10, is of the opinion that the case is one in respect of which the conditions specified in Part I of Schedule 2

are likely to be satisfied, he shall refer the case to the appropriate officer, who shall—

(a)   *if the conditions specified in Part I of Schedule 2 are not satisfied, return the case to the supervising officer;*

(b)   *if the conditions specified in Part I of Schedule 2 are satisfied—*

(i)   *certify the case as a special case and refer it to a hearing, or*

(ii)   *if the circumstances are such as, in his opinion, make such certification inappropriate, return the case to the supervising officer.*

(4)   Where a case is not referred to a hearing no reference to it shall be made on the member concerned's personal record.

(5)   Proceedings at or in connection with a hearing to which a case is referred under this regulation shall, for the purposes of section 65 of the 1996 Act (interpretation of Chapter I of Part IV), be disciplinary proceedings.

Practice Note

If it is the *supervising* officer's opinion that the case is *likely* to satisfy the 'special case' conditions (see below), he/she must refer the case to the 'appropriate' officer. 'Appropriate officer' means (reg. 4(1)):

- where the member concerned is a member of the Metropolitan Police or the City of London Police, an assistant commissioner *in that force*, and
- in any other case, an assistant chief constable.

The appropriate officer will then need to determine whether the conditions in relation to 'special cases' are satisfied or not. If they are not, he/she must return the case to the supervising officer. If the conditions are satisfied, the appropriate officer must then either certify the case as a 'special case' (under reg. 11(3)(b)(i)) and refer it to a hearing or, if in his/her opinion it is not appropriate to make such a certification, refer it back to the supervising officer.

Any proceedings resulting from a referral under reg. 11 will be 'disciplinary proceedings' for the purposes of Part IV of the Police Act 1996 (reg. 11(5)).

No sanction may be imposed — under reg. 31 (see below) — unless a case has been referred to a hearing (reg. 14).

Withdrawal

The Police (Conduct) Regulations 1999, reg. 12 provides that:

(1)   At any time before the beginning of the hearing the supervising officer may direct that the case be withdrawn, unless the chief officer has a duty to proceed under section 75(7) or 76(2) or (5) of the 1996 Act.

(2)   Where a case is withdrawn it shall be treated as if the supervising officer had decided not to refer it to a hearing.

Practice Note

For the 'duty to proceed' under the relevant sections of the Police Act 1996, see above.

The effect of reg. 12(2) is that cases withdrawn before the beginning of a hearing will be treated as if they had never been referred in the first place and therefore no reference to them can be made on the member's personal record (see reg. 11(4) above).

Referral of cases to hearing

The Police (Conduct) Regulations 1999, reg. 13 provides that:

> *(1)   The supervising officer shall ensure that, as soon as practicable, the member concerned is given written notice of a decision to refer the case to a hearing and that, not less than 21 days before the date of hearing, the member concerned is supplied with copies of—*
>
> > *(a)   any statement he may have made to the investigating officer; and*
> >
> > *(b)   any relevant statement, document or other material obtained during the course of the investigation.*
>
> *(2)   The notice given under paragraph (1) shall specify the conduct of the member concerned which it is alleged failed to meet the appropriate standard and the paragraph of the Code of Conduct in respect of which the appropriate standard is alleged not to have been met.*
>
> *(3)   In this regulation any reference to a copy of a statement shall, where it was not made in writing, be construed as a reference to a copy of an account thereof.*

Regulation 14 provides that:

> *No sanction may be imposed under regulation 31 unless the case has been referred to a hearing.*

Practice Note

Regulation 13(1) makes two requirements. The first requirement is that the member be given written notice of the decision to refer the case to a hearing *as soon as practicable* (see also reg. 9 above). As with reg. 9, the wording suggests that the member must be served personally with the written notice here. This view is further reinforced by the modified wording used in reg. 13 in relation to 'special cases' (see below, and Appendix 4). This notice must specify the relevant conduct that allegedly failed to meet the appropriate standard, together with the relevant paragraph of the Code of Conduct (as to which, see above) (reg. 13(2)).

The second requirement is that, not less than 21 days before the date of the hearing, the member concerned be supplied with copies of the documents set out at reg. 13(1)(a) and (b), including a copy of any account or statement given verbally (reg. 13(3)).

Unless there is a hearing, no sanction under reg. 31 can be imposed (reg. 14).

Notice of hearing

The Police (Conduct) Regulations 1999, reg. 15 provides that:

(1)   The supervising officer shall ensure that at least 21 days in advance the member concerned is notified of the time, date and place of the hearing.

(2)   In a case to which this paragraph applies the hearing may, if the supervising officer considers it appropriate in the circumstances, take place before the expiry of the 21 days referred to in paragraph (1).

(3)   Paragraph (2) applies where the member concerned is given a written notice under regulation 13(1) of a decision to refer the case to a hearing and—

(a)   at the time he receives such a notice he is detained in pursuance of the sentence of a court in a prison or other institution to which the Prison Act 1952 applies, or has received a suspended sentence of imprisonment; and

(b)   having been supplied under regulation 13 with the documents therein mentioned he does not elect to be legally represented at the hearing.

Practice Note

Generally the member concerned must be given at least 21 days' notice of the time, date and place of any proposed hearing. However, in the (very unusual) circumstances set out at reg. 15(3)(a) and (b), the supervising officer may allow the hearing to take place earlier if he/she considers it appropriate in the circumstances. Regulation 15(1) does not specify the manner or form in which that notification is to be given (e.g. in writing, delivered personally, etc.) although the most easily proven method practicable under the circumstances might be preferred.

Regulation 16 provides that:

If the supervising officer is of the opinion that the hearing should have available the sanctions of dismissal, requirement to resign or reduction in rank, he shall cause the member concerned to be given notice in writing, at the same time as he is given notice of the hearing under regulation 15, of the opportunity to elect to be legally represented at the hearing and of the effect of section 84(1) to (3) of the 1996 Act.

Practice Note

Under reg. 16, if the supervising officer is of the opinion that the sanctions of

- dismissal,
- requirement to resign, or
- reduction in rank

should be available to the hearing, the supervising officer *must* make sure that any member concerned is given written notice that

- he/she is entitled to elect legal representation at the hearing, and
- the hearing cannot reduce the member in rank, require the member to resign or dismiss him/her unless he/she has been given the opportunity to elect such representation, and
- unless the member has so elected, the member may only be represented at the hearing by a 'friend' (that is a police officer).

This further notice must be given at the same time as the reg. 15 notice. Failure to notify the member of this entitlement will mean that the sanctions above will not be available and will also lead to the case being remitted under reg. 29 (see below).

Practically, this means that, if the opportunity to be legally represented is not given to the member concerned the only options open to the hearing are a fine, reprimand or caution (reg. 31(1)).

Regulation 17 provides that:

> *(1)   The member concerned shall be invited to state in writing, within 14 days of the date on which he is notified that the last of the documents required by regulation 13(1) to be supplied to him have been so supplied—*
>
> *(a)   whether or not he accepts that his conduct did not meet the appropriate standard;*
>
> *(b)   in a case where regulation 16 applies, whether he wishes to be legally represented at the hearing;*
>
> *(c)   whether he proposes to call any witnesses to relevant facts at the hearing and the names and addresses of any such witnesses whose attendance he wishes the supervising officer to take steps to secure.*
>
> *(2)   Any witness whose attendance the member concerned wishes the supervising officer to take steps to secure who is a member of a police force shall be ordered to attend at the hearing of the case, and the supervising officer, where so requested, shall cause any other such witnesses to be given due notice that their attendance is desired and of the time and place of the hearing.*
>
> *(3)   Nothing in this regulation shall require a hearing to be adjourned where a witness is unable or unwilling to attend the hearing.*

Practice Note

Under reg. 17(1), the member concerned will be 'invited' to state in writing:

- whether or not he/she accepts that his/her conduct did not meet the appropriate standard;
- whether he/she wishes to be legally represented (if reg. 16 applies);
- whether he/she proposes to call any witnesses and, if so, the names and addresses of those whose attendance he/she wishes the supervising officer to secure.

It does not appear to be necessary to give the details of any witnesses that the officer concerned proposes to call without the assistance of the supervising officer (contrast the situation in relation to efficiency hearings, see Chapter 3).

It is not compulsory for the officer concerned to make any written response and it would seem wrong to apply any pressure to do so. The regulations do not say who will make the 'invitation' to give such a response or when.

Any written response must be made within 14 days of the member being 'notified' that the last of the documents under reg. 13(1) have been supplied (reg. 17(1)). Presumably, the documents must also have *been* supplied otherwise the member will not be in a position to make a full evaluation of the case against him/her.

As with a statement made under reg. 9 (see above), any admission made under reg. 17 may have significant consequences for the member concerned, particularly as an admission can, without more, amount to a finding against him/her (see below).

Any witnesses who are police officers will be ordered to attend the hearing (reg. 17(2)). The member concerned will also be ordered to attend the hearing (reg. 24(1)). If he/she fails to attend the hearing, it may proceed and be concluded in his/her absence (reg. 24(2)) and any requirement under the 1999 Regulations that cannot be complied with because the member is absent will be dispensed with (reg. 24(4)). In other words, the hearing does not *have* to be adjourned simply because the member concerned is prevented from attending — either by ill-health or any other cause — and may proceed to conclusion without him/her. If any requirement under the 1999 Regulations cannot be complied with because the member concerned has not attended the hearing, that does not mean that the procedure will be delayed; it means that the requirement is dispensed with.

If, however, the member informs the officer presiding over the hearing in advance that he/she is unable to attend as a result of ill-health, *or some other unavoidable reason*, the hearing *may* be adjourned (reg. 24(3)). (For guidance on situations involving the officer's poor health, see Appendix 1, para. 3.67 and annex J).

The supervising officer must cause any other witnesses whose details have been given under reg. 17(1) to be notified that their attendance is required and to advise them of the time and place (and the date) of the hearing (reg. 17(2)).

A hearing does not *have* to be adjourned simply because a witness is unable or unwilling to attend (reg. 17(3)); however, the officers conducting a hearing have a discretionary power to do so in the appropriate circumstances.

The hearing

The Police (Conduct) Regulations 1999, reg. 18 provides that:

> *(1)   Where a case is referred to a hearing it shall be heard by three officers appointed by the chief officer concerned who shall not be interested parties.*

(2)   Subject to regulation 29, one such officer shall be of the rank of assistant chief constable or, where the member concerned is a member of the City of London or metropolitan police force of at least the rank of commander, who shall be the presiding officer.

(3)   Subject to paragraph (4), the presiding officer shall be assisted by two officers of at least the rank of superintendent who shall be from the same force as the member concerned.

(4)   Where the member concerned is a superintendent, the presiding officer shall be assisted by two officers of the rank of assistant chief constable or, if the assisting officers are members of the City of London or metropolitan police force, of at least the rank of commander, who shall be from a different force or forces from the member concerned.

Practice Note

Regulation 18 requires that the hearing be conducted by three officers who are not 'interested parties' (as to which, see reg. 7 above). This requirement attempts to remove any potential conflict of interest between the panel members and the officer concerned, but only extends to those having some form of direct interest *in the case itself*. However, care should be taken at all stages in the disciplinary process to avoid any such conflict or the appearance thereof, whether directly arising from the conduct case, or from any other matters outstanding against that officer. For example, where a chief officer is the respondent in pending employment tribunal proceedings brought by a particular individual, the chief officer should not hear any disciplinary proceedings against that individual officer (*R* v *Chief Constable of Merseyside Police, ex parte Carol Anne Bennion* (2000) LTL 29 June 2000). In that case the Divisional Court held that, by hearing a disciplinary case against an officer who was also bringing an action against him in the Employment Tribunal, the chief constable was acting as a judge in his own cause or, at best, was acting as judge where there was a real possibility of bias. The court held that the legal principle preventing anyone from so acting was well established (see e.g. *R* v *Bow Street Metropolitan Stipendiary Magistrate, ex parte Pinochet Ugarte (No. 2)* [2000] 1 All ER 577) and that there was no reason to believe that this principle did not apply to police disciplinary cases. It did not matter that the two types of proceedings were distinctly different, nor that there was no evidence of *actual* bias against the officer. Further submissions by the chief officer that the individual officer concerned must first exhaust all the relevant avenues under the disciplinary process before bringing the action for judicial review also failed and the decision of the disciplinary hearing was quashed. Although under the new conduct provisions set out in this chapter, chief constables/commissioners themselves will rarely, if at all, hear a case at first instance, the same principles could apply to an assistant chief constable/commissioner and will clearly apply to other stages where the chief constable/commissioner is involved.

Subject to reg. 29 dealing with 'remission of cases' (see below), under reg. 18(2) the 'presiding officer' at the hearing must be:

- an assistant chief constable, or
- in the case of a Metropolitan Police or City of London Police officer, a commander.

Generally, the other two assisting officers must be at least the rank of superintendent and must be from the same force as the member concerned (reg. 18(3)). However, under reg. 18(4), where the member concerned is a superintendent, the assisting officers must be assistant chief constables (or commanders in the case of Metropolitan Police and City of London Police officers) in different forces from that of the member concerned.

Documents to be supplied

The Police (Conduct) Regulations 1999, regs 19 and 20 provide that:

19.—(1)   Where the member concerned accepts, in accordance with regulation 17, that his conduct fell short of the appropriate standard a summary of the facts of the case shall be prepared, a copy of which shall be supplied to the member concerned at least 14 days before the hearing.

(2)   If the member concerned does not agree with the summary of facts he may submit a response within 7 days of receipt of the summary.

(3)   Where the member concerned does not accept that his conduct fell short of the appropriate standard no summary of facts shall be prepared.

20.   There shall be supplied to the officers conducting the hearing—

(a)   a copy of the notice given under regulation 13; and

(b)   where a summary of facts has been prepared under regulation 19, a copy of that summary and of any response from the member concerned.

Practice Note

Where the member concerned accepts, *in writing*, in accordance with reg. 17, that his/her conduct fell short of the 'appropriate standard' (i.e. the Code of Conduct), a summary of the facts of the case will be prepared and a copy supplied to the member at least 14 days before the hearing (reg. 19(1)). The 1999 Regulations do not say who is responsible for the preparation and supply of the summary.

If the member disagrees with the summary, he/she may submit a response within seven days *of receiving it* (reg. 19(2)). If the member has not accepted that his/her conduct fell short of the appropriate standard, there is no need for a summary (reg. 19(3)).

Where a summary of facts has been prepared, a copy of it will be supplied to the officers conducting the hearing in addition to a copy of the reg. 13 notice (reg. 20). Nothing is stipulated about furnishing a copy of any written acceptance made by the officer under reg. 17.

Representation

The Police (Conduct) Regulations 1999, reg. 21 provides that:

(1)   Unless the member concerned has given notice in accordance with regulation 17 that he wishes to be legally represented, the supervising officer shall appoint a member of a police force to present the case.

(2)   The member concerned may conduct his case either in person or by a member of a police force selected by him or, if he has given notice in accordance with regulation 17 that he wishes to be legally represented, by counsel or a solicitor.

Practice Note

Unless the member has given notice (under reg. 17) that he/she wishes to be legally represented, the *supervising officer* must appoint another police officer to present the case (reg. 21(1)). This would generally be someone of at least inspector rank from any police force. Where the member concerned has elected to be legally represented, this regulation leaves it open for the case to be presented by a solicitor/counsel.

The member concerned may conduct his/her own case in person or by another police officer chosen by him/her from any police force. If the member has given notice under reg. 17, he/she may then be represented by a solicitor/counsel (reg. 21(2)).

The government proposes to allow adverse inferences to be drawn from an officer's silence by extending the scope of s. 34 of the Criminal Justice and Public Order Act 1994 to police conduct proceedings (see clause 124 of the Criminal Justice and Police Bill which had not, at the time of writing, received Royal Assent). This does not appear to include a similar provision in relation to an officer's refusal or failure to give evidence at any hearing (s. 35 of the 1994 Act).

Procedure at hearing

The Police (Conduct) Regulations 1999, regs 22 and 23 provide that:

22.—(1)   The officers conducting the hearing may from time to time adjourn if it appears to them to be necessary or expedient to do so for the due hearing of the case.

(2)   Any decision of the officers conducting the hearing shall be based on a simple majority, but shall not indicate whether it was taken unanimously or by a majority.

23.—(1)   Subject to the provisions of these Regulations, the officers conducting the hearing shall determine their own procedure.

(2)   The officers conducting the hearing shall review the facts of the case and decide whether or not the conduct of the member concerned met the appropriate

standard and, if it did not, whether in all the circumstances it would be reasonable to impose any, and if so which, sanction.

(3)   The officers conducting the hearing shall not find that the conduct of the member concerned failed to meet the appropriate standard unless the conduct is—

(a)   admitted by the member concerned; or

(b)   proved by the person presenting the case on the balance of probabilities, *to have failed to meet that standard.*

Practice Note

The officers conducting the hearing will, subject to the provisions of the 1999 Regulations, determine their own procedure (reg. 23(1)). Any question as to whether any evidence is admissible, or whether any question should be put to a witness will also be determined by the officers conducting the hearing (reg. 28(1)). These widely drafted discretionary powers will, however, be subject to general principles of law (e.g. natural justice and human rights considerations).

Additionally, the presiding officer may, *with the consent of the member concerned*, allow any document to be adduced in evidence, even though no copy of it was supplied to the member under reg. 13 (reg. 28(2)).

The officers conducting the hearing may adjourn from time to time if it appears to them to be *necessary or expedient for the due hearing of the case* (reg. 22(1)). Any decision of the officers need only be based on a simple majority but must not indicate whether it was so decided or whether it was reached unanimously (reg. 22(2)). No provision is made for the presiding officer to have any form of 'casting vote' or for his/her view to carry any more weight than the assisting officers.

The job of the officers conducting the hearing (set out under reg. 23(2)) is threefold:

- they must first review the facts of the case and decide whether or not the member's conduct met the 'appropriate standard' (the Code of Conduct);
- if they decide that the member's conduct did not meet that standard, the officers must then decide whether, in all the circumstances, it would be reasonable to impose a sanction and, if so;
- they must determine which sanction to impose.

Therefore, a finding that the conduct fell short of the required standard does not automatically mean that any sanction must be imposed.

Under reg. 23(3) the officers conducting the hearing can only find that the member's conduct failed to meet the appropriate standard if:

- it is admitted by the member concerned; or
- it is proved by the person presenting the case *on the balance of probabilities*.

Thus, the standard of proof required in such hearings has been reduced to that of an ordinary civil trial (and that required of a defendant where the burden of proof falls on him/her). Although much attention has been given to this lowering of the standard of proof required, it is a general common law rule that the greater the consequences being faced by the defendant, the greater the degree of evidence that will be required to tip the balance of probabilities against him/her. In a case involving a disciplinary action against a fire officer the court held that:

> . . .the standard of proof depends on the nature of the issue. The more serious the allegation, the higher the degree of probability that is required; but it need not in a civil case reach the very high standard required by the criminal law.

(*R* v *Hampshire County Council, ex parte Ellerton* [1985] ICR 317).

Therefore, in setting the standard of proof in cases under the 1999 Regulations, it will be necessary to have regard to the precise nature of the allegations involved. A case arising out of a failure to observe the required standards of dress will attract a lower degree of probability than say a case where there is an allegation involving the officer's integrity or honesty.

Support for this view can be found in another case, *Bhandari* v *Advocates' Committee* [1956] 1 WLR 1442, this time concerning disciplinary proceedings against an advocate from Kenya, where the Privy Council said that:

> . . . in every allegation of professional misconduct involving an element of deceit or moral turpitude, a high standard of proof is called for and we cannot envisage any body of professional men [sic] sitting in judgment on a colleague who would be content to condemn on a mere balance of probabilities.

A verbatim record of the proceedings must be taken and, if the member concerned lodges notice of appeal (see below) and applies for a copy or transcript of the record within the time limit, it will be supplied to him/her (reg. 30).

Attendance at hearing

The Police (Conduct) Regulations 1999, regs 24 and 25 provide that:

24.—(*1*)   *The member concerned shall be ordered to attend the hearing.*

(2)   *If the member concerned fails to attend the hearing, it may be proceeded with and concluded in his absence.*

(3)   *Where the member concerned informs the presiding officer in advance that he is unable to attend due to ill-health or some other unavoidable reason, the hearing may be adjourned.*

(4)   *Where, owing to the absence of the member concerned, it is impossible to comply with any of the procedures set out in these Regulations, that procedure shall be dispensed with.*

25.—*(1)   This regulation shall apply where there has been a complaint against the member concerned.*

(2)   Notwithstanding anything in regulation 26(1), but subject to paragraphs (3) and (5), the complainant shall be allowed to attend the hearing while witnesses are being examined, or cross-examined, and may at the discretion of the presiding officer be accompanied by a friend or relative.

(3)   Where the complainant or any person allowed to accompany him is to be called as a witness at the hearing, he and any person allowed to accompany him shall not be allowed to attend before he gives his evidence.

(4)   Where the member concerned gives evidence, then, after the presenting officer has had an opportunity of cross-examining him, the presiding officer shall put to him any questions which the complainant requests should be so put and might have been properly so put by the presenting officer or, at the presiding officer's discretion, may allow the complainant to put such questions to the member concerned.

(5)   Subject as aforesaid, the complainant and any person allowed to accompany him shall neither intervene in, nor interrupt, the hearing; and if he or such a person shall behave in a disorderly or abusive manner, or otherwise misconduct himself, the presiding officer may exclude him from the remainder of the hearing.

(6)   In this regulation a reference to the complainant is a reference to the originator of the complaint notwithstanding that it was transmitted to the chief officer concerned by some other person or by the Authority or some other body.

Practice Note

Attendance at a hearing will be a duty commitment for the officer concerned and he/she will be ordered to attend. Failure to obey that order may therefore be an offence itself under the Code of Conduct (see above).

Regulations 24(2) and (4) make it quite clear that a hearing can take place without the officer concerned being present. However, in cases where the officer is unable to attend as a result of ill health or, 'some other avoidable reason', reg. 24(3) makes provision for the adjournment of the hearing where the officer so informs the presiding officer in advance. For further guidance see Appendix 1, section 3.

Regulation 25 provides that the originator of a complaint ('the complainant') will, as a general rule, be allowed to attend the hearing *while witnesses are being examined or cross-examined*. The complainant may also be accompanied by a friend or relative at the discretion of the presiding officer (reg. 25(2)). If the complainant or any accompanying friend/relative is to give evidence, neither will be allowed to attend the hearing before *he/she* gives evidence (reg. 25(3)). It is unclear whether this restriction applies to:

- the presence of either the complainant or the accompanying person before the *latter* gives evidence; or
- the presence of either the complainant or the accompanying person before *either* gives evidence.

In the interests of fairness it would seem that the second interpretation might be preferred, particularly if the purpose of the provision is to prevent the complainant from learning of any detail (through the testimony of others) that might influence his/her own evidence-in-chief.

If the member concerned gives evidence, he/she may be asked questions by the presiding officer on behalf of the complainant after the cross-examination. He/she may also be asked questions *by the complainant* at the presiding officer's discretion (reg. 25(4)). Contrast this with the much more 'closed' procedure where senior officers are concerned (see Chapter 8).

Notwithstanding these provisions, the complainant and anyone accompanying him/her must not intervene in or interrupt the hearing. If any of these people misconduct themselves or behave in a disorderly or abusive manner, the presiding officer may exclude them from the hearing (reg. 25(5)). Although the regulation does not extend the specific power to exclude people beyond the complainant and those accompanying him/her in the event of disruption or misconduct, there may be a residual power to do so under reg. 23(1).

Regulations 26 and 27 provide that:

26.—*(1)   Subject to regulation 25 and paragraphs (2) and (3), the hearing shall be in private:*

Provided that it shall be within the discretion of the presiding officer to allow any solicitor or any such other persons as he considers desirable to attend the whole or such part of the hearing as he may think fit, subject to the consent of all parties to the hearing.

(2)   Any member of the Authority shall be entitled to attend the hearing in a case to which regulation 25 applies or which arises from a matter to which section 72 of the 1996 Act applies.

(3)   The member concerned may be accompanied at the hearing by a member of a police force.

(4)   The presiding officer may allow witnesses to be accompanied at the hearing by a friend or relative.

27.   *Where it appears to the presiding officer that a witness may, in giving evidence, disclose information which, in the public interest, ought not to be disclosed to a member of the public he shall require any member of the public including the complainant and any person allowed to accompany the complainant or any witness to withdraw while the evidence is given.*

Practice Note

Generally, hearings will be conducted in private (reg. 26(1)). However, there are some exceptions:

* The member concerned may be accompanied by another police officer (reg. 26(3)).

- The presiding officer may allow witnesses to be accompanied by a friend or a relative (reg. 26(4)).

Where there has been a complaint made against the member concerned, whether directly or through the Police Complaints Authority or some other person/body, the person who originated the complaint will generally be allowed to attend parts of the hearing. (For a discussion of the term 'complaint' see the Practice Note to reg. 5 above.)

If it appears to the presiding officer that a witness may disclose in evidence information which, in the public interest, ought not to be disclosed to the public, he/she must require any member of the public (including complainants and their accompanying friends) to withdraw while the evidence is given (reg. 27).

The presiding officer has discretion to allow the presence of any solicitor or other person that he/she considers desirable to attend the whole or part of the hearing, subject to the consent of all parties to the hearing (reg. 26(1)).

Members of the Police Complaints Authority are entitled to attend hearings where there has been a complaint against the member concerned or where the case arose from a matter requiring the mandatory supervision of the investigation by the Authority (reg. 26(2)). Home Office guidance also advises that members of the Authority be allowed to attend hearings where they have exercised their authority under the Police Act 1996, s. 76 (recommending or directing that a chief officer bring proceedings against an officer).

Statements in lieu of oral evidence

The Police (Conduct) Regulations 1999, reg. 28 provides that:

> *(1)   Any question as to whether any evidence is admissible, or whether any question should or should not be put to a witness, shall be determined by the presiding officer.*
>
> *(2)   With the consent of the member concerned the presiding officer may allow any document to be adduced in evidence during the hearing notwithstanding that a copy thereof has not been supplied to the member concerned in accordance with regulation 13(1).*

Practice Note

The discretion of the presiding officer granted by reg. 28 is subject to the rules of natural justice (as to which, see Chapter 10).

Documents that were not copied to the officer concerned under reg. 13 (see above) may still be admitted in evidence provided that both the presiding officer and the officer concerned agree.

Remission of cases

The Police (Conduct) Regulations 1999, reg. 29 provides that:

(1)   The hearing of the case—
(a)   shall, in the circumstances mentioned in paragraph (2); or
(b)   may, in the circumstances mentioned in paragraph (5),
be remitted by the presiding officer concerned to an officer of equivalent rank in the force concerned or to an officer of equivalent rank in another force who, at the presiding officer's request, has agreed to act as the presiding officer in the matter.

(2)   A case shall be so remitted if—
(a)   the presiding officer is 'an interested party otherwise than in his capacity as such; or
(b)   there would not, because the member concerned was not given notice under regulation 16 of the opportunity to elect to be legally represented at the hearing, be available on a finding against him any of the sanctions referred to in that regulation, and it appears to the presiding officer concerned that those sanctions ought to be so available and that accordingly it would be desirable for there to be another hearing at which the member concerned could, if he so wished, be so represented.

(3)   Where a case is remitted to another officer under paragraph (2)(b) notice in writing shall be served on the member concerned inviting him to elect, within 14 days of the receipt thereof, to be legally represented at the hearing before that officer.

(4)   An officer remitting a case under paragraph (2)(b) shall not give to the officer to whom the case has been remitted any indication of his assessment of the case or of the sanction which might be imposed.

(5)   A case not falling within paragraph (2) may be remitted by the presiding officer in accordance with paragraph (1) if, either before or during the hearing, the presiding officer concerned considers remission appropriate.

Practice Note

Remission of a hearing really means passing it over to another officer of equivalent rank, either in the force concerned or of another force.

The hearing of a case *must* be remitted if:

- the presiding officer is an 'interested party'; or
- if the member was not given the opportunity to elect legal representation under reg. 16 (see above), thereby limiting the sanctions available to the hearing

and the presiding officer feels that those sanctions ought to be available.

In addition, the hearing of a case *may* be remitted if, either before or during the hearing, the presiding officer considers it appropriate (reg. 29(5)).

If the case is remitted under the second item above, the member must be served in writing with a notice inviting him/her to elect *within 14 days of receipt*, to be legally represented. Further, in such cases, the officer remitting the case must not give any indication of his/her assessment of the case, nor of the sanction that might be imposed to the 'new' officer. This suggests that, in cases where the hearing is remitted under the first item above, or in cases where discretionary remission is adopted, the presiding officer *may* indicate his/her assessment of the case so far and also any sanctions that he/she thinks ought to be imposed.

Record of hearing

The Police (Conduct) Regulations 1999, reg. 30 provides that:

> *A verbatim record of the proceedings at the hearing shall be taken and, if the member concerned so requests within the time limit for any appeal and after he has lodged notice of appeal in accordance with rules made under section 85 of the Police Act 1996, a transcript of the record or a copy thereof shall be supplied to him by the presiding officer.*

Practice Note

For the procedures relating to appeals generally, see Chapter 7.

The sanctions

The Police (Conduct) Regulations 1999, reg. 31 provides that:

> *(1)   Subject to section 84(1) of the 1996 Act, the officers conducting the hearing may impose any of the following sanctions, namely—*
> *(a)   dismissal from the force;*
> *(b)   requirement to resign from the force as an alternative to dismissal taking effect either forthwith or on such date as may be specified in the decision;*
> *(c)   reduction in rank;*
> *(d)   fine;*
> *(e)   reprimand;*
> *(f)   caution.*
> *(2)   Any sanction imposed under paragraph (1), except a requirement to resign, shall have immediate effect.*
> *(3)   A fine imposed under paragraph (1) shall be such that, if it were recovered by way of deductions from the pay of the member concerned during the period of thirteen weeks following the imposition of the sanction, the aggregate sum which might be so deducted in respect of any one week (whether on account of one or more fines) would not exceed one seventh of his weekly pay.*

Regulations 32 and 33 provide that:

> **32.**   *Where the question of the sanction to be imposed is being considered, the officers conducting the hearing—*
> *(a)   shall have regard to the record of police service of the member concerned as shown on his personal record and may receive evidence from any*

witness whose evidence would, in the opinion of the officers conducting the hearing or member concerned, assist in determining the question; and

(b)   the member concerned, or his representative, shall be afforded an opportunity to make oral or, if appropriate, written representations as respects the question or to adduce evidence relevant thereto.

33.   *The member concerned shall be informed orally of the finding and of any sanction imposed at the conclusion of the hearing and shall be provided with a written notification and summary of the reasons within three days.*

Practice Note

The reference to s. 84(1) of the Police Act 1996 in reg. 31 is to the general prohibition on imposing a reduction in rank, requirement to resign or dismissal without having first given the officer an opportunity to elect legal representation.

Any of the above sanctions *except a requirement to resign,* will have immediate effect (reg. 31(2)). This immediate effect will not be delayed by any appeal procedure.

If a fine is imposed, it is subject to a maximum limit (set out under reg. 31(3)). To work out the maximum amount of the fine you must first assume that it is to be recovered from the officer concerned by weekly deductions over the next 13 weeks. The overall sum — whether one fine or a number of fines — when spread across these 13 weeks must not exceed one-seventh of the officer's weekly pay (i.e. 13 weeks is the figure to be used in calculating the amount of the fine rather than the means of paying it). In other words, the fine(s) cannot exceed 13 days' pay — though reg. 31 does not say whether that is gross pay or net pay. Neither does reg. 31 appear to require the fine *to be paid* over the 13-week period following the imposition of the sanctions.

In considering what sanction to impose, the officers conducting the hearing *must* have regard to the officer's service record (reg. 32(a)). In doing so, they *may* receive evidence from witnesses if the officers are of the opinion that such evidence would help them (reg. 32(a)).

The officer concerned must be given the opportunity to make oral or written representations in respect of any sanction (either in person or through his/her representative (reg. 32(b)).

At the time of writing there was no provision requiring an officer reduced in rank to 're-qualify'. Therefore an officer who has passed the relevant qualifying examinations to the rank of sergeant or inspector (under the Police Promotion Regulations 1996 (SI 1996 No. 1685)) retains his/her qualification and will be eligible for promotion in the future.

At the end of the hearing the officer concerned must be informed *orally* of:

- the finding; and
- any sanction imposed.

He/she must also be provided with:

- *written notification*, and
- a *summary of the reasons*

within three days of the end of the hearing (reg. 33). Presumably responsibility for giving this information rests with the presiding officer though the 1999 Regulations do not say so.

However this notification is provided, it is important to be able to prove receipt of it as this will be the trigger for the time limit on any review process (as to which, see Chapter 6).

Once a particular sanction has been imposed, any later action by a chief officer superseding that sanction (whether by intention or effect) may amount to an unlawful frustration of the legitimate expectations of the officer concerned (see e.g. *R* v *Chief Constable of Merseyside Police, ex parte O'Leary* (2001) LTL 9 February). In such circumstances the officer concerned may apply for a judicial review of the decision (as to which see Chapter 10).

A Police Authority does not have the power to pay the costs of a police officer of the rank of superintendent or below in relation to internal disciplinary proceedings (*R* v *South Yorkshire Police Authority, ex parte Andrew Booth* (2000) *The Times*, 10 October 2000). A Police Authority does, however, have the power to provide financial assistance to police officers in relation to criminal proceedings and applications for judicial review by virtue of s. 6(1) of the Police Act 1996 and s. 111(1) of the Local Government Act 1972 (see *R* v *Director of Public Prosecutions, ex parte Duckenfield* [2000] 1 WLR 55).

Record of proceedings

Under the Police (Conduct) Regulations 1999, reg. 38, chief officers must keep a book recording details of every case brought against a member of their force. The entry in that book must include details of the findings, together with any other decisions reached in proceedings connected with the case (e.g. any sanction imposed).

Special cases

The Police (Conduct) Regulations 1999, reg. 39, makes provision for very serious cases involving criminal offences. It modifies the 1999 Regulations for those cases (see sch. 2) and the modified text appears in Appendix 4.

KEY STAGES: MISCONDUCT (NON-COMPLAINT)

What	Who	How	When
Suspension of officer concerned	Chief officer (police officer) — may delegate to assistant chief constable/ commander	Exercise power given by reg. 5	On report, complaint or allegation that officer's conduct does not meet appropriate standard
Notice of investigation	Investigating officer (police officer)	Give notice to officer concerned in accordance with reg. 9	As soon as practicable (without prejudicing *any* investigation of the matter)
Written report	Investigating officer (police officer)	Submit written report to supervising officer and, if relevant, the Police Complaints Authority	At the end of the investigation or if it appears that it will be a 'special case', as soon as that becomes apparent to the investigating officer
Notice of decision to refer to hearing	Supervising officer (police officer from same force as officer concerned)	Give written notice to officer concerned	As soon as practicable
Copy of documents	Supervising officer (police officer from same force as officer concerned)	Ensure that officer concerned is served with copies of documents set out in reg. 13	Not less than 21 days before date of hearing

What	Who	How	When
Response after receipt of reg. 13 documents	Officer concerned	Written statement saying: • whether or not he/she accepts that conduct did not meet appropriate standard • whether he/she wishes to be legally represented (if reg. 16 applies) • whether he/she proposes to call any witnesses • names and addresses of those witnesses whose attendance he/she wants supervising officer to secure	Within 14 days of the date on which notified that last of reg. 13 documents has been supplied
Notice of time, date and place of hearing	Supervising officer (police officer from same force as officer concerned)	Ensure that officer concerned is 'notified' (no specified method)	At least 21 days in advance of hearing (unless officer concerned has been sentenced to term of imprisonment and circumstances in reg. 15(3) apply
Notice of opportunity to be legally represented	Officer concerned	Give officer concerned notice in writing if supervising officer is of opinion that sanctions of dismissal, requirement to resign or reduction in rank should be available	At same time as notice of hearing under reg. 15

What	Who	How	When
Appointment of presiding officer and assisting officers	Chief officer (police officer)	Three officers appointed under requirements of reg. 18 (e.g. one assistant chief constable/commander and two superintendents)	Before the hearing
Summary of facts	Not specified	Where officer concerned accepts allegation per reg. 17, summary of facts is to be prepared and supplied to officer	At least 14 days before hearing
Appointment of presenting officer	Supervising officer (police officer from same force as officer concerned)	Appoint another police officer to present case unless officer concerned has given notice that he/she wishes to be legally represented	Before the hearing
Review facts of case and decide whether conduct met appropriate standard	Officers conducting hearing (police officers)	By simple majority but without stating ratio of votes	By conclusion of hearing
Impose sanction if appropriate	Officers conducting hearing (police officers)	• By simple majority but without stating ratio of votes • Impose relevant sanction in accordance with reg. 31	After making decision that conduct of officer concerned did not meet the appropriate standard
First notification of finding and sanction	Not specified	Orally	At the conclusion of the hearing

What	Who	How	When
Confirmation of finding/ sanction and summary of reasons	Not specified	Provide officer concerned with written notification and summary of reasons	Within three days of conclusion of the hearing

5 COMPLAINTS AGAINST POLICE

THE COMPLAINTS SYSTEM

Any effective and credible police complaints system has to provide a transparent, thorough and truly impartial fact-finding process, while at the same time affording proper protection to individual police officers and those who deploy them. Steering a course between the rights of those who feel aggrieved at the conduct of the police on the one hand, and the operational realities of providing an effective police service on the other, is notoriously difficult. In an attempt to do just that, various measures have been introduced in the police complaints system over recent years but there are several areas where there is continuing dissatisfaction. There are also areas where there is mutual agreement among the many 'stakeholders' in the process.

One of the statutory developments in the recent history of the police complaints system has been the creation and growth of the Police Complaints Authority (PCA). Since its inception the PCA has tried to provide a framework for the transparent supervision of alleged police misconduct, particularly in relation to the more serious complaints against police officers. The role of the PCA within the current framework is set out below. However, despite what some claim to be the relative success of the present system for investigating complaints against the police, there have been many calls for a change in the law governing this area (see *Independent Investigations and Improving Public Confidence*, a paper by Sadiq Khan, Capita Conference 8th June 2000). By way of response, the government recently began a long consultation process during which alternative schemes were proposed by consultants KPMG and Liberty. Having some significant misgivings of their own, the PCA have also proposed changes to the present system (see *Police Review*, 26 May 2000). The consultation process was, at the time of writing, still underway and in February 2001 the government published draft proposals for substantive changes in the supervision and investigation of police complaints. These are summarised below.

The key areas of the current system which have attracted particular criticism are:

Independence

The present system involves police officers investigating other police officers. The issue of non-police investigators and panel members at conduct hearings has been hotly debated for some time and there are those who feel that this is the only way in which to achieve independence — real and perceived. To an extent this has been introduced for the investigation of the conduct of the most senior officers (see Chapter 9) and also in the creation of the Police Ombudsman scheme in Northern Ireland. In support of the case for non-police Investigating Officers (IOs), proponents cite the fact that, despite their name, such officers do not actually *investigate* anything, but rather manage and direct a team of trained investigators. This removes any need for the IO to hold the office of 'constable' as opposed to being given the relevant *powers*, together with training in their use.

In addition, the *name* of the PCA suggests that it is a police organisation or is in some way directly connected with the officers whose conduct has been complained about, thus compounding any perceived lack of independence.

The need to involve independent roles in the initiation of disciplinary investigations and the bringing of disciplinary hearings (as to which, see Chapter 4) has also found support among many commentators and practitioners.

As many of the more serious complaints against police officers often include criminal allegations, the consideration of prosecuting the officer(s) concerned is often in issue. The decision as to whether a police officer (or anyone else) should face prosecution or not is taken by the Crown Prosecution Service (CPS), a department staffed and controlled by the Lord Chancellor's Department and working in close proximity to the police (particularly now that some CPS lawyers work inside police stations). Again this has been viewed as representing a lack of independence — whether perceived or actual.

The making of complaints

The *locus standi* or right to bring a complaint against a police officer is currently restricted and, arguably, restrictive. The present system (set out below) gives little opportunity for third parties to bring a complaint on another's behalf, nor for members of the public having a generic or communal interest in the behaviour of the police (e.g. those who witness an incident involving alleged misconduct on the part of the police). Moreover, even where someone does have sufficient *locus*, the system provides no redress should the police decide not to record a reported matter as a 'complaint'.

Similarly, concerns have been raised over the inability of organisations such as the PCA to appeal against the findings of conduct hearings.

Transparency

Many commentators and practitioners have expressed concern at the lack of transparency in the current system — or at least the presence of some significant 'blindspots' (e.g. the disclosure of the IO's report). The question of transparency is central to many of the issues arising from independence (above). Taken together, these shortcomings have been cited as evidence that the current statutory system surrounding police complaints does not provide 'an effective remedy' as required by the European Convention on Human Rights (*Govell* v *United Kingdom* [1999] EHRLR 121).

The future

Within its consultation paper, the government has suggested the following modifications to the police complaints system:

- The creation of a replacement for the PCA — the Independent Police Complaints Commission (IPCC). It is envisaged that the IPCC would have a much more independent and proactive role, extending to the provision of advice and guidance on bringing complaints. The IPCC would have its own trained investigation managers who would be civilians, co-ordinating teams of police and non-police investigators. The IPCC would have discretionary powers to observe and present discipline cases, and to work with HMIC in inspecting police forces' performance in complaints handling. The IPCC would also be responsible for determining whether cases are submitted to the CPS (although the decision to bring a prosecution would remain with the CPS).
- A revised complaints system to include all ranks, special constables and civilian employees and to allow complaints about the way in which a police force is directed and controlled.
- The provision of a right of appeal to the IPCC against any refusal to record a complaint.
- A greater degree of discretion for the IPCC, chief officers and police authorities to disclose information to complainants.
- The introduction of new procedures for processing criminal and disciplinary issues when civil claims are lost or settled by the police.
- 'Informal resolutions' would be retained but renamed 'local' resolutions and the IPCC would have powers to review and monitor the use of the system.

Clearly these proposals, if accepted, would address some (though not all) of the issues discussed above. Although the detail has yet to be agreed, these substantive changes, set against the backdrop of individual Convention rights reinforced by the Human Rights Act 1998 (see Chapter 1), may go some considerable way to achieving the critical balance between the police service's accountability and its operational effectiveness.

Part IV of the Police Act 1996 sets out the provisions for the recording and investigation of complaints against police officers. Every police authority and Her Majesty's Inspectorate of Constabulary (HMIC) is under a statutory duty to 'keep themselves informed' as to the workings of the relevant sections of the 1996 Act relating to the recording and investigation of complaints (s. 77). Further detail as to HMIC responsibilities in relation to complaints is set out at Appendix 1, annex K.

Provisions are also made for the making of regulations in respect of non-Home Office police forces under s. 78 of the 1996 Act (such as the British Transport Police and the Ministry of Defence Police).

The Police Act 1996, s. 65, defines a complaint as:

> . . . *a complaint about the conduct of a member of a police force which is submitted—*
>
> (a) *by a member of the public, or*
> (b) *on behalf of a member of the public and with his written consent.*

Practice Note

Therefore a complaint so defined must emanate from a member of the public and must be made about the conduct of a 'member of a police force'. As special constables and cadets are not members of a police force, the definition — and the attendant procedures — do not apply to them.

The definition allows for the reporting of complaints by third parties acting on behalf of the member of the public, for example, MPs, Citizens Advice Bureaux or friends/family. If a complaint is made by another person/ organisation, there must be some form of writing that indicates the complainant's willingness for that person/organisation to submit the complaint on their behalf. This would presumably include e-mails and other electronically generated messages. It is clear from other parts of the 1996 Act (e.g. s. 67 below) that complaints need not be in writing and can be made orally.

Clearly there will be occasions where there may be an overlap in the procedures relating to complaints, conduct and performance. Local advice should be sought from the relevant complaints department (see Appendix 7 for contact details) in the recording and investigation of such incidents.

There is no requirement for the officer concerned to have been on duty at the time of the conduct complained of and again local guidance should be sought in relation to the recording and investigation of 'complaints' of off-duty police officers.

The definition does not extend to complaints in so far as they relate to the *direction or control* of a police force by the chief officer (s. 67(4)).

Where the conduct complained of is (or has been) wholly or partly the subject of criminal or disciplinary proceedings, none of the provisions relating to the recording and investigation of complaints under Chapter 1 of Part IV of the 1996 Act applies (s. 67(5)).

Steps to be taken

The Police Act 1996, s. 67 provides that:

(1)   Where a complaint is submitted to the chief officer of police for a police area, he shall take any steps that appear to him to be desirable for the purpose of obtaining or preserving evidence relating to the conduct complained of.

(2)   After complying with subsection (1), the chief officer shall determine whether he is the appropriate authority in relation to the member of a police force whose conduct is the subject of the complaint.

(3)   If the chief officer determines that he is not the appropriate authority, he shall—

(a)   send the complaint or, if it was submitted orally, particulars of it, to the appropriate authority, and

(b)   give notice that he has done so to the person by whom or on whose behalf the complaint was submitted.

Practice Note

The first duty to fall on a chief officer on receipt of a complaint is to obtain and preserve evidence. This duty is not dependent on the complaint having any prima facie foundation, neither is it dependent on the determination as to who is the 'appropriate authority'. Under s. 65, that 'authority' will be:

- in relation to a Metropolitan Police officer — the commissioner;
- in relation to an officer above the rank of superintendent from another force — the police authority for that force;
- in relation to an officer of superintendent rank or below from another force — the chief officer of that force.

The procedure to be followed in respect of senior officers above the rank of superintendent is set out in s. 68 (see Chapter 8).

If the chief officer receiving the complaint determines that he/she is not the appropriate authority, he/she must follow the requirements set out at s. 67(3)(a) and (b) above.

Steps to obtain or preserve evidence relating to the conduct complained of might include:

- taking possession of pocket notebooks or incident report books, custody records, etc.;
- securing recordings made by CCTV cameras or tapes/logs of control-room messages;
- taking initial witness statements and photographs;
- obtaining information stored on police computer systems.

Once these steps in relation to the preservation of evidence and determination of the appropriate authority have been completed, the complaint must be recorded (s. 69(1)).

After recording a complaint, the chief officer must decide whether it is suitable for informal resolution (see below) and may appoint another member of the force to assist (s. 69(2)). If the complaint is suitable for informal resolution, the chief officer must seek to resolve it informally and may appoint another officer from that force to do so (s. 69(4)).

If, after attempts have been made to resolve a complaint informally (see below), it appears to the chief officer that such informal resolution is 'impossible' or that the complaint is, for any other reason not suitable for informal resolution, he/she must appoint another officer of that, or some other force, to investigate it (s. 69(6)). 'Impossible' is a finite term that is much greater than mere 'impracticability'. It is more likely then that informal resolution would be found to be unsuitable for some other reason.

Under s. 69(3), a complaint will not be suitable for informal resolution unless:

- the member of the public consents; and
- the chief officer is satisfied that the conduct complained of, even if proved, would not justify criminal *or disciplinary* proceedings.

If the complaint is not suitable for informal resolution, the chief officer must appoint another member of that, or some other force, to investigate it (s. 69(5)). Any request by a chief officer for the chief officer of another force to provide an officer to investigate a complaint (under s. 69(5) or (6)) must comply with the request (s. 69(8)).

Any officer who has previously been appointed to resolve a complaint informally may not later investigate the complaint (s. 69(7)).

Unless the investigation of the complaint is supervised by the Police Complaints Authority under s. 72 (see below), the investigating officer must submit any report on the complaint to the chief officer who appointed him/her (s. 69(9)).

Informal resolution

As one of the few areas under the current complaints system for which there is general approbation, the informal resolution procedures are built on the principles of flexibility and simplicity and they are intended to prevent cases of a minor nature from receiving the full attentions of formal investigation. The procedure for the informal resolution of complaints is to be found mainly in the Police (Complaints) (Informal Resolution) Regulations 1985 (SI 1985 No. 671) (see Appendix 8).

In addition to the restrictions placed on informal resolution under s. 69(3) of the Police Act 1996 above, a complaint that is supervised by the Police Complaints Authority, under its mandatory or discretionary remit, may not be informally resolved (reg. 3 of the 1985 Regulations).

Appointed officers

If it is decided that informal resolution is appropriate, the officer initially deputed to handle the question may act as the 'appointed officer' (as defined in the 1985 Regulations) and seek an informal resolution. Alternatively, the case might be referred to another officer to undertake the role of appointed officer.

As soon as practicable after the decision to resolve the complaint informally, the appointed officer should seek the views of both the complainant and also the officer whose conduct has been complained of (reg. 4(1)). The officer should be allowed to speak to a 'friend' about the matter first if he/she wishes. For further discussion on the role of 'friend', (see Chapter 2).

At the same time, or thereafter, the appointed officer may take any steps that appear to be appropriate to resolve the complaint.

Early resolution

Regulation 4(1) of the 1985 Regulations allows a supervisory officer of whatever rank to deal speedily with a complaint if it appears to them that it can be resolved in an informal manner at the time it is made.

Regulation 4 allows a supervisory officer to receive a complaint and, if the officer complained about is both present and willing to explain his/her understanding of the incident giving rise to the complaint, to deal with it at the time. In order to do this, the complainant must accept the explanation given or, if appropriate, any apology as a satisfactory outcome.

There is no requirement imposed on an officer to give an apology and the supervisor cannot do so on the officer's behalf unless the officer agrees that his/her conduct fell below the required standard. However, that does not prevent the supervisor apologising on behalf of the force.

If any explanation or apology is accepted, the supervisory officer should report the matter to the officer who has delegated responsibility for the informal resolution of complaints. If satisfied with the handling of the complaint, that officer may make a record in the complaints register and write to the complainant noting the way in which the complaint was handled and indicating the intention of recording it as having been informally resolved.

Where it appears to the appointed officer that the resolution of a complaint is likely to be assisted by a meeting between the complainant and the officer concerned — or also with any other person considered appropriate — then suitable arrangements may be made.

There will be no obligation on the officer who is the subject of the complaint to attend such a meeting. A meeting may provide an opportunity for the complainant and the officer to exchange views and for any misunderstandings to be cleared up. It will also allow the officer, where there is an admission to the conduct complained of, to offer an explanation or an apology to the complainant. If in the course of the informal resolution procedure evidence comes to light of a more serious complaint which might require a formal investigation, the informal procedures should be terminated and the matter reported to the chief officer immediately, whereupon the provisions of Part IV of the 1996 Act will apply.

Where there has been an attempted or a successful informal resolution of a complaint, no record must be made of it in the personal record of the officer concerned. Where informal resolution appears to be impossible or it is apparent that the complaint is for any other reason not suitable to be so resolved, arrangements must be made for it to be investigated formally.

Admissibility of statements

Generally a statement made for the purpose of an informal resolution of a complaint will not be admissible in any criminal, civil or disciplinary hearing (Police Act 1996, s. 86(1)). Where an officer makes a voluntary statement — oral or written — to the appointed officer, that officer must be told that this is the case. However, where the statement made consists of, or includes an admission relating to any matter that is not part of that complaint, s. 86(1) will *not* prevent it from being so used (s. 86(2)). Therefore informed consideration should be given by the officer before he/she makes any admissions in relation to the attempted informal resolution of a complaint.

The Police Complaints Authority

The Police Complaints Authority (PCA) is an independent body set up to oversee, among other things, the investigation of complaints against the police. It replaced the former Police Complaints Board. The PCA was originally established under s. 83 of the Police and Criminal Evidence Act 1984. Its role has become increasingly important in ensuring the thorough and impartial investigation and supervision of sensitive and serious matters involving police conduct. If there is any doubt as to whether or not the PCA ought to be informed of any matter involving the conduct of police officers, advice should be sought from the relevant force complaints and discipline department or from the PCA itself. (For contact details, see Appendix 7.)

The PCA is made up of at least eight members plus a chair who is appointed by the Crown. Its constitution can be found in sch. 5 to the Police Act 1996 (see Appendix 9).

Certain complaints made against police officers must be *referred* to the PCA. There are also provisions as to which investigations the PCA either may, or must, *supervise*.

Referral

The Police Act 1996, s. 70(1)(a) requires that the following complaints be *referred* to the PCA, i.e. complaints alleging that the conduct complained of resulted in:

- the death of, or serious injury to, some other person; or

- assault occasioning actual bodily harm, bribery or a serious arrestable offence

(Police (Complaints) (Mandatory Referrals etc.) Regulations 1985 (SI 1985 No. 673)).

Section 70(2) allows the PCA to 'call in' any complaint not referred to them, irrespective of whether it meets the above criteria or not. An example of such a complaint might be where there has been an allegation of the discriminatory use of police powers to stop and search (as to which, see Blackstone's Police Manuals).

Section 71 allows chief officers to refer to the PCA other serious or exceptional matters not arising from a complaint but which indicate that an officer may have committed a criminal offence. An example here would be the investigation of accidents involving police vehicles.

Supervision

It appears from the wording of s. 72 of the Police Act 1996 that any complaint involving the conduct set out in the bullet points above must be supervised by the PCA. It must also supervise any other complaint that is not within those criteria but which it determines is in the public interest for it to supervise.

Where the PCA supervise an investigation, it may place certain conditions on the appointment, or continued appointment, of a particular investigating officer (s. 72(3)). It may also make reasonable requirements in relation to the direction of the investigation and the resources committed to it. However, the PCA may not make any requirement relating to the obtaining and preserving of evidence in connection with a complaint where the possibility of criminal proceedings arises unless it has the consent of the Crown Prosecution Service. It must also seek the views of the relevant chief officer before making a requirement as to the commitment of his/her resources to an investigation.

At the end of a supervised investigation, the investigating officer must submit a report to the PCA as well as sending a copy to the 'appropriate authority' (the chief officer or police authority) (s. 73(1)). After considering the report, the PCA will send a statement to the appropriate authority and, if it is practicable to do so, send a copy to the officer whose conduct is being investigated and to the complainant. That statement will say whether the investigation has been carried out to the PCA's satisfaction and specify any respect in which it has not been so carried out (s. 73(9)).

Ordinarily, no disciplinary proceedings or criminal proceedings may be brought until the PCA's statement has been submitted (s. 73(6) and (7)) but, in exceptional circumstances, the Director of Public Prosecutions may bring criminal proceedings before the submission if it is undesirable to wait (s. 73(8)).

Procedure after investigation

At the end of any investigation, supervised or not, the chief officer must determine whether the report indicates that a criminal offence may have been committed by the officer. If he/she does conclude that a criminal offence may have been committed, the chief officer must send a copy of the report to the Director of Public Prosecutions (Police Act 1996, s. 75(2) to (3)).

Once the question of criminal proceedings has been dealt with, the chief officer will send a memorandum to the PCA stating whether or not it is proposed to bring disciplinary proceedings against the officer and if not, why not (s. 75(4)). This memorandum will be accompanied by a copy of the complaint and a copy of the report of the investigation. Where a memorandum from the chief officer indicates that no disciplinary proceedings are to be brought, the PCA may 'recommend' to him/her that such proceedings *are* brought (s. 76(1)). If, having made such a recommendation and consulted with the chief officer, he/she still does not bring disciplinary proceedings, the PCA may *direct* him/her to do so, giving written reasons (s. 76(3) to (4)). The chief officer must then (s. 76(7)):

- comply with this direction unless it is withdrawn (s. 76(5) to (6));
- advise the PCA of any action taken; and
- supply the PCA with such other information as it may reasonably require in discharging its functions.

Withdrawn or ill-founded complaints

Although there is no specific legal remedy available against someone who makes a false complaint against a police officer, there are a number of options open to investigating officers in relation to withdrawn or ill-founded complaints.

If it is apparent from the outset that a complaint cannot or should not be investigated, dispensation from the requirement to investigate may be sought from the PCA (under reg. 3 of the Police (Dispensation from Requirement to Investigate Complaints) Regulations 1985 (SI 1985 No. 672)). A full list of grounds whereby that dispensation can be sought is set out in the 1985 Regulations (see Appendix 10). Broadly, cases where dispensation is sought will generally come under one or more of the following (D.I.S.P.) categories:

- Delay — where more than 12 months have elapsed between the incident giving rise to the complaint and its being reported *and* either no good reason is given for that delay or it would be unjust to the officer concerned to investigate it.
- Identity — where there is an anonymous complainant who cannot reasonably be contacted or identified.
- Same — in the case of repetitious complaints where the complainant has no fresh allegation/evidence but has made the same complaint before and it has been finalised.
- Practicable — where the investigation is not reasonably practicable (e.g. because of the complainant's own conduct) or where complaint is vexatious, abusive or oppressive.

Even where a complaint falls into one of these categories, it might not receive dispensation, in which case a normal investigation would have to follow.

A complaint may be withdrawn at any time but should only be regarded as withdrawn when a signed statement is received from the complainant (or someone authorised to act on his/her behalf). Withdrawal of a complaint would not necessarily amount to an end to the investigation which might still be pursued under the internal conduct procedures (see Chapter 4).

In cases where it seems to the investigating officer that the complaint is ill-founded or that it would require a disproportionate amount of effort to investigate it, he/she may submit a report to the appropriate complaints department (or the PCA if supervised) to that effect. Then the only possible recourse would be judicial review, which would be unlikely to succeed.

KEY STAGES: INFORMAL RESOLUTION OF COMPLAINTS (GENERAL)

What	Who	How	When
Complaint deemed suitable for informal resolution	Chief officer (or deputee)	Chief officer applies conditions set out in s. 69 of the Police Act 1996 and the Police (Complaints) (Informal Resolution) Regulations 1985	After determining that he/she is the appropriate authority
Seek views of complainant *and* officer concerned	Appointed officer (police officer)	Personal contact. Allow officer to speak to 'friend' if he/she desires	As soon as practicable after decision to resolve informally
Arrange for formal investigation	Appointed officer (police officer)	Initiate formal investigation	If informal resolution appears to be impossible/ unsuitable

KEY STAGES: EARLY RESOLUTION

What	Who	How	When
Receive complaint and resolve informally	Supervisory officer of any rank (police officer)	If officer is both present and willing to explain understanding of incident. Complainant willing to accept explanation and/or apology. Consider meeting between officer and complainant	At time of complaint
Report to chief officer/person having delegated authority	Supervisory officer (police officer)	Submission of report outlining facts and outcome	?
Conclusion of matter	Chief officer/person having delegated authority	Make record in complaints register. Write to complainant indicating that matter has been resolved	?
Evidence of more serious complaint comes to light during process	Supervisory officer or person having delegated authority	Terminate informal resolution proceedings — report matter to chief officer	Immediately

6 REVIEWS

INTRODUCTION

The Police (Efficiency) Regulations 1999 and the Police (Conduct) Regulations 1999 make provision for cases to be reviewed. Although set out within the different 1999 Regulations themselves, the procedures are almost identical but have a small number of minor differences. These differences are discussed below.

REVIEW UNDER THE POLICE (EFFICIENCY) REGULATIONS 1999

The Police (Efficiency) Regulations 1999, regs 19 to 21 provide that:

19.—(1) Where the officers conducting the inefficiency hearing have imposed a sanction under regulation 17, the member concerned shall be entitled to request the chief officer of the police force concerned, or where the member concerned is a member of the metropolitan police force an assistant commissioner, ('the reviewing officer') to review the finding or the sanction imposed, or both the finding and the sanction.

(2) A request for a review must be made to the reviewing officer in writing within 14 days of the date on which a copy of the decision sent under regulation 16(4) is received by the member concerned unless this period is extended by the reviewing officer.

(3) The request for a review shall state the grounds on which the review is requested and whether a meeting is requested.

20.—(1) The reviewing officer shall hold a meeting with the member concerned if requested to do so.

(2) Where a meeting is held, the member concerned may be accompanied by a member of a police force and by counsel or a solicitor.

21.—*(1)   The member concerned shall be informed of the finding of the reviewing officer in writing within three days of completion of the review.*

(2)   The reviewing officer may confirm the decision of the hearing or he may impose a different sanction but he may not impose a sanction greater than that imposed at the hearing.

(3)   The decision of the reviewing officer shall take effect by way of substitution for the decision of the hearing and as from the date of that hearing.

(4)   Where as a result of the decision of the reviewing officer the member concerned is required to resign or reduced in rank he shall be notified in writing of his right of appeal to a Police Appeals Tribunal.

Practice Note

An officer may request a review of his/her case where a sanction has been imposed at an efficiency hearing (see Chapter 3). However, the review requested may consider both the sanction and/or the finding itself. The same is true of a review under the Police (Conduct) Regulations 1999 (see below).

'Sanction' here would appear to mean any of the three options set out under reg. 17(1)(a) to (c). Therefore, the member concerned may request a review where the hearing only imposes a written warning without any further punishment.

The request will be made to the member's chief officer or, in the case of a Metropolitan Police officer, to the assistant commissioner for the time being authorised under s. 8 of the Metropolitan Police Act 1856 (see reg. 3(1)). This person is referred to as the 'reviewing officer'. Regulation 22 makes special provisions for situations where the chief officer or assistant commissioner is an 'interested party' or where there is an assistant chief officer deputising under s. 12 of the Police Act 1996.

For some reason the 1999 Regulations do not define 'interested party' but reg. 4 of the Police (Conduct) Regulations 1999 (see Chapter 4) define it as:

. . . a witness or any person involved in the conduct which is the subject of the case or who otherwise has a direct interest in the case.

In cases falling under reg. 22, the review will be carried out as follows:

- Generally, by the assistant chief constable designated under s. 12(4) of the Police Act 1996.
- Where that assistant chief constable is absent or is an interested party, the review will be carried out by the chief officer of another force.
- Where the officer concerned is a Metropolitan Police officer and the review officer is absent or an interested party, the review will be carried out by the commander designated under para. 4(7) of sch. 6 to the Police Regulations 1995 (SI 1995 No. 215). If that commander is absent or an interested party, the review may be carried out by another assistant commissioner (reg. 22(3)).

- Where the member concerned is a City of London Police officer and the commissioner is absent or an interested party, the review will be carried out by the chief officer of another force or an assistant commissioner in the Metropolitan Police (reg. 22(4)).

The request must be made to the reviewing officer in writing within 14 days of the date on which the member *receives* the notification sent out under reg. 16(4). The period may be extended by the reviewing officer without the need for the member to apply for such an extension.

The purpose of the review may be to consider the finding, the sanction or both. The reviewing officer may confirm the decision of the hearing or he/she may impose a different sanction. However, the reviewing officer may not impose a sanction greater than that imposed at the hearing (reg. 21(2)). Given the wording of reg. 21, the reviewing officer appears able to impose *any* other sanction (provided it is no greater in its effect than the original sanction) and is not limited to those sanctions listed at reg. 17. This is different from the situation in relation to cases under the Police (Conduct) Regulations 1999 (see Chapter 4 and below) where the alternative sanctions available to the reviewing officer are specifically restricted to those under the relevant regulation (reg. 31). It is difficult to see what other sanction a reviewing officer might wish to substitute beyond those set out under the Police (Efficiency) Regulations 1999, reg. 17, but it may allow him/her greater latitude in, say, requiring an officer to move locations or to leave a tenured post as an alternative to the original sanction imposed by the efficiency hearing.

The request must state the grounds on which it is made and whether a meeting is requested. If a meeting is requested, the reviewing officer must hold one (reg. 20(1)) — although the regulation does not specify when. Presumably such a meeting would have to be held within a reasonable time after the relevant hearing reached its decision.

However, a review can be carried out without holding such a meeting. Where a meeting is held, the member may be accompanied by a 'friend' (police officer) *and* a solicitor/counsel (reg. 20(2)). This is a broader entitlement than that available under the Police (Conduct) Regulations 1999 (see below).

The finding of the review

The officer concerned must be informed of the finding of the reviewing officer in writing and within three days of the completion of the review (reg. 21(1)). The 1999 Regulations do not specify how the officer must be informed, neither does it make clear whether the information needs to be sent or received within the three-day period. It would seem sensible that the reviewing officer take responsibility for this task and that the information be served on the officer personally. It may not be practicable for the three-day requirement to be complied with, particularly if the officer is on leave or otherwise unavailable.

The reviewing officer's decision is substituted for that of the hearing and takes effect from the same date (reg. 21(3)). If there is a finding that the performance of the member concerned had not been unsatisfactory the original sanction will be expunged forthwith.

If the reviewing officer's decision results in the member concerned being required to resign or his/her reduction in rank, the member must be notified of the right to appeal to a Police Appeals Tribunal (reg. 20(4)) (see Chapter 7). Again the 1999 Regulations do not specify who is to take responsibility for such notification or when it should be made. It would seem practical for the interviewing officer to issue the notification at the same time as the decision.

Hearing in absence of chief officer

The Police (Efficiency) Regulations 1999, reg. 22 provides that:

(1)   Subject to paragraphs (2) to (4), where the chief officer is an interested party or the circumstances in section 12(4)(a) or (b) of the 1996 Act apply, the review shall be conducted by the assistant chief constable designated under section 12(4) of the 1996 Act.

(2)   Where the designated assistant chief constable is absent or an interested party, the review shall be conducted by the chief officer of another force who has agreed to act in that capacity.

(3)   Where the member concerned is a member of the metropolitan police force, the review shall be conducted by an assistant commissioner.

(4)   Where the member concerned is a member of the City of London police force, the review shall be conducted by the Commissioner or, if he is absent or an interested party, by a chief officer of another force who has agreed to act in that capacity or an assistant commissioner of the metropolitan police force who has agreed to act in that capacity.

Practice Note

'Interested party' is defined above.

The circumstances in s. 12(4)(a) or (b) of the Police Act 1996 are as follows:

(4)   A chief constable shall, after consulting his police authority, designate a person holding the rank of assistant chief constable to exercise all the powers and duties of the chief constable—

(a)   during any absence, incapacity or suspension from duty of the chief constable, or

(b)   during any vacancy in the office of chief constable.

Regulation 22 makes provision for the delegation of a chief officer's reviewing function — with relevant amendments for an officer within the

Metropolitan Police and City of London Police forces — and then makes further provision for cases to be reviewed in that officer's absence.

Regulation 23 makes the relevant amendments to the Police Regulations 1995 to take account of the imposition of sanctions and findings under the Police (Efficiency) Regulations 1999 generally.

REVIEW UNDER THE POLICE (CONDUCT) REGULATIONS 1999

The Police (Conduct) Regulations 1999, regs 34 to 36 provide that:

34.—(1)   Where a sanction is imposed under regulation 31, the member concerned shall be entitled to request the chief officer of the force concerned or, where the member concerned is a member of the metropolitan police force, an assistant commissioner ('the reviewing officer'), to review the finding or the sanction imposed or both the finding and the sanction.

(2)   A request for a review must be made to the reviewing officer in writing within 14 days of receipt of the written summary of reasons given in accordance with regulation 33 unless this period is extended by the reviewing officer.

(3)   The request for a review shall state the grounds on which the review is requested and whether a meeting is requested.

35.—(1)   The reviewing officer shall hold a meeting with the member concerned if requested to do so.

(2)   Where a meeting is held the member concerned may be accompanied by a member of a police force and, in a case where regulation 16 applies, by counsel or a solicitor.

36.—(1)   The member concerned shall be informed of the finding of the reviewing officer in writing within three days of completion of the review.

(2)   The reviewing officer may confirm the decision of the hearing or he may impose a different sanction which is specified in regulation 31(1) but he may not impose a sanction greater than that imposed at the hearing.

(3)   The decision of the reviewing officer shall take effect by way of substitution for the decision of the hearing and as from the date of that hearing.

(4)   Where as a result of the decision of the reviewing officer the member concerned is dismissed, required to resign or reduced in rank he shall be notified in writing of his right of appeal to a Police Appeals Tribunal.

Practice Note

As with the Police (Efficiency) Regulations 1999 (above), the Police (Conduct) Regulations 1999 provide for a review of any finding and any sanction imposed under reg. 31. The reviewing officer's decision is substituted for that of the hearing and takes effect from the same date (reg. 36(3)).

The time by which the request for a review must be made to the reviewing officer is 14 days from receipt of the written summary of reasons under reg. 33. The member concerned may be accompanied at any review meeting by a fellow officer but can only be additionally accompanied by a solicitor/counsel where reg. 16 (in relation to the availability of the sanctions of dismissal, requirement to resign or reduction in rank) applies (reg. 35(2)). This is in contrast to a review meeting in relation to unsatisfactory performance (see above) where there are no restrictions on the member concerned being accompanied by a solicitor/counsel in addition to a 'friend'.

Hearing in absence of chief officer

The Police (Conduct) Regulations 1999, reg. 37 provides that:

> *(1)   Subject to paragraphs (2) to (4), where the chief officer is an interested party or the circumstances in section 12(4)(a) or (b) of the 1996 Act apply, the review shall be conducted by the assistant chief constable designated under section 12(4) of the 1996 Act.*
> *(2)   Where the designated assistant chief constable is absent or an interested party, the review shall be conducted by the chief officer of another force who has agreed to act in that capacity.*
> *(3)   Where the member concerned is a member of the metropolitan police force the review shall be conducted by an assistant commissioner who is not an interested party.*
> *(4)   Where the member concerned is a member of the City of London police force, the review shall be conducted by the Commissioner or, if he is absent or an interested party, by the chief officer of another force who has agreed to act in that capacity or an assistant commissioner of the metropolitan police force who has agreed to act in that capacity.*

Practice Note

'Interested party' is defined above.

The circumstances in s. 12(4)(a) or (b) of the Police Act 1996 are the same as for the Police (Efficiency) Regulations 1999 (see above).

Regulation 37 makes provision for the delegation of a chief officer's reviewing function — with relevant amendments for an officer within the Metropolitan Police and City of London Police forces — and then makes further provision for cases to be reviewed in that officer's absence.

KEY STAGES: REVIEW (EFFICIENCY AND CONDUCT)

What	Who	How	When
Request for review of finding and/or sanction	Officer concerned	Written request to reviewing officer stating grounds and whether meeting requested or not	Within 14 days of receiving copy of original decision/written summary of reasons (unless extended by reviewing officer)
Meeting with officer concerned	Reviewing officer (police officer)	Hold meeting if requested	Not specified
Inform of finding of review	Reviewing officer (police officer)	Written information to be provided to officer concerned	Within three days of completion of review
Notification of right of appeal to Police Appeals Tribunal	Not specified	Where officer concerned is required to resign or reduced in rank by reviewing officer	Not specified

7 APPEALS

INTRODUCTION

Where an officer has been dismissed, required to resign or reduced in rank following a hearing or chief officer's review in relation to unsatisfactory performance or misconduct, that officer has the right of appeal. The right to appeal is widely regarded to be a crucial part of any disciplinary proceedings and a basic principle of natural justice. For these reasons, it is important both that officers are notified of their right to appeal and that the appeal is carried out in accordance with the procedures set down.

The importance of an individual's right to appeal disciplinary action taken against him/her (particularly dismissal) has been strongly asserted by employment tribunals on many occasions. The House of Lords went as far as ruling that the failure to permit an employee to exercise a contractual right of appeal was itself capable of rendering an otherwise fair dismissal unfair (*West Midlands Co-operative Society* v *Tipton* [1986] ICR 192) and the Court of Appeal has held that a dismissal was unfair when there was a contractual right to have three individuals on an appeal panel and there were only two (*Westminster City Council* v *Cabaj* [1996] IRLR 397).

Furthermore, under the principles of natural justice and fair trial, that an individual should not be a judge in his/her own cause (i.e. the rule against bias), courts have decided that the body hearing the appeal should not be the same body who took the original disciplinary decision. Although this will generally depend on the extent of involvement in the original decision, care should be taken that the appeal panel was not (as far as is possible) involved in the original decision.

ACAS CODE OF PRACTICE

The Code of Practice on Disciplinary and Grievance Procedures issued by ACAS (the Arbitration Conciliation and Advisory Service) gives practical guidance on the drafting and operation of disciplinary rules and procedures. It does not have statutory force but is widely used as a guide to what is and is not fair for the purposes of employment legislation. The Code emphasises that disciplinary procedures should not be viewed primarily as a means of imposing sanctions but should be designed to emphasise and encourage improvements in individual conduct. To that end, section 9(xiv) of the Code states that disciplinary procedures should 'provide a right of appeal — normally to a more senior manager — and specify the procedure to be followed'.

THE POLICE APPEALS TRIBUNAL

The Police Appeals Tribunal is a new feature for the police service. The rules of the constitution of the Police Appeals Tribunal are set out in sch. 6 to the Police Act 1996. In the case of appeals by a senior officer, the appeal tribunal will consist of:

- A person chosen from a list of persons with a seven-year qualification within the meaning of the Courts and Legal Services Act 1990, s. 71, and who has been nominated by the Lord Chancellor for the role of sitting on a Police Appeals Tribunal.
- A member of a police authority other than the relevant authority.
- A person who is or has within the past five years been an inspector or person who has within the past five years been (and is no longer) the Metropolitan Police Commissioner.

In the case of appeals by other officers, the appeal tribunal will consist of:

- A person chosen from the list set out above and similarly nominated by the Lord Chancellor.
- A member of the authority (or if the authority is the Secretary of State a person nominated by the Secretary of State).
- A person chosen from a list maintained by the Secretary of State of former (within the last five years) and current chief officers of police, so long as that person is/was not the chief officer of police maintained by the relevant authority.
- A retired officer of appropriate rank.

In both cases, the person nominated from the list of persons qualified under the Courts and Legal Services Act 1990 will be the chairman and will have the casting vote if the vote is tied.

A tribunal does not need to have a hearing in all cases (Police Act 1996, sch. 6, para. 6). It may determine an appeal without the formality of a hearing, provided the appellant and respondent are given the opportunity to make representations as to the holding of a hearing and provided also that those representations have been considered.

THE POLICE APPEALS TRIBUNALS RULES 1999

The Police Appeals Tribunals Rules 1999 (SI 1999 No. 818) (see Appendix 11) were introduced under the Police Act 1996, s. 85. However, the Police (Appeals) Rules 1985 (SI 1985 No. 576) still apply to appeals against disciplinary decisions made under the 1985 disciplinary regulations.

Note that the Act referred to in the 1999 Rules below is the Police Act 1996.

Procedure before the hearing

The Police Appeals Tribunals Rules 1999, r. 5 provides that:

(1)   Subject to rule 7 and paragraph (2), the time within which notice of an appeal under section 85 of the Act shall be given is 21 days from the date on which the decision appealed against was notified to the appellant in pursuance of regulations made in accordance with section 50(3) of the Act.

(2)   In a case to which regulation 39 of the Police (Conduct) Regulations 1999 or regulation 25 of the Police (Conduct) (Senior Officers) Regulations 1999 applies where the decision appealed against was given in pursuance of those Regulations as modified by Part II of Schedule 2 or, as the case may be, by Part II of the Schedule to those Regulations, the time within which notice of an appeal under section 85 of the Act shall be given is 28 days from—

(a)   the conclusion of any criminal proceedings in which the appellant is charged with an offence in respect of the conduct to which the decision appealed against related; or

(b)   a decision that no such criminal proceedings will be instituted or taken over by the Director of Public Prosecutions has been communicated to the appellant.

(3)   The notice of appeal shall be given in writing to the relevant police authority and a copy of the notice shall be sent to the respondent.

Practice Note

Rule 5 sets out a fairly strict timetable for applying for an appeal against a decision and for the taking of the various preparatory steps before the appeal hearing. Ordinarily, an officer who wishes to appeal will have to give notice of his/her intention to appeal within 21 days of the date *on which the decision appealed against was notified* to the member concerned (r. 5(1)), i.e. the date on which notification was actually received. Note that for senior officers (see Chapter 8) the time limit is slightly longer. In cases where the offence complained of at the original hearing was an imprisonable offence or one which might justify dismissal from the force, the officer wishing to appeal is given 28 days from the end of any criminal proceedings brought against him/her as a result of the offence or from the date that the decision is taken not to bring criminal proceedings (r. 5(2)).

These time limits (and those set out below) may be extended by the Police Authority on the application of the officer bringing the appeal, although the 1999 Rules state that an extension will only be given where it is just to do so according to the circumstances of the case (see r. 7 below).

The officer should give notice in writing to his/her police authority who will pass a copy of it to the respondent to the appeal (i.e. the person who will represent the police authority at the appeal hearing) (r. 5(3)). Where the officer in question is a senior officer, the respondent to the appeal will be designated by the police authority. Otherwise the respondent will be the chief officer of the force.

Procedure on notice of appeal

The Police Appeals Tribunals Rules 1999, r. 6 provides that:

(1)   As soon as practicable after receipt of a copy of the notice of appeal, the respondent shall provide to the relevant police authority—

(a)   a copy of the report of the person who made the decision appealed against;

(b)   the transcript of the proceedings at the original hearing; and

(c)   any documents which were made available to the person conducting the original hearing.

(2)   A copy of the transcript mentioned in paragraph (1)(b) shall at the same time be sent to the appellant.

(3)   Subject to rule 7, the appellant shall, within 28 days of the date on which he receives a copy of the transcript mentioned in paragraph (1)(b), submit to the relevant police authority—

(a)   a statement of the grounds of appeal;

(b)   any supporting documents; and

(c)   either—

(i)   any written representations which the appellant wishes to make under paragraph 6 of Schedule 6 to the Act or, as the case may be, any request to make oral representations under that paragraph; or

(ii)   a statement that he does not wish to make any such representations as are mentioned in paragraph (i):

Provided that, in a case where the appellant submits a statement under sub-paragraph (c)(ii), nothing in this paragraph shall prevent representations under paragraph 6 of Schedule 6 to the Act being made by him to the chairman of the tribunal.

(4)   The documents submitted to the police authority under paragraph (3) shall, as soon as practicable, be copied to the members of the tribunal and to the respondent.

(5)   The respondent shall, not later than 21 days from the date on which he receives the copy documents sent to him under paragraph (4), submit to the relevant police authority—

(a)   a statement of his response to the appeal;

(b)   any supporting documents; and

(c)   either—

(i)   any written representations which the respondent wishes to make under paragraph 6 of Schedule 6 to the Act or, as the case may be, any request to make oral representations under that paragraph; or

(ii)   a statement that he does not wish to make any such representations as are mentioned in paragraph (i):

Provided that, in a case where the respondent submits a statement under sub-paragraph (c)(ii), nothing in this paragraph shall prevent representations under paragraph 6 of Schedule 6 to the Act being made by him to the chairman of the tribunal.

(6)   The respondent shall at the same time send a copy of the documents referred to in paragraph (5)(a) and (c) to the appellant, together with a list of the documents (if any) referred to in paragraph (5)(b).

(7)   The documents submitted to the police authority under paragraph (5) shall, as soon as practicable, be copied to the members of the tribunal.

(8)   So far as applicable, rules 8 and 9 shall apply in relation to the hearing of any oral representations under paragraph 6 of Schedule 6 to the Act as they apply in relation to the hearing of an appeal under section 85 of the Act; and the appellant and the respondent shall be entitled to be represented at the hearing of such oral representations as if it were the hearing of such an appeal.

Practice Note

The 'original hearing' is the conduct or inefficiency hearing which concluded that the appellant failed to meet the appropriate standard or that his/her performance was unsatisfactory (r. 3(1)).

As soon as practically possible after receiving the copy of the notice of appeal, the respondent must send to the police authority the following documents (r. 6(1)):

- A copy of the report of the person who made the original decision (which is being appealed against).
- The transcript of the original hearing (which must also be sent to the officer bringing the appeal under r. 6(2)).
- All documents which were available to the person who made the original decision.

The officer bringing the appeal has 28 days from the date on which he/she receives the transcript to send the following documents to the police authority (r. 6(3)):

- A statement of the grounds of appeal.
- Any supporting documents.
- Either any written representation or a request to make oral representations or a statement that he/she does not wish to make such representations.

The documents should then, as soon as achievable, be copied to the respondent and to the members of the tribunal (r. 6(4)).

The respondent then has 21 days after receiving these documents to send the following documents to the officer bringing the appeal (r. 6(6)) and to the police authority (r. 6(5)) who must make copies for the appeal tribunal (r. 6(7)):

- A response to the grounds of appeal.
- Any supporting documents.
- Either any written representation or a request to make oral representations or a statement that he/she does not wish to make such representations.

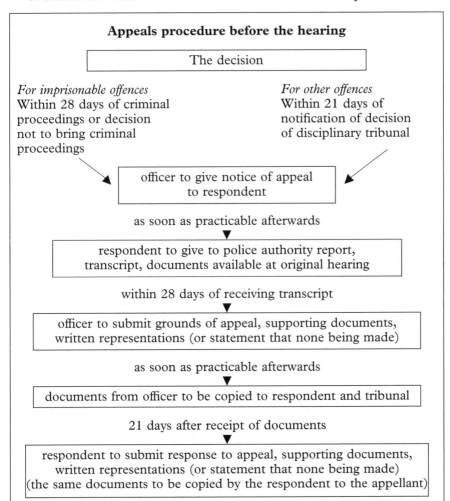

Appeals procedure before the hearing

The decision

For imprisonable offences
Within 28 days of criminal proceedings or decision not to bring criminal proceedings

For other offences
Within 21 days of notification of decision of disciplinary tribunal

officer to give notice of appeal to respondent

as soon as practicable afterwards

respondent to give to police authority report, transcript, documents available at original hearing

within 28 days of receiving transcript

officer to submit grounds of appeal, supporting documents, written representations (or statement that none being made)

as soon as practicable afterwards

documents from officer to be copied to respondent and tribunal

21 days after receipt of documents

respondent to submit response to appeal, supporting documents, written representations (or statement that none being made)
(the same documents to be copied by the respondent to the appellant)

It should also be noted that a negative statement in relation to the making of representations will not prevent the respondent from making representations to the chair of the tribunal where it has been decided to proceed without a hearing.

Extensions of time limits

The Police Appeals Tribunals Rules 1999, r. 7 provides that:

(1)   The relevant police authority may extend the period referred to in rule 5(1) or (2) or 6(3) in any case where the authority is satisfied, on the application of the appellant, that by reason of the special circumstances of the case it is just to do so; and in such a case rules 5 and 6 shall have effect as if for that period there were substituted such extended period as the authority may specify.

(2)   Where the relevant police authority refuses an application by the appellant under paragraph (1), it shall give the appellant notice in writing of the reasons for the decision and of the right of appeal conferred by paragraph (3).

(3)   An appellant whose application under paragraph (1) is refused may, not later than 14 days after receiving notice under paragraph (2), appeal in writing to the chairman of the tribunal against the decision of the relevant police authority.

(4)   The chairman may, on such an appeal, make any decision which the relevant police authority had power to make under paragraph (1); and, where he extends the period referred to in rule 5(1) or (2) or 6(3), rules 5 and 6 shall have effect as if for that period there were substituted such extended period as the chairman may specify.

Practice Note

If the authority does not grant an extension, the officer bringing the appeal has the right to appeal that decision to the chairman of the appeal tribunal (although this must be done within 14 days of receiving the decision of the authority) (r. 7(3)). In these circumstances, the chairman will have the same rights to extend time as the police authority.

Extensions of time may only be given at the discretion of the police authority, i.e. they will not grant a request as a matter of course. The sorts of circumstances in which an authority may find it just to extend time are, for example, where the police officer has been ill, where he/she did not know that there was a right of appeal (although this might depend on the authority's view of whether he/she should have known) or new facts or documents coming to light after the original hearing. However, this is not an exhaustive list and there is no limit to the categories of circumstances in which the authority may consider extending time for compliance with the 1999 Rules. The authority may also take into account factors such as whether the evidence will have been affected by the delay or how quickly the officer bringing the appeal acted once he/she knew of the possibility of taking action.

Procedure at the appeal hearing

The Police Appeals Tribunals Rules 1999, r. 8 provides that:

(1)   Where a case is to be determined at a hearing, the chairman of the tribunal shall cause the appellant and the respondent to be given notice of the date of the hearing not less than 28 days, or such shorter period as may with the agreement of both parties be determined, before the hearing begins.

(2)   Subsections (2) and (3) of section 250 of the Local Government Act 1972 (powers in relation to local inquiries) shall apply to the hearing as if—

(a)   references to a local inquiry were references to a hearing held under Schedule 6 to the Act;

(b)   references to the person appointed to hold the inquiry, or to the person holding the inquiry, were references to the chairman of the tribunal; and

(c)   references to that section were references to this rule.

(3)   The tribunal may proceed with the hearing in the absence of either party, whether represented or not, if it appears to be just and proper to do so, and may adjourn it from time to time as may appear necessary for the due hearing of the case.

(4)   Subject to these Rules, the procedure at a hearing shall be determined by the tribunal.

Practice Note

The parties to the appeal hearing must receive 28 days' notice of the hearing (unless both sides agree to a shorter period before the hearing) (r. 8(1)). This is the same period of notice required to be given to the complainant in cases where the disciplinary proceedings arise from a complaint (see r. 12(2) below).

Under the Local Government Act 1972, s. 250(2) (to which r. 8(2) refers), an individual may be ordered to attend the hearing as a witness or to produce documents which relate to the hearing. The individual must be sent a witness summons which states the time and place where he/she must attend or produce the relevant documents. The necessary expenses of attendance must be paid. If the individual does not attend or fails to produce the documents, he/she will (on summary conviction) be liable to a fine not exceeding level 3 on the standard scale, to six months' imprisonment or to both.

Procedure at the hearing

The Police Appeals Tribunals Rules 1999, r. 9 provides that:

(1)   Subject to paragraph (3) and rule 12, the hearing shall be held in private:

Provided that it shall be within the discretion of the tribunal to allow such person or persons as it considers desirable to attend the whole or such part of the hearing as it may think fit.

(2)   Notwithstanding that the tribunal has allowed a person to attend the hearing, where it appears to the tribunal that a witness may in giving evidence disclose information which, in the public interest, ought not to be disclosed to a member of the public, the tribunal shall require any member of the public present to withdraw while that evidence is given.

(3)   A member of the Council on Tribunals shall be entitled to attend the hearing.

Practice Note

The hearing will be in private unless the appeal tribunal decides that it is desirable for a particular person (or particular persons) to attend the hearing (r. 9(1)). If the tribunal does allow a member of the public to attend, it may still require him/her to leave if evidence is being given which it would not be in the public interest to be heard (r. 9(2)).

Evidence at the hearing

The Police Appeals Tribunals Rules 1999, r. 10 provides that:

(1)   Unless the tribunal otherwise determines, the evidence adduced by the respondent shall be given first.

(2)   All oral evidence given at the hearing shall be given on oath.

(3)   All witnesses giving evidence at the hearing shall be subject to examination and cross-examination.

(4)   Any question as to whether any evidence is admissible, or whether any question should or should not be put to a witness, shall be determined by the tribunal.

(5)   A verbatim record of the evidence given at the hearing shall be taken and kept for a period of not less than seven years from the date of the end of the hearing unless the chairman of the tribunal requests that a transcription of the record be made.

Practice Note

The party against whom the appeal is being raised will adduce its evidence first (unless the tribunal decides otherwise) (r. 10(1)). All witnesses giving evidence will do so on oath (r. 10(2)) although the tribunal may also admit written evidence (see r. 11(1) below). The witnesses may then be cross-examined (r. 10(3)). After this, the officer bringing the appeal will bring evidence in support of his/her case. The appeal tribunal has the power to decide for itself whether or not evidence is admissible (r. 10(4)).

Written statements

The Police Appeals Tribunals Rules 1999, r. 11 provides that:

(1)   Subject to the provisions of this rule, the tribunal may admit evidence by way of a written statement made by a person, notwithstanding that he may not be called as a witness, so, however, that evidence shall not be admissible under this rule if it would not have been admissible had it been given orally.

(2)   For the purposes of this rule, a written statement purporting to be made and signed by a person and witnessed by another person shall be presumed to have been made by that person unless the contrary be shown.

(3)   Nothing in this rule shall prejudice the admission of written evidence which would be admissible apart from the provisions of this rule.

Practice Note

As in court proceedings, written statements may be admitted in evidence without the maker of the statement being called to give oral evidence. However, in these circumstances, the appeal tribunal may not give the statement as much weight as it might have had the maker of the statement been present at the hearing to be cross-examined on his/her evidence. The weight the tribunal will attach may depend, to some extent, on the reason for the witness not attending and the nature of the evidence (e.g. the likelihood that the witness might be mistaken or whether there was plausible contrary evidence from another witness who was cross-examined at the hearing).

The role of the complainant at the hearing

The Police Appeals Tribunals Rules 1999, r. 12 provides that:

(1)   This rule shall apply in relation to a hearing where the decision appealed against arose from a complaint and the appeal is not against sanction only.

(2)   The chairman of the tribunal shall cause notice of the date of the hearing to be sent to the complainant, at the same time as such notice is sent to the appellant and the respondent in pursuance of rule 8(1).

(3)   Notwithstanding anything in rule 9(1) but subject to paragraph (5), the tribunal shall allow the complainant to attend the hearing while witnesses are being examined, or cross-examined, on the facts alleged and, if the tribunal considers it appropriate so to do on account of the age of the complainant, or otherwise, shall allow him to be accompanied by a personal friend or relative who is not to be called as a witness at the inquiry:

Provided that—

(a)   where the complainant is to be called as a witness at the hearing he and any person allowed to accompany him shall not be allowed to attend before he gives his evidence; and

(b)   where it appears to the tribunal that a witness may in giving evidence disclose information which, in the public interest, ought not to be disclosed to a member of the public, it shall require the complainant and any person allowed to accompany him to withdraw while that evidence is given.

(4)   Where the appellant gives evidence, then, after the person representing the respondent has had an opportunity of cross-examining him, the chairman of

the tribunal shall put to him any questions which the complainant requests should be so put and might have been properly so put by way of cross-examination and, at his discretion, may allow the complainant himself to put such questions to the appellant.

(5) Subject as aforesaid, the complainant and any person allowed to accompany him shall neither intervene in, nor interrupt the hearing; and if he or such a person should behave in a disorderly or abusive manner, or otherwise misconduct himself the chairman of the tribunal may exclude him from the remainder of the hearing.

Practice Note

Rule 12 only applies where the decision appealed against arose from a complaint (as to which, see Chapter 5) and the appeal is not simply against the sanction imposed earlier. In these cases, the tribunal must allow the complainant to attend the hearing during the relevant stages. In such cases, that entitlement only extends to occasions *while witnesses are being examined and cross-examined about the facts alleged* (r. 12(3)). This would not appear to give a complainant any entitlement to be present during the giving of any antecedents, mitigation or extraneous background evidence relating to the appellant.

If the complainant is going to give evidence, he/she must not attend before giving that evidence and, if the tribunal feels that a witness is going to give information that ought not to be disclosed to the public, it must require the complainant (and anyone accompanying him/her) to withdraw (r. 12(3)).

If the complainant attends the hearing (in cases where proceedings were started as a result of a complaint by him/her) the tribunal should allow the complainant to hear all the evidence. The complainant is allowed to be accompanied by a friend or relative if the tribunal considers it appropriate (for example, if the complainant is elderly) (see r. 12(3) below). However, that person may not attend before the complainant gives evidence (r. 12(3)(a)) and may also be excluded from the hearing if the evidence being given should not be disclosed to a member of the public (r. 12(3)(b)).

The complainant has an indirect role in the cross-examination of the officer bringing the appeal. Under r. 12(4), the chairman must put to the officer any (relevant) question which the complainant asks him to. Furthermore, the chairman also has the discretion to allow the complainant to put questions to the officer directly. However, other than in this context, the complainant (or the accompanying person) may not interrupt the hearing and he/she is liable to be excluded from the remainder of the hearing if the chairman so decides (r. 12(4)).

As with conduct hearings (see Chapter 4), there is a specific power to exclude the complainant and anyone accompanying him/her if they interrupt the hearing or behave in a disorderly or abusive manner (r. 12(5)). Although that power does not extend to anyone else, the fact that hearings will generally be held in private means that there should be little opportunity for any other disruption or disorder.

Many sets of disciplinary proceedings will have been commenced because of complaints by members of the public. Just as in the original hearings, provision is made for the complainant to give evidence at the hearing. However, the complainant is also given a form of representation at the hearing by having the right to require the chairman of the appeal tribunal to put questions to the police officer. Thus members of the public who do bring complaints will have an active role in participating in all the stages of disciplinary proceedings conducted against an officer. However, there are two checks on the manner in which a complainant may contribute to the appeal hearing. First, and most importantly, the chairman only has the duty to ask questions which are proper (and therefore may be expected to use his/her discretion not to put questions which are irrelevant or abusive). Secondly, the chairman has the power to make the complainant leave if he/she interrupts proceedings or is otherwise disruptive.

The decision

The Police Appeals Tribunals Rules 1999, r. 13 provides that:

(1) The chairman of the tribunal shall prepare a written statement of the tribunal's determination of the appeal and of the reasons for the decision.

(2) The statement prepared under paragraph (1) and a record of any order made under section 85(2) of the Act shall be submitted to the relevant police authority and, in the case of an appeal by a senior officer, to the Secretary of State within a reasonable period after the determination of the appeal.

(3) The relevant police authority shall, as soon as practicable, copy the statement and any record of an order submitted to it under paragraph (2) to the appellant and the respondent.

(4) In a case where the decision appealed against arose from a complaint, the relevant police authority shall notify the complainant of the outcome of the appeal.

Practice Note

A Police Appeals Tribunal may make an order which appears to it to be *less* severe than the decision appealed against and which could have been imposed by the person making that decision.

It is an important aspect of natural justice that any party to proceedings be given reasons for any decision. Therefore, under r. 13(1), the chairman's decision must be in writing and reasons for the decision must be given. Within a reasonable time after the appeal, the chairman must also give a copy of the decision to the relevant police authority (or in the case of an appeal by a senior officer, to the Secretary of State) (r. 13(2)) which must, as soon as possible, send it to the officer bringing the appeal and to the respondent (r. 13(3)). Under r. 13(4), the original complainant must also be notified of the outcome of the appeal.

After the decision of the appeal tribunal, there is no further right of appeal within the police disciplinary system. If the officer in question wishes to pursue the matter further formally, he/she will have to do so in court or in the employment tribunal through use of the common law or those Acts of Parliament which are applicable to police officers (see Chapter 2).

KEY STAGES: APPEALS

What	Who	How	When
Notice of appeal given	Appellant	Lodge notice with relevant police authority (and copy to respondent)	Generally within 21 days of being notified of decision appealed against (unless extension granted). If 'special case' under relevant conduct regulations, within 28 days of the end of related criminal proceedings or date when Director of Public Prosecution's decision not to prosecute was communicated to appellant (unless extension granted)
Provision of documents to relevant police authority	Respondent	Send documents required by r. 6(1)	As soon as practicable after receipt of copy of notice of appeal

What	Who	How	When
Submission of statement of grounds of appeal, supporting documents and representations/ requests	Appellant	Submit documents and requests as set out in r. 6(3) to relevant police authority	Within 28 days of receiving copy of transcript required by r. 6(1)(b) (unless extension granted)
Copy of above documents to tribunal members and respondent	Not specified	Copy above documents to relevant parties	As soon as practicable
Statement of response, supporting documents and other representations/ statements	Respondent	Submit statements and documents set out in r. 6(5) to relevant police authority	Not later than 21 days from receipt of copy of documents under r. 6(4)
Copy of written representations/ requests or statements	Respondent	Send copy of representations/ requests or statements under r. 6(5)(a) and (c) to appellant	Same time as submission to relevant police authority
Copy of documents submitted to relevant police authority by respondent to be sent to tribunal members	Not specified	Send copy of documents etc. submitted by respondent to relevant police authority under r. 6(5) to tribunal members	Not less than 28 days before hearing begins or such shorter period as determined with agreement of both parties

What	Who	How	When
Notice of hearing where decision appealed against arose from complaint and appeal is not against sanction only	Chair of tribunal	Cause notice to be sent to complainant	Same time as notice of hearing given to respondent and appellant under r. 8
Written statement of determination	Chair of tribunal	Prepare written statement including reasons for decision	Reasonable period after determination
Submit statement	Not specified	Written statement prepared under r. 13(1) submitted to relevant police authority/Secretary of State as appropriate	Reasonable period after determination
Notification where decision appealed against arose from complainant	Relevant police authority	Notify complainant of outcome	Not specified

8 SENIOR OFFICERS

INTRODUCTION

In addition to the general provisions relating to complaints against police officers (see Chapter 5), Part IV of the Police Act 1996 also makes specific provision for the investigation and disposal of complaints against senior officers, that is, officers above the rank of superintendent (s. 65).

Section 68 of the Police Act 1996 provides that:

(1)   Where a complaint about the conduct of a senior officer—
  (a)   is submitted to the appropriate authority, or
  (b)   is sent to the appropriate authority under section 67(3),
the appropriate authority shall record and, subject to subsection (2), investigate it.
(2)   If satisfied that the conduct complained of, even if proved, would not justify criminal or disciplinary proceedings, the appropriate authority may deal with the complaint according to the apprpriate authority's discretion.

Practice Note

Unlike cases involving complaints against other officers (as to which, see Chapter 5), there is no *duty* on the appropriate authority to take steps to obtain or preserve evidence where the person complained about is a senior officer. The appropriate authority here will be the Commissioner in the case of Metropolitan police officers and the relevant police authority in other cases (s. 65). If the appropriate authority is not satisfied that the complaint falls into the category outlined in s. 68(2), he/she must appoint a police officer of the same (or higher) rank as the person whose conduct is the subject of the complainant to investigate the matter and that investigating officer may be from the same force or a different force.

Unless any investigation is supervised by the Police Complaints Authority (PCA; see Chapter 5), the investigating officer must submit his/her report to the 'appropriate authority' as above (s. 68(6)).

On receiving either a report concerning the conduct of a senior officer submitted under s. 68(6), or a copy of a report from the PCA concerning such conduct, the appropriate authority must send a copy of it to the Director of Public Prosecutions unless the report satisfies the appropriate authority that no criminal offence has been committed (s. 74).

Provision for the investigation and resolution of allegations of misconduct against senior officers is made in the Police (Conduct) (Senior Officers) Regulations 1999 (SI 1999 No. 731) (see Appendix 12). However, in the case of the Metropolitan Commissioner s. 9E of the Police Act 1996 will apply (see Chapter 9).

THE POLICE (CONDUCT) (SENIOR OFFICERS) REGULATIONS 1999

Definitions

The main terms referred to throughout the 1999 Regulations are defined in reg. 4.

'Senior officers' are not specifically defined in reg. 4 but the 1999 Regulations only apply to conduct by a chief constable or assistant chief constable or, in the case of the City of London Police and the Metropolitan Police forces, by an officer of or above the rank of commander (reg. 3).

'Appropriate authority' — the Commissioner of Police for the Metropolis in the case of Metropolitan Police officers and, in any other case, the police authority for the relevant police area. This definition clearly indicates that the 1999 Regulations do not apply to the Metropolitan Police Commissioner, who is dealt with under s. 9E of the Police Act 1996 (see Chapter 9).

'Appropriate standard' — the standard set out in the Code of Conduct contained in sch. 1 to the Police (Conduct) Regulations 1999 (see Chapter 4).

'Authority' — the Police Complaints Authority (see Chapter 5).

'Complaint' has the meaning assigned to it by the Police Act 1996, s. 65 (see Chapter 5).

'Investigating officer' — an officer appointed under the Police Act 1996, s. 68(3), or under reg. 7 (see below) to investigate a complaint or any other matter relating to the conduct of the senior officer.

'Representative' — counsel, a solicitor or a member of a police force selected by the senior officer for the purpose of proceedings under the 1999 Regulations.

Suspension

The Police (Conduct) (Senior Officers) Regulations 1999, reg. 5(1) provides that:

(1) Where it appears to the appropriate authority, on receiving a report, complaint or allegation which indicates that the conduct of a senior officer does not meet the appropriate standard, that the senior officer concerned ought to be

suspended from membership of the force and from his office as constable, the appropriate authority may, subject to the following provisions of this regulation so suspend him.

Practice Note

The wording here imposes two requirements before suspension can take place. The first requirement is that the report, complaint or allegation must indicate that the senior officer's conduct does not meet the appropriate standard as defined above. This — relatively undemanding — requirement is the same as that under the equivalent Regulations for other ranks; see Chapter 4). The second requirement is that it must appear to the police authority that the senior officer *ought* to be suspended from both his/her membership of the force *and* from his/her office as constable. 'Constable' here has nothing to do with rank and simply refers to the holding of the public office of constable which applies to all officers attested under the Police Act 1996, s. 29. The wording of reg. 5(1) therefore suggests that there should be some form of *objective* assessment by the police authority as to whether or not the senior officer ought to be relieved of his/her office and membership of the relevant police force. This is a more stringent requirement than that which attaches to the power of chief officers to suspend their more junior ranks.

Regulation 5 goes on to provide that:

(2)   *The appropriate authority shall not so suspend a senior officer unless it appears to them that either of the following conditions ('the suspension conditions') is satisfied:*

(a)   *that the effective investigation of the matter may be prejudiced unless the senior officer concerned is so suspended;*

(b)   *that the public interest, having regard to the nature of the report, complaint or allegation, and any other relevant considerations, requires that he should be so suspended.*

(3)   *If the appropriate authority determine that a senior officer ought to be suspended under this regulation, they shall forthwith notify the Authority of their decision and of the suspension condition appearing to them to justify their decision.*

(4)   *If, upon being so notified of the decision of the appropriate authority, the Authority are satisfied that the suspension condition in question is fulfilled, they shall as soon as practicable notify their approval of the suspension of the senior officer concerned to the appropriate authority; and the suspension of the officer shall not have effect unless the approval of the Authority is so given.*

(5)   *Where the Authority give their approval to the suspension of a senior officer, his suspension shall take effect from the time he receives notice of that approval from the appropriate authority and he shall be suspended until—*

(a)   *the Authority decide otherwise; or*

(b)   *the appropriate authority decide otherwise; or*

(c)   *it is decided that the conduct of the senior officer concerned shall not be the subject of proceedings under regulation 11; or*

(d)   the notification of a finding that the conduct of the senior officer concerned did not fail to meet the appropriate standard or notification that, in spite of a finding that his conduct did fail to meet the appropriate standard, no sanction should be imposed; or

(e)   a sanction has been imposed,
whichever first occurs.

Practice Note

A senior officer cannot be suspended unless it appears to the relevant authority that one of the 'suspension conditions' set out at reg. 5(2) applies. The first suspension condition is that the effective investigation of the matter may be prejudiced unless the senior officer concerned is suspended. This condition would apply if the continued presence of the senior officer concerned may prejudice the effective investigation of what has been reported, complained about or alleged.

The second and alternative suspension condition is more stringent. This condition is that the public interest *requires* the senior officer concerned to be so suspended, having regard to the nature of the report, complaint or allegation *and* any other relevant considerations. This condition might be satisfied where the person's continued presence in office creates an *appearance* of interference with or obstruction of the effective investigation of the matter in hand, a less onerous condition than the first. However, the provision that the public interest also *requires* the senior officer's suspension suggests that, unless it can be shown that the nature of the case together with any other relevant considerations demand it, the senior officer's suspension cannot be ordered under this head.

Notification to police complaints authority

If the appropriate authority determines that a senior officer ought to be suspended and that a suspension condition does apply, they must notify the Police Complaints Authority (PCA) *forthwith* (reg. 5(3)). That notification must specify the suspension condition but it need not be in writing. On receipt of that notification, the PCA must determine whether or not it is satisfied that the suspension condition is fulfilled (reg. 5(4)). If the PCA is satisfied, it must *as soon as practicable* (see Chapter 4) notify the appropriate authority of its approval of the senior officer's suspension. If this approval is not given, the senior officer's suspension cannot take effect (reg. 5(4)). Once the PCA notifies the appropriate authority of its approval for the suspension, the suspension does not take effect until *the senior officer concerned receives notice of that approval* (reg. 5(5)). The 1999 Regulations do not specify the time or method by which the senior officer must be so notified.

The senior officer will be suspended until the first of any of the following events occurs:

- the PCA decides that the senior officer should no longer be suspended; or

- the appropriate authority decides that the senior officer should no longer be suspended; or
- it is decided that the conduct concerned will not be the subject of proceedings under reg. 11 (see below); or
- notification that the senior officer's conduct did not fail to meet the appropriate standard; or
- notification that, although the senior officer's conduct *did* fail to meet the appropriate standard, no sanction should be imposed; or
- a sanction has been imposed.

Although it is not explicit in the 1999 Regulations, 'notification' would appear to mean notification to the senior officer concerned.

Urgent cases

In cases of urgency a senior officer may be suspended with immediate effect (reg. 6(1)). The power is available to police authorities in relation to the suspension of a chief officer and to the chief officer in any other case (reg. 6(1)(a) and (b)). Where this power is used, the PCA must be notified *forthwith* (reg. 6(2)).

This provision for urgent cases is subject to some significant savings. First, the power to suspend is not a separate power from that set out at reg. 5 and therefore it must be subject to the same requirements in relation to both the objective test and the existence of a 'suspension condition' (see above). Secondly, the suspension will automatically cease after 24 hours *unless the PCA has notified its approval* (reg. 6(3)).

Urgent cases are not defined in the 1999 Regulations and they would probably only extend to occasions where the risk of harm or loss to people, property or evidence demands the utmost expediency.

Investigating officers

The Police (Conduct) (Senior Officers) Regulations 1999, reg. 7 provides that:

> *(1)   Where a report, complaint or allegation is received which indicates that the conduct of a senior officer did not meet the appropriate standard, the following provisions of this regulation shall have effect for the purpose of investigating the matter.*
>
> *(2)   The provisions of paragraphs (3) and (4) shall have effect—*
>
> *(a)   in relation to cases arising otherwise than from a complaint to which Chapter I of Part IV of the 1996 Act applies; and*
>
> *(b)   in cases arising from such a complaint when the requirements of that chapter are dispensed with by or under regulations made under section 81 of the 1996 Act.*
>
> *(3)   Unless the appropriate authority decide, in the light of such preliminary enquiries is they may make, that no proceedings under regulation 11 need be*

taken, the matter shall be referred to an investigating officer who shall cause it to be investigated.

(4)   The investigating officer shall be—

(a)   a member of the police force concerned; or

(b)   if the chief officer of some other force is requested and agrees to provide an investigating officer, a member of that other force,

and of at least the rank of the senior officer concerned.

(5)   Neither—

(a)   the chief officer concerned; nor

(b)   any member of the police force concerned serving in the same division as the senior officer concerned,

shall be appointed as the investigating officer for the purposes of paragraph (3) or section 68(3) of the 1996 Act.

(6)   The provisions of this regulation are without prejudice to the powers of the Authority with regard to the approval of the investigating officer under section 72(3) (a) or (b) of the 1996 Act in a case where the Authority are required, or have determined, to supervise the investigation of a complaint or other matter under that section.

Practice Note

Although reg. 7(1) uses the expression 'report, *complaint* or allegation', the provisions of reg. 7(3) and (4) only apply to cases that are not the subject of a 'complaint' as defined in Part IV of the Police Act 1996 (as to which, see Chapter 5) or cases where the requirements to investigate such a 'complaint' have been, dispensed with (reg. 7(2)).

The wording of reg. 7(3) makes it clear that the appropriate authority may make its own preliminary inquiries before deciding whether or not the report or allegation need to become the subject of any proceedings. If the authority does so decide, it must refer the matter to an investigating officer who will cause it to be in investigated. The investigating officer does not need to carry out the investigation personally.

The investigating officer can either be a member of the police force to which the senior officer belongs or can be provided by the chief officer of some other force if he/she is requested to do so. In any case the investigating officer must be of at least the same rank as the senior officer concerned.

Under reg. 7(5), some people may not be appointed as the investigating officer. These are:

- the chief officer of the senior officer's force; and
- any officer serving in the same division as the senior officer.

Presumably the reference to a 'division' would also include any other organisational segment or administrative subsection such as an 'area' or 'sector'. Whether the expression would extend to the *areas* that are used to divide up the Metropolitan Police district is not clear.

These restrictions on the appointment of an investigating officer are also applied by reg. 7(5) to the investigation of 'complaints' under the Police Act 1996 (see Chapter 5). The restrictions are also applied without prejudice to the general powers of the Police Complaints Authority to approve the appointment of an investigating officer under s. 72(3) of the 1996 Act (see Chapter 5).

Regulation 8 provides that:

The investigating officer shall as soon as is practicable (without prejudicing his or any other investigation of the matter), cause the member concerned to be given written notice—

    (a)   that there is to be an investigation into the case;

    (b)   of the nature of the report, complaint or allegation;

    (c)   informing him that he is not obliged to say anything concerning the matter, but that he may, if he so desires, make a written or oral statement concerning the matter to the investigating officer or to the appropriate authority; and

    (d)   informing him that if he makes such a statement it may be used in any subsequent proceedings under these Regulations.

Practice Note

The wording of reg. 8 is identical to the corresponding regulation (reg. 9) in respect of other ranks (see Chapter 4). However, there are some significant differences in the extent of reg. 8. Whereas the heading for reg. 8 refers to this part of the process as the '*initial personal explanation*', the corresponding regulation (reg. 9) for other ranks calls it simply the 'notice of investigation'. There seems to be an expectation that senior officers will be more ready to make a personal statement at this stage of an investigation, and to do so without having taken advice (see below). Given the extent of the sanctions available (see reg. 22 below), together with the effect of reg. 10 (below), the making of such a statement in the absence of competent advice may carry a substantial risk.

The most significant difference between the provision of reg. 8 and its counterpart for lower ranks is the omission of any requirement to advise the senior officer of:

- his/her right to seek advice from a staff association; or
- his/her right to be accompanied at any future meeting, interview or hearing by a 'friend'.

Article 6 of the European Convention on Human Rights provides that:

In the determination of his civil rights and obligations . . ., everyone is entitled to a fair and public hearing within a reasonable time by an independent and impartial tribunal established by law.

It is, however, thought unlikely that this could be used to attack the 1999 Regulations as unfair here, especially given the decision in *Pellegrin* v *France* (application 28541/99, 8 December 1999), which casts some doubt on whether police disciplinary matters are covered at all.

The written notice must be given 'as soon as is practicable'. Practicable has been accepted as meaning 'possible to be accomplished with known means or resources' (see *Adsett* v *K & L Steelfounders* [1953] 1 All ER 97). However, the giving of such a notice must not be to the prejudice of the investigation of the matter — whether by the investigating officer or someone else — therefore there may be some justifiable delay in the provision of a reg. 8 notice.

The wording 'cause to be given' — as opposed to 'sent' — suggests that personal service is required.

The making of a statement in response to the receipt of a reg. 8 notice may have significant implications for the member concerned and serious consideration ought to be given to making any response in the absence of legal advice.

Regulation 9 provides that:

(1)   Where, following or, where paragraph (2) applies, during the investigation of a report, complaint or allegation, it appears that the conduct of a senior officer may not have met the appropriate standard, the appropriate authority shall consider whether proceedings under regulation 11 need be taken.

(2)   This paragraph applies where, before the end of the investigation, it appears to the investigating officer that the case is one in respect of which the conditions specified in Part I of the Schedule to these Regulations are likely to be satisfied and informs the appropriate authority accordingly.

(3)   Unless the appropriate authority decide that no such proceedings need be taken, the appropriate authority shall inform the senior officer in writing of the report, allegation or complaint and give him a written notice—

(a)   asking him whether or not he accepts that his conduct did not meet the appropriate standard;

(b)   informing him that he is not obliged to say anything concerning the matter, but that he may, if he so desires, make a written or oral statement concerning the matter to the authority; and

(c)   informing him that if he makes such a statement it may be used in any subsequent proceedings under these Regulations.

(4)   If the appropriate authority decide that no proceedings under regulation 11 need be taken, they shall so inform the senior officer in writing forthwith.

(5)   In a case where paragraph (2) applies, the appropriate authority shall—

(a)   determine whether the case is one in respect of which the conditions specified in Part I of the Schedule to these Regulations are satisfied; and

(b)   if they determine that the case is one in respect of which those conditions are satisfied and unless they are of the opinion that the circumstances are such that it would be inappropriate to do so, certify the case as a special case: and where the appropriate authority certify the case under sub-paragraph (b), the notice given under paragraph (3) shall inform the senior officer concerned that it has been so certified.

Practice Note

The wording of reg. 9(1) is confusing. It would appear to say that there are two occasions where the appropriate authority must consider whether proceedings under reg. 11 (see below) need to be taken. Those occasions are:

- *following* an investigation, where it appears that the conduct of a senior officer may not have met the appropriate standard;
- *during* an investigation where reg. 9(2) applies (i.e. 'special cases') and it appears that the conduct of a senior officer may not have met the appropriate standard.

Therefore, in the majority of cases (i.e. not 'special cases') the appropriate authority must await the outcome of the investigation before considering whether or not proceedings under reg. 11 need to take place.

Regulation 9(2) applies to 'special cases', that is, those very serious cases where the conditions set out in Part I of the schedule to the 1999 Regulations are met (see below). In cases where reg. 9(2) applies, the appropriate authority must:

- determine whether the conditions in Part I are satisfied; and
- if they are so satisfied, decide whether, *in their opinion*, the circumstances of the case are such that it would be inappropriate to certify it as a 'special case' (see reg. 25)

(reg. 9(5)).

If the authority decide that the case is a 'special case', it must certify the case as such (reg. 9(5)(b)) and include that fact in the written notice given to the senior officer under reg. 9(3) (reg. 9(5)).

Unlike the written notice in reg. 8 above, reg. 9 makes no requirement for the written notice to be given to the senior officer *as soon as practicable*, in fact it places no requirement on the time for service of such a notice.

As with the response to the reg. 8 notice, any reply made on being served with a written notice under reg. 9 may have serious consequences for the officer concerned and ought not to be given without obtaining legal advice (see reg. 10).

If, having considered the matter, the appropriate authority decide that no proceedings need be taken, they must inform the senior officer in writing *forthwith* (reg. 9(4)). The wording of this provision, i.e. that the authority might decide that no proceedings *need* be taken as opposed to *ought* to be taken, gives the authority a degree of latitude in making their decision. It is arguable that, although an objective assessment would say that proceedings ought to be brought against the officer, the appropriate authority determine that such proceedings are not in fact *needed*.

Sanction without hearing

The Police (Conduct) (Senior Officers) Regulations 1999, reg. 10 provides that:

(1)   If the senior officer concerned accepts that his conduct did not meet the appropriate standard, the appropriate authority may impose a sanction under regulation 22 without the case being dealt with in accordance with regulations 11 to 21.

(2)   Notwithstanding that the senior officer concerned accepts that his conduct did not meet the appropriate standard, the appropriate authority may, after considering the report of the investigation, deal with the matter according to the appropriate authority's discretion if they are satisfied that it does not justify the imposition of any sanction under these Regulations.

Practice Note

Regulation 10 allows for the various sanctions set out in reg. 22 to be imposed without a hearing provided the senior officer accepts that his/her conduct did not meet the appropriate standard. Given that the sanctions available include the requirement to resign and summary dismissal, the acknowledgement of such an allegation in relation to his/her conduct puts a senior officer in a very precarious position. This is one reason that the making of any response in answer to the notices provided for under regs 8 and 9 should be considered carefully. In addition, such admissions may also attract further liability (both personal and vicarious), particularly in relation to civil actions against the police. Although reg. 10 goes on to allow the authority to exercise its discretion in disposing of the case notwithstanding any admission or acceptance by the senior officer, the dangers of making any such response should not be underestimated. As most senior officers are covered by some form of liability insurance, there may also be provisions within their policy that have a material effect on the making of any admissions.

Notice of proceedings

The Police (Conduct) (Senior Officers) Regulations 1999, reg. 11 provides that:

(1)   This regulation shall apply where the senior officer concerned—

(a)   accepts that his conduct did not meet the appropriate standard but the appropriate authority do not proceed as mentioned in regulation 10(1) or (2); or

(b)   does not accept that his conduct failed to meet the appropriate standard but the appropriate authority, after taking into account any statement he may have made in pursuance of notice given under regulation 8 or 9, are not satisfied that his conduct did meet the appropriate standard.

(2)   Subject to paragraph (4), where this regulation applies the appropriate authority shall refer the case to a hearing and instruct an independent solicitor to give written notice to the senior officer concerned—

(a)   that the case is being referred to a hearing, and

(b)   specifying the conduct of that senior officer which it is alleged failed to meet the appropriate standard and the paragraph of the Code of Conduct in respect of which the appropriate standard is alleged not to have been met.

(3)   The reference in paragraph (2) to an independent solicitor is a reference to a solicitor who is not a member, officer or servant of the appropriate authority or of any local authority which appoints any member of the appropriate authority.

(4)   Notwithstanding that a case is one to which this regulation applies by virtue of paragraph (1)(b), if, after considering the report of the investigation, the appropriate authority are satisfied that the conduct in question, even if found to have failed to meet the appropriate standard, would not justify the imposition of any sanction under these Regulations, the steps mentioned in paragraph (2) need not be taken and the matter may be dealt with according to the appropriate authority's discretion.

(5)   Proceedings at or in connection with a hearing to which a case is referred under this regulation shall, for the purposes of section 65 of the 1996 Act (interpretation of Chapter I of Part IV) be disciplinary proceedings.

Practice Note

Regulation 11 envisages two types of situation. The first is where the senior officer accepts that his/her conduct did not meet the appropriate standard but the appropriate authority does not dispose of the case under reg. 10. The second type of situation is where the senior officer does *not* accept that his/her conduct did not meet the appropriate standard but the appropriate authority (having taken into account any statement that the senior officer made under reg. 8 or 9) are not satisfied that the officer's conduct met the appropriate standard. In each of these cases, the appropriate authority must (unless reg. 11(4) applies):

- refer the case to a hearing; and
- instruct an independent solicitor to give written notice to the senior officer

(reg. 11(2)).

An 'independent solicitor' is a solicitor who is not a member, officer or employee of the appropriate authority or of any local authority that appoints any member of the appropriate authority (reg. 11(3)). This excludes any solicitor who works for the police authority or, in the case of the Metropolitan Police force, who works for the commissioner (and probably anyone associated with such a firm); it also excludes any solicitor (or firm) working for the particular local authority that appoints *any* member of the police authority or the Metropolitan Police commissioner.

The expression 'given' here suggests, as elsewhere in the Regulations covered by this book, personal service rather than any other form of communication.

Proceedings brought at, or in connection with a hearing to which a case is referred under reg. 11 will be 'disciplinary proceedings' for the purpose of Part IV of the Police Act 1996 (reg. 11(5)).

Although the heading to reg. 11 says 'Notice of proceedings', it is in fact reg. 13 (see below) which imposes the requirement for notifying the senior officer concerned of the hearing itself.

Discretionary disposal of case

If, however, after considering the report of the investigation, the appropriate authority are satisfied that the conduct in question, *even if found to have failed to meet the appropriate standard,* would not justify the imposition of any sanction under the 1999 Regulations, they may deal with the matter according to their discretion and do not need to comply with the requirements under reg. 11(2) (reg. 11(4)).

Withdrawal of cases

The Police (Conduct) (Senior Officers) Regulations 1999, reg. 12 provides that:

> *(1)   At any time before the beginning of the hearing referred to in a notice under regulation 11, the appropriate authority may direct that the case be withdrawn.*
>
> *(2)   Where a direction is given under paragraph (1), the appropriate authority shall, as soon as possible, cause the senior officer concerned to be served with a written notice of the direction and the case shall be treated as if it had not been referred to a hearing.*

Practice Note

The appropriate authority may direct that a case be withdrawn and they can do so at any time *before the beginning of the hearing* (reg. 12(1)).

Where the appropriate authority makes such a direction for a case to be withdrawn, they must, *as soon as possible,* cause the senior officer concerned to be served with a written notice to that effect (reg. 12(2)).

After such a direction for withdrawal has been given, the case will be *treated* 'as if it had not been referred to a hearing' (reg. 12(2)). It is unclear whether this provision means that a case so withdrawn disposes of it absolutely or whether the appropriate authority can still deal with the senior officer at their discretion under the provisions of reg. 11(4) (see above).

Notice of hearing

The Police (Conduct) (Senior Officers) Regulations 1999, reg. 13 provides that:

> *(1)   Where a senior officer is given notice under regulation 11, he shall, at least 21 days before the date of the hearing referred to in that notice, be notified of the time, date and place of the hearing and be supplied with copies of—*
>
> *(a)   any statement he may have made under regulation 8 or 9;*
>
> *(b)   any relevant statement, document or other material obtained during the course of the investigation.*

(2)   In this regulation any reference to a copy of a statement shall, where it was not made in writing, be construed as a reference to a copy of an account thereof.

Practice Note

Although the heading to reg. 13 refers to the documents that are to be supplied to the senior officer concerned, it also makes provision for notifying the officer of the bearing itself. The regulation does not specify who will be responsible for ensuring that this is carried out but it may be helpful if the independent solicitor were to do it at the same time as discharging the other notification requirements under reg. 11.

Where a senior officer is given notice under reg. 11, he/she must be notified of the:

- time,
- date, and
- place

of the proposed hearing, at least 21 days before the bearing referred to (reg. 13(1)). He/she must also be supplied with copies of:

- any statement that he/she may have made under reg. 8 or 9 (see above); and
- any relevant statement, document or other material obtained during the course of the investigation.

The expression 'statement' here will include an account of any verbal statement (reg. 13(2)).

There is discretion for those documents which have not been supplied to the senior officer concerned to be adduced in evidence at a hearing provided that the officer consents (see reg. 16 below).

The hearing

The Police (Conduct) (Senior Officers) Regulations 1999, reg. 14, sets out the people who will make up the tribunal. Regulation 14 provides that:

(1)   Where a case is referred to a hearing it shall be heard by a tribunal consisting of a single person selected and appointed by the appropriate authority from a list of persons nominated by the Lord Chancellor.

(2)   To assist the tribunal on matters pertaining to the police there shall also be appointed by the appropriate authority one or more assessors selected by that authority with the approval of the tribunal one of whom is or has been a chief officer of police, so, however, that there shall not be so appointed—

(a)   a person who is one of Her Majesty's inspectors of constabulary;

(b)   the chief officer of the force of which the senior officer concerned is a member; or
(c)   a member, officer or servant of the appropriate authority or of any local authority which appoints any member of the appropriate authority.

Practice Note

Where a case against a senior officer is referred to a hearing, the 'tribunal' will consist of a single person appointed by the appropriate authority from a list of people nominated by the Lord Chancellor (reg. 14(1)). They will usually be senior barristers. When selecting from the people named on the list, care will need to be taken to avoid any conflict of interest that might arise from previous knowledge of/involvement with the senior officer concerned. In the event of such a conflict the person, though named on the list, would not be able to sit on the tribunal.

Regulation 14(2) provides that one or more 'assessors' *shall* be selected (again, by the appropriate authority) to help the tribunal *on matters pertaining to the police*. This wording suggests that, although there must be at least one such assessor, the assessors' remit is only to assist in relation to police-specific matters. The nature of the assessors' function is reinforced by the fact that one of their number must be, or have been, a chief officer of police. There is no express requirement that the assessor must be/have been a chief officer of police in England or Wales, and the expression chief officer of police would appear to include assistant chief constables and commanders. Under reg. 14(2), certain people are excluded from acting as an assessor, namely:

- one of Her Majesty's inspectors of constabulary;
- the chief officer of the senior officer's own force; and
- a member, officer or servant of the appropriate authority or of any local authority which appoints any member of that appropriate authority.

Any assessor chosen under reg. 14 must be selected with the approval of the 'tribunal', i.e. the person presiding over the hearing.

Conduct of hearing

The conduct of any hearing is provided for under the Police (Conduct) (Senior Officers) Regulations 1999, regs 15–19. Regulation 15 provides that:

(1)   The hearing shall be in private.
(2)   The case shall be presented—
    (a)   by the independent solicitor mentioned in regulation 11(2); or
    (b)   by some other independent solicitor.
(3)   In paragraph (2)(b), 'independent solicitor' has the same meaning as in regulation 11.
(4)   The senior officer concerned may conduct his case either in person or by a representative.

(5)   Any question as to whether any evidence is admissible, or whether any question should or should not be put to a witness, shall be determined by the tribunal.

(6)   A verbatim record of the proceedings before the tribunal shall be taken and a transcript of the record shall be made and sent to the appropriate authority; and, if a sanction is imposed by that authority and the senior officer concerned so requests within the time limit for any appeal and after he has lodged notice of appeal in accordance with rules made under section 85 of the 1996 Act, a copy of the transcript shall be supplied to him.

Practice Note

The hearing must be in private (reg. 15(1)). This contrasts with the position relating to hearings of cases for other ranks (see Chapter 4). For the situation relating to the presence of the complainant, see reg. 19 below.

The case will be presented either by the independent solicitor referred to in reg. 11 (above) or by some other independent solicitor as defined in that regulation (reg. 15(2)). The senior officer concerned may conduct his/her own case or may be represented (reg. 15(4)).

Any question as to whether any evidence is admissible, or whether any question should or should not be put to any witness, will be determined by the tribunal (reg. 15(5)) although this must be subject to the principles of natural justice (as to which, see Chapter 10).

A verbatim record of the proceedings must be made and a transcript sent to the appropriate authority (reg. 15(6)). If a sanction is imposed on the senior officer and he/she lodges an effective notice of appeal, a copy of this transcript must be supplied to him/her.

The tribunal may allow any document to be adduced in evidence during the hearing even though a copy of it has not been supplied to the senior officer concerned, provided that he/she consents (reg. 16).

The tribunal may adjourn the hearing from time to time if it appears to it to be necessary or expedient to do so for the due hearing of the case (reg. 17).

The tribunal may proceed with the hearing in the absence of the senior officer concerned *if it appears just and proper to do so* and, where the absence of the senior officer makes compliance with any procedure under the 1999 Regulations impossible, that procedure will be dispensed with (reg. 18). Although reg. 18 is designed to prevent senior officers from defeating the disciplinary process by absenting themselves from a hearing, the regulation raises some Human Rights Act 1998 implications since it may be said to deny the senior officer a fair trial (see Chapter 1).

Complaints

In cases where there has been a 'complaint' against the senior officer (under the Police Act 1996, s. 65), there will be a 'complainant'. The Police (Conduct) (Senior Officers) Regulations 1999, reg. 19 makes provision for the attendance of that complainant at a hearing, notwithstanding the general requirement under reg. 15 (above) that any hearing must be held in private. Regulation 19 provides that:

(1)   This regulation shall apply where there has been a complaint against the senior officer concerned.

(2)   Notwithstanding anything in regulation 15(1) but subject to paragraphs (3), (4) and (6), the tribunal shall allow the complainant to attend the hearing while witnesses are being examined, or cross-examined, and the complainant may at the discretion of the tribunal be accompanied by a friend or relative.

(3)   Where the complainant or any person allowed to accompany him is to be called as a witness at the hearing, he and any person allowed to accompany him shall not be allowed to attend before he gives his evidence.

(4)   Where it appears to the tribunal that a witness may, in giving evidence, disclose information which, in the public interest, ought not to be disclosed to a member of the public, it shall require the complainant and any person allowed to accompany him to withdraw while the evidence is given.

(5)   Where the senior officer concerned gives evidence, then after the person presenting the case has had an opportunity of cross-examining him, the tribunal shall put to him any questions which the complainant requests should be so put and might have been properly so put by way of cross-examination and, at its discretion, may allow the complainant himself to put such questions to the senior officer concerned.

(6)   Subject as aforesaid, the complainant and any person allowed to accompany him shall neither intervene in, nor interrupt, the hearing; and if he or such a person should behave in a disorderly or abusive manner, or otherwise misconduct himself, the tribunal may exclude him from the remainder of the hearing.

(7)   In this regulation, a reference to the complainant is a reference to the originator of the complaint notwithstanding that it was transmitted to the appropriate authority by some other person or by the Authority or some other body.

Practice Note

A 'complainant' for this purpose means the originator of the complaint, irrespective of whether that complaint was made to the appropriate body by some other person or by the Police Complaints Authority (see Chapter 5) (reg. 19(7)).

The provisions of reg. 19 are similar to the corresponding provisions for the attendance of complainants at hearings for other ranks (see Chapter 4). Under reg. 19(2) the tribunal must generally allow the complainant to be present *while witnesses are being examined or cross-examined*. This general entitlement does not appear to extend to other parts of the hearing such as the giving of antecedents. In addition, the tribunal *may* permit the complainant to be accompanied by a friend or relative. This is a discretionary power of the tribunal rather than an enforceable right of the complainant.

Where the complainant or anyone permitted to accompany him/her is to be called as a witness, neither person will be allowed to attend the hearing before giving that evidence (reg. 19(3)).

Notwithstanding these provisions, the complainant and anyone accompanying him/her must not intervene in or interrupt the hearing. If any of these people misconduct themselves or behave in a disorderly or abusive manner, the presiding officer may exclude them from the hearing (reg. 19(6)).

One significant omission from these 1999 Regulations in comparison with their counterpart for other ranks is the specific provision allowing the Police Complaints Authority (PCA) to attend a hearing. Whereas the relevant conduct Regulations for more junior ranking officers provide specifically for the attendance of a member of the PCA in certain cases (see Chapter 4), the 1999 Regulations relating to senior officers make no such provision, neither do they allow the tribunal discretion to admit other parties (e.g. other solicitors or witnesses' friends).

Where it appears to the tribunal that a witness may, in giving evidence, disclose information that ought not in the public interest to be publicly disclosed, the tribunal must require the complainant and any person accompanying him/her to withdraw while that evidence is given (reg. 19(4)). Although the initial question as to the likelihood of such a sensitive disclosure being made rests with the tribunal, once the tribunal has decided that such a disclosure *may* occur, it has an obligation to require the complainant and any accompanying person to withdraw. It is unclear whether the withdrawal must be for the whole of the period while that particular witness gives their evidence or only for such part of it as is likely to disclose the sensitive information.

Under reg. 19(5), where the senior officer concerned gives evidence and the person presenting the case has had an opportunity to cross-examine, the tribunal *must* put to him/her any questions that:

- the complainant requests be put; and
- which might have properly been put in cross-examination.

The tribunal *may*, at its discretion, allow the complainant to put such questions to the senior officer.

The tribunal's report

The Police (Conduct) (Senior Officers) Regulations 1999, reg. 20 provides that:

> *(1)   The tribunal shall review the facts of the case and decide whether or not the conduct of the senior officer concerned met the appropriate standard.*
>
> *(2)   The tribunal shall not find that the conduct of the senior officer concerned failed to meet the appropriate standard unless the conduct is—*
>
> *(a)   admitted by the senior officer concerned; or*

(b)   proved by the person presenting the case on the balance of probabilities, to have failed to meet that standard.

Practice Note

Once the hearing is complete, the tribunal must review the facts of the case and decide whether or not the conduct of the senior officer concerned met the appropriate standard (reg. 20(1)).

Under reg. 20(2) the tribunal can only find that the conduct of the senior officer concerned failed to meet the appropriate standard if:

- the senior officer concerned admits that the conduct failed to meet the standard; or
- it is proved, on the balance of probabilities, by the person presenting the case that the conduct failed to meet that standard.

Under reg. 20(3) as soon as possible after the hearing, the tribunal must submit a report to the appropriate authority setting out:

- its finding under reg. 20(1);
- a recommendation as to any sanction (if the case was found to have been proved); and
- any other matter arising out of the hearing that it desires to bring to the attention of the authority.

Clearly, if the tribunal did not find that the senior officer's conduct failed to meet the appropriate standard, there will be no recommendation as to a sanction. Where such a recommendation is made, however, the appropriate authority are not bound to implement it and may impose any of the sanctions set out in reg. 22 (see below).

The tribunal must also send a copy of its report to the senior officer concerned but there is no explicit requirement as to the time limit within which this must be done (reg. 20(4)).

Under reg. 21, on receiving the tribunal's report, the relevant authority must decide whether to:

- dismiss the case;
- record a finding that the senior officer's conduct failed to meet the appropriate standard but to take no further action; or
- record such a finding and impose a sanction.

After the authority has so decided, the senior officer concerned must be notified *in writing* and *as soon as possible* (reg. 21(2)) although the regulation does not specify by whom.

Sanctions

The Police (Conduct) (Senior Officers) Regulations 1999, reg. 22 provides that:

(1)   For the purposes of regulation 10, 20 or 21, the sanctions which may be recommended or imposed shall be—
    (a)   dismissal from the force;
    (b)   requirement to resign from the force as an alternative to dismissal taking effect forthwith or on such date as may be specified in the recommendation or decision;
    (c)   reprimand.
(2)   Where the question of the sanction to be imposed is being considered by the appropriate authority under regulation 10 or 21—
    (a)   they shall have regard to the record of police service of the senior officer concerned as shown on his personal record and may receive evidence from any witness whose evidence would, in their opinion, assist them in determining the question; and
    (b)   the senior officer concerned, or his representative, shall be afforded an opportunity to make oral or, if appropriate, written representations as respects the question or to adduce evidence relevant thereto.
(3)   Regulation 15(5) shall apply to proceedings at which such evidence as is referred to in paragraph (2)(a) or (b) or such oral representations as are referred to in paragraph (2)(b) is given or are made as it applies to the proceedings before the tribunal.

Practice Note

The relevant sanctions in reg. 22 are available under the following circumstances:

- reg. 10 — where a senior officer accepts, without a hearing, that his/her conduct did not meet the appropriate standard;
- reg. 20 — the recommendation of a tribunal following a hearing; and
- reg. 21 — imposition of a sanction by the appropriate authority on receipt of the tribunal's report.

These sanctions are:

- dismissal from the force;
- requirement to resign as an alternative to dismissal;
- reprimand.

Where the sanction or requirement to resign applies, the requirement may take effect immediately or on such a date as may be specified in the recommendation or decision (reg. 22(1)(b)).

If the sanction is being considered under reg. 10 (admission by the senior officer) or reg. 21 (decision by appropriate authority on receiving tribunal's report), reg. 22(2) makes certain additional provisions. Those provisions are that:

- the appropriate authority *must* have regard to the senior officer's record of police service (as shown on his/her personal record) and *may* receive

evidence from any witness whose evidence would, in the authority's opinion, assist them in deciding which sanction to impose; and
* the senior officer concerned (or his/her representative) must be given an opportunity to make oral representations (or written representations if 'appropriate') or to adduce relevant evidence with regard to 'the question' — presumably the question of which sanction to impose.

It would appear from the wording of reg. 22(2) and of reg. 21 that, other than in cases of an admission by the senior officer (reg. 10), these provisions only apply to circumstances set out at reg. 21(1)(b) — namely, when deciding *which* of the available sanctions ought to be imposed, as opposed to whether the case should be dismissed (reg. 21(1)) or whether no sanction should be imposed, even though the senior officer's conduct did not meet the appropriate standard (reg. 21(1)(a)).

The decisions as to whether any evidence is admissible or whether any question should or should not be put under reg. 22(2) will be made by the appropriate authority in the same way as they are made by a tribunal under reg. 15(5) and will be subject to the same caveats (see above) (reg. 22(3)).

Report to the Secretary of State

The Police (Conduct) (Senior Officers) Regulations 1999, reg. 23 provides that:

A copy of the report of the tribunal together with the decision of the appropriate authority shall be sent to the Secretary of State.

Practice Note

No specific time requirement is imposed by reg. 23 on the sending of the report(s) to the Secretary of State and no individual/body is specifically given responsibility for doing so. All the expenses of a hearing, *including the costs of the senior officer concerned*, will be paid out of the police fund, subject to taxation in such a manner as the Secretary of State may direct (reg. 24).

KEY STAGES: SENIOR OFFICERS' CONDUCT

What	Who	How	When
Notification of suspension	Appropriate authority	Give notification together with the relevant 'suspension condition'	Forthwith
Notification of approval	Police Complaints Authority	If satisfied that relevant 'suspension condition' is fulfilled, notify the appropriate authority	As soon as practicable
Notification of decision to suspend in urgent cases	'Appropriate authority'	Notify the Police Complaints Authority	Forthwith
Notice of investigation	Investigating officer (police officer)	Give written notice of investigation, nature of report etc. and 'caution' in accordance with reg. 8	As soon as practicable
Notice seeking response	Appropriate authority	Give written notice in accordance with reg. 9	Following investigation (or during investigation if 'special case') unless appropriate authority decides no proceedings to be taken
Notification of no proceedings	Appropriate authority	Inform the senior officer concerned in writing that no proceedings need to be taken	Forthwith

What	Who	How	When
Notice of proceedings	Independent solicitor instructed by the 'appropriate authority'	Give written notice that case is being referred to hearing and specifying relevant conduct in accordance with reg. 11	Not specified (but see reg. 11)
Notice of decision to withdraw case	'Appropriate authority'	Serve written notice on senior officer concerned when direction for case to be withdrawn is given under reg. 12(1)	As soon as possible
Notice of hearing	Not specified	Serve written notice on senior officer concerned stating time, date and place of hearing	At least 21 days before date of hearing set out in reg. 11 notice
Supply documents and relevant material	Not specified	Supply senior officer concerned with documents and material in accordance with reg. 13	At least 21 days before date of hearing set out in reg. 11 notice
Report of finding (and recommended sanction where appropriate)	Tribunal	• Submit report in accordance with reg. 20 to 'appropriate authority' • Send copy to senior officer concerned	As soon as possible after hearing
Decision to dismiss, take no further action or impose sanction	Appropriate authority	Decide to dismiss or make record of finding(s) under reg. 21	On receipt of tribunal's report
Notification of decision	Not specified	Senior officer concerned to be notified in writing	As soon as possible after decision has been taken

What	Who	How	When
Copy report and decision to Secretary of State	'Appropriate authority'	Send copy of tribunal's report and decision of 'appropriate authority' to Secretary of State	Not specified
Request for review of finding and/or sanction	Officer concerned	Written request to reviewing officer stating grounds and whether meeting requested or not	Within 14 days of receiving copy of original decision/written summaries of reasons (unless extended by reviewing officer)
Meeting with officer concerned	Reviewing officer	Hold meeting if requested	Not specified
Inform of finding of review	Reviewing officer	Written information to be provided to officer concerned	Within three days of completion of review
Notification of right of appeal to Police Appeals Tribunal	Not specified	Where officer concerned is required to resign or reduced in rank by reviewing officer	Not specified

9 SPECIAL GROUPS

INTRODUCTION

There are many individuals working within the police force who, by virtue of their status, are not covered by the 1999 Regulations and whose discipline and conduct is covered by other Regulations and statutes.

CHIEF OFFICERS

Issues of efficiency and effectiveness concerning a Chief Officer must be dealt with by the relevant police authority and the Secretary of State under the Police Act 1996. Section 11 of that act provides:

11.—(1) The chief constable of a police force maintained under section 2 shall be appointed by the police authority responsible for maintaining the force, but subject to the approval of the Secretary of State and to regulations under section 50.

(2) Without prejudice to any regulations under section 50 or under the Police Pensions Act 1976, the police authority, acting with the approval of the Secretary of State, may call upon the chief constable to retire in the interests of efficiency or effectiveness.

(3) Before seeking the approval of the Secretary of State under subsection (2), the police authority shall give the chief constable an opportunity to make representations and shall consider any representations that he makes.

Section 42 provides:

(1) The Secretary of State may require a police authority to exercise its power under section 11 to call upon the chief constable to retire in the interests of efficiency or effectiveness.

(2)   Before requiring the exercise of that power or approving the exercise of that or the similar power exercisable with respect to an assistant chief constable, the Secretary of State shall give the chief constable or assistant chief constable an opportunity to make representations to him and shall consider any representations so made.

(3)   Where representations are made under this section the Secretary of State may, and in a case where he proposes to require the exercise of the power mentioned in subsection (1) shall, appoint one or more persons (one at least of whom shall be a person who is not an officer of police or of a Government department) to hold an inquiry and report to him and shall consider any report made under this subsection.

(4)   The costs incurred by a chief constable or assistant chief constable in respect of an inquiry under this section, taxed in such manner as the Secretary of State may direct, shall be defrayed out of the police fund.

Under s. 11(2) of the Police Act 1996, a police authority has the power to call upon its chief constable to retire in the interests of efficiency or effectiveness. This power may only be exercised with the approval of the Secretary of State (s. 11(2)). However, the Secretary of State also has the authority to *require* the relevant police authority to exercise this power (s. 42(1)).

Whether it is the Secretary of State who is requiring the authority to exercise its power or the police authority who is requesting approval for such a step, the Chief Officer must be allowed to make representations on his/her behalf. If it is the police authority who is seeking approval for its exercise of power, the representation should be made to the authority and it must consider them (s. 11(3)). However, if it is the Secretary of State who is requiring the authority to act, the representations should be made to the Secretary of State and he/she must consider them (s. 42(2)).

Where representations are made and the Secretary of State intends to require the police authority to exercise its power to call upon the chief constable to retire, the Secretary of State must appoint one or more persons to hold an inquiry and report to him/her (s. 42(4)). At least one of the members of the inquiry should be someone who is outside the police force or any government department. The costs of this enquiry may be paid from the police fund (s. 42(5)). It appears that a decision will then be taken by the Secretary of State on the basis of the Chief Officer's representations and the report of the inquiry.

THE NATIONAL CRIME INTELLIGENCE SERVICE

Section 9E, Removal of Commissioner or Deputy Commissioner, of the Police Act 1996 (as inserted into the Police Act by amendment by s. 318 of the Greater London Authority Act 1999) provides:

(1)   The Metropolitan Police Authority, acting with the approval of the Secretary of State, may call upon the Commissioner of Police of the Metropolis to retire in the interests of efficiency or effectiveness.

(2)   Before seeking the approval of the Secretary of State under subsection (1), the Metropolitan Police Authority shall give the Commissioner of Police of the Metropolis an opportunity to make representations and shall consider any representations that he makes.

(3)   Where the Commissioner of Police of the Metropolis is called upon to retire under subsection (1), he shall retire on such date as the Metropolitan Police Authority may specify or on such earlier date as may be agreed upon between him and the Authority.

(4)   This section shall apply in relation to the Deputy Commissioner of Police of the Metropolis as it applies to the Commissioner of Police of the Metropolis.

This section brings the provisions relating to the Metropolitan Police Commissioner and the Deputy Police Commissioner into line with that of chief officers under s. 11 of the Police Act 1996 (see above). However, there is no corresponding amendment to s. 42 of the Police Act such that the Metropolitan Police Commissioner or the Deputy Police Commissioner are given the opportunity to make representations.

The National Crime Intelligence Service (NCIS) was established under the Police Act 1997, s. 2, and its functions are to gather, store and analyse information in order to provide criminal intelligence, to provide such intelligence to police forces and to support these police forces and the National Crime Squad (NCS). Other than its Director General, full-time members of the NCIS, before their appointment, must have:

- held the rank of assistant chief constable or higher in a police force;
- held the rank of commander or higher in the Metropolitan Police or the City of London Police forces; or
- eligibility under the Police Act 1996, s. 50, for any such rank (Police Act 1997, s. 9).

Functions of the NCIS

- Gather, store and analyse information in order to provide criminal intelligence.
- Provide criminal intelligence to police forces.
- Support police forces, the NCS and other law enforcement agencies in carrying out their criminal intelligence activities.

Disciplinary Regulations

The disciplinary provisions relating to officers in the NCIS are set out in the NCIS (Complaints) Regulations 1998 (SI 1998 No. 641) as amended, and the NCIS (Discipline) (Senior Police Members) Regulations 1998 (SI 1998 No. 636).

THE NATIONAL CRIME SQUAD

The National Crime Squad (NCS) was established under the Police Act 1997, s. 48, and its functions are the prevention and detection of serious crime which is of relevance to more than one police area in England and Wales. The requirements of appointment to the NCS are the same as those for the NCIS.

Functions of the NCS

- Prevent and detect serious crime which is relevant to more than one police area.
- At the request of a chief officer of police, act in support of the activities of a police force in the detention and prevention of serious crime.

Disciplinary Regulations

The disciplinary provisions relating to officers in the NCS are set out in the National Crime Squad (Complaints) Regulations 1998 (SI 1998 No. 638) as amended, and the National Crime Squad (Discipline) (Senior Police Members) Regulations 1998 (SI 1998 No. 637).

The Race Relations (Amendment) Act 2000 makes special provisions for liability of the Director General of the National Criminal Intelligence Service to be the chief officer of police for officers seconded to that force, and similarly the Director General of the National Crime Squad for officers seconded to that force (new s. 76B Race Relations Act 1976). Any compensation is to be paid by the NCIS and NCS service funds respectively.

Complaints against the NCIS or the NCS

Complaints against seconded police members of the NCS are dealt with under the National Crime Intelligence Service (Complaints) Regulations 1999 (SI 1999 No. 641) as amended by the National Crime Intelligence Service (Complaints) (Amendment) Regulations 1999 (SI 1999 No. 1273).

Complaints against seconded police members of the NCS are dealt with under the National Crime Squad (Complaints) Regulations 1999 (SI 1999 No. 638) as amended by the National Crime Squad (Complaints) (Amendment) Regulations 1999 (SI 1999 No. 1266). These Regulations are set out in Appendix 6.

SECONDED OFFICERS

In addition to officers working for the special authority organisations such as the NCS and the NCIS, there are several hundred police officers throughout England and Wales who are seconded temporarily to central services. Examples of central services can be found in National Police Training and

Crime Prevention College. Such central services are provided for under the Police Act 1996, s. 57. Further, there are other opportunities for police officers to be attached to overseas departments (s. 26 of the 1996 Act), to Her Majesty's Inspectorate of Constabulary (HMIC) as well as other units within the Police Policy and Crime Reduction Unit at the Home Office.

The applicability of many parts of the Police Act 1996 to such officers is governed by s. 97 (set out below). Section 97 is generally intended to make provision for those police officers who, while serving temporarily in one or more of the specialist roles set out in s. 97(1) may otherwise not be treated as members of a police force for a number of important purposes: calculation of length of service, entitlement for promotion and enjoyment of powers as a police officer. Section 97 provides that:

(1)   For the purposes of this section 'relevant service' means—

(a)   temporary service on which a person is engaged in accordance with arrangements made under section 26;

(b)   temporary service under section 56 on which a person is engaged with the consent of the appropriate authority;

(c)   temporary service under the Crown in connection with the provision by the Secretary of State of—

  (i)   such organisations and services as are described in section 57, or

  (ii)   research or other services connected with the police,

on which a person is engaged with the consent of the appropriate authority;

(ca)   temporary service with the National Criminal Intelligence Service on which a person is engaged with the consent of the appropriate authority;

(cb)   temporary service with the National Crime Squad on which a person is engaged with the consent of the appropriate authority;

(cc)   temporary service with the Police Information Technology Organisation on which a person is engaged with the consent of the appropriate authority;

(d)   temporary service as an adviser to the Secretary of State on which a person is engaged with the consent of the appropriate authority;

(e)   service the expenses of which are payable under section 1(1) of the Police (Overseas Service) Act 1945, on which a person is engaged with the consent of the appropriate authority;

(ea)   temporary service with the Police Ombudsman for Northern Ireland on which a person is engaged in accordance with arrangements made under paragraph 8 of Schedule 3 to the Police (Northern Ireland) Act 1998;

(f)   service in the Royal Ulster Constabulary, on which a person is engaged with the consent of the Secretary of State and the appropriate authority; or

(g)   service pursuant to an appointment under section 10 of the Overseas Development and Co-operation Act 1980, on which a person is engaged with the consent of the appropriate authority.

(2)   In subsection (1) 'appropriate authority', in relation to a member of a police force, means the chief officer of police acting with the consent of the police authority, except that in relation to the chief officer of police it means the police authority.

(3)   Subject to subsections (4) to (8), a member of a police force engaged on relevant service shall be treated as if he were not a member of that force during that service; but, except where a pension, allowance or gratuity becomes payable to him out of money provided by Parliament by virtue of regulations made under the Police Pensions Act 1976—

(a)   he shall be entitled at the end of the period of relevant service to revert to his police force in the rank in which he was serving immediately before the period began, and

(b)   he shall be treated as if he had been serving in that force during the period of relevant service for the purposes of any scale prescribed by or under regulations made under section 50 above fixing his rate of pay by reference to his length of service.

(4)   In the case of relevant service to which subsection (1)(e) refers, the reference in subsection (3) to regulations made under the Police Pensions Act 1976 shall be read as including a reference to regulations made under section 1 of the Police (Overseas Service) Act 1945.

(5)   A person may, when engaged on relevant service, be promoted in his police force as if he were serving in that force; and in any such case—

(a)   the reference in paragraph (a) of subsection (3) to the rank in which he was serving immediately before the period of relevant service began shall be construed as a reference to the rank to which he is promoted, and

(b)   for the purposes mentioned in paragraph (b) of that subsection he shall be treated as having served in that rank from the time of his promotion.

(6)   A member of a police force who—

(a)   has completed a period of relevant service within paragraph (a), (b), (c), (ca), (cb), (cc), (d) or (g) of subsection (1), or

(b)   while engaged on relevant service within paragraph (e) of that subsection, is dismissed from that service by the disciplinary authority established by regulations made under section 1 of the Police (Overseas Service) Act 1945 or is required to resign as an alternative to dismissal, or

(c)   while engaged on relevant service within paragraph [(ea) or] (f) of that subsection, is dismissed from that service or is required to resign as an alternative to dismissal,

may be dealt with under regulations made in accordance with section 50(3) for anything done or omitted while he was engaged on that service as if that service had been service in his police force; and section 85 shall apply accordingly.

(7)   For the purposes of subsection (6) a certificate certifying that a person has been dismissed, or required to resign as an alternative to dismissal, shall be evidence of the fact so certified, if—

(a)   in a case within paragraph (b) of that subsection, it is given by the disciplinary authority referred to in that paragraph, or

(b)   in a case within paragraph (c) of that subsection, it is given by or on behalf of the Police Ombudsman for Northern Ireland or (as the case may be) the chief constable of the Royal Ulster Constabulary, or such other person or authority as may be designated for the purposes of this subsection by order of the Secretary of State.

(8)   A member of a police force engaged on relevant service within paragraph (b), (c), (ca), (cb), (cc), or (d) of subsection (1)—
   (a)   shall continue to be a constable, and
   (b)   shall be treated for the purposes of sections 30, 59, 60, 64 and 90 as if he were a member of his police force.
(9)   The Secretary of State shall be liable in respect of torts committed by a member of a police force engaged on relevant service within paragraph (b), (c) or (d) of subsection (1) in the performance or purported performance of his functions in like manner as a master is liable in respect of torts committed by his servants in the course of their employment, and shall in respect of any such tort be treated for all purposes as a joint tortfeasor.

Practice Note

Section 97(6) makes particular provision for the application of disciplinary procedures in respect of officers who have completed a period of service in the roles set out under (a), (b), (c), (ca), (cb), (cc), (d) or (g) or who, while engaged in such roles as are set out under (e), (ea) or (f), were dismissed or required to resign.

The wording of s. 97(8) makes it clear that officers engaged in certain seconded roles are only to be treated as members of their police force for certain specified purposes under the 1996 Act. The roles identified are those falling under (b), (c), (ca), (cb), (cc) or (d) of subsection (1) above. Police officers seconded to these temporary duties continue to be constables and therefore enjoy all the powers and privileges relating to that office (regardless of rank). They are to be treated as members of the police force only in respect of specified sections of the Police Act 1996 (ss. 30, 59, 64 and 90). Thus officers seconded to those duties are not to be treated as members of the police force for other purposes and are not caught by the Police (Efficiency) Regulations 1999 and Police (Conduct) Regulations 1999, neither are they able to perform any of the various functions set out in those Regulations.

Section 97(6) makes specific provision in relation to seconded officers returning to their forces after a period of relevant service. Section 97(6) allows chief officers to deal with such officers as if they had been serving back in their respective force at the time of any act or omission which may have occurred while on secondment. This provision clearly envisages the situation where the conduct of a seconded officer gives rise to concern and he/she is then returned to his/her own force under the terms of secondment.

The guidance provided by the Home Office (see Appendix 1, annex L) suggests that, in cases of poor performance, the preliminary stages of the developmental process designed for other officers (see Chapter 3) should be followed. However, if there is no improvement, the guidance advocates that the officer should be returned to his/her parent force.

Most contracts for secondment will be terminable on the giving of four weeks' notice by either side. Misconduct or poor performance is not generally required for a seconded officer's contract to be terminated, however, the consequences of returning a seconded officer early can be considerable, particularly as many such officers move their homes great distances outside their own force area on taking up a post or even move into accommodation provided by the particular organisation to which they are attached.

Once a seconded officer has returned to his/her force, s. 97(6) allows him/her to be dealt with under regulations made under s. 50(3). Section 50(3) allows for regulations for the establishment of procedures for cases in which a member of a police force may be dealt with by dismissal, requirement to resign, reduction in rank, reduction in rate of pay, fine, reprimand or caution. Clearly these sanctions are available under each of the conduct or efficiency procedures and therefore it may be argued that those procedures in their entirety can be brought into effect in respect of officers who have returned from their secondment. On the other hand, the authority to make regulations in relation to the conduct, efficiency and effectiveness of members of police forces and the maintenance of discipline is found under s. 50(2)(e) of the 1996 Act and not s. 50(3). Therefore, it might also be argued that, although the sanctions set out under s. 50(3) are available to chief officers in respect of their returning secondees, the relevant procedures set out in the Police (Efficiency) Regulations 1999 and the Police (Conduct) Regulations 1999 are not. The Regulations themselves do not help as the explanatory notes (which, in any event, is not part of the Regulations) state only that they are made under s. 50 of the Police Act 1996.

PROBATIONARY CONSTABLES

The provisions relating to probationary constables are set out in the Police Regulations 1995 (SI 1995 No. 215), regs 14 and 15 (see Appendix 13). Regulation 14(2) states that probationary constables will generally be on probation for the first two years of their service as a constable in the police force. However, the chief officer of police may extend the probationary period by up to a year if the probationary period of a particular individual was 'seriously interrupted by a period of absence from duty by reason of injury or illness'. In its Report of Police Training and Recruitment (1999), the Home Affairs Committee recommended that probationer constables are not sworn in (or 'attested') until they have completed six months' service. The Court of Appeal has held that it is critical to observe that the probationary period ceases at the end of the two-year period unless a decision has by then been made to extend it (*R v Chief Constable of Greater Manchester Police, ex parte Lainton* [2000] ICR 1324). If no extension has been made by the time the two-year period elapses, the officer becomes a permanent appointee and a chief officer does not have the power to return such an appointee to their former probationary status.

Discharge of a probationer

The Police Regulations 1995, reg. 15(1) provides that during the period of a constable's probation, he/she may be dispensed with at any time if the chief officer of police (which, under reg. 15(5) includes the assistant commissioner of police) considers that he/she is not fitted, physically or mentally, to perform the duties of his/her office, or that he/she is not likely to become an efficient or well-conducted constable.

When a probationary constable is discharged, under reg. 15(2), he/she will be entitled to receive a month's notice or a month's pay in lieu of notice.

Regulation 15(3) adds that a probationer's service shall not be dispensed with in circumstances in which he/she gives notice of his/her intention to retire from the police force (and does in fact retire before the date on which his/her services would otherwise have been dispensed with). Where a constable has been given notice that his/her services are to be dispensed with and gives notice of his/her intention to retire, one month's pay from the date of the notice that his/his services are being dispensed with. Whereas the power to extend a probationer's two-year period under reg. 14 above can be delegated to another senior officer, there is no power to delegate the decision to dismiss under reg. 15 (see *Lainton* above). In the *Lainton* case, the decision was taken by the Assistant Chief Constable for Personnel and Training.

CADETS

The provisions relating to cadets are set out in the Police Cadets Regulations 1979 (SI 1979 No. 1727). Regulation 5 sets out three ways in which a police cadet's service may be terminated, namely by:

- resignation on two weeks' notice to the police authority (or such shorter period as the authority accepts) (reg. 5(1));
- on appointment as a member of a police force (reg. 5(2)); or
- on termination by the chief officer of police (reg. 5(3)).

Termination by the chief officer

When a police cadet's service is terminated for misconduct, he/she will not be entitled to any notice or pay in lieu of notice. Where the termination is for any other reason, he/she will be entitled to two weeks' notice or two weeks' pay in lieu of notice (reg. 5(4)).

Where the chief officer is considering terminating a police cadet's service for misconduct, the cadet must be given the opportunity of a personal interview with the chief officer, the deputy/assistant chief constable or the assistant commissioner (as relevant) (reg. 5(5)). At this interview, the cadet will be entitled to:

- be accompanied by anyone he/she chooses; and
- make any representations.

There are no specific provisions about how the interview should be conducted. However, any decision made by a police authority will be judicially reviewable so that, for example, any interview or hearings which take place must be conducted in accordance with principles of natural justice (see Chapter 10).

SPECIAL CONSTABLES

The provisions relating to special constables are set out in the Special Constable Regulations 1965 (SI 1965 No. 536).

Suspension and dismissal

Regulation 2(1) of the 1965 Regulations provides that, where there is a report or complaint received from which it appears that a special constable has been negligent in the discharge of his/her duties as a special constable or deemed to be otherwise unfit for these duties, the chief constable may suspend the special constable from office. This suspension will last until either it is decided that no action needs to be taken as a result of the report or allegation or that further action needs to be taken.

Regulation 2(1) gives the police authority a wide discretion in the sanctions which it may use in dealing with special constables and includes the power to dismiss the constable. However, as above, decisions relating to the service of special constables will be judicially reviewable.

Retirement

Regulation 3(2) of the 1965 Regulations provides that the chief constable may also require a constable to retire on the grounds of:

- age;
- a disability which is likely to be permanent and affects the performance of the ordinary duties of a special constable; or
- as an alternative to dismissal, where the constable has been negligent in the discharge of his/her duties or otherwise unfit for them.

CIVILIAN EMPLOYEES

Civilian employees within a police force, although employed by a police authority, are under the direction and control of the chief constable. Like employees outside the police force, they are entitled to protection from dismissal as set out in the Employment Rights Act 1996, s. 98. Thus when an employee is being dismissed for a reason connected with capability or conduct, the police authority must act reasonably in treating his/her conduct as being a sufficient reason for dismissal.

Whether or not an employment tribunal takes the view that an employer has acted reasonably in dismissing an individual depends to a great extent, not only on the nature of the individual's wrongdoing, but also on the procedure followed by the employer. Factors which can be considered are:

- for capability dismissals, whether the employee's performance has been appraised and whether he/she has been given an opportunity to improve;
- for conduct dismissals, whether the employee has been warned that his/her conduct might lead to dismissal and what opportunity has been given to assess his/her conduct after having been warned (the number of warnings which a tribunal considers reasonable will depend on the seriousness of the offence).

The police authority may, in certain circumstances, dismiss an individual for a single act of misconduct where the seriousness of that misconduct justifies it (e.g. when an employee in a position of trust acts dishonestly). However, the tribunal will still look at whether dismissal was a fair sanction in the circumstances. The question for the tribunal will always be the reasonableness of the decision to dismiss in the circumstances of the particular case having regard to equity and the substantial merits.

The ACAS Code of Conduct

The ACAS Code of Practice on Disciplinary and Grievance Procedures, which does not have statutory force but is widely used by employment tribunals as a guide to good practice and the reasonableness of the procedure followed by an employer, states that disciplinary procedures should not be viewed primarily as a means of imposing sanctions but should also be designed to emphasise and encourage improvements in individual conduct. It emphasises the following essential features of a good disciplinary procedure:

- deal quickly with matters;
- provide for individuals to be informed of the case against them and an opportunity to state their case before a decision is reached;
- give individuals the right to be accompanied;
- ensure careful investigation of allegations;
- explain sanctions; and
- provide a right of appeal.

10 THE ROLE OF THE HIGHER COURTS

INTRODUCTION

Where an officer is dissatisfied with the decision of a police tribunal and has exhausted any other relevant internal appeals procedure, he/she may, in certain circumstances, seek remedy in the civil courts: the County Court, the High Court, the Court of Appeal and the House of Lords. Claims may be made under the common law, for breach of statutory duty or in judicial review.

COMMON LAW

In general, it will be difficult for an officer with a grievance about internal proceedings to found a claim under the common law: the tort of negligence will generally not apply to such proceedings and the tort of misfeasance in public office will be difficult to establish. We will examine each aspect in turn.

Negligence

A person may bring a claim for negligence where another person who owes him/her a duty of care acts in breach of that duty (one simple example is that of a person who is injured as a result of another's negligent driving). In general, a person will not owe a duty of care unless the following criteria are fulfilled:

- that the damage which arises from breach is foreseeable;
- that there is a sufficiently close relationship between the parties; and
- that it is just and equitable to impose a duty of care

(see *Caparo Industries* v *Dickman* [1990] 1 All ER 568).

One example of the duty of care is the duty of an employer both to a former employee and to a prospective employer of that employee not to provide a misleading reference about that former employee. The House of Lords, in the case of *Spring* v *Guardian Royal Exchange* [1994] 3 WLR 354, emphasised that their decision on the duty of employer's liability to a former employee was founded on the fact that the relationship was in an employment context but stated that the duty was not limited to 'employees' but could also apply to someone employed under a contract for services. Therefore, it would appear that a police authority is also under a duty not to provide a misleading reference to a constable.

An officer who is the subject of internal proceedings and alleges that those proceedings have been misconducted will not generally be able to found a claim in negligence against the chief constable or commissioner. In the case of *Calveley* v *Chief Constable of Merseyside Police* [1989] 2 WLR 624, the House of Lords decided that the chief constable did not owe a duty of care in common law to an officer in the conduct of disciplinary proceedings because the requirement that the damage must be foreseeable was not fulfilled. A comparison was made with the relationship between an investigating officer and a suspect under investigation. The House of Lords found that, if there was no duty of care owed to a civilian suspect, it was hard to see why a police officer should be in a better position. In *L (a child) and P* v *Reading Borough Council and the Chief Constable of the Thames Valley Police*, LTL 12 March 2001, the court held that there was sufficient proximity between a police officer and a child victim arising out of an interview. However, the House of Lords has recently held it to be at least arguable that the relationship between a police officer and his/her chief constable (or commissioner) produced duties that were analogous to those owed by an employer to an employee (*Waters* v *Metropolitan Police Commissioner* [2000] 1 WLR 1607). That relationship, together with the provisions of s. 88(1) of the Police Act 1996 (making chief constables liable for the torts of an officer under their direction or control) meant that a police officer could have a valid cause of action in negligence against the chief constable where that chief constable had failed to protect the officer against victimisation and harassment from fellow officers leading to injury.

Misfeasance in public office

Misfeasance in public office is another common law cause of action which arises when an authority (such as a police authority) causes a person loss by an administrative action which the authority in question knew to be unreasonable or unlawful. Although this might apply to police disciplinary and efficiency proceedings, it would in practice be very difficult for an officer to succeed on such a claim as he/she would have to show that the police authority had acted in bad faith or without reasonable cause. In *Calveley* (above), the action for misfeasance in public office failed because no 'bad faith' had been alleged, let alone proved and no absence of reasonable cause had been shown. For the indictable offence of misfeasance, see Chapter 11.

BREACH OF STATUTORY DUTY

Where internal police proceedings have been breached, an officer may bring a claim for breach of the statute or the relevant Regulation. In the case of *Ridge* v *Baldwin* [1964] AC 40, a chief constable was himself dismissed after being prosecuted on conspiracy and corruption charges. The relevant committee dismissed him under the Municipal Corporations Act 1882 which stated that the committee 'may' dismiss an officer whom it thought had been negligent. The House of Lords held that the dismissal was null and void for the following two reasons. First, the committee had a duty to observe the principles of natural justice (i.e. the right to be heard and the right to an unbiased hearing) in dismissing any officer under the 1882 Act and it had breached this duty by not informing the chief constable of the charges against him and not affording him the opportunity to be heard. Secondly, the relevant disciplinary regulations had themselves been interpreted incorrectly.

Although the principles of natural justice (which are set out in more detail below) have their origins in the common law, they are commonly raised in judicial review proceedings and, in general, the appropriate course of action for an officer bringing a complaint about the conduct of internal proceedings (along with claims under the Human Rights Act 1998 — see Chapter 1) is to make an application for judicial review.

JUDICIAL REVIEW

Judicial review is a central feature of public/administrative law (the law relating to the administrative acts of public bodies such as the government, local councils and tribunals). It allows the courts to supervise the activities of public bodies and brings before the courts issues ranging from commercial disputes (such as patent rights and import duty assessments), to self-contained points of procedure (for example, in magistrates' courts and extradition proceedings) through to social concerns (such as housing, prisoners' rights and health). Police authorities are public bodies for these purposes and are therefore susceptible to judicial review provided that the matter being reviewed is within the scope of review.

To be subject to judicial review, however, the subject matter of the decision to be reviewed must be public in nature. In *R* v *Derbyshire County Council, ex parte Noble* [1990] IRLR 332, a police surgeon applied for judicial review when his contract was terminated on the basis that the termination was unfair. The Court of Appeal held that this was not an appropriate subject for an application of judicial review, finding that:

- the remedies the surgeon sought did not arise from a breach from any public duty placed upon the Council;
- the Council was not performing a public function in terminating the surgeon's contract;
- a public law element could not be injected into the case simply by showing that police surgeons have public functions.

Procedure

The rules of procedure governing judicial review are set out in RSC, ord. 53 of sch. 1 to the Civil Procedure Rules 1998. Before applying for judicial review, the permission of the court must be obtained to make such an application (r. 3). The judge can grant or refuse permission without a hearing (r. 3(3)). If permission to apply is granted, the court can impose conditions on the application, for example, requiring the applicant to give security for costs (r. 3(9)).

Applications for judicial review must be brought promptly and in any event within three months from the date when the grounds for the application first arose (unless the court considers that there is good reason for extending the period within which the application can be made) (r. 4). Applications may be brought only in the Administrative Court and should be made by completion of a claim form (r. 5). The claim form should be accompanied by written evidence (usually a witness statement) in support of the application (r. 6).

At the hearing of the application, any person who wishes to be heard in opposition to the application (and appears to the court to be a proper person to be heard) may be heard. The costs of judicial review proceedings will generally be paid by the losing party. A Police Authority has the power to provide financial assistance to police officers in relation to applications for judicial review by virtue of s. 6(1) Police Act 1996 and s. 111(1) Local Government Act 1972 (see *R v Director of Public Prosecutions, ex parte Duckenfield* (2000) 1 WLR 55). (*Cf.* the situation in relation to police disciplinary cases, e.g. *R v South Yorkshire Police Authority, ex parte Andrew Booth* (2000) *The Times*, 10 October 2000 — see Chapter 4.)

Remedies

The remedies for judicial review are entirely within the court's discretion and this includes whether to grant any relief at all. The judicial review remedies comprise:

- a quashing order (formerly an order of *certioriari*) (quashing a decision);
- a mandatory order (formerly an order of *mandamus*) (rectifying inaction); and
- a prohibiting order (formerly an order of prohibition) (restraining threatened action).

Remedies also include the following private law remedies:

- declaration (making a finding that a particular state of affairs exists or that a person has a particular right);
- injunction (normally to prevent action taking place but including, in unusual situations, mandatory injunctions forcing a party to carry out a particular act); and
- damages.

Note that the terminology above (e.g. quashing order) is that introduced by the Part 54 of the new Civil Procedure Rules 1998.

An applicant for judicial review may be granted a combination of two or more of these remedies. A useful example in the police context is the case of *R v Chief Constable of Devon & Cornwall, ex parte Hay and the Police Complaints Authority* [1996] 2 All ER 711. The chief constable's decision to drop disciplinary proceedings against an officer arising out of a fatal shooting was found to be unlawful. The court made an order of *certiorari* to quash the decision and an order of *mandamus* directed to the chief constable to hear and determine the charge against the officer. It is common for a successful application for judicial review to result in the matter being remitted (sent back) to the original decision-making body for further consideration.

Grounds for judicial review

It is not possible to categorise rigidly the possible grounds for an application for judicial review. The most widely used classification is under the following heads:

- illegality;
- irrationality/unreasonableness; and
- procedural impropriety.

However, these limbs are neither exhaustive nor mutually exclusive and the grounds of intervention should be flexible enough to accommodate the circumstances of the particular case.

Illegality

A finding of illegality may be made where a public body makes a decision (including one which is an exercise of its discretion) but misinterprets the law which it is applying, makes a relevant error in applying the law, takes into account irrelevant considerations or wholly ignores relevant considerations. It encompasses circumstances in which a public body has acted outside its lawful authority. Where the court finds that there has been illegality, this may render the relevant decision of the public body a nullity.

Abuse of power is related to (but not generally considered to be the same as) illegality: for example, this may comprise improper motive on the part of the decision maker, improper delegation of power, bad faith and frustrating the purpose of the legislation under whose authority the decision under review is purportedly made. In *R v Hull University Visitor, ex parte Page* [1993] AC 682, Lord Griffiths (referring to a previous decision of his) described 'abuse of power' as follows: 'I used the phrase "abuse of power" to connote some form of misbehaviour that was wholly incompatible with the judicial role that the judge was expected to perform.' It may also be noted that 'bad faith', as for the tort of misfeasance in public office, may be very difficult for an applicant for judicial review to prove (and should not be alleged lightly).

In *R v Deputy Chief Constable of Nottinghamshire Constabulary, ex parte Street*, *The Times*, 16 July 1983, it was held that, although the chief constable could delegate administrative matters, under the (now superseded) Police Regulations 1979 (SI 1999, No. 1470) he could not delegate the final decision to dispense with the probationer's services. Thus, it is important to note that, where the Regulations specify that an officer of a certain rank must make a particular decision, this cannot be delegated to a more junior officer.

Irrationality/unreasonableness

The court may also review a decision if it considers that a public body has done something which may not be done by a public body in the same situation, having the same function, understanding its duties and acting reasonably. In short, it entitles an applicant to bring a claim where a public authority has gone badly wrong. In *Champion v Chief Constable of the Gwent Constabulary* [1990] 1 WLR 1, for example, an officer made an application for judicial review when his chief constable refused him permission to sit as a school governor, on the basis that holding such a position might give rise to the impression amongst the general public that this could interfere with the impartial discharge of his duties as a police officer (contrary to para. 1 of sch. 2 to the Police Regulations 1979). The House of Lords held that the chief constable had applied an unrealistic standard to the matter which was being considered and, as a result, 'came to a conclusion so unreasonable that no reasonable Chief Constable could ever have come to it'.

Failure to give reasons for a decision may also amount to 'irrationality'. An officer conducting an appeal hearing who did not give any reasons for his decision to uphold a complaint might, therefore, be susceptible to judicial review. The reasons need not, however, be so detailed as would be expected from a court of law. When an application is made under the head of 'irrationality', it should be kept in mind that the decision or activity in question must appear extremely unsatisfactory before the courts will intervene on the grounds of irrationality/unreasonableness. The reviewing court will thus give a wide margin of appreciation to the tribunal or other body deciding the issue 'first time round'.

Procedural impropriety

Procedural impropriety/unfairness may arise where a public body has failed to comply with procedural requirements imposed by an Act, statutory instrument or the common law. A typical example occurs when an Act or statutory instrument sets out procedural safeguards which are not followed. It is closely linked to the concepts of 'natural justice' and fair trial. As stated above, 'natural justice' is concerned with procedural safeguards founded in the common law, in particular the right to be heard and the requirement that no person should be a judge in his/her own cause (the rule against bias). These common law rights may be extended or restricted by judges within the general doctrine of precedent. The right to be heard includes the right to be provided with relevant information (for example, in disciplinary proceedings, the nature of the allegation and the evidence which gives rise to the allegation). In *R* v *Chief Constable of Thames Valley, ex parte Stevenson, The*

Times, 22 April 1987, the failure to accord to a probationer constable the opportunity to deal with a report prepared by the assistant chief constable which contained recommendations as to his dismissal amounted to a procedural impropriety. The rule against bias includes circumstances where there is the *appearance* of bias as well as those where there is actual bias.

In general, the extent and scope of the duty of a public body to ensure procedural fairness depends on all the circumstances of the case and, therefore, the following factors may be taken into account by the court in determining whether there should be a review:

- the importance of the decision to the applicant;
- whether he/she raised a complaint at the time; and
- whether the applicant agreed to the procedure.

The question of whether internal police proceedings are fair thus goes beyond the issue of whether the express provisions of the particular Regulations have been complied with, and proceedings may still be procedurally unfair when such provisions are followed but, for example, there is bias or insufficient information is provided. In *Chief Constable of North Wales Police* v *Evans* [1981] 1 WLR 1155, the House of Lords ordered the reinstatement of a probationer constable (who had been discharged) on the basis of the failure of the chief constable to put to the constable various factors which had formed part of the basis of the decision to discharge him. This constituted a breach of the principles of natural justice.

Accompaniment and natural justice

Under the Police (Conduct) Regulations 1999 (SI 1999 No. 730), an officer may be accompanied at a disciplinary hearing only by another officer (i.e. the Regulations do not expressly permit legal representation). In *Maynard* v *Osmond* [1976] 3 WLR 711 (which was an ordinary High Court action and not judicial review), the court held that there was no breach of natural justice as a result of the failure to permit legal representation and that the right to representation may be excluded provided that fairness can be achieved without it. The Police (Conduct) (Senior Officers) Regulations 1999 allow an officer to be accompanied by a friend or relative. According to *R* v *Metropolitan Police Force Disciplinary Tribunal, ex parte Lawrence, The Times*, 13 July 1999, which arose from the disciplinary proceedings after the Stephen Lawrence inquiry, this 'friend or relative' may be a legally qualified person.

Furthermore, the Police Complaints Authority may have the right to attend a stage of proceedings. In *R* v *Police Complaints Authority, ex parte Thompson, The Times*, 24 October 1989, the Authority insisted on one of its members being present at a disciplinary interview. The court had regard to the fact that the complaint was one which had to be reported to the Authority under the Police and Criminal Evidence Act 1984, s. 89, and ruled that a member of the Authority could attend such an interview. It added that the attendance of the Authority at such hearings could be valuable protection for an officer as well as for a member of the public.

No technical breach of natural justice

There will not be a breach of natural justice where the individual concerned has not suffered any prejudice. For example, in *R v Chief Constable of South Wales, ex parte Thornhill* [1987] IRLR 313, where the alleged breach was the fact that the investigating officer had come into the hearing room during an adjournment to discuss another police matter with the chief constable, the court accepted that the work of the police force had to go on during the course of proceedings and held that this discussion could not amount to a breach of natural justice. This feature was emphasised in *R v Chief Constable of the Thames Valley, ex parte Cotton* [1990] IRLR 344, in which the Court of Appeal stated that there was no such thing as a 'technical' breach of natural justice.

APPEALS

The right of appeal against a final decision of the County Court or the High Court (including judicial review) lies to the Court of Appeal. Before an application to appeal can be made, permission to appeal must be granted by either the trial judge or the Court of Appeal itself. The Court of Appeal is generally constituted by three Lord Justices.

Although the Court of Appeal is not limited to overturning errors of law (and may look at the whole of the evidence at the hearing), it will give great weight to findings of fact made by the judge at the original hearing and it will therefore be in exceptional circumstances only that it differs from a judge in relation to a finding of fact. However, the Court of Appeal will be more willing to differ from the judge on the question of inferences to be drawn from those findings of fact. Where the judge is wrong on a matter of law crucial to the decision, then an appeal will succeed unless the decision can be upheld on the basis of some alternative and sound proposition of law. The right of appeal from decisions of the Court of Appeal lies to the House of Lords where the matter will be heard by five Law Lords. However, there is no right of appeal to the House of Lords for the refusal of permission to make an application for judicial review.

From 2 May 2000, the rules governing procedure in relation to appeals are set out in Part 52 of the Civil Procedure Rules 1998.

11 MISCELLANEOUS OFFENCES AND REGULATIONS

INTRODUCTION

Restrictions on private lives

The Police Regulations 1995 (SI 1995 No. 215) impose restrictions on the private lives of officers. Regulation 10 of the 1995 Regulations provides that the restrictions contained in sch. 2 shall apply to all members of a police force. It also provides that no restrictions other than those designed to secure the proper exercise of the functions of a constable shall be imposed by the police authority or the chief officer of police on the private lives of members of a police force except such as may temporarily be necessary or such as may be approved by the Secretary of State after consultation. This ability to impose restrictions on the private lives of police officers will now have to be read in the light of the European Convention on Human Rights (as to which, see Chapter 1).

Schedule 2

The Police Regulations 1995, sch. 2, provides that a member of a police force:

- Shall at all times abstain from any activity which is likely to interfere with the impartial discharge of his/her duties or which is likely to give rise to the impression amongst members of the public that it may so interfere (this does not include serving as a school governor), and in particular a member of a police force shall not take any active part in politics.
- Shall not reside at premises which are not for the time being approved by the chief officer of police.

- Shall not, without the previous consent of the chief officer of police, receive a lodger in a house or quarters with which he/she is provided by the police authority, or sub-let any part of the house or quarters.
- Shall not, unless he/she has previously given written notice to the chief officer of police, receive a lodger in a house in which he/she resides and in respect of which he/she receives a rent allowance, or sub-let any part of such a house.
- Shall not wilfully refuse or neglect to discharge any lawful debt.

Business interests

The Police Regulations 1995, reg. 10, provides that, if a member of a police force or a relative included in his/her family proposes to have, or has, a 'business interest', the member shall forthwith give written notice of that interest to the chief officer of police unless that business interest was disclosed at the time of the officer's appointment as a member of the force.

On receipt of such a notice, the chief officer shall determine whether or not the interest in question is compatible with the member concerned remaining a member of the force and shall notify the member in writing of his/her decision.

Within 10 days of being notified of the chief officer's decision (or within such longer period as the police authority may in all the circumstances allow), the member concerned may appeal to the police authority against that decision by sending written notice to the police authority.

If a business interest is felt to be incompatible, the chief officer may dispense with the member's services after giving them an opportunity to make representations.

For the purposes of reg. 10, a member of a police force or relative has a business interest if:

- the member holds any office or employment for hire or carries on any business;
- a shop is kept or a like business carried on by the member's spouse (not being separated) at any premises in the area of the police force in question or by any relative living with him/her; or
- the member, his/her spouse (not being separated) or any relative living with them has a pecuniary interest in any licence or permit granted in relation to liquor licensing, refreshment houses or betting and gaming or regulating places of entertainment in the area of the police force in question.

'Relative' includes a reference to a spouse, parent, son, daughter, brother or sister. For officers seconded to the Home Office under Central Service conditions (as to whom, see Chapter 9), there are further restrictions imposed by the Civil Service Business Appointment Rules, which should be provided for them *before* entering into a contract with the relevant Home Office departments.

OFFENCES

Offence — Malfeasance in a Public Office — Common Law
Triable on indictment. Imprisonment at large.
(*Arrestable offence*)

It is a misdemeanour at common law for the holder of a public office to do anything that amounts to a malfeasance or a 'culpable' misfeasance (*R* v *Wyatt* (1705) 1 Salk 380).

Practice Note

This offence can only be tried on indictment and the court has a power of sentence 'at large', that is, there is no limit on the sentence that can be passed (making this an arrestable offence under the Police and Criminal Evidence Act 1984, s. 24).

The conduct can be separated into occasions of *mal*feasance and *mis*-feasance. The first requires some degree of wrongful motive or intention on the part of the officer concerned while the second is more likely to apply where there has been some form of wilful neglect of duty. Although many of the earlier cases involved an element of corruption, this is not a requirement for the offence (*R* v *Dytham* [1979] 2 QB 722). This offence might be committed where a police officer wilfully neglects to prevent a criminal assault (as in *Dytham*), or possibly where a supervisory officer fails to intervene in a situation where one of his/her officers is carrying out an unlawful act. The neglect has to be 'wilful' and not simply inadvertent. It also has to be done without reasonable excuse or justification.

The offence is a very serious one and therefore the conduct must have been sufficiently damaging to the public interest that it merits condemnation and criminal punishment.

Offence — Constables on Licensed Premises — Licensing Act 1964, s. 178
Triable summarily. Fine.
(*No specific power of arrest*)

The Licensing Act 1964, s. 178 provides that:

If the holder of a justices' licence—
(a) knowingly suffers to remain on the licensed premises any constable during any part of the time appointed for the constable's being on duty, except for the purposes of the execution of the constable's duty, or
(b) supplies any liquor or refreshment, whether by way of gift or sale, to any constable on duty except by authority of a superior officer of the constable, or
(c) bribes or attempts to bribe any constable,
he shall be liable . . .

Practice Note

To prove the offence at s. 178(a), you must show that the licensee committed the offence 'knowingly'. That knowledge must apply both to the fact that the person is a constable *and* that the constable was on duty. That requirement does not explicitly apply to the other offences.

Offence — Impersonating a Police Officer — Police Act 1996, s. 90(1)
Triable summarily. Six months' imprisonment.
(No specific power of arrest)

The Police Act 1996, s. 90 provides that:

(1)   Any person who with intent to deceive impersonates a member of a police force or special constable, or makes any statement or does any act calculated falsely to suggest that he is such a member or constable, shall be guilty of an offence and liable . . .

Practice Note

This is a crime of 'specific intent' and an intention to deceive must be proved.

Offence — Wearing or Possessing Uniform — Police Act 1996, s. 90(2) and (3)
Triable summarily. Fine.
(No specific power of arrest)

The Police Act 1996, s. 90 provides that:

(2)   Any person who, not being a constable, wears any article of police uniform in circumstances where it gives him an appearance so nearly resembling that of a member of a police force as to be calculated to deceive shall be guilty of an offence . . .
(3)   Any person who, not being a member of a police force or special constable, has in his possession any article of police uniform shall, unless he proves that he obtained possession of that article lawfully and has possession of it for a lawful purpose, be guilty of an offence . . .

Practice Note

'Article of police uniform' means:

- any article of uniform, or
- any distinctive badge or mark, or
- any document of identification

usually issued to members of police forces or special constables (s. 90(4)).

Offence — Causing Disaffection — Police Act 1996, s. 91(1)
Triable either way. Two years' imprisonment on indictment;
six months' imprisonment and/or a fine summarily.
(No specific power of arrest)

The Police Act 1996, s. 91(1) provides that:

(1)   Any person who causes, or attempts to cause, or does any act calculated to cause, disaffection amongst the members of any police force, or induces or attempts to induce, or does any act calculated to induce, any member of a police force to withhold his services, shall be guilty of an offence . . .

Appendix 1 Home Office: Guidance on Police Unsatisfactory Performance, Complaints and Misconduct Procedures

SECTION 6 — PROCEDURES FOR SENIOR OFFICERS [Not yet issued]

INTRODUCTION

(a) This guidance contains the Code of Conduct for police officers and sets out the procedures for dealing with unsatisfactory performance, complaints from members of the public, misconduct matters, Chief Officer's review and appeals to Police Appeals Tribunals. A number of annexes provide more detailed guidance on specific points relating to the individual procedures. The procedures described in this guidance are designed to accord with the principles of natural justice and the basic principles of fairness, and should be administered accordingly.

(b) The guidance is issued by the Secretary of State in accordance with the provisions of sections 83 and 87 of the Police Act 1996. As such, those who are responsible for administering the procedures described in this guidance are reminded that they are required to take its provisions fully into account when discharging their functions. Whilst it is not necessary to follow its terms exactly in all cases, the guidance should not be departed from without good reason. This guidance is not a definitive interpretation of the relevant legislation. Interpretation is ultimately a matter for the courts.

(c) The guidance on the individual procedures is designed to further the twin aims of being fair to the individual officer and of arriving at a correct assessment of the matter in question. The procedures are intended as means to this end, not as ends in themselves. Thus, a departure from the procedures described in this guidance will be justified if — and only if — it can be shown that it led to a truer and fairer result than observing them would have done.

(d) If, at a Chief Officer's review or on appeal to a Police Appeals Tribunal, an appellant raises the issue of an apparent failure to follow any of the provisions of this guidance, the respondent can be required to explain and justify this. The weight and significance to be attached to any departure from the guidance will vary from case to case. However, it is to be expected that Chief Officers and/or Police Appeals Tribunals will wish to be satisfied that any departure from the procedures set out in this guidance has not proved detrimental to the correct assessment of the fitness of the officer concerned to continue in his or her former rank or office.

(e) The procedures set out in this guidance apply to all police officers, most sections relating to those of or below the rank of superintendent, whilst guidance on the procedures for senior officers is in section 6. Whilst probationers are not subject to the procedures for dealing with unsatisfactory performance (since there are separately established procedures for dealing with the performance of probationers), they are subject to the misconduct procedures. The provision for a chief officer to dispense with the services of a constable during his or her probationary period should not be used as an alternative means of dismissing a probationer who should properly face misconduct proceedings. Where misconduct proceedings are appropriate and justified, they should be brought; where they are not brought, a probationer should not be left with the impression that he or she has been suspected of misconduct and been given no chance to defend him or herself.

CODE OF CONDUCT FOR POLICE OFFICERS[1]

(a) The primary duties of those who hold the office of constable are the protection of life and property, the preservation of the Queen's peace, and the prevention and detection of criminal offences. To fulfil these duties police officers are granted extraordinary powers; the public and the police service therefore have the right to expect the highest standards of conduct from them.

[1 See Schedule 1 to the Police (Conduct) Regulations 1999.]

(b)   This Code sets out the principles which guide police officers' conduct. It does not seek to restrict officers' discretion: rather, it aims to define the parameters of conduct within which that discretion should be exercised. However, it is important to note that any breach of the principles in this Code may result in action being taken by the organisation, which, in serious cases, could involve dismissal.

(c)   This Code applies to the conduct of police officers in all ranks whilst on duty, or whilst off duty if the conduct is serious enough to indicate that an officer is not fit to be a police officer. It will be applied in a reasonable and objective manner. Due regard will be paid to the degree of negligence or deliberate fault and to the nature and circumstances of an officer's conduct. Where off duty conduct is in question, this will be measured against the generally accepted standards of the day.

Honesty and integrity
1.   It is of paramount importance that the public has faith in the honesty and integrity of police officers. Officers should therefore be open and truthful in their dealings; avoid being improperly beholden to any person or institution; and discharge their duties with integrity.

Fairness and impartiality
2.   Police officers have a particular responsibility to act with fairness and impartiality in all their dealings with the public and their colleagues.

Politeness and tolerance
3.   Officers should treat members of the public and colleagues with courtesy and respect, avoiding abusive or deriding attitudes or behaviour. In particular, officers must avoid: favouritism of an individual or group; all forms of harassment, victimisation or unreasonable discrimination; and overbearing conduct to a colleague, particularly to one junior in rank or service.

Use of force and abuse of authority
4.   Officers must never knowingly use more force than is reasonable, nor should they abuse their authority.

Performance of duties
5.   Officers should be conscientious and diligent in the performance of their duties. Officers should attend work promptly when rostered for duty. If absent through sickness or injury, they should avoid activities likely to retard their return to duty.

Lawful orders
6.   The police service is a disciplined body. Unless there is good and sufficient cause to do otherwise, officers must obey all lawful orders and abide by the provisions of Police Regulations. Officers should support their colleagues in the execution of their lawful duties, and oppose any improper behaviour, reporting it where appropriate.

Confidentiality
7.   Information which comes into the possession of the police should be treated as confidential. It should not be used for personal benefit and nor should it be divulged to other parties except in the proper course of police duty. Similarly, officers should respect, as confidential, information about force policy and operations unless authorised to disclose it in the course of their duties.

Criminal offences
8.   Officers must report any proceedings for a criminal offence taken against them. Conviction of a criminal offence may of itself result in further action being taken.

Property

9. Officers must exercise reasonable care to prevent loss or damage to property (excluding their own personal property but including police property).

Sobriety

10. Whilst on duty[2] officers must be sober[3]. Officers should not consume alcohol when on duty unless specifically authorised to do so or it becomes necessary for the proper discharge of police duty.

Appearance

11. Unless on duties which dictate otherwise, officers should always be well turned out, clean and tidy whilst on duty in uniform or in plain clothes.

General conduct

12. Whether on or off duty, police officers should not behave in a way which is likely to bring discredit upon the police service.

SECTION 1
UNSATISFACTORY PERFORMANCE PROCEDURES

1.1 This section of the guidance describes the procedures for managing unsatisfactory work performance by officers up to and including the rank of Superintendent which do not fall to be dealt with by way of the formal misconduct procedures.

1.2 The procedures outlined below do not apply to officers above the rank of Superintendent and nor do they apply to probationers, for whom there is an established separate procedure.

1.3 The purpose of these procedures is to enable line managers and officers to discuss in an objective and systematic way any perceived failures to meet performance standards. In this way it is intended that any such failures and appropriate remedial action can be identified and implemented early enough to avoid the need for formal action.

I. SOURCES OF INFORMATION

Internal

1.4 Poor work performance will most often first be identified by the immediate supervisors of the officer concerned as part of their normal management responsibilities.

From the public

1.5 It is also possible that managers may be alerted to poor work performance on the part of one of their officers as a result of information from a member of the public. The information from the member of the public may be in the form of a formal complaint. Where it is, it must be dealt with in accordance with the established procedures for the handling of complaints (see Section 2).

1.6 During the handling of a complaint, performance — as opposed to misconduct — issues will often be identified. Where such a complaint is formally investigated it will be appropriate for the chief officer to identify those issues in the memorandum to the Police Complaints Authority (PCA) (see Section 2 paragraph 2.69) and to

---

[2 For superintendents, 'on duty' includes any period when the officer is off duty but has agreed to be available for recall to duty to deal with matters which might occur within the area(s) he/she has agreed to cover. It does not apply to the general 24-hour responsibility superintendents have for their own command area/department.]

[3 An officer who is unexpectedly called out for duty should be able, at no risk of discredit, to say that he or she has had too much to drink.]

indicate whether the unsatisfactory performance procedures are to be invoked. Where a complaint has been finalised other than by formal investigation, the unsatisfactory performance procedures will need to be considered where appropriate.

1.7 A single complaint from a member of the public about an officer's perform-ance will not of itself be sufficient to trigger the unsatisfactory performance pro-cedures, which are designed to deal with a pattern of poor work performance. Where, though, the complaint adds to existing indications of poor performance it may be appropriate to institute the unsatisfactory performance procedures or, if the officer concerned is already subject to the procedures, continue with those procedures. For example, a pattern of complaints may give rise to managerial concerns about the work performance of the officer concerned. Any such concerns should first be addressed by means of normal managerial methods which may, for example, after discussion with the officer concerned, include words of advice or further training. Only where such methods fail to achieve the necessary improvement in performance should consider-ation be given to the use of the unsatisfactory performance procedures.

II. INITIAL ACTION

1.8 It is an essential part of effective line management that managers should be aware of the contribution being made to meeting the aims and objectives of the unit by each of the individuals they manage. This means that managers should be sure to let an individual know when he or she is doing well or, if the circumstances arise, when there are the first signs that there is a need for improvement in work performance. This aspect of line management is an integral part of a line manager's responsibilities, and it is neither necessary nor desirable to impose a formal framework dictating how this process should be conducted; managers will deal with such issues in the light of their knowledge of the individual and the circumstances giving rise to concern about work performance.

1.9 There are, though, some generally well understood principles which should apply in such circumstances:

(a) an especially important function of line management is to establish and maintain standards of performance. Occasional lapses below acceptable standards will normally be dealt with informally and should not involve the application of the formal unsatisfactory performance procedures, which are designed to cover persistent failure to meet such standards;

(b) the manager must discuss any shortcoming with the individual at the earliest possible opportunity — it would be quite wrong for the line manager to store up a list of grievances about the work performance of an individual and say nothing about them until, for example, the occasion of the officer's performance appraisal;

(c) the reason for dissatisfaction must be made clear to the individual and there must be a factual basis for discussing the issues;

(d) the manager must seek to establish the underlying reasons for poor perform-ance (e.g. a failure to perform a task correctly may be because the individual was never told how to do it), and it may be appropriate for the manager to arrange further training or guidance, or perhaps suggest that the individual should seek welfare or medical advice;

(e) in cases where the difficulty appears to stem from a personality clash with a colleague or senior officer, or where for other reasons a change of duties might be appropriate, the officer's line management may, in consultation with the appropriate personnel department/officer, consider that he or she should be given the opportunity to improve his or her performance among other colleagues or in another work environment (where an officer is moved in this way his or her new line management should be informed of the reasons for the move and of the assessment of his or her performance); and

(f)   the manager must make it clear to the officer that he or she is available to give further advice and guidance if needed, that future work performance will be monitored carefully and that, if there is no, or insufficient, improvement then the matter will be dealt with under the unsatisfactory performance procedures.

1.10   The principles outlined above cover the position when a manager first becomes aware of some aspect(s) of less than satisfactory work performance and is dealing with the issue as an integral part of normal line management responsibilities. At this stage it will be appropriate for the manager to put on record the advice given, or other steps taken to address the issue, and to inform his or her line manager of the facts of the matter. These steps are important to ensure continuity in circumstances where one or more members of the management chain may move on.

1.11   Ideally, as a result of this management action, performance will improve and continue at an acceptable level, in which case no further action will need to be taken.

1.12   If there is no improvement, or insufficient improvement, or the improvement is not sustained over a reasonable period of time, preferably agreed between the manager and the officer, it will then be appropriate to start the formal unsatisfactory performance procedure. The period of time agreed between the manager and the officer or, if necessary, determined by the manager, must be sufficient to provide a reasonable opportunity for the desired improvement to take place, taking into account the circumstances of the particular case. At this stage, and indeed throughout these procedures, the period of time in which an improvement is expected may be extended if, due to some unforeseen or unavoidable circumstance (e.g. a prolonged absence), the officer is unable to demonstrate whether or not the required improvement has been achieved.

III.   FORMAL INTERVIEW PROCEDURES

1.13   The following paragraphs outline each stage of the formal unsatisfactory performance interview procedures, with the detailed procedure being preceded by a brief overview of the arrangements.

1.14   The procedures described below include references to interviews conducted by the reporting and countersigning officers, who are assumed to be the immediate line manager and that person's line manager respectively. However, because a crucial aspect of managing unsatisfactory performance by a police officer will be relating the performance to police service professional standards, the overriding consideration in identifying which of the officer's line managers should conduct the interviews is that he or she must be a police officer. That is not to say that civilian line managers will have no part to play.

1.15   *Civilian line managers* will, of course, be responsible for the day to day management of any police officers working for them. This will include identifying and dealing with any instances of poor work performance on the part of those officers, using normal managerial methods such as the provision of advice and further training. It is only in those cases where the unsatisfactory performance procedures are to be instituted that a police officer in the management chain must be involved. The police officer manager will, however, still need to liaise closely with the civilian manager since he or she will have the best knowledge of the officer concerned and the grounds for dissatisfaction with the officer's performance.

1.16   The following paragraphs also assume that, in order to manage the unsatisfactory performance procedures fairly and effectively, managers will need to listen to what others may have to say about an officer's performance at each stage of the procedure. The interview procedures include periods of time in which to allow the officer concerned to improve his or her performance. During these periods it is important that the officer's performance is monitored and for the officer to be told at regular intervals whether or not there is considered to have been an improvement and, if not, how such an improvement might be achieved.

First interview

General

1.17   The reporting officer or, if the officer concerned so requests, the countersigning officer will interview the officer concerned; explain in which respect(s) the officer's work performance is considered to be less than satisfactory; give the officer an opportunity to give his or her version of events and to be accompanied by a 'friend' (see paragraph 1.21 below); say what is required to improve to an acceptable standard; and set a reasonable timescale, not normally less than three months and not normally more than six months, by the end of which the improvement must be effected.

1.18   The interviewer will record the substance of the interview and provide the officer concerned with a copy of the record. This will not be a verbatim record of the interview. Rather, it will be a note summarising the substance of the interview. A copy of this note, together with any comments made by the officer concerned, will be sent to the appropriate personnel department (or officer) via the Superintendent (or the Chief Inspector, where there is no Superintendent) with line management responsibility for the relevant area of work (or, where the officer concerned is a Superintendent, via the officer with line management responsibility for the Superintendent).

Informing the officer concerned

1.19   The reporting officer will write to the officer concerned informing him or her that for stated explicit reasons he or she is subject to the unsatisfactory performance procedures and is required to attend for interview in order to discuss the cause(s) of concern and any subsequent action.

1.20   The written communication from the manager, which will be copied to the countersigning officer, will refer to the right of the officer concerned to have the interview with the countersigning officer if he or she prefers. It will also explain that the officer has the right to be accompanied by a 'friend', who must be a serving police officer and not otherwise involved in the procedures.

1.21   *The role of the 'friend'*, throughout the procedures described in this guidance, is to advise and assist the officer concerned, including speaking on the officer's behalf, calling and/or questioning witnesses, and/or producing witness statements or other documentation or exhibits to assist the officer's case. The 'friend' should be considered on duty when attending interviews or meetings relating to the officer concerned's case.

1.22   Information which needs to be checked by the manager may emerge during the course of the interview. In such circumstances, the interview may be adjourned whilst this is done.

At the interview

1.23   At the interview the line manager will:

(a)   explain fully the reasons for dissatisfaction with the officer concerned's work performance;

(b)   listen to what the officer (and his or her 'friend') has to say, and comment as appropriate;

(c)   where appropriate, decide that no further action need be taken;

(d)   say what action is required on behalf of the officer to improve his or her performance to an acceptable standard;

(e)   agree or, if necessary, impose an action plan with a timescale within which the officer should improve his or her performance to an acceptable standard;

(f)   remind the officer of the seriousness of the situation and, in particular, that if work performance continues to fall short of an acceptable standard, then the second stage of the formal procedure will come into effect (see paragraph 1.26 below); and

(g)   where appropriate, recommend that the officer should seek welfare, medical or counselling advice.

Following the interview

1.24   Within seven days of the interview the line manager will send the officer concerned a written note recording the substance of the interview, together with a copy for his or her 'friend', if applicable. The officer will be invited to acknowledge receipt of this record and to comment if he or she wishes in writing, normally within seven days of receipt of the note. The documents will be copied to the countersigning officer and to the appropriate personnel department (or officer) via the senior manager (usually the Superintendent, or the Chief Inspector where there is no Superintendent) with line management responsibility for the relevant area of work (or, where the officer concerned is a Superintendent, via the officer with line management responsibility for the Superintendent). Any written comments provided by the officer concerned will be retained with the note recording the substance of the interview.

1.25   If, during the course of the two years following the action taken (after which time a record of unsatisfactory performance will be expunged — see 1.56), the performance again drops to an unsatisfactory level, the initial action described in paragraphs 1.8 to 1.12 above need not be repeated; the procedure may restart at the first interview stage.

Second interview

General

1.26   If, after the time set in the first formal interview (paragraph 1.23(e) above), the officer's performance has improved and been maintained to an acceptable standard he or she should be informed by the line manager that this is the case and that no further action will be taken, stressing that it will be important for the officer to continue to maintain the improved work performance. However, if the officer's performance has not improved to an acceptable standard, the countersigning officer will consult the personnel department (or relevant personnel officer) with a view to holding a second interview, which will be conducted by the countersigning officer with advice from a representative from the personnel department (or the relevant personnel officer), who will be present at the interview and who need not be a police officer.

1.27   At the second interview the officer concerned will be given the opportunity to give his or her version of events and may be accompanied, and assisted, by a 'friend' as described in paragraph 1.21 above. As with the first interview, this interview may be discontinued temporarily if the interviewers need to check any additional information which may emerge.

1.28   After the interview, if appropriate, the countersigning officer and the personnel department representative (or relevant personnel officer) jointly will give the officer concerned a written warning that continued failure to improve his or her work performance (described in specific terms) will ensure that the next stage of the unsatisfactory performance procedure will come into effect, which could result in the officer being required to resign or, if relevant in addressing the reasons for poor performance, being reduced in rank. A written warning of this kind may only be given on two occasions within a period of two years before resulting in a hearing. (A written warning in these circumstances should not be confused with a written warning under the misconduct procedures; the two are not the same.)

Informing the officer concerned

1.29   The countersigning officer will write to the officer concerned saying that for the stated explicit reasons his or her work performance is still considered to be less than satisfactory, that consideration is now being given to what further action could be taken, including whether it is in the force's interest to continue to employ the officer, and requiring the officer to attend for interview with both the countersigning officer and a representative from the personnel department (or the relevant personnel officer).

1.30   The written communication from the countersigning officer will refer to the right of the officer to seek advice from a staff association representative and to be accompanied to the interview by a 'friend'. The role of the 'friend' would be as described in paragraph 1.21 above.

At the interview

1.31   At the second interview the countersigning officer will:

(a)   explain fully the reasons for continued dissatisfaction with the officer's work performance;

(b)   listen to what the officer (and his or her 'friend') has to say, commenting as appropriate;

(c)   where appropriate, agree that no further action need be taken;

(d)   agree or impose a final timescale for improvement, which should not normally be less than three months and not normally more than six months;

(e)   make it clear that continued failure to respond to the opportunities which have been given to improve to an acceptable standard of performance will ensure that the next stage of the unsatisfactory performance procedure will come into effect, which may result in the officer being required to resign or, if relevant in addressing the reasons for the poor performance, being reduced in rank.

Following the interview

1.32   Within seven days of the interview the countersigning officer and the personnel department representative (or relevant personnel officer) jointly will send the officer concerned a written note recording the substance of the interview, together with a copy for his or her 'friend', if applicable. The officer will be invited to acknowledge receipt of this note and to comment, if he or she wishes, in writing normally within seven days of receipt of the record. The documents will be copied to the personnel department (or the relevant personnel officer) and to the senior manager (normally the Superintendent, or the Chief Inspector where there is no Superintendent) with line management responsibility for the relevant area of work (or, where the officer concerned is a Superintendent, via the officer with line management responsibility for the Superintendent). Any written comments provided by the officer will be retained with the note recording the substance of the interview.

1.33   If, during the course of the two years following the action taken (after which time a record of unsatisfactory performance will be expunged — see 1.56), the performance again drops to an unsatisfactory level, the initial action and first stage interview described in paragraphs 1.8 to 1.12 and 1.17 to 1.25 above need not be repeated; the procedure may restart at the second interview stage.

IV.   HEARINGS

General

1.34   If, after the time set in the second formal interview (paragraph 1.31(d) above), the officer's performance has improved and been maintained to an acceptable standard, he or she should be informed by the countersigning officer that this is the case and that no further action will be taken, stressing that it will be important for the officer to continue to maintain the improved work performance. However, if there is still no, or insufficient, improvement, the countersigning officer will recommend to the senior manager (normally the Superintendent, or Chief Inspector where there is no Superintendent) that the officer concerned should now be the subject of a formal unsatisfactory performance hearing. The senior manager will initiate the necessary action with the personnel department. The hearing will be presided over by an Assistant Chief Constable, preferably with responsibility for personnel, in conjunction with two assessors of Superintendent rank where the officer concerned is of a rank below that of Superintendent. Where the officer concerned is a Superintendent, the two assessors will normally be Assistant Chief Constables from another force or forces (or Metropolitan Police Commanders), in which case the presiding officer will normally be an Assistant Chief Constable from the officer concerned's force.[4] See also Annex E — Officers appointed to conduct hearings.

1.35 The officer concerned will be given the opportunity to state his or her case and to be assisted by a 'friend'. The role of the 'friend' would be as described in paragraph 1.21 above. Since the hearing could lead to the officer concerned being required to resign or reduced in rank, he or she will be advised of the right to elect to be legally represented at the hearing. See Annex D — Legal representation.

Purpose of hearing

1.36 The purpose of the hearing is to determine whether the officer concerned has, in the matter in question, performed his or her work to an acceptable standard and, if not, what is to be done about it. The principal matter to be considered at the hearing is the officer's performance as a police officer.

Basis of decision making

1.37 The hearing is a consideration of the officer's work performance and how it relates to the officer's future in the police service or current rank, if performance in a particular rank is relevant. In deciding this issue, the hearing will apply the test of reasonableness. In particular, the officers taking the hearing will have to decide whether, on the evidence before them, it would be reasonable to conclude that the officer's work performance had failed to meet an acceptable standard and, if so, what should be done about it. If there is a difference of view between the three officers taking the hearing, the decision will be based on a simple majority vote between them. Before reaching their final decision, the officers will wish to satisfy themselves that what was alleged did indeed take place, on at least the balance of probabilities, and that this amounted to unsatisfactory performance; that the correct procedures were followed and, if so, have been exhausted or whether further remedial action might be successful. The officer and his or her representative will be given a further opportunity to address the officers holding the hearing on the possible outcome.

Officer's rights

1.38 The officer concerned and his or her 'friend' will be given adequate duty time to deal with any matters arising from the unsatisfactory performance procedures. The officer will be given copies of all relevant documentation at least 21 days before the

---

[4 In the Metropolitan Police (and City of London Police), the hearing will be presided over by a Commander, with two Superintendents acting as assessors, where the officer concerned is below the rank of Superintendent; or by a Commander from the same Area as the officer concerned, with two Commanders from another Area acting as assessors, where the officer concerned is a Superintendent (in the City of London Police, by a Commander or the Assistant Commissioner with two Assistant Chief Constables or Metropolitan Police Commanders).]

hearing, unless the officer agrees, in writing, to a shorter timescale. Hearings will be carried out in accordance with the principles of natural justice. Since any unsatisfactory performance hearing could potentially result in the officer concerned being required to resign or reduced in rank, the opportunity to elect to be legally represented must be offered in all cases (see Annex D).

Informing the officer concerned

1.39   Within two weeks of the end of the period of time set at the second interview for improvement, the officer concerned must be informed whether he or she is currently considered to be meeting an acceptable standard of work performance. If it is not up to standard, the officer will be advised of a date for the unsatisfactory performance hearing.

1.40   The date of the hearing will be not less than three, and should be no more than eight, weeks ahead. On being notified of the date for the hearing, the officer will also be advised of his or her right to be legally represented at the hearing and/or to be accompanied by a 'friend'.

1.41   Not less than three weeks in advance of the date of the hearing, the officer concerned will be provided with the relevant papers (see 1.42). The officer will be reminded that the hearing has the authority to decide that the officer should be required to resign or, if relevant in addressing the reasons for poor performance, be reduced in rank on grounds of unsatisfactory performance.

Conduct of the hearing

1.42   The officers conducting the hearing will be supplied with a full report, including supporting statements and papers, at least 21 days before the date of the hearing in order for them to be considered properly. A copy of these papers will, at the same time, be sent to the officer concerned. The officers taking the hearing will also be advised of any witnesses that the officer concerned would wish to speak on his or her behalf.

1.43   The purpose of the hearing is to review the facts of the case, listen to and question the officer concerned, and decide on the outcome of the case. Within these guidelines, it will be for the presiding officer to determine the course of the hearing. In opening the hearing he or she should indicate that all three officers conducting the hearing have read the papers, refer to any matters which they consider to be particularly relevant and invite the officer to say anything he or she wants to say about the work performance and its causes.

The officer's 'friend' and/or legal representative may speak on his or her behalf, and the presiding officer will, at all times during the hearing, give the officer concerned the opportunity to speak personally. The role of the 'friend' (and/or the legal adviser) will be as described for the interview stages of the procedure. If, during the course of the hearing, the presiding officer considers it necessary to seek legal advice on a particular point, the hearing may be adjourned whilst such advice is obtained. A verbatim record of the proceedings at the hearing must be taken, normally by means of a tape-recording.

Witnesses

1.44   In many cases it may be possible to agree that the documentary information before the hearing, together with the officer's account and any representations made by his or her 'friend' and/or legal representative, provide the officers taking the hearing with sufficient information on which to reach their conclusions. In other cases, such agreement may not be possible, and the officer concerned may decide to call witnesses to speak at the hearing (provided that prior notification of this has been given to the personnel officer responsible for arranging the hearing). There may also be cases where the officers taking the hearing consider that they require more information and would thus wish to hear the officer concerned's line manager(s) in person. Any witnesses appearing before a hearing may be subject to examination and cross-examination.

1.45   The hearing will be conducted in private. Those present will, apart from the presiding officer and the two panel members, include a representative of the personnel department. Also, presiding officers may, at their discretion and with the consent of the officer concerned, permit other persons to be present if they have good reason to think that their presence would be beneficial (e.g. for training or monitoring purposes). See Annex H — Other persons who may attend hearings.

Presence of the officer concerned

1.46   The officer subject to the unsatisfactory performance procedure does not have to be present for the hearing to be valid. If an officer fails to appear at a hearing without prior warning or without reason being given sufficient to excuse his or her absence, the hearing may proceed and decisions be made in the absence of the officer. It will be for the presiding officer to decide, in any case where the officer has failed to appear, whether to proceed or adjourn the hearing to another date. The relevance of any reasons given for the officer's absence will be taken into account when deciding whether to proceed or adjourn.

1.47   *Ill-health.* Attendance at a hearing is not subject to the same considerations as reporting for duty, and the provisions of Regulation 35 (sick leave) of the Police Regulations 1995 do not apply. An illness or disability may render an officer unfit for duty without affecting his or her ability to attend a hearing. However, if the officer concerned is incapacitated, the hearing may be deferred until he or she is sufficiently improved to attend. A hearing will not be deferred indefinitely because a sick officer is unable to attend, although every effort should be made to make it possible for the officer to attend if he or she wishes to be present. For example:

(a)   if the officer suffers from a physical injury — a broken leg, for instance — it may be possible to hold the hearing at a location convenient to him or her;

(b)   the acute phase of a serious physical illness is usually fairly short-lived, and the hearing may be deferred until the officer is well enough to attend.

Where, despite such efforts having been made and/or the hearing having been deferred, the officer either persists in failing to attend the hearing or maintains his or her inability to attend, the presiding officer will need to decide whether to continue to defer the hearing or whether to proceed with it, if necessary in the absence of the officer concerned. The presiding officer must judge which is the most appropriate course of action in all the circumstances of the case. Nothing in this paragraph should be taken to suggest that, where an officer's medical condition is found to be such that he or she would normally be retired on medical grounds, the unsatisfactory performance proceedings should prevent or delay retirement. (See also Annex J — Ill health.)

V. OUTCOME OF THE HEARING

Range of possible outcomes

1.48   There are four possible outcomes as a result of an unsatisfactory performance hearing:

(a)   the hearing decides that the circumstances reported by line management do not constitute unsatisfactory performance on the part of the officer concerned (though they may decide that the performance had been correctly assessed up to a previous stage), in which case no further action is called for. Any records relating to performance adjudged at the hearing to have been satisfactory will be expunged from the officer's personal file;

(b)   the officer remains in post with a specific written warning that failure to improve his or her performance within a stated time may, following a second hearing, result in termination of service on the grounds of unsatisfactory performance;

(c)   the officer is reduced in rank with a written warning (as described in (b) above); or

(d)   the officer is required to resign on the grounds of unsatisfactory performance.

1.49   Where the officers taking a hearing decide on the outcome listed at (b) above this will, in effect, be a final opportunity for the officer concerned to improve his or her work performance. The time allowed for the required improvement will normally be not less than three months and normally not more than six months. If, after the time set at the hearing, the officer's performance has improved and been maintained to an acceptable standard he or she should be informed that this is the case and that no further action will be taken, stressing that it will be important for the officer to continue to maintain the improved work performance. However, if no such improvement has been achieved or maintained, a further hearing will be convened to decide the officer's future in the police service. This further hearing will not be preceded by the two interviews with the officer's line managers which would precede a first hearing. Where the officers taking the hearing decide on the outcome listed at (c) above, any further failure by the officer concerned to perform to the required standard in the reduced rank will be dealt with on its merits, with the full unsatisfactory performance procedures being applied from the beginning.

1.50   Where the officers taking a hearing decide on either of the outcomes listed at (b) or (c) above, they may at the same time also recommend that the officer be given guidance by his or her line managers and/or receive further training in order to help the officer to improve his or her performance.

Notification of decision

1.51   The officers taking the hearing will retire or, if considered necessary, adjourn the hearing in order to consider their decision. The officer concerned will be told of the hearing's decision by the presiding officer. The officer concerned will also be informed in writing by the presiding officer of the decision of the hearing, and the reasons for that decision, no more than three days after the completion of the hearing. The officer concerned will, at the time of being notified of the decision of the hearing, also be advised that it is open to him or her to exercise the right to ask the Chief Officer of the force to review the decision of the hearing (see paragraph 1.54 below).

1.52   If a hearing is adjourned the officers conducting it should not discuss the details of the case with anyone else, whether connected with the case or not. It is only in this way that the impartiality of the proceedings can be seen to be protected adequately.

Implementation of decision

1.53   A decision that the officer concerned should be required to resign will allow one month's notice of termination of service (or such longer period as may be determined by the Chief Constable to enable him or her to complete the review before the officer concerned's resignation takes effect) commencing from the day that the officer is informed in writing of the decision. A decision to reduce an officer in rank will have immediate effect, and will not be deferred pending a Chief Constable's review. The implementation of either type of decision will, proceed whether or not there is a subsequent appeal to a Police Appeals Tribunal.

VI. AVENUES OF APPEAL

Chief Constable's review

1.54   An officer will have a right to seek the Chief Constable's review of the decision of a hearing. The request for a review should be made within 14 days of the receipt of the written notification of the hearing's decision, and should be accompanied by written grounds in support of the request. See Section 4.

Appeal to Police Appeals Tribunal

1.55   If, after the Chief Constable's review, an officer who was required to resign or reduced in rank still believes that the decision of the hearing was unjustified, it will be open to the officer to appeal to a Police Appeals Tribunal. See Section 5.

VII. OTHER MATTERS

Expunging of records

1.56   Records of any part of the unsatisfactory performance procedure will be expunged from an officer's personal file or other record after a period of two years has elapsed since the last action was taken, or the outcome of a hearing or Chief Constable's review was that the performance in question was satisfactory, or following a successful appeal to a Police Appeals Tribunal.

Relationship with misconduct procedures

1.57   The misconduct and unsatisfactory performance procedures are separate but complementary. They should ensure that both poor conduct and poor performance on the part of police officers are dealt with effectively, having regard to the public interest, the interests of the police service and the interests of individual officers.

1.58   During the course of misconduct enquiries it may emerge that all or part of the matter in question relates more to issues of poor performance than poor conduct on the officer concerned's part. In such circumstances it may be appropriate for the case, or at least that aspect of it relating to performance, to be dealt with by the officer's line management. In many cases, this will probably take the form of advice and/or further training being provided to the officer. However, if the misconduct enquiries have disclosed further evidence of a pattern of poor performance by the officer concerned, it may be appropriate to institute or, if the officer is already subject to the procedures, continue the formal unsatisfactory performance procedures at whatever stage is applicable to the officer concerned.

SECTION 2
COMPLAINTS PROCEDURES

I. INTRODUCTION

2.1   This section describes the application of statutory procedures for dealing with complaints against the police by members of the public. However, forces are reminded of the benefits, in terms both of goodwill and resource management, of practices to resolve problems which have occurred and pre-empt complaints from being made in the first place. There are obvious advantages in offering an apology on behalf of the force and making amends for any loss by means of an *ex gratia* payment. Where complaints are recorded, maximum use should be made of the informal resolution procedure wherever it is possible to do so.

II. DEFINITIONS

2.2   For the purpose of the procedures set out in Part IV of the Police Act 1996, section 65 of that Act[1] defines 'complaint' as any complaint made about the conduct of a police officer which is submitted either by a member of the public or on behalf of the member of the public and with his or her consent. Under section 67(5), the provisions of Part IV of the Act relating to the recording or investigation of complaints are not applicable to matters which are, or have been, the subject of criminal or disciplinary (referred to in this guidance as misconduct proceedings — see Section 3) proceedings. Each aspect of this definition is explored below.

2.3   'conduct' — Section 67(4) states that, for the purposes of Part IV of the Act, the definition of a complaint does not extend to complaints relating to the direction or control of a police force by its chief officer or the person performing the chief officer's functions. Moreover, by virtue of section 67(5), none of the procedures set out in or under Part IV of the Act apply to any conduct which forms the whole or a part of a complaint where that complaint has already been the subject of criminal or disciplinary proceedings.

2.4   'member of the public' — Complaints alleging misconduct can be received only from members of the public who have had occasion to be well informed as to the facts of the incident. There is no need to record and process complaints from persons not involved in the incident. Complaints should, though, be recorded if the member of the public was either personally involved in the incident, or is the relative or friend of someone who was and who is acting on their behalf. However, while other approaches from members of the public will not provide a basis for recording a complaint under Part IV of the Act, forces will no doubt wish to consider whether they provide grounds for investigation and should arrange for them to be replied to and the matter explained, so far as this is practicable.

2.5   'on behalf of' — It is not necessary for the person who has been (or might have been) affected by the alleged misconduct to approach the force personally. The matter may be referred to the force by a third party including, for example, a Citizens Advice Bureau or a Member of Parliament, or by any other individual or organisation. No form of consent is prescribed and any words which can reasonably be taken as indicating the complainant's willingness for the complaint to be passed on should be taken as sufficient for the purpose. Discretion should be exercised before asking a third party for evidence of the person involved's written consent to the passing on of a complaint. In particular, where a solicitor indicates in forwarding details of an incident that he or she is doing so on instructions from a client, the complaint should be treated without challenge as having been made by the client direct to the chief officer.

2.6   Where the Police Complaints Authority (PCA) express a view on whether a particular matter which comes to their attention in the report of an investigation should or should not be treated as a complaint, chief officers will no doubt take account of such a view. However, subject to any determination by the courts, the decision remains one for the chief officer concerned.

III. IMMEDIATE ACTION

2.7   The following immediate steps are required to be taken on receipt of a complaint alleging misconduct on the part of a police officer:

(a)   preservation of evidence;

[1 All subsequent references to sections relate to the 1996 Act, unless the context indicates otherwise.]

(b) determination of the appropriate authority;
(c) recording of the complaint; and
(d) determination as to whether the complaint is required to be referred to the PCA.

Preservation of evidence

2.8   Section 67(1) places on chief officers the duty to take whatever preliminary steps are necessary to obtain or preserve evidence. This duty must be carried out whether or not the complaint appears *prima facie* to be one whose investigation should eventually be supervised by the PCA and whether or not it appears that the chief officer will be the appropriate authority in respect of the complaint.

2.9   The duty to preserve evidence should be broadly defined to include, for example, any immediate searches or observations which may be necessary. Where there might be a long delay, for example in a case which is *sub judice*, consideration should be given to the need to preserve relevant records which might otherwise be destroyed as a matter of force routine.

2.10   Where the complaint is one of assault by a police officer it is advisable to make immediate arrangements to have the victim and the officer medically examined, with their consent. The examination should, whenever possible, be carried out by a police surgeon, or at a hospital if medical attention is required urgently. In addition, a note should be made of the general condition of the victim and the officer and this should include references to any visible signs of injury or discomfort. Photographs of both parties can also be useful.

Determination of the 'appropriate authority'

2.11   Certain statutory duties are placed on the 'appropriate authority' for an officer against whom a complaint is made. These duties are discussed fully below. After taking any action necessary to preserve evidence, the chief officer who has received a complaint should determine whether he or she is the appropriate authority in relation to the officer concerned.

2.12   Wherever the act under consideration may have been committed and irrespective of the command the officer is currently serving under (for instance if loaned to another force under mutual aid or to conduct an investigation), for disciplinary purposes an officer answers to his or her own chief officer and it is in his or her own force that any disciplinary issues fall to be recorded and considered. Nevertheless, if the complaint relates to the conduct of an officer while serving with another force, it may well be appropriate for that force to undertake any criminal investigation (if appropriate) and also to supply the officer's own force with the detail necessary for the consideration of any misconduct issues.

2.13   Officers on central or relevant service are subject to misconduct proceedings by their own force on their return to it for any breach of the code of conduct committed before or during the period of central or relevant service. It is not always necessary for the officer to return to his or her force while the investigation is being undertaken but the officer concerned will always need to be returned to his or her parent force for any misconduct proceedings to take place (see Annex L — Officers on central/seconded service).

2.14   For all officers of Superintendent rank and below the appropriate authority will be the chief officer of the force. Above the rank of Superintendent, the appropriate authority will be the police authority for the officer's parent force, except in the case of senior officers of the Metropolitan Police, where the Commissioner is invariably the appropriate authority.

Recording of complaints

2.15   The appropriate authority in relation to the complaint should record the matter as soon as possible after it is received. Entries should be made in a general register of complaints, which should be kept under the following headings:

(a)   the date, time and place the complaint or information was received, and by whom;

(b)   the name and address of the reporting member of the public and/or details of the reporting officer;

(c)   the date/time/place/nature of the incident or conduct reported;

(d)   the particulars of the officer concerned;

(e)   the name of the investigating officer, or appointed officer in a case disposed of by informal resolution;

(f)   the date of any referrals to the PCA under section 70 and whether referred under subsection 1(a)(i) or 1(a)(ii) or 1(b) or 2;

(g)   the date of any request to the PCA for a dispensation from the requirement to investigate, specifying whether the complaint was anonymous, repetitious, incapable of investigation etc;

(h)   whether the investigation was supervised by the PCA under section 72 and, if so, whether supervision was under subsection 1(a) or 1(b) or 1(c);

(i)   the date on which the investigating officer's report was submitted to the chief officer/police authority/Crown Prosecution Service(CPS)/PCA;

(j)   (for officers other than senior officers) the date on which the chief officer's memorandum sent to the PCA under the provisions of section 75;

(k)   the result of the disposal of the complaint, including particulars of any sanction imposed; and

(l)   the means by which the member of the public has been told of the result.

2.16   Chief officers should keep the record centrally and may also find it useful to keep corresponding records at a local level. (A central record will also need to be maintained of all misconduct cases arising from internal reporting — see Section 3 paragraph 3.75.)

2.17   It may not always be immediately clear from initial contact by a member of the public with the police whether the matter of concern amounts to a complaint alleging misconduct for the purposes of Part IV of the Act. In these circumstances, it may be appropriate for the member of the public to be seen by a supervisory officer to discuss their concerns and see how best they may be addressed. Where, as a result of this discussion, it is apparent that a complaint within the meaning of section 67 was intended but that the member of the public wishes to withdraw it, or does not want it to be pursued, the matter should still be recorded and be shown as having been withdrawn or not proceeded with. A signed written statement by a complainant is required before a complaint can be regarded as withdrawn. The statement should reflect that the complainant understands that no misconduct proceedings will follow.

2.18   Whether a complaint is substantiated or unsubstantiated does not depend on proceedings being brought against an officer or on the outcome of any such proceedings, but on the extent to which evidence has been forthcoming to support the allegation made in the complaint. There will be circumstances in which a complaint is shown to have been justified but misconduct proceedings are not possible or are inappropriate. In such cases, the complaint should be recorded as substantiated and shown within that category in statistical returns as having been dealt with other than by criminal or misconduct proceedings. However, no record of the incident would be kept on the officer's service record.

2.19   In deciding how individual matters should be recorded in cases of doubt, and in considering what matters have been complained of in any particular situation, it is suggested that chief officers should have regard to the following guidance.

2.20   Where a complainant alleges, on one occasion or in one letter, several different matters (for example, that an officer assaulted the complainant and stole some money) these should be recorded as separate complaints.

2.21   The main object of distinguishing and separately recording different matters in this way is to enable the figures for substantiated and unsubstantiated complaints to be given properly. If it is established that a police officer assaulted but did not steal from a complainant, this would make one substantiated and one unsubstantiated complaint: if the matters were not recorded separately, there would be no satisfactory way of arriving at the number of substantiated complaints, nor of distinguishing them from less serious matters.

2.22   Where a person complains of a series of like actions, whether or not involving more than one officer, in the course of one continuing incident (for example, assault on arrest and again in the car on the way to the station) this should be recorded as a single item, which will be recorded as substantiated if investigation establishes that any one of the alleged actions in fact took place.

2.23   Where a complaint relates to an alleged assault, it should be recorded by the most serious aspect of that possible assault. If more than one officer is complained against and different actions are imputed to each officer, the complaint against each officer should be recorded according to the nature of the complaint against him or her, and not by the most serious complaint against any of the officers involved.

2.24   Where a group of people make similar complaints about the treatment they have received on a single occasion (for example, where a number of persons are arrested in a single operation and several of them subsequently complain separately that they were assaulted), each person's complaint should be recorded and counted separately.

2.25   Where several complaints are made by different people about one incident (for example, in addition to the victim, witnesses may independently make complaints regarding an assault by a police officer) this should be recorded and counted as one matter, since only one action is complained about.

2.26   Where a complaint is couched in general terms but the subsequent investigation reveals a number of instances of apparent misconduct, all of which arose directly from the incident which gave rise to the complaint and which affected the complainant, each should be treated as a separate item and be so recorded and dealt with, unless the reporter of the complaint specifically states otherwise.

2.27   None of this implies that a number of matters complained of cannot be dealt with together so far as investigation, consideration of criminal or misconduct action and reference to the CPS or to the PCA are concerned. However, if the investigation or other actions relate to a number of separate matters complained of, it is desirable that the documents sent to the PCA should make this clear. For example, the PCA will need to know whether or not a misconduct hearing is proposed in respect of any and, if so, which of the matters referred to. The outcome of each complaint should be recorded separately.

Officers not on duty

2.28   The mere fact that the investigation of an incident (e.g. a traffic accident) reported by a member of the public shows that the other person involved is a police officer will not normally be a sufficient reason to justify the matter being recorded as a complaint against a police officer. Whether such a matter should be so recorded will be very much a matter of judgement in the light of the circumstances of the particular case, taking account in particular of the apparent reason for the report by the member of the public and the nature and substance of the allegation. Usually such an allegation relating to off duty conduct will need to be recorded as 'against a member of a police force' only if the fact of being a police officer is essential to the burden of the complaint.

2.29   There will be other cases which do not involve any allegation of, for instance, a criminal offence, nor arise out of an officer's duty, for instance complaints arising from domestic quarrels, matrimonial difficulties, disputes between landlord and tenant and other civil disputes. These will not normally fall within the provisions of Part IV of the Act.

Special constables and police cadets

2.30   Complaints against special constables and cadets do not come within Part IV of the Act since they are not members of a police force. However, chief officers may well consider it appropriate to investigate complaints made against special constables and cadets as if they were complaints falling within Part IV of the Act. In a case where a report containing complaints against a regular and a special constable jointly, or against a police officer and a cadet jointly, is required to be referred to the PCA, it is recommended that they should be sent the whole of the investigation report, even though that part of it dealing with the conduct of the special constable or cadet is not their direct concern.

Civilian members of the force

2.31   Any complaint made against a civilian member of the force is to be dealt with under the agreed procedure for such personnel. If a complaint is made against both a police member of a force and a civilian member arising from the same incident, there will need to be liaison between those with personnel responsibility for each and consideration given to appointing a single investigating officer, who must be a police officer.

Complaints by civilian employees

2.32   Whether an allegation by a civilian employee should be treated as a complaint falling within Part IV of the Act will depend largely upon its nature and circumstances. There may be occasions on which the status of a civilian employee is irrelevant to the subject matter of the allegation and this will apply particularly where the matter arises from an alleged incident which occurred outside work. Conversely, an allegation arising from everyday working relationships between civilian employees and police officers should normally be treated as an internal matter (and frequently one for resolution by management and industrial relations techniques) since the civilian is not then in the same position as a member of the public but is one employee among others. If the allegation involves apparent misconduct on the part of the officer concerned it will, of course, have to be handled as an internal misconduct matter, even if it is not handled as a complaint from a member of the public.

2.33   Although section 65 makes it clear that the statutory complaints process is intended for complaints from members of the public, there may be circumstances in which a complaint is received from a serving member and it is considered appropriate to record the matter because the incident was unrelated to the officer's employment, for example where the complainant was from another force and was off duty at the time of the incident.

Police officers and public interest disclosure

2.34   Police officers have an obligation, in the public interest, to disclose wrong-doing by others in the force. However, some may be concerned that they could be victimised by colleagues or senior management, or be at risk of misconduct proceedings for disclosure of information. It is important to provide protections, both to the officer and to the service, which encourage police officers to come forward and report wrongdoing to an appropriate authority. Where police officers act in accordance with the following framework, they are entitled to protection against victimisation and misconduct proceedings.

2.35   Police officers who disclose information in the public interest, which they reasonably and genuinely believe to breach or be likely to breach the code of conduct (or similar code for non-police members), should:

(a)   where the disclosure relates to the conduct, or alleged conduct, of officers up to and including the rank of superintendent, make the disclosure to the chief officer with responsibility for the discipline of the police force;

(b)   where the disclosure relates to the conduct or alleged conduct of a chief officer, to the clerk to the police authority or to HM Inspectorate of Constabulary for referral to the relevant police authority;[2]

(c)   where the disclosure relates to the conduct or alleged conduct of a non-police member of a police force, to the appropriate disciplinary authority.

2.36   Supervisors and managers should ensure that any police officer who makes such a disclosure is not victimised, whether by act or omission, as a consequence of making the disclosure. Any officer who is thought to have victimised another officer may themselves be found to have breached the code of conduct.

IV.   FIRST DECISIONS ON HANDLING OF COMPLAINTS

Informal resolution

2.37   Where a complainant alleges misconduct of an apparently minor nature, consideration should first be given to whether or not the matter, if proved, would warrant a criminal charge or misconduct proceedings. If not, a positive attempt should be made to resolve the complaint informally. The procedures for doing so are covered in Appendix A to this Section.

2.38   If it has proved possible to resolve a complaint by informal resolution, it should be made clear to the complainant that this will normally bring action on the complaint to an end and that it will not normally be possible for him or her to reopen it. The necessary steps should then be taken to ensure that the complainant signs the informal resolution record or otherwise signifies their acceptance that the complaint has been resolved to their satisfaction and that no further action will be undertaken in connection with it. Whilst it is necessary to consider the question of *sub judice* when undertaking an informal resolution, it must be borne in mind that the intention of the legislation is that minor matters can be dealt with as quickly as possible.

Dispensations

2.39   With some complaints it may be apparent from the outset either that they cannot be investigated or that there are other reasons why further action should not be taken. Where such cases meet the criteria set down in the regulations, application may be made to the PCA for a dispensation from the requirement to investigate. The procedures for doing so are covered in Appendix B to this Section.

[2 Where an officer discloses conduct to a police authority or HMIC this may relate only to the conduct of a chief officer or equivalent civilian grade. It may not be used in an attempt to appeal against a decision in respect of any internal policy or procedure, unless that decision encapsulates or is in itself the breach of conduct alleged to be in contravention of the code of conduct.]

Complaints covering several issues

2.40   While internal reports of apparent poor conduct are likely to have distinguished in advance between those issues requiring management action and those potentially requiring formal misconduct action, a member of the public's complaint may well raise a variety of issues, each needing to be distinguished and dealt with appropriately. For example, the member of the public's account of an incident may also contain elements complaining about the force's policing style, about the organisation of the force as a whole or of a particular operation, about quality of service or other matters. These are separate issues from that of the conduct of individual police officers and each chief officer should have in place arrangements to record and deal with such complaints.

Complaints which cannot be resolved informally

2.41   Where informal resolution procedures have failed or are inappropriate, an investigating officer must be appointed and consideration given as to whether the case should be referred to the PCA regarding supervision.

V.   REFERRAL TO THE PCA

2.42   Where it has been decided that a complaint from a member of the public — or, indeed, any matter which indicates that a police officer may have breached the Code of Conduct — should be investigated formally, consideration will need to be given to whether it is necessary or desirable for reference to be made to the PCA for supervision of the investigation.

Mandatory referral to the PCA

2.43   Once a complaint has been recorded, it must be referred to the PCA if it alleges conduct by a police officer falling within either section 70(1)(a)(i) or Regulation 4(1) of the Police (Complaints) (Mandatory Referrals Etc) Regulations 1985.

Mandatory supervision

2.44   The conduct specified in section 70(1)(a)(i) is any resulting in death or serious injury. 'Serious injury' is defined in section 65 as 'a fracture, damage to an internal organ, impairment of bodily function, a deep cut or laceration'. The PCA are statutorily required to supervise the investigation of all complaints of this kind.

Discretionary supervision

2.45   The conduct specified in Regulation 4(1) of the Police (Complaints) (Mandatory Referrals Etc) Regulations 1985 is: assault occasioning actual bodily harm; an offence under section 1 of the Prevention of Corruption Act 1906 (that is, bribery); or a serious arrestable offence. The PCA have discretion whether or not to supervise the investigation of such cases.

Discretionary referral to the PCA

2.46   It should also be borne in mind that the PCA are empowered under section 72(1)(c) to supervise the investigation of any other complaint not falling within the criteria for mandatory supervision. Under section 71 they may also supervise any non-complaint matter regarding possible misconduct referred to them voluntarily where the public interest makes it desirable for them to do so.

2.47   It may therefore be appropriate to invite the PCA to consider supervising the investigation of any case — whether involving a complaint or not — that is likely to undermine confidence in the police, either locally or nationally, and where independent testimony to the thoroughness of the investigation could help to meet that concern.

Matters 'called in' by the PCA

2.48   Section 70(2) provides that the PCA may require any complaint of misconduct to be sent to them for consideration, even though the complaint does not meet the criteria for mandatory supervision.

Uncertainty as to whether to refer a case

2.49   If there is uncertainty over whether a particular complaint should be referred to the PCA, it will generally be appropriate to let the PCA decide the issue. Most forces will be aware of the type of cases which are likely to interest the PCA.

2.50   Where there is doubt as to whether a complaint of injury constitutes 'serious injury' (but there is no doubt that it would amount to actual bodily harm) the PCA's view on the question of referral should be sought or the case should simply be referred to them under section 70(1)(a).

Timing of referrals

2.51   Mandatory referrals are required to be submitted to the PCA by the end of the day after the one on which it became clear that the complaint fell within the criteria for referral. There may be cases where it is not immediately apparent that the complaint falls within these criteria. Such a situation would arise if, for instance, a medical report showed that an injury was more serious than had originally been supposed.

2.52   There is no time limit for voluntary referrals to the PCA, but the value of the PCA's independent supervision may depend upon them being involved from a very early stage.

Complaints covering less serious matters as well as matters which must be referred

2.53   Where a complaint covers a variety of allegations of misconduct arising from a single incident, not all of which fall within the criteria for mandatory referral, the PCA should be told of all the allegations which have been made. The PCA will supervise the investigation of all the allegations which arise from the same incident.

Approval of investigating officer

2.54   If the PCA supervise the investigation of a complaint, they may choose to exercise their right to approve the appointment of the investigating officer. The PCA should be provided at the time of referral with the name, rank and force of the officer whom it is proposed to appoint as the investigating officer. Where this information is not immediately available, the PCA should be told that it will follow as soon as possible. In the interests of bringing greater independence to the investigation of complaints, forces are encouraged to consider the appointment of investigating officers from another force.

2.55   If the appointment has already been made (e.g. because of the need to begin the investigation urgently) and the PCA are not satisfied with that appointment, they may ask the force to propose the appointment of another officer. The force is obliged to comply with such a request and should not formally make a new appointment until the PCA have approved it.

Conduct of investigation

2.56   Where the PCA supervise an investigation they have the power to impose reasonable requirements affecting its conduct, including the resources employed to carry it out. This power is subject to the following restrictions:

(a)   where the possibility of criminal proceedings arises, the PCA may not make any requirement relating to the obtaining or preservation of evidence of a criminal offence without the prior consent of the CPS; and

(b)   before making any requirement affecting the resources to be employed in an investigation, the PCA must seek the views of the chief officer responsible for making those resources available, and have regard to any views so expressed.

2.57   The fact that an investigation is being supervised by the PCA does not absolve police forces from the requirement to have regard to those parts of this guidance which apply generally to the recording and investigation of complaints. At the same time it should be recognised that the PCA are not similarly bound to have regard to the guidance.

2.58   If the PCA are supervising an investigation into a complaint which is then withdrawn, the investigating officer is not required to submit a report to the PCA under section 73(1), and nor will the PCA be required to make a statement to the appropriate authority under section 73(2). The PCA should however be supplied on request with any information bearing on the circumstances in which the complaint was withdrawn, together with a copy of the complainant's notice of withdrawal.

2.59   An officer investigating a complaint under the supervision of the PCA should bear in mind not only the need to observe the formal requirements of the PCA in relation to the supply of information and the conduct of the investigation, but also the desirability of keeping the PCA abreast of any significant developments in the investigation. In particular, the investigating officer should bear in mind the requirement to inform the PCA if the CPS is to be consulted and to advise them of the outcome of any such consultation.

VI.   ILL-FOUNDED, WITHDRAWN OR NOT PROCEEDED WITH COMPLAINTS

2.60   If it becomes clear to the investigating officer that the complaint is ill-founded, or that the effort required to pursue it would be disproportionate, he or she may prepare a report to the Superintendent (or more senior officer) in charge of complaints and discipline (or to the PCA if the investigation is being supervised) recommending that the complaint be pursued no further. In such cases, the original complaint and the investigating officer's report will still have to be referred to the PCA (under section 75), and this should be done with the minimum of delay so that, if the PCA agree, the matter may be brought to a swift conclusion.

2.61   A complaint should be regarded as withdrawn only when a signed written statement is received from the complainant (or someone authorised to act on his or her behalf) that he or she withdraws the complaint, or that he or she does not wish any further steps to be taken in connection with it.

2.62   To avoid doubt and subsequent argument, the statement should be worded in unequivocal terms (but it is suggested that the use of an expression such as 'unreservedly withdrawn' is best avoided). It should be made clear to the originator of the complaint that this will normally bring action on the complaint to an end and that it will not normally be possible for him or her to reopen it.

2.63   If the case has been referred to the PCA, they should be informed that the complaint has been withdrawn, enclosing a copy of the statement of withdrawal. Where only part of the complaint is withdrawn, the other parts must still be pursued in the normal way.

2.64   There is nothing to prevent the investigating officer, if he or she thinks it necessary in the circumstances of a particular case, from pursuing inquiries into a complaint despite the withdrawal of the original report by the member of the public concerned. (In such a case, since the member of the public no longer wishes to pursue the matter, the provisions of section 90 no longer operate to require reference to the CPS. In deciding whether the case should nevertheless go to the CPS, it will be appropriate to use the normal test applicable where an allegation of crime is received against a police officer otherwise than in a complaint from a member of the public.)

2.65   Where the member of the public has decided to pursue the matter no further, but the investigation of the complaint is nevertheless continued, the investigation becomes a purely internal matter and the PCA will no longer be involved in the case (unless it is decided that it would be appropriate to refer the case to the PCA under the provisions of section 71).

VII.   PROCEDURES FOLLOWING INVESTIGATION

The investigation report

2.66   In a *supervised* investigation the investigating officer should submit the investigation report simultaneously to the PCA, the CPS (if it appears that a crime may have been committed) and the officer in charge of complaints and discipline.

2.67   In an *unsupervised* investigation a copy of the investigation report need not be sent to the PCA until a decision has been taken as to whether or not misconduct proceedings are appropriate, although it should be sent to the CPS if there is a possibility that a crime may have been committed.

The PCA's statement

2.68   At the end of a supervised investigation the PCA must make a statement (which will be sent to the chief officer, the complainant and any officer whose conduct has been investigated) saying whether they are satisfied with the conduct of the investigation, and specifying any respect in which they are not. It is open to the PCA to enter certain qualifications when recording a satisfactory verdict on an investigation, without implying that they are dissatisfied with the investigation as a whole. They may also mention any matter arising from the investigation or its supervision which they think should be brought to the attention of the appropriate authority, the complainant or the officer whose conduct was investigated, or be dealt with in the public interest. No misconduct proceedings may be brought until the PCA's statement is received.

Memorandum to be submitted to the PCA

Supervised investigations

2.69   After receiving the report of any investigation supervised by the PCA, the chief officer must submit to the PCA a memorandum setting out his or her opinion on the misconduct issues raised or other related matters; indicating whether or not misconduct proceedings have been or are to be brought and, if not, the reasons for not doing so.

Unsupervised investigations

2.70   Similar requirements apply when a report is received of an investigation which was not supervised. In such cases the chief officer's memorandum to the PCA should be accompanied by a copy of the complaint or, if it was made orally, a copy of the record of the complaint; and a copy of the investigating officer's report, with the relevant supporting statements and other documents annexed to it by the investigating officer.

Requests by the PCA for additional information

2.71   Under section 76(7)(b) chief officers are required to provide the PCA with any information which they may reasonably require for the exercise of their functions under section 76, which relates to the PCA's powers in respect of disciplinary proceedings (referred to in this guidance as misconduct proceedings — see Section 3). Such information may be in addition to that contained in the investigation report and other documents submitted to them. If, however, the chief officer is of the opinion that to comply with such a request would be prejudicial to the interests of justice, or that the required information is not obtainable without disproportionate effort on the part of the police, then representations may be made to the PCA to this effect.

The PCA's decision

2.72   The PCA may concur with a decision not to bring misconduct proceedings and, if so, will notify the force and the member of the public involved. However, if the PCA are dissatisfied with the decision not to bring misconduct proceedings they may recommend or, in the last resort, direct that such proceedings be brought. In all cases where the hearing follows the PCA's recommendation or direction they should be given an opportunity to satisfy themselves as to the case that is to be presented at the hearing and to comment on it if they wish. Any comments made by the PCA should be taken into consideration before proceeding with the case. The PCA may, if they wish, ask to send a representative to act as an observer at a hearing which follows a recommendation or direction, and this request should normally be granted.

Recommendation by the PCA

2.73   Where the PCA make a recommendation that misconduct proceedings should be held they will specify the matters which they consider should be the subject of misconduct proceedings and will give the reasons for their recommendation.

Direction by the PCA

2.74   Where the PCA's recommendation is not accepted they must be given an explanation. The PCA may accept this; or they may enter into further discussions; or they may direct that such proceedings (that is, normally a hearing) be brought as they may specify, again giving reasons for their direction in writing. If a direction is made, misconduct proceedings should be instituted forthwith and the officer and the member of the public concerned should be informed that this has been done at the direction of the PCA. The PCA will supply a statement, to form part of the case papers, specifying why they considered that proceedings should be brought and the grounds for their decision. In such a case, the hearing should be advised that the proceedings follow a direction from the PCA, but should not be informed of the PCA's reasons for the direction.

Withdrawal of misconduct proceedings before the hearing

2.75   There may be cases where it is considered that misconduct proceedings brought against an officer following a complaint made by a member of the public should be withdrawn before the hearing. Where the proceedings follow a direction from the PCA, the PCA must be invited to withdraw their direction.

Officer concerned ceasing to serve

2.76   The fact that an officer who is the subject of a complaint, or is involved in other matters referred to the PCA, ceases to serve as a police officer (or had already ceased to serve before the complaint was received) does not put the matter outside the purview of the PCA. The case should, therefore, be treated in accordance with the normal procedures as far as is practicable and a report sent to the PCA, notwithstanding that there could be no question of misconduct proceedings.

2.77   The PCA should also be informed if an officer ceases to serve while a report under section 75 is under their consideration, or if an officer ceases to serve before a misconduct hearing is held, whether or not the case had been referred to the PCA. The PCA would find it helpful to be informed of the circumstances in which an officer left the police service after a complaint had been made.

Disclosure of outcome of misconduct proceedings

To the PCA

2.78   The PCA should be informed in writing of the outcome of the proceedings. If convenient, this may be done by sending the PCA a copy of the presiding officer's account of the hearing.

To the complainant

2.79   In many cases the complainant will have attended the hearing, and may have acted as a witness but, unless he or she was present, will not know the outcome of the hearing. Provided it would be in the public and the force's interest and if no clear objection can be perceived, the complainant should be notified of the outcome of the misconduct proceedings as soon as possible after their conclusion.

2.80   Normally, any notification to the complainant should be confined to a statement to the effect that the conduct complained of was found to have been established and that suitable misconduct action has been taken against the officer concerned. Although there may be some exceptional cases where a complainant should not be informed of the nature of the sanction imposed against an officer found to have breached the Code of Conduct, forces should normally take all reasonable steps to provide this information to the complainant (though where the sanction was a fine it would not be necessary to specify the precise amount).

APPENDIX A TO SECTION 2
INFORMAL RESOLUTION OF COMPLAINTS

1.   Section 69(2) of the Police Act 1996 provides that the first step to be taken after the recording of a complaint is to consider whether informal resolution might be appropriate. Chief officers should therefore give positive consideration to the appointment of an officer or officers whose task it will be, once complaints have been recorded, to address the issue of informal resolution.

2.   Informal resolution is intended to provide a flexible and simple procedure for dealing with complaints of a minor nature which would otherwise attract the full length and formality of the investigation process. Complaints are suitable for informal resolution only if the conduct complained of, even if established, would not justify a criminal charge or misconduct proceedings, and if the complainant is content for the case to be handled in this way. Informal resolution is not available in cases where the PCA are required or decide to supervise the investigation.

3.   If the officer deputed to consider the case thinks that informal resolution is a possibility, he or she will have to see the complainant to establish the latter's views. When the decision is taken that informal resolution is appropriate, the case may be referred to another officer to undertake the informal resolution (that is, to act as the 'appointed officer' as defined in the Regulations), or the officer initially deputed to handle the question might act as the appointed officer and seek an informal resolution. The latter course may in many cases prove the simpler and more straight forward way to proceed.

Consulting the parties concerned

4.   Regulation 4(1) of the Police (Complaints) (Informal Resolution) Regulations requires that, as soon as practicable after the decision to attempt to resolve a complaint informally, the appointed officer should seek the views of both the complainant and the officer against whom the complaint has been made (who should be given access to a 'friend' if he or she wishes) about the matter. The appointed

officer may at the same time or thereafter take any steps which appear to him or her to be appropriate to resolve the complaint. (If the appointed officer does not have management responsibility for the officer concerned he or she should report the matter to the officer's line management on completion of the informal resolution procedure.)

Aim of informal resolution

5. It should be noted that the appointed officer's task is to achieve a position in which the complainant is satisfied that his or her complaint has been dealt with in an appropriate manner. This will not necessarily require an apology on behalf of either the force or the officer concerned. In some instances it will be sufficient to explain the law or the procedures under which the officer was operating at the time of the incident which gave rise to the complaint. In yet others it will be clear to the appointed officer that there is an irreconcilable difference between the complainant's and the officer's descriptions of the incident which gave rise to the complaint. In such a case it may be sufficient to explain the position to the complainant and invite him or her to accept that nothing further can be done.

6. The only limit placed on the appointed officer's freedom to approach the resolution of the complaint in the most appropriate way is that he or she may not render any apology on behalf of the officer concerned unless that officer has admitted the conduct complained of and agreed that it fell below the proper standards. The appointed officer may, however, offer an apology on behalf of the force, if it is felt appropriate.

Admissibility of statements

7. An officer volunteering an oral or written statement to the appointed officer must be informed that any statement made for the purpose of informal resolution will not be admissible in subsequent criminal, civil or disciplinary proceedings under the provisions of section 86(1). However, any material which consists of, or includes, an admission relating to a matter which is not subject to or part of the informal resolution may still be admissible under section 86(2). It thus follows that:

(a) If an officer or a complainant makes any statement in the course of an attempt to resolve a complaint informally then, whether or not the attempt is successful, provided the statement contains only material concerned with matters which may be resolved informally, no use may subsequently be made of that statement by either party in criminal, civil or misconduct proceedings. If the attempt at informal resolution fails and a formal investigation takes place, fresh statements must be taken specifically for the purpose of the formal investigation if they may eventually be required for criminal, civil or misconduct proceedings.

(b) If, however, in the course of an attempt to resolve a complaint informally a statement is made which consists of an admission relating to any matter which does not fall to be resolved informally, or merely includes such an admission, then that statement is admissible in subsequent proceedings.

Scope for immediate handling

8. Regulation 4(1) of the Police (Complaints) (Informal Resolution) Regulations provides that a supervisory officer of any rank may deal speedily with a complaint if it appears to him or her that it can be resolved informally there and then. This will, for example, permit the supervisory officer to receive a complaint and, if the officer concerned is present or readily available and is willing to explain his or her understanding of the incident which has given rise to the complaint, to deal with it at the time if the complainant accepts the explanation or, if appropriate, the apology as a satisfactory outcome.

9.   In a case handled in this way, the supervisory officer should report the matter to the officer to whom the chief officer has delegated his functions under Regulation 13(3) of the Police (Complaints) (General) Regulations 1985. If that officer is satisfied with the handling of the complaint, he or she may make a record in the complaints register and write to the complainant recording briefly his or her understanding of the way in which the complaint was handled and indicating the intention of recording it as having been resolved informally. It is recommended that criteria should be established in each force as to the extent to which junior officers may deal with complaints in this manner. Where the supervisory officer does not have management responsibility for the officer concerned the matter should also be reported to the officer's normal line management.

Meetings
10.   Where it appears to the appointed officer that the resolution of a complaint is likely to be assisted by a meeting between the complainant and the officer concerned — or between those persons together with any other person considered appropriate — arrangements for such a meeting may be made. The officer concerned will not, however, be obliged to attend such a meeting.

11.   A meeting may provide an opportunity for the complainant and the officer concerned to exchange points of view and for any misunderstandings to be cleared up. It will allow the officer, where he or she admits the conduct complained of, to apologise for it, or give an explanation of it to the complainant in person if he or she wishes to do so. If the officer concerned considers that the conduct in question was reasonable in all the circumstances, a meeting will allow the officer to state his or her case to the complainant.

12.   The appointed officer should make every effort to ensure that the meeting is conducted in a civil and orderly manner. The parties concerned may find it reassuring to have a lay person or a 'friend' present at the meeting as an independent presence, and this should not be discouraged. Whilst there can be no objection to the complainant being accompanied by a solicitor, the officer concerned should normally be advised of this if it is known in advance of the meeting. In such a case, care should be taken that the meeting does not become over-formalised in a way which might inhibit the resolution of the complaint.

Addition of more serious matters
13.   If in the course of the informal resolution procedure (whether by reason of a fresh allegation by the complainant, an admission by the officer concerned, or some other means) evidence comes to light of a more serious complaint which might require a formal investigation, the procedures should be terminated.

Failure of informal resolution
14.   Where it appears that informal resolution is impossible, or that the complaint is for any other reason not suitable for informal resolution, arrangements must be made for it to be investigated formally.

Copy of record
15.   Under Regulation 5 of the Police (Complaints) (Informal Resolution) Regulations a complainant is entitled to obtain a copy of the record (that is, the information contained in the formal register) relating to the complaint if he or she applies for it within three months of the date on which either it was resolved or it ceased for any other reason to be dealt with by way of informal resolution. The complainant should be informed of this right at the conclusion of the informal resolution procedure. Whether or not the complainant requests a copy of the record, the officer concerned

should, in all cases, be given a copy of the record or a written notification of the complaint and its outcome.

Officer's personal record

16.   No entry relating to the attempted or successful informal resolution of a complaint should be made in the personal record of the officer concerned, or be referred to in future misconduct proceedings.

APPENDIX B TO SECTION 2
DISPENSATIONS FROM THE REQUIREMENT TO INVESTIGATE COMPLAINTS

1.   A dispensation from the requirement to investigate a complaint may be sought from the PCA under Regulation 3 of and the Schedule to the Police (Dispensation from Requirement to Investigate Complaints) Regulations 1985 where a complaint, which has been recorded under section 69, appears to fall into one of the following categories.

Anonymous

2.   A complaint may be regarded as anonymous where it bears no indication of the maker's identity (or, where the complaint is in respect of conduct towards another person, of that other person's identity, or of how such a person can be contacted), or where, after reasonable inquiries, it proves impossible to contact him or her, or to establish his or her identity within a reasonable time or by reasonable means. If a dispensation is sought, the PCA must be told what inquiries were made.

Where investigation is not reasonably practicable

3.   This would apply if, for example, the complainant (or, where the complaint is in respect of conduct towards another person, that other person) refuses to co-operate with the police in their inquiries and it is, therefore, not possible to carry out a meaningful investigation. Investigation may not be reasonably practicable where, for example, the complainant fails after the completion of related criminal proceedings to reply to requests asking him or her to see the investigating officer, or to provide other specified assistance, and the investigation cannot proceed without more information. Wherever possible a letter should be sent to the complainant by recorded delivery explaining that a dispensation will be sought from the PCA if he or she fails to provide further assistance within a specified time, normally 21 days. If a dispensation is sought, the PCA should be given details of the action taken to attempt to secure an interview, or otherwise establish contact with the person concerned, and should be given a copy of any letter sent to the complainant.

Repetitious

4.   A complaint may be regarded as repetitious where it repeats, without any additional grounds and containing no fresh allegations or evidence, the substance of a previous complaint which has either been dealt with or withdrawn or resolved informally. If a dispensation is sought, the PCA should be given a copy of the original complaint (or a reference to previous correspondence with the PCA) for purposes of comparison and, where appropriate, a copy of the statement of withdrawal or a copy of the outcome of the informal resolution.

Vexatious, oppressive or otherwise an abuse of the procedure

5.   If a dispensation is sought under this heading, a full explanation must be given to the PCA of the reasons for the request.

Delay

6. A dispensation may be sought where more than 12 months have elapsed between the incident which gave rise to the allegation and the making of the complaint, and that either no good reason for the delay has been given, or it would be unjust to the officer concerned to initiate an investigation after the events concerned have faded from memory. Where possible, a letter should be sent to the complainant by recorded delivery explaining that consideration is being given to seeking a dispensation from the PCA and inviting him or her to set out the reasons for the delay within 21 days. If a dispensation is sought, the PCA should be given details of any reasons for the delay which the complainant has provided.

Handling

7. After establishing that the complaint under consideration falls into one or other of the categories described above, the PCA should be sent a copy of the complaint with a memorandum explaining why it is considered to fall into the category it does, giving reasons for this view, and inviting them to agree that there is no need for any further action under Part IV of the Act. It should be noted that a request under this provision is not precluded because an investigation of the complaint, or an attempt at informal resolution, has already been started.

8. The PCA may ask for further information before reaching a decision on whether to grant a dispensation but, if they agree to the request, no further action need be taken except to record the outcome in the complaints register. If the PCA do not agree with the view taken of the complaint it should be investigated or, if appropriate, be the subject of an attempt at informal resolution in the normal way.

9. Even where a complaint fails into one of the categories described above it may be decided that the complaint nevertheless merits investigation or some other appropriate action. For example, an anonymous complaint may contain serious allegations which clearly require investigation. In such circumstances, the investigation and subsequent action will proceed in the normal way.

SECTION 3
MISCONDUCT PROCEDURES

I. RECEIPT OF AND ACTION ON INFORMATION

General

3.1 It is an essential part of effective line management that managers should be aware of the conduct and performance of the individuals they manage. It is an integral part of a line manager's normal responsibilities to decide how to respond to any information which gives rise to concerns about an individual's conduct or perform- ance. Information about an officer's conduct may come from any one of a number of sources, either internal or external. Where the information comes in the form of a public complaint the case will be dealt with in accordance with the established procedures for dealing with complaints cases. The complaints procedures are sum- marised very briefly in paragraphs 3.8 and 3.9 below and described more fully in Section 2 of this guidance. Procedures for dealing with non-complaints cases are described in paragraphs 3.10 to 3.15 below.

3.2 There may be cases where, although the matter is not in itself serious, it nevertheless amounts to further evidence of a pattern of apparently poor work performance on the part of the officer concerned. In such a case, it might be appropriate to instigate the unsatisfactory performance procedures (see Section 1). In a case where the officer concerned is already subject to these procedures, the further information about his or her work performance might justify moving on to the next stage in the process, or it might simply need to be taken into account should the officer concerned proceed to the next stage.

3.3   In all cases, and at each stage of a case, the officer concerned should be reminded that he or she has a right to seek advice from a staff association representative, if he or she has not already done so, and to be accompanied to any meeting, interview or hearing by a 'friend', who must be a serving police officer and not otherwise involved in the case. The role of the 'friend' will be to advise and assist the officer, including speaking on the officer's behalf, producing either witnesses, witness statements or other documentation to assist the officer's case. A 'friend' should be considered to be on duty when attending meetings, interviews or hearings.

3.4   In addition to consulting a 'friend', the officer concerned may feel that he or she should seek legal advice, either generally or in respect of, for example, some aspect of an interview during any informal enquiries or formal investigation. There is no objection to this. Where this occurs during the course of an interview, it will be for the interviewing officer to decide whether to proceed with other aspects of the interview or whether to suspend the interview until the officer has been able to obtain the relevant legal advice.

3.5   At any stage of a case, up to and including a formal hearing, the officer concerned may submit that there are insufficient grounds upon which to base the case and/or that the correct procedures have not been followed. It will be for the officer responsible for the relevant stage of the case to consider any such submission and determine how best to respond to it, bearing in mind the need to ensure fairness to the officer concerned.

3.6   In cases where it is clear that there will need to be legal arguments based, say, on the way the force has applied the procedures, consideration should be given to holding a preliminary hearing. If the case is one in which the officer concerned has elected to be represented, the force may decide to appoint a lawyer to present its case. For reasons of effectiveness and economy, though, the force may consider that their own need for a lawyer could be confined to the legal arguments stage.

Fast track procedures (special cases)

3.7   Guidance on fast track procedures which do not follow all of the procedures set out for all other cases in this Section may be found in the Appendix to this Section.

Complaints Cases

3.8   Information about an officer may come in the form of a complaint by a member of the public. This paragraph and the one that follows briefly summarise the procedures for dealing with complaints cases. Fuller guidance is given in Section 2 of this guidance. The first steps on receipt of a complaint will be the preservation of evidence, the determination of the appropriate authority, the recording of the complaint and deciding whether it needs to be referred to the Police Complaints Authority (PCA). After the complaint has been recorded, it will be necessary to decide whether it can be dealt with by way of informal resolution (unless the case has been referred to the PCA), whether a dispensation should be sought from the PCA, or whether it needs to be investigated formally.

3.9   The PCA have the power to supervise investigations, to approve the appointment of investigating officers in supervised cases, to review the decision as to whether misconduct proceedings should be brought in any case referred to them, and to recommend or direct that misconduct proceedings be brought. In a case where the

PCA have recommended or directed that proceedings be brought there will be an informal consultation with the PCA which will give them an opportunity to satisfy themselves as to the case that is being brought and to comment upon it if they wish. Any comments made by the PCA should be taken into consideration before proceeding further with the case. The PCA may, if they wish, also send a representative to the subsequent hearing as an observer.

Non-Complaints Cases

3.10   Other information may arise from matters referred to the PCA by reason of its gravity or in other exceptional circumstances. Where information is received other than by way of a public complaint, it will normally be for the officer's line management to consider initially how best to deal with the matter, having regard to its potential seriousness. In many cases an officer's line management might consider that the matter can and should be dealt with and resolved locally using normal managerial methods, that is, words of advice backed up subsequently, where applicable, by further guidance and/or training. In other cases local enquiries might be considered appropriate, at least as a first step. In yet other cases it will be clear that the matter is potentially so serious that no local enquiries would be possible or appropriate and that it should be referred to the force's complaints and discipline department. In such circumstances, the case should be referred to the Superintendent[1] (or, where there is no Superintendent, the Chief Inspector) with line management responsibility for the particular area of work to decide whether or not it should be sent to the complaints and discipline department.[2] (For appropriate action relating to officers on central service and secondment, see Annex L.)

3.11   On receiving the information which gives rise to concern about a possible failure to meet the standards set out in the Code of Conduct, the line management of the officer concerned may decide that the matter is one which can and should be enquired into locally. Depending on the outcome of those enquiries, the line manager may decide that it should also be dealt with locally by means of words of advice (once the words of advice have been given, the line manager will then need to consider what else may need to be done in order to help the officer, for example, further guidance and/or training). This would normally be because it was clear to the line manager that the matter in question was not sufficiently serious to justify formal action under the misconduct procedures. The officer concerned will be informed of the details of the allegation or information which gives cause for concern and be given a full opportunity to respond to the allegation or information and to offer an explanation. The officer may consult a 'friend' before deciding whether to respond to the allegation.

3.12   The officer's line manager, having considered the matter either before or after having made preliminary enquiries, might decide that a more senior officer should be involved. The more senior officer might decide (again, where appropriate, after making preliminary enquiries) to take no action; to arrange for the officer to receive words of advice; or to recommend that a written warning be given to the

[1 Where the officer concerned is a Superintendent all decisions in the case at its various stages will need to be taken by an Assistant Chief Constable. This applies throughout the remainder of this section.]

[2 Cases where there is no Superintendent or Chief Inspector with management responsibility for the officer concerned are unlikely to be common. However, in any such cases an appropriate officer, depending on the particular circumstances of the officer concerned and his or her post, will need to be appointed to fill this management role. It may be advisable to identify those situations where this problem could arise and nominate an officer to fill the management role in advance of possible need.]

officer. A written warning, which would be recorded and would normally have to be administered by a Superintendent or above[3] (or, exceptionally where there is no Superintendent, by a Chief Inspector), may be given only where the officer concerned has admitted the failure to meet standards. Where the officer does not admit the failure, and the case cannot be dealt with locally, a formal investigation will take place.

3.13   Where an officer admits a failure to meet standards which would normally be dealt with by way of written warning but already has two valid written warnings recorded, then the matter must be referred to a formal hearing. This will apply whether or not the previous warnings related to similar conduct. (Written warnings are valid only for twelve months, from the date they are administered.) In such a case the officers taking the hearing would be made aware that it followed two written warnings. Cases where an officer does not admit a failure will be referred to a formal investigation.

3.14   Where an apparent failure to meet standards requires more investigation than can be carried out locally, or is potentially so serious that a formal misconduct hearing is likely, the line manager (or the more senior officer referred to above) should refer the case to the Superintendent (or, where there is no Superintendent, the Chief Inspector) with line management responsibility for the particular area of work to decide whether or not it should be sent to the complaints and discipline department. If it is so referred, the complaints and discipline department then takes over responsibility for any further investigation and for subsequent action, including any misconduct hearing.

3.15   Where it is either clear from the outset or it emerges during the course of an informal investigation (or interview under the unsatisfactory performance procedures) that there is a conduct issue serious enough to warrant formal investigation and the possibility of a misconduct hearing, the informal process will not be appropriate. If already begun it must cease immediately. No interviews or further interviews will take place until an investigating officer has been appointed to conduct them in accordance with the guidance contained in paragraphs 3.20 to 3.23 below.

II.   FORMAL INVESTIGATION

3.16   Where it has been decided that a misconduct case, whether or not it involves a complaint, should be investigated formally, responsibility for the investigation will normally be assumed by the complaints and discipline department.

3.17   The investigation should be completed as quickly as is practicable. The investigating officer should ensure that the officer concerned and, if there is one, the complainant are kept informed as to the progress of the investigation, particularly if there is some delay, provided that to do so would not prejudice the investigation.

Suspension and removal from normal duties

3.18   In serious cases, it might be decided that the officer concerned should be removed from his or her normal duties or be suspended during the course of the formal investigation or pending the outcome of misconduct proceedings. Such a course of action should be taken only where it was necessary and in the public interest to do so. In all cases, unless it was impossible or positively undesirable to do so, consideration should first be given to a temporary transfer to other duties rather than suspension. Where an officer is suspended this will be with pay, except where the officer is in custody following conviction, or is absent and his or her whereabouts are unknown, when the suspension will normally be without pay. Neither removal from normal duties nor suspension implies any decision about the misconduct case.

[3 An Assistant Chief Constable if the officer concerned is a Superintendent.]

The investigating officer

3.19   The investigating officer should be of a rank not lower than Inspector and of at least the same rank as the officer concerned,[4] and should normally be from a different command or unit from the officer concerned and his or her line management. He or she should have had no previous involvement in the case or close connection with the individuals associated with the case such as might give rise to doubts about his or her impartiality. An investigating officer from another force may be appointed where the circumstances of the case indicate that this would be appropriate. In cases being supervised by the Police Complaints Authority (PCA), they may choose to exercise their right to approve the appointment of the investigating officer. The investigating officer's task will be to collect evidence, and he or she will be responsible for ensuring that the investigation is carried out impartially and confidentially. See also Annex A — Appointment of investigating officer from another force — and paragraphs 2.47 and 2.48 of Section 2.

Notification of investigation

3.20   The investigating officer will need to consider at the outset of the investigation whether there is any reason why the officer concerned should not be informed that an alleged failure to meet the standards set out in the Code of Conduct is being investigated. The presumption is that the officer should be notified of the investigation and the reasons for it at the outset unless it would be prejudicial to the investigation to do so. Any decision not to inform the officer will be kept under regular scrutiny and review in order to avoid undue delay.

3.21   The notification of the investigation to the officer concerned will be the responsibility of the investigating officer. Unless there are good reasons for not doing so, the officer concerned should be notified in writing of the investigation as soon as reasonably practicable and should be informed of his or her rights. As soon as the officer has been notified of the investigation he or she will be given an opportunity to give his or her account of the conduct or event(s) in question, if he or she wishes to do so. Where the officer concerned has (or should have) been notified, he or she should not be required to make a duty statement regarding the matter under investigation (this also applies where an officer has or should have been cautioned in relation to the investigation of a criminal allegation). See also Annex B — Notification of investigation to officer concerned.

3.22   Where an officer is alleged or appears to have committed a criminal offence a normal criminal investigation will take place, with the officer being cautioned in accordance with the PACE Code of Practice for the Detention, Treatment and Questioning of Persons by Police Officers. However, the officer need not be informed immediately of the criminal allegation if doing so would impede the criminal investigation.

Interviews

3.23   The object of interviewing an officer about a possible failure to meet standards is twofold: first, to provide the officer concerned with an opportunity to give his or her account of the matter and, second, to enable the officer to offer any explanatory detail which might serve to explain or defend the matter. The officer may not be compelled to answer any question put to him or her during the course of the interview. Interviews should be tape recorded.

[4 Where the officer concerned is a Superintendent, the investigating officer must be of at least the rank of Assistant Chief Constable (or the equivalent). In such a case, the investigating officer would be responsible for the conduct and report of the investigation but could delegate the actual investigative work to other officers.]

III. INVESTIGATION REPORTS

3.24   When the investigating officer has completed the investigation, or where it cannot be taken any further, he or she will submit a report to the officer in charge of the complaints and discipline department. In an investigation supervised by the PCA the report should be copied to the PCA for their interim statement.

3.25   The report should include a short statement of the original complaint or information, a summary of events, the conclusions drawn and the recommendations for future action. The report should contain all material relevant to the question of whether the officer has performed his or her duty in accordance with the standards set out in the Code of Conduct, as well as examine any matters relevant to the criminal law, and should include any medical or welfare considerations which may have had a bearing on the officer's behaviour at the tune. Copies of all statements or other documents obtained by the investigating officer should be attached to the report.

3.26   It may at times be proper and appropriate to disclose to an accused officer in misconduct proceedings (or to his or her 'friend' or legal representative) material in an investigation report which could assist in demonstrating the officer's innocence or in mitigating any sanction which may be imposed. Such an occasion might arise where misconduct proceedings are started where an investigating officer has recommended none or has recommended that factors mitigating the accused officer's culpability be taken into account before a decision is made to start misconduct proceedings.

Consideration of investigation report

3.27   On receiving the investigation report, the Superintendent (or more senior officer) in charge of complaints and discipline[5] will need to consider whether the officer's conduct, as disclosed by the investigation, appears to have fallen below the standards as set out in the Code of Conduct and, if it does, what would be the most appropriate way to deal with the matter. Where a decision is taken that there should be no further action, the officer concerned should be informed of this. Criminal matters will be the subject of a report to the Crown Prosecution Service (CPS) in accordance with the relevant statutory provision.

3.28   Where information from a source other than a report indicates that an officer may have committed a criminal offence and ought to be charged with it, the case should be referred to the CPS for advice, even though the circumstances of the offence have in any case required a charge to be preferred forthwith.

3.29   Misconduct proceedings will almost always be deferred until after the completion of any related criminal proceedings against the officer concerned. However, there may be exceptional circumstances — for example, in special cases where the fast track procedure is invoked (for which guidance is provided in the appendix to this Section) or where the defence to the criminal charge is in itself an admission of misconduct — where this would not be appropriate. In these exceptional cases it would be appropriate for the misconduct proceedings to take place in advance of the criminal proceedings. However, where the criminal proceedings relate to conduct which is the same as that for which misconduct proceedings are being brought, it is essential that the misconduct proceedings do not prejudice the outcome of the criminal proceedings. It would be appropriate to proceed with misconduct action in such a case, prior to the completion of the criminal proceedings, only where the officer's representative has been informed and the CPS has no objections, and where there was no other reason to believe that the criminal proceedings might be prejudiced by the instigation or continuation of misconduct proceedings.

[5 For Superintendents, at least an Assistant Chief Constable.]

3.30   Whether or not there are criminal proceedings, all cases will need to be considered individually and discretion should be used when deciding whether a particular case requires a formal misconduct hearing. In deciding whether a hearing is required, it will be necessary to consider the seriousness of the possible failure to meet standards and whether there is any evidence that it arose, for example, through inadequate training or knowledge. Where an officer has declined to answer questions when being interviewed this in itself should not be considered as evidence of a possible failure to meet standards: the evidence available will need to be considered to be sufficient, in its own right, before a decision is taken to hold a formal hearing. Similarly, any misleading statement contained in a response by an officer to the notification of investigation, or in any written or oral statement made earlier, should not in itself normally be considered as evidence of a failure to meet standards. However, where such a misleading statement is of greater seriousness than the original conduct in question (for example, if it is intended as a means of falsely implicating another officer) it would be reasonable to take account of it in reaching any decisions regarding the officer's conduct.

3.31   Where criminal proceedings have taken place for an offence arising out of the matter under investigation and those proceedings have resulted in the acquittal of an officer, that determination will be relevant to a decision on whether to discipline the officer:

(a)   where the conduct under investigation is in substance the same as the criminal charge so determined, and where the alleged failure is serious and the likely sanction serious such that it would be reasonable to look for proof to a high degree of probability (see paragraph 3.70), it will normally be unfair to institute disciplinary proceedings; or

(b)   where the conduct under investigation is not in substance the same as the criminal charge so determined, it may nevertheless be unfair to proceed where a matter essential to the proof of the misconduct was in issue in criminal proceedings and had been resolved in the officer's favour.

3.32   Where an officer has been found guilty of a criminal offence there is discretion whether or not to institute misconduct proceedings. Generally speaking, the officer having been sentenced by the court, the only matter outstanding is his fitness for the responsibilities of his rank or as a member of a police force. There may be cases where some lesser sanction than dismissal or reduction in rank, such as a fine, reprimand or caution would be appropriate. In some cases involving conviction of relatively trivial offences, however, no misconduct proceedings need be taken. In particular, in the case of minor traffic and other offences, where the officer's fitness for the responsibilities of his rank or as a member of a police force is not in question, misconduct action might only rarely be necessary.

3.33   Where the conduct under investigation is in substance the same as a criminal charge and where a decision has been taken by the CPS not to proceed with that charge because of insufficiency of evidence, it will be relevant to take such a decision into account when considering whether it is appropriate to institute misconduct proceedings.

Timing of investigations

Criminal proceedings

3.34   Special considerations arise in regard to the timing of an investigation of a complaint against a police officer where the complaint is related to some aspect of pending criminal proceedings against a member of the public; for example, against the complainant or the complainant's associates. There may also be difficulty in investigating a complaint where the related trial has been completed but an appeal is pending. Consultation with the CPS on the handling of cases of special difficulty is unaffected by this guidance.

3.35   There will be rare and exceptional occasions when the investigation into possible misconduct is taken forward while criminal proceedings are in progress. Where the investigation brings to light any material which is likely to assist a complainant or any other person in defending criminal proceedings, or which suggests that such proceedings are unsafe or ill-founded, the relevant material should immediately be drawn to the attention of the CPS (headquarters). This also applies where there is an outstanding appeal. Where the information calls into question the safety of a conviction where the proceedings, including any appeal, are completed, the information should be reported to the Criminal Cases Review Authority.

Civil proceedings

3.36   Where a member of the public has initiated civil proceedings in respect of a member of a police force or has indicated an intention to do so, the matter should not automatically be regarded as a complaint. Instead, efforts should be made to determine whether the person concerned wishes the matter also to be treated as a complaint and is willing to cooperate in its investigation. If the complainant wishes a complaint to be recorded but is unwilling to cooperate in the investigation it should be made clear that, as civil proceedings are often protracted, it is unlikely that a satisfactory investigation will be possible once they are completed, and that the delay may, in certain circumstances, preclude misconduct proceedings being brought against an officer. The wishes of the complainant should also be established if the complaint was made before civil proceedings were started in respect of the same matter. If in such a case, for instance on legal advice, the complainant wishes to withdraw the complaint, this should be recorded. If the complainant refuses further cooperation but declines to withdraw the complaint, the possible consequences of delay should be explained.

3.37   Where the complainant asks for the matter to be recorded or maintained as a complaint and is willing to cooperate in the investigation, the normal procedures should be followed, including submission to the CPS and the PCA as appropriate, with a note that there are extant civil proceedings and a view as to whether any misconduct action should be delayed until the civil proceedings have concluded. In deciding whether misconduct proceedings should be deferred, the effect of such a deferment, on both the maintenance of force discipline and on the interests of the officer concerned, should be considered.

3.38   Nothing in these paragraphs should be taken as precluding investigation of matters raised in a civil action where this is necessary to prepare for the legal proceedings.

Action on investigation report

3.39   Following consideration of the investigation report, it might be decided that a formal hearing was not required but that it would be more appropriate for the matter to be dealt with by the officer's line management by way of words of advice. There might also be cases, where the officer admitted the failure to meet the standards set out in the Code of Conduct, in which it would be appropriate for a Superintendent (or above) to administer a written warning to the officer, in line with the guidance given in paragraphs 3.12 and 3.13 above (see also Annex C — Written warnings in complaints cases). In some cases it may be decided that no further action should be taken, and the officer should be informed in writing accordingly.

3.40   Other than in a case where two written warnings have already been given, there will generally be little value, where the officer admits the failure to meet standards, in holding a formal hearing unless the failure to meet standards is considered to be such that some sanction, other than a reprimand or caution, would be appropriate. In all other cases, line managers should normally deal with the matter, including, where appropriate, by arranging for the officer to receive a written warning (in line with the guidance contained in paragraphs 3.12 and 3.13 above).

Complaints cases

3.41   Where the case arose originally from a public complaint, whether or not the investigation was supervised, the PCA must be informed of the view taken of the case and be given details of any misconduct action that is proposed or, where no misconduct action is proposed, the reasons for this decision. In an unsupervised case the PCA should, at the same time, be supplied with a copy of the original complaint and a copy of the investigation report together with the relevant supporting statements and documents. The PCA may agree with the proposed course of action or, where no misconduct hearing is proposed, may recommend or, if necessary, direct that a hearing be held.

IV.   FORMAL HEARINGS

Appointment of case officer

3.42   Where it is decided that a hearing should be held, the first step will be for the Superintendent (or more senior officer) in charge of complaints and discipline to nominate an officer (normally from the complaints and discipline department) to be the case officer. The case officer will be responsible for putting together the material that is to be presented to the hearing, and for making the necessary arrangements for the hearing. The investigating officer may be nominated as the case officer, if this is thought convenient, although there may be cases where it is appropriate for these roles to be separated.

Appointment of presenting officer

3.43   An officer, normally of no lower rank than inspector, will also need to be appointed to act as the presenting officer at the hearing. The presenting officer's role is to help the officers taking the hearing to establish the facts of the case; he or she will not act as a prosecutor. Although the roles of the case officer and presenting officer are different, they may be undertaken by the same officer.

PCA recommendation/direction

3.44   Where a hearing is to be held on the recommendation or direction of the PCA they should be given an opportunity to satisfy themselves as to the case that is to be brought and to offer any comment upon it. Any comments made by the PCA should be taken into consideration before proceeding further with the case.

Notifying the officer concerned

3.45   The case officer will notify the officer concerned that a decision has been taken to hold a formal misconduct hearing. This notification will be in writing and will include:

(a)   the time(s), date(s) and place(s) of the alleged misconduct;

(b)   details of the behaviour or actions which is/are alleged to have breached the standards set out in the Code of Conduct; and

(c)   the particular section(s) of the Code of Conduct that the officer concerned is alleged to have breached.

3.46   At the same time, the case officer should arrange for the officer concerned to receive copies of all statements, documents or other material obtained by the investigating officer (including any which relate to the officer's character) which appear to him or her to be relevant to the case, whether or not they are to be used in support of the presenting officer's case at the hearing, any evidence that is to be given at the hearing by the officer's line management, and copies of the papers that are to be supplied to the officers taking the hearing prior to the hearing (see paragraph 3.51 below). If the officer concerned seeks further disclosure of material that does not, to the case officer, appear relevant to the alleged misconduct, the officer concerned should indicate in what way such material is relevant to the case. Where relevance is shown, the material should be disclosed.

3.47   Within 14 days of the receipt of these papers the officer concerned must indicate whether he or she admits or denies the failure to meet standards. Thereafter, the case officer will notify the officer concerned of the time and date of the hearing. This should be done at least 21 days before the date of the hearing. In a complex case it would be appropriate to consider giving a longer period of notice. It is clearly desirable, once the decision to hold a hearing has been taken, for the hearing to take place as soon as possible thereafter.

Joint hearings

3.48   Cases will arise where two or more officers are to appear before a hearing in relation to apparent failures to meet the standards set out in the Code stemming from the same incident. In any such incident, each officer will most likely have played a different part and any misconduct will be different for each officer involved. In some circumstances it may be considered necessary to deal with all the cases together in order to disentangle the various strands of action, and this might extend to the holding of a single hearing. However, any request from the officers concerned for separate hearings should normally be granted unless it is clear that a joint hearing is necessary for the proper examination of the incident in question and that such a hearing can be held without causing injustice to any of the individual officers. Where a joint hearing is held it will be the duty of the officers taking it, once the outline of events is clear, to consider each officer individually and deal with him or her accordingly.

Legal representation

3.49   Where the Superintendent (or more senior officer) in charge of complaints and discipline has decided that a hearing should be held, he or she will then need to decide whether the hearing is likely to want at its disposal the outcomes of dismissal, requirement to resign or reduction in rank. If this is so, the officer concerned must be given the opportunity to elect to be legally represented at the hearing, at the same time as he or she is notified of the decision to hold a hearing. The officer will be required to indicate his or her decision on the matter of legal representation within 14 days of receiving the notification of the decision to hold a hearing or of receiving the copies of the papers for the hearing, if this is later. If the officer fails within this period, without reasonable cause, to indicate his or her decision, this will be taken as indicating a decision not to be legally represented. See Annex D — Legal representation.

3.50   Where the officer concerned is to be legally represented at a hearing, the case to be put to the hearing may be presented by a lawyer, who would assume the role of presenting officer and carry out that role as if it was being performed by a police officer. The lawyer would not act as prosecutor. Where an officer has given notice that he or she wishes to be legally represented, but in the event is not so represented, the case against him or her may still be presented by a lawyer. However, forces may consider that their own need for representation by a lawyer could be restricted to dealing with any legal arguments, normally dealt with in the first stages of a hearing (see also paragraph 3.57).

Documents for hearing

3.51 Where the officer concerned admits the failure to meet standards the case officer will prepare a summary of the facts of the case. A draft of this summary will be made available to the officer concerned at least two weeks before the hearing, seeking agreement to it within one week. Any disagreement with the contents of the summary must be recorded. Where the officer concerned does not admit the failure to meet standards no such summary will be prepared. Where an officer is considered to have failed to meet standards in more than one respect and, for example, admits one failure but not another, the case should proceed as if the officer had admitted none of the failures.

3.52 The papers that will need to be circulated in advance to the officers taking the hearing will depend on whether the officer admits or denies the failure to meet standards. Where the officer denies the failure, the officers taking the hearing will be given a copy of the document which notified the officer concerned of the decision to hold a hearing, which will set out only the allegation(s) against the officer concerned. Where the officer admits the failure, the officers taking the hearing will, in addition, receive a copy of the agreed summary prepared by the case officer.

Appointment of officers to take hearing

3.53 Hearings will be presided over by an Assistant Chief Constable, with two officers of Superintendent rank acting as assessors.[6] Where the officer concerned is a Superintendent, the two assessors will be Assistant Chief Constables (or Metropolitan Police Commanders) from outside the home force.[7] None of the officers taking the hearing should have had any previous involvement in the case and nor should they have so close a connection with the officer concerned as might give rise to suspicions of bias. The presiding officer, in conjunction with the two assessors, will be responsible for the conduct of the hearing, the determination of the hearing and the decision as to outcome. If there is a difference of view between the officers taking the hearing, the decisions of the hearing will be based on a simple majority vote between them. See also Annex E — Officers appointed to conduct hearings.

Witnesses

3.54 Prior to the hearing the presenting officer will decide which witnesses to call. The officer concerned may agree to the reading of statements from witnesses whose evidence is not in dispute. Any witnesses called to give evidence to the hearing may be subject to examination and cross-examination (see also Annex F — Evidence at hearings). It is good practice to give reasonable notice of witnesses to be called. (The officer concerned will be given the opportunity to say whether he or she wishes the case/presenting officer to call any witnesses and, if so, which.) See also Annex G — Witnesses.

The 'friend'

3.55 Whether or not the officer is to be legally represented he or she should be reminded at an early stage of the right to be accompanied to the hearing by a 'friend' or, where applicable, a legal representative. The role of the 'friend' or legal representative will be to advise and assist the officer concerned, including speaking on the officer's behalf, calling and/or questioning witnesses, and/or producing witness

---

[6] In the Metropolitan and City of London forces, a Commander and two Superintendents.]
[7] In the Metropolitan Police, a Commander as presiding officer with two Commanders from another Area acting as assessors; in the City of London Police, a Commander or the Assistant Commissioner with two Assistant Chief Constables or Metropolitan Police Commanders.]

statements, other documentation or exhibits to assist the officer's case. Both the 'friend' and the officer concerned should be given adequate duty time to prepare for the hearing (at which the 'friend' may wear plain clothes).

Purpose and conduct of hearing

3.56   The purpose of the hearing is to review the facts of the case, listen to and (if appropriate) question the officer concerned and, where applicable, any witnesses who may be called, and decide the outcome of the case. It will be for the presiding officer to determine the course of the hearing, in accordance with the principles of natural justice and fairness. The officer's 'friend' and/or legal representative may speak on the officer's behalf and the presiding officer will, at all stages of the hearing, give the officer concerned the opportunity to speak personally.

3.57   In cases where there are to be legal arguments based on, for example, the way the procedures have been applied during the course of the investigation, it is normally advisable to dispose of these at the start of the hearing as far as is possible. The parties may find it helpful to submit written skeleton arguments, to each, other and to the officers conducting the hearing, in readiness for this part of the proceedings. In the event that, whether in the light of skeleton arguments or after hearing oral arguments, the presiding officer decides that he or she needs to obtain legal advice, this advice may be provided in private but should in due course be summarised to the parties concerned at the hearing.

3.58   The officer concerned will, throughout the hearing, be given the opportunity to speak personally, or have his or her 'friend' or legal representative to do so on their behalf, and may be called upon to give his or her account of the events in question, though he or she may not be compelled to do so.

3.59   Hearings will be conducted in two parts. The first part of a hearing will consider the incident(s) and/or action(s) which gave rise to concerns about the officer's conduct, and will end with a decision as to whether the officer's conduct fell below the standards set out in the Code of Conduct. If the officers taking the hearing decide that there has been no failure to meet the standards in the Code the officer should be told that this is the case, the hearing should be concluded and no entry should be made in the officer's personal record.

3.60   If the officers taking the hearing find that the officer's conduct did fail to meet the standards, the second part of the hearing will determine the appropriate outcome. Where the officer concerned admits the failure to meet the standards in the Code the officers taking the hearing may, if they wish, dispose of the case without hearing witnesses, the facts of the case being outlined by the presenting officer, although they should agree to any request from the officer concerned for witnesses as to mitigation, character and antecedents to be heard. In considering the question of outcome, the officers taking the hearing will need to take into account any aggravating or mitigating factors and have regard to evidence as to the officer's character and record of service.

3.61   Hearings will be conducted in private. However, a presiding officer may, at his or her discretion and with the consent of the officer concerned, permit other persons to be present if there is good reason to believe that their presence would be beneficial (e.g. for monitoring or training purposes). In addition, there may be cases where it would be appropriate, again at the presiding officer's discretion, to allow witnesses and other individuals to be accompanied to the hearing by a friend or relative. See also Annex H —Other persons who may attend hearings.

3.62   Where a hearing stems from a complaint by a member of the public, the complainant may be present if he or she wishes throughout the hearing and until a finding is reached; provided that, if he or she is to be called as a witness, he or she should not be allowed to attend before this point. If the presiding officer considers it appropriate, the complainant may be accompanied by a friend or relative, to whose presence the same rules and restrictions will apply.

3.63   The PCA may, if they wish, ask to send a representative to act as an observer at any hearing which follows a recommendation or direction, and this request should normally be granted.

3.64   The presiding officer may require any member of the public present to withdraw if evidence is to be given which, in the presiding officer's view, might disclose information which ought not to be disclosed to a member of the public. In addition, any members of the public present, will be required to withdraw once the hearing has decided that the case against the officer concerned has been established and before it moves on to consider the question of outcome. This requirement will not apply to any PCA observer at the hearing.

3.65   A verbatim record of the proceedings at the hearing must be taken, normally by means of a tape-recording.

Presence of officer concerned

3.66   It is not necessary for the officer concerned to be present at the hearing for it to be valid. If the officer concerned fails to appear at a hearing without prior warning or without reason being given sufficient to excuse his or her absence, the hearing may proceed and decisions be made in the officer's absence. It will be for the presiding officer to decide in such a case whether to proceed or to adjourn the hearing to another date. See paragraph 3.68 below.

Attendance at hearings — Ill health

3.67   Attendance at a hearing is not subject to the same considerations as reporting for duty and the provisions of Regulation 35 (sick leave) of the Police Regulations 1995 do not apply. An illness or disability may render an officer unfit for duty without affecting his or her ability to attend a hearing. However, if the officer concerned is incapacitated there is no objection to the hearing being deferred until he or she is sufficiently improved to attend. A hearing will not be deferred indefinitely because a sick officer is unable to attend, although every effort should be made to enable the officer to attend if he or she wishes to be present. For example:

(a)   if the officer suffers from a physical injury — a broken leg, for instance — it may be possible to hold the hearing at a location convenient to him or her;

(b)   the acute phase of a serious physical illness is usually fairly short-lived, and the hearing may be deferred until the officer is well enough to attend.

3.68   Where, despite such efforts having been made and/or the hearing having been deferred, the officer either persists in failing to attend the hearing or maintains his or her inability to attend, the presiding officer will need to decide whether to continue to defer the hearing or whether to proceed with it, if necessary in the absence of the officer concerned. The presiding officer must judge which is the most appropriate course of action in all the circumstances of the case. Nothing in this paragraph should be taken to suggest that, where an officer's medical condition is found to be such that he or she would normally be retired on medical grounds, the misconduct proceedings should prevent or delay retirement. However, there may be some cases, especially those where the conduct in question is very serious, where it may not be in the public or the force's interest to proceed with medical retirement in advance of a misconduct hearing, held in the absence of the officer concerned if necessary. In the event of medical retirement the misconduct proceedings will automatically lapse. (See also Annex J — Ill health.)

V. OUTCOMES OF HEARINGS

3.69   There will, essentially, be three issues for the hearing to decide; what actually happened on the occasion in question, did the officer's conduct on that occasion fail to meet the standards set out in the Code of Conduct and, if so, what should be done about it? In considering the first two of these issues, the officers taking the hearing will make every effort to discover the truth and to assess the situation impartially. Their consideration of the issues before them will involve a number of factors, only some of which may require individual actions on the part of the officer concerned to be established.

3.70   In deciding matters of fact the burden of proof lies with the presenting officer, and the tribunal must apply the standard of proof required in civil cases, that is, the balance of probabilities. The straightforward legal definition of the civil standard of proof is that the adjudicator is convinced by the evidence that it is more likely or probable that something occurred than that it did not occur. Relevant case law makes it clear that the degree of proof required increases with the gravity of what is alleged and its potential consequences. It therefore follows that, where an allegation is likely to ruin an officer's reputation, deprive them of their livelihood or seriously damage their career prospects, a tribunal should be satisfied to a high degree of probability that what is alleged has been proved.

3.71   Misconduct tribunals should always bear in mind the fact that police officers are required to deal with people who may have a particular motive for making false allegations against them. An officer facing serious consequences is entitled to expect a tribunal to give very careful consideration to the evidence before an allegation is found to be proved, and tribunals should always look for other evidence which supports that given by a complainant.

3.72   Where the officers taking the hearing decide that the officer concerned has acted in a way which falls below the required standards, they will then need to consider how best to deal with the matter. In considering this question, the hearing will have regard to the officer's record of police service as shown on his or her personal record (normally with oral evidence being given by the Superintendent or Chief Inspector with management responsibility for the unit in which the officer concerned works), and will take into account any mitigating or aggravating factors.

3.73   Evidence given by the line manager will normally include details of the officer's current work performance, and care must be taken to ensure that any such details are relevant to the issue before the hearing, accurate and known to the officer. The evidence given by the line manager should cover all relevant matters, including those which are to the officer's credit, and must be fair and accurate. The officer who is to present the evidence should therefore exercise considerable care in its preparation and, in particular, should ensure that nothing is included in the evidence which cannot be substantiated. The evidence should not include details of any misconduct matters which have been expunged from the officer's personal record, details of informally resolved complaints or other misconduct matters which are not formally recorded on the officer's personal record.

3.74   In addition, the officer concerned or his or her 'friend' (or legal representative) will be given the opportunity to make representations on the question of the most appropriate way of disposing of the case and to produce witnesses as to the officer's character, whether or not witnesses have been heard in the main body of the hearing.

3.75   Where an officer has mounted a defence of public interest disclosure, the tribunal should have regard to whether the correct procedure was followed (see Section 2, paragraphs 2.34 to 2.36).

3.76   The full range of sanctions available to a hearing is:

(a)   *Dismissal* — effective immediately;

(b)   *Requirement to resign* — either immediately or after such other period as the tribunal may specify;

(c)   *Reduction in rank* — effective immediately;

(d)   *Fine* — of not more than 13 days' pay recoverable over a minimum of 13 weeks;

(e)   *Reprimand* — which would be recorded in the officer's personal record;

(f)   *Caution* — which would not be recorded in the officer's personal record;

3.77   In addition, in a case where it has been established that there was a failure to meet standards, it is open to the hearing to decide that no further action need be taken in relation to the officer concerned.

3.78   The officers taking the hearing will retire or, if necessary, adjourn the hearing (normally only overnight) in order to consider their decisions. The officer concerned will be informed of the hearing's decisions orally, in person, by the presiding officer. He or she will then be notified in writing by the presiding officer of the decisions of the hearing not more than three days after the completion of the hearing. Together with this notification, the officer will also be informed of the right to seek a Chief Constable's review of the decisions of the hearing. The notification of the decisions of the hearing will be accompanied by a copy of the presiding officer's account of the hearing's conclusions about the failure to meet standards, its views on any mitigating or aggravating factors, and the reasons for the decisions of the hearing as to finding and outcome.

3.79   If a hearing is adjourned the officers conducting it should not discuss the details of the case with anyone else, whether connected with the case or not. It is only in this way that the impartiality of the proceedings can be seen to be protected adequately.

VI.   AVENUES OF APPEAL

Chief Constable's review

3.80   An officer has the right to require the decisions of the hearing to be reviewed by his or her Chief Constable. The request for a review should be made within 14 days of the written notification of the hearing's decision, and should be accompanied by written grounds in support of the request. See Section 4.

Appeal to Police Appeals Tribunal

3.81   An officer who has been dismissed, required to resign or reduced in rank following a hearing and the Chief Constable's review will have a right of appeal to a Police Appeals Tribunal. See Section 5.

VII.   RECORDS

3.82   Where an officer is found not to have fallen below the standards set out in the Code of Conduct, or receives a caution from a hearing, or the hearing decides to take no action, no entry should be made in the officer's service record. Where a record is made of the outcome of any misconduct hearing it will be expunged from the officer's service record after a period of three or five years, depending on the punishment imposed (regulation 17(2) of the Police Regulations 1995 refers). Records of written warnings will be expunged after 12 months. Where written warnings or the outcome of any misconduct hearings have been expunged from an officer's service record they should not be referred to in any future misconduct proceedings.

Misconduct books

3.83   Regulations require that each force keeps a record of misconduct hearings held to deal with alleged breaches of the Code of Conduct, including the outcome of any such action. Forces may also wish to keep records of other action taken which falls short of formal proceedings.

APPENDIX TO SECTION 3
FAST TRACK PROCEDURES (SPECIAL CASES)

Introduction

1.   The following paragraphs provide guidance on the operation of the fast track misconduct procedures, referred to as 'special cases' in the Conduct Regulations. Schedule 2 of the Police (Conduct) Regulations 1999 gives the statutory provisions for special cases.

2.   In almost all circumstances, the procedures set out in the main part of section 3 will be applied. However, in a small number of cases, and only exceptionally, it will be appropriate to use the fast track procedures. They are designed to deal with cases of gross misconduct where an officer has been caught 'red handed' committing a serious crime, either as a single incident (for instance, a serious assault) or, more likely, after a long-running inquiry which uncovers serious apparent wrongdoing by a police officer (for instance, corruption).

3.   Even where the criteria for fast track (see below) are met there may be circumstances where it would not be appropriate to apply it. For instance, where it was more likely than not to prejudice a criminal prosecution, or where it might prematurely alert others (police officers or non-police officers) who are, or may be, the subject of investigation. Another factor might be where more than one officer is involved, where the alleged conduct of one is suitable for fast tracking but not that of the other(s).

4.   Briefly, the effect of fast track will be to deal swiftly with an officer in advance of any criminal proceedings which may in due course be brought, and would normally expect to result in an officer's dismissal from the force. From the decision to put the case onto fast track it is expected that the procedure will be completed within six weeks. The case will be heard by the officer's Chief Constable (Commissioner in the Metropolitan Police) with a right of review by another chief officer and, in due course and in accordance with the provisions of the Police Act 1996, right of appeal to a Police Appeals Tribunal. Unlike standard track cases, there will be no oral witness testimony at first hearings of fast track cases, but the appeal to a Police Appeals Tribunal will afford full rights to call witnesses.

5.   A case may be transferred from standard track to fast track, or from fast track to standard track, but on only one occasion either way. A referral of a case by the head of complaints and discipline to a chief officer for consideration of fast track does not count as a transfer for these purposes, and nor does a decision by the chief officer, having had a case so referred, that a case will not be fast tracked. Where fast track procedures are used and do not result in a finding against an officer, proceedings under the 'standard track' may not be used for what is effectively the same breach of the Code of Conduct.

Complaints cases

6.   Where a matter which meets the criteria for fast track has arisen from a complaint by a member of the public, the complainant will have the right to attend the fast track hearing. However, since the officer concerned will not be giving

evidence, the complainant will have no right or opportunity to put questions to the officer concerned. This will need to be explained carefully to the complainant in advance of the hearing.

Evidence

7. There will be no oral witness testimony at the fast track hearing. There will be the initial written record of the report, allegation or complaint accompanied by supporting evidence which might typically be written statements, supported by photographs, video or audio tapes, computer records and documentary evidence such as bank statements.

Fast track process

Timing

8. A decision to fast track may be made at any stage during an inquiry into a report, allegation or complaint. In some cases this will be simultaneous with a decision to lay a criminal charge and pass the file to the CPS for consideration of prosecution. In others, particularly during a long running surveillance operation, the point may be reached where the criteria for fast track are met and it would clearly be right to invoke the procedure and lay a criminal charge, but those carrying out the investigation need to continue to gather evidence before submitting a file to the CPS. (See also Section 3 paragraph 3.29.)

Criteria

9. Each of the following criteria must be met for the fast track procedure to be applied.
- The alleged breach of the Code of Conduct must be serious, criminal in nature such that, if the officer concerned was convicted, a period of imprisonment would be likely to result; and
- if proved, the conduct would in all probability attract a sanction of dismissal; and
- the evidence is overwhelming and does not rely solely on oral witness testimony; and
- the gravity of the alleged conduct is such that it is in the public interest, if proved, for the officer to be removed from the service as quickly as possible.

Procedure for consideration in advance of the hearing

10. The trigger to consider fast tracking a case will be evidence which goes to show that the above criteria are met. The head of the force complaints and discipline department will submit the case to the chief officer responsible to the Chief Constable (or responsible to the Commissioner in the Metropolitan Police) for complaints and discipline matters for consideration of invoking the fast track procedures. That officer will make the decision whether the case is to be fast tracked, based on the above criteria, the available evidence and any other relevant information.

11. If the chief officer decides that the case will not be fast tracked, he or she will refer it back to the complaints and discipline department to proceed under standard track procedures. This referral back will not count as transferring from fast track to standard track (see paragraph 5 above).

12. If the chief officer decides that the case will be fast tracked, he or she will sign a 'Fast track Notice' and arrangements should be made for the officer concerned to attend a meeting with the chief officer as soon as possible. At that meeting the officer concerned will be advised of the nature of the report, allegation or complaint, the decision to invoke the fast track procedures and the nature of the evidence being relied

on, copies of which will be handed to him or her. The officer concerned will also be told the date of the hearing and of his or her right to legal representation and to advice from a 'friend'.

13.   The date of the hearing will be not less than 21 days and not more than 28 days from the date the 'Fast track Notice' is served. The date of service starts the six week period for completion of the fast track process.

14.   If for any reason the 'Fast track Notice' and accompanying papers are not served on the officer concerned in person, they should be taken by hand or sent by recorded delivery to the officer concerned's registered address not more than 24 hours after the date that the meeting was scheduled to have taken place.

15.   Not later than two weeks prior to the date of the hearing, the officer concerned should signify his or her intention to admit or deny the alleged breach of the Code of Conduct.

Procedure for the hearing

16.   The fast track hearing will be presided over by the Chief Constable (Commissioner in the Metropolitan Police) or, if that person is not appropriate, by the Chief Constable of another force. The Chief Constable will be provided with the papers seven days prior to the hearing.

17.   In addition to the Chief Constable and the officer concerned, those entitled to be present at the hearing are: the head of complaints and discipline or more senior officer, to present the case as far as is necessary; the officer's legal representative and/or 'friend', a verbatim note taker (unless the proceedings are tape recorded), any complainant, and any other persons at the discretion of the Chief Constable and with the consent of the officer concerned. The hearing may take place in the absence of the accused officer.

18.   There will be no oral witness testimony. Unless the officer concerned has admitted, or admits at the hearing, the alleged breach of the Code of Conduct, the Chief Constable will invite the officer's legal representative and/or 'friend' to address him or her as to why the officer concerned should not be found to have breached the Code as alleged on the basis of the evidence provided. After hearing submissions the Chief Constable will:

(a)   find that the conduct has not been proved; or

(b)   decide that the matter requires further inquiry or testing of the evidence and refer it back for standard track proceedings (which is likely to await the outcome of criminal proceedings) to the stage of the appointment of the investigating officer; or

(c)   decide that the conduct has been proved.

19.   If the officer had admitted the allegation or the Chief Constable finds it proved on the balance of probabilities (see paragraph 3.70), written evidence of mitigation and antecedents are presented. After consideration of this evidence, the Chief Constable may impose punishment from the range available under the standard misconduct procedures (see paragraph 3.76), though it is likely that the most severe punishment of dismissal will normally be imposed. The Chief Officer will then advise the officer concerned or his or her rights of appeal.

20.   The Chief Constable's decisions and the reasons for those decisions are to be confirmed in writing to the officer concerned not more than 24 hours after the conclusion of the hearing.

Absence of officer concerned

21.   The hearing may proceed in the absence of the officer concerned, but the Chief Constable should ensure that a legal representative and/or 'friend' have the opportunity to be present to speak as necessary on behalf of the officer concerned.

Adjournment of the hearing
22.   The hearing may be adjourned by the Chief Constable for up to seven days, but this option may be exercised only once. If the officer concerned or his or her representative seeks an adjournment or adjournments, this may be for an aggregated period up to four weeks. If either time expires and the hearing does not proceed, the case is to be referred back to the complaints and discipline department for standard track procedures to be applied or resumed (which is likely to await the outcome of criminal proceedings).

Discipline book
23.   Where there has been a finding of breach of the Code of Conduct, the police authority will be informed and an entry made in the force discipline book.

Publication of outcomes
24.   Forces should bear in mind that it would be inadvisable for the outcome of a fast track hearing to be publicised. Questions from the media should therefore be handled with caution and in the light of legal advice.

Chief Constable's review
25.   The review by the Chief Constable afforded by the standard track procedures (see Section 4) is replicated in the fast track procedures by a review by a Chief Constable from another force.
26.   The review may concern either the finding that the Code of Conduct had been breached or the level of sanction imposed, or both. The process of the review should be as described in Section 4, summarised below and with exceptions as necessary. Schedule 2 of the Police (Conduct) Regulations 1999 gives the statutory provisions of the review.

Timing
27.   The notice requiring a review is to be lodged in writing by or on behalf of the officer concerned to the Chief Constable (Commissioner in the Metropolitan Police) within fourteen days of receiving written notification of the decisions of the hearing. This notice should state whether the officer wants the review to be carried out on the papers or for there to be a meeting. In either case, the officer concerned is to be provided without delay access to such parts of the recording or verbatim notes of the hearing as are necessary to establish the specific grounds for the request for the review.
28.   The review should be carried out by the Chief Constable within 30 days of receiving the written notification of the decision the hearing.

Review on the papers or at a meeting
29.   The review may be conducted either on the papers or at a meeting.
30.   If the officer concerned asks for the review to be carried out on the papers, he or she will be responsible for ensuring that the reviewing officer receives the grounds on which the review is sought not later than seven days after lodging the notification for the review.
31.   If the officer concerned asks for a meeting, he or she should be given seven days' written notice of the date for the review. Those present at the review will be the Reviewing Officer, the officer concerned and/or his or her legal representative and/or the officer concerned's 'friend', a verbatim note taker, the complainant, where applicable, and any other person at the discretion of the Reviewing Officer and the officer concerned. The review may take place in the absence of the officer concerned.

Review meeting
32.   The Reviewing Officer will hear oral submissions put by the officer concerned and/or his or her legal representative and/or 'friend' before reaching a decision.

Outcomes of the review

33. The Reviewing Officer will reach one of the following decisions as to the outcome of the review:

(a) that the conduct had not been proved to the required standard; or

(b) that the case should not have been fast tracked; or

(c) that the conduct was proved but the sanction imposed was too severe; or

(d) that the decision was correct.

34. These outcomes should then be taken forward in accordance with the following:

(a) the earlier decision will be quashed and the officer concerned reinstated;

(b) the outcome will be quashed and the case referred back to the officer concerned's force complaints and discipline department for consideration of standard tracking the matter;

(c) the Reviewing Officer will substitute another, less severe, sanction. Where this lesser sanction is requirement to resign or reduction in rank, the Reviewing Officer will advise the officer concerned of his or her right to appeal to a Police Appeals Tribunal;

(d) where the sanction was dismissal, requirement to resign or reduction in rank, the Reviewing Officer will advice the officer concerned of his or her right to appeal to a Police Appeals Tribunal (see paragraphs 36 to 38 below).

Notification in writing

35. The decisions and reasons for them are to be confirmed in writing to the officer concerned not more than 24 hours after the conclusion of the review.

Appeal to Police Appeals Tribunal

36. The right of appeal to a Police Appeals Tribunal is available to those officers who have been dismissed, required to resign or reduced in rank. Section 5 of this guidance describes the procedure to be followed.

37. In fast track cases, the Chief Constable's Review having been carried out by a Chief Constable from another force, the right of appeal is to a Tribunal set up by the officer concerned's own police authority.

38. In the light of the special circumstances of the fast track process, an officer eligible to appeal to a Police Appeals Tribunal may defer exercising that right until four weeks after the conclusion of criminal proceedings or a CPS decision not to bring criminal proceedings. An extension of this period may be granted at the discretion of the police authority.

SECTION 4
CHIEF CONSTABLE'S REVIEW

I. SCOPE

4.1 A police officer will have a right to ask his or her Chief Constable[1] to review any decision of an unsatisfactory performance hearing or a misconduct hearing.

4.2 The review will provide the opportunity for a Chief Constable to take quick action to rectify clear errors or inconsistencies in process or determination by the earlier hearing.

[1 The Commissioner in the City of London Police; in the Metropolitan Police, the officer's Assistant Commissioner (but see paragraph 4.11).]

II. THE REQUEST FOR A REVIEW

4.3   An officer will be told of his or her right to request a Chief Constable's[2] review when given the official notice of the hearing decisions (see paragraph 3.70). An officer who wishes his or her Chief Constable to review the decisions of the hearing in his or her case must ask the Chief Constable to do so within 14 days of receiving the written notification of the decisions of the hearing. In exceptional circumstances this period may be extended at the discretion of the Chief Constable. The request must be made in writing to the Chief Constable, whose office will copy it immediately to the case officer or personnel officer with responsibility for the case. Where an officer intends to seek a review he or she will be given access to such parts of the recording of the hearing as are necessary to establish the specific grounds for a review.

4.4   The request must make clear what aspects of the hearing's decisions the officer concerned wishes the Chief Constable to review and give the name(s) of the case/presenting officer or the relevant personnel officer, the date of the hearing and the name of the presiding officer. It must also give the decisions as to the officer's future taken by the hearing. It must be accompanied by written grounds in support of the request.

4.5   The case/presenting officer or personnel officer will return the request for a review to the Chief Constable's office, as soon as practicable, together with the account of the officer who presided at the hearing (which will have detailed the reasons for the hearing's decisions and will have been copied to the officer concerned following the conclusion of the hearing). No further action on the case/presenting officer's or personnel officer's part will normally be required, unless the request for a review contains important new statements whose accuracy needs to be checked.

4.6   The aim should be for the presiding officer's account to be in the Chief Constable's possession within one week of receiving the request for a review. Chief Constables will be expected to deal with requests for review as soon as practicable. This should be within one week of the Chief Constable receiving the presiding officer's account. However, there may be exceptional circumstances where this period should be extended, in particular where an officer has been dealt with for a breach of the Code on criminal conduct and has notified that an appeal against criminal conviction is pending.

III. THE REVIEW

4.7   Unless the officer concerned requests a personal hearing, which must be granted, the Chief Constable will conduct the review on the basis of the account of the hearing prepared by the presiding officer and the representations made by the officer concerned in the request for a review. Before or during the review it will be open to the Chief Constable to seek extra information from the presiding officer if this is considered necessary (e.g. the officer concerned may have raised a matter in the request for a review which is not adequately covered in the presiding officer's account of the hearing). Where this is done, both the request for the information and the information itself should be in writing, and copies of the request and the presiding officer's response should be supplied to the officer concerned.

4.8   Where a personal hearing takes place, this will not amount to a fresh re-hearing of the case. Rather, it will be an opportunity for the officer concerned to state his or her grounds for seeking a review of the hearing's decisions in person, and will allow the Chief Constable to question the officer concerned about those grounds or any other relevant points.

[2 Where a case has been dealt with under the fast track (special cases) procedure, the review will be carried out by another Chief Constable.]

4.9   The officer concerned may be accompanied to a personal hearing by a 'friend'. Where the officer concerned was entitled to be legally represented at the original hearing he or she may also be accompanied to any personal hearing by his or her legal representative. The role of the 'friend' or legal representative will be to advise and assist the officer concerned, including speaking on the officer's behalf. The Chief Constable will, throughout any personal hearing, give the officer concerned the opportunity to speak personally. Any other person may be present at the personal hearing at the Chief Constable's discretion. The review may proceed in the absence of the officer concerned.

4.10   The Chief Constable must have had no previous involvement in the case under review, and nor must he or she have any detailed knowledge of the case prior to the request for a review.

4.11   If the Chief Constable (Commissioner in the City of London, Assistant Commissioner in the Metropolitan Police) is absent, unavailable or was previously involved in the case, the review will be conducted by their designated Deputy. If the designated Deputy has previously been involved in the case or has overall responsibility for complaints and discipline matters, the case will be reviewed by another Chief Constable or, in the Metropolitan Police, another Assistant Commissioner. A Chief Constable from another force conducting the review will consider the case and make a recommendation as to whether to uphold or vary the decisions of the hearing to the Chief Constable of the officer concerned, who will remain responsible for the implementation of the decision. In the Metropolitan Police another Assistant Commissioner will review the case and uphold or vary the decisions as if he or she were the Assistant Commissioner for the area in question.

4.12   The task of the Chief Constable in conducting the review will be to determine whether the original hearing was conducted fairly and whether the outcome decided upon appears to have been justified and appropriate to the nature of the case. Reviews must be carried out fairly and in accordance with the principles of natural justice. The Chief Constable will be responsible for determining the course of the review.

4.13   The Chief Constable will read or hear the grounds put forward by the officer concerned in his or her request for a review, together with any representations made at a personal hearing by the officer and his or her 'friend' or legal representative, and will consider the presiding officer's account of the hearing. The Chief Constable may also consider any further information requested from the presiding officer (paragraph 4.7 refers). Where there is some dispute about an element of the original hearing the Chief Constable may call for and consider the relevant part of the recording of the hearing or a transcript of the relevant part of the recording.

IV. THE OUTCOME

4.14   The Chief Constable, having read or heard the matters put forward by the officer concerned in his or her request for a review, in conjunction with the presiding officer's account and any further information provided by the presiding officer, may concur fully with the decisions of the hearing, or may conclude that the decisions of the hearing should be varied. The Chief Constable may thus decide to overturn a decision at the original hearing that the conduct of officer concerned did not meet the standard required, or decide that the sanction imposed was not appropriate. It will not be open to the Chief Constable to increase the seriousness of the outcome.

4.15   Once the Chief Constable has reached a decision, he or she will inform the officer concerned of the outcome of the review. The Chief Constable will make a written record of the reasons for his or her determination and, in the case of a variation of the decisions of the hearing, specify the revised outcome. It will be the responsibility of the case officer or personnel officer to arrange for copies of the note recording the Chief Constable's decision to be sent, within seven days of the completion of the review, to the officer concerned and to the personnel officer responsible for implementing the decision as to outcome.

4.16   Whether or not there is a personal hearing, the aim should be for the review to have been conducted and the result notified to the officer concerned within four weeks of the receipt of the request for the review, and in no case should this be later than 30 days (in an unsatisfactory performance case) or 60 days (in a misconduct case) after the date of the original hearing.

4.17   Where the outcome of the Chief Constable's review is that the officer concerned is to be dismissed, required to resign or reduced in rank, the officer will be notified in writing of his or her right of appeal against this decision to a Police Appeals Tribunal (see Section 5). This will be done at the same time as the officer is notified of the outcome of the review.

4.18   Where the outcome of the Chief Constable's review is a decision to vary any part of the outcome of a misconduct hearing, his or her decision will have effect from the date of the decision of the original hearing.

SECTION 5
APPEALS TO POLICE APPEALS TRIBUNALS

I. SCOPE

5.1   An officer who has been dismissed, required to resign or reduced in rank following a hearing and the Chief Constable's review of the hearing's decisions has a right of appeal to a Police Appeals Tribunal. An appeal may be lodged in respect of the finding of the hearing and the sanction imposed or in respect of the sanction alone. There is no right of appeal to a Police Appeals Tribunal where any of the lesser sanctions have been imposed, whether at the original hearing or as a result of a Chief Constable's review.

5.2   A Police Appeals Tribunal has the power to overturn a finding of a breach of the Code of Conduct, to reinstate an officer in his or her force and/or former rank (but not to a particular post or appointment, such as detective), or to impose a less severe sanction than that being appealed against, provided that such a sanction was available to the original hearing.

II. NOTIFICATION OF RIGHT OF APPEAL

5.3   Where the outcome of the Chief Constable's review is that the officer concerned is to be dismissed, required to resign or reduced in rank, the officer must be advised of the right of appeal to a Police Appeals Tribunal. This must be done in writing at the same time as the notification to the officer of the outcome of the Chief Constable's review.

III. NOTICE AND GROUNDS OF APPEAL

5.4   If the officer concerned (hereafter referred to as the appellant) wishes to exercise the right of appeal he or she must give notice of this in writing to the police authority,[1] who are responsible for appointing a Police Appeals Tribunal, with a copy

[1 The designated Home Office official of The Metropolitan Police Committee in Metropolitan Police cases.]

to his or her chief officer. This notice must be submitted within 21 days of the date on which the appellant was notified in writing of the outcome of the Chief Constable's Review.

5.5   Having lodged a notice of appeal, the appellant must submit to the Tribunal (via the police authority) a full statement of the grounds on which the appeal is based, and any supporting documents or statements, within 28 days of the date on which he or she received a copy of the transcript of the original hearing (see paragraph 5.8).

5.6   A Police Appeals Tribunal may decide to determine a case without a hearing provided that all parties to the appeal have been given an opportunity to make written or oral representations for the holding of a hearing. The grounds of appeal will therefore need to be accompanied by any written representations that the appellant wishes to make in support of an oral hearing of the appeal, or any request to make oral representations to the Chairman of the Tribunal for the holding of a hearing, or a statement to the effect that the appellant does not wish to make any such representations. Where, having decided originally not to make any such representations, the appellant considers that there has been a material development in the case which causes him or her to wish to reverse that decision, it will be open to the appellant to make representations to the Chairman of the Tribunal for the holding of an oral hearing of the appeal.

Extensions of time limits

Notice of appeal

5.7   There may be circumstances where the notice of appeal just fails to meet the deadline for its submission (see paragraph 5.4). In such a case it will be within the discretion of the police authority to accept the notice.

5.8   Where the officer concerned has been dealt with under the fast track procedures (see the Appendix to Section 3) the standard time limit for notice of appeal to a Police Appeals Tribunal does not apply. An officer in this category may exercise his or her right of appeal up to four weeks after the conclusion of criminal proceedings or decision by the CPS not to proceed with criminal prosecution, sending the notice of appeal in the normal way to the police authority (see paragraph 5.4) but clearly identifying the case as one which was dealt with under the fast track (special cases) procedures. If the officer concerned does not meet this time limit for lodging a notice of appeal, he or she may seek an extension in accordance with paragraph 5.7.

Grounds of appeal

5.9   If the appellant has particular reasons for seeking an extension of the period for submitting the grounds of appeal (see paragraph 5.5) he or she should submit them to the police authority and give a clear indication as to when he or she is likely to be able to submit the grounds of appeal. The police authority will invite a Tribunal Chairman to consider the application for an extension and decide whether it should be granted, either for the full period requested by the appellant or for such other period as the Chairman considers reasonable. This will not, however, preclude the appellant from subsequently amending the grounds of appeal where there is a material change in the circumstances of his or her case, for instance, new evidence or witnesses. In such circumstances, the Chairman of the Tribunal will have discretion to allow the amendment to be made.

5.10   There may be special circumstances, for example the emergence of significant new evidence at a later date, which cause an officer to reverse an earlier decision not to appeal. In such a case it will be open to the officer to lodge a notice of appeal with the police authority, notwithstanding the fact that the time limit for doing so may have long passed. The notice must be accompanied by the reasons for wishing to lodge an 'out of time' appeal. Where such a notice is received the police authority will appoint a Tribunal Chairman to consider whether or not the appeal should be heard. If it is decided that the appeal should not be heard, the officer concerned must be informed in writing by the police authority of the reasons for this decision. If it is decided that the appeal should be heard, the procedures for doing so will be as if the appeal was 'in time'.

IV. THE RESPONDENT

5.11   In appeals by officers of or below the rank of Superintendent, the respondent is the officer's Chief Constable. When the respondent receives a copy of the notice of appeal he or she must make available to the police authority a copy of the report of the officer who presided at the hearing, which sets out the decisions of the hearing and the reasons for them; the relevant case papers (which is those papers that were presented to the original hearing); a copy of the note recording the outcome of the Chief Constable's review; and a copy of the transcript of the original hearing (which should at the same time be copied to the appellant). This should be done as soon as practicable. The respondent should then, within 21 days of receiving the copy of the grounds of appeal, submit to the Tribunal (via the police authority) the response to the arguments put forward in the appellant's grounds of appeal, with a copy to the appellant (who will have received a copy of the presiding officer's report of the original hearing and the note recording the outcome of the Chief Constable's review). The response to the appeal should normally be drafted by the officer who presided at the original hearing in the case.

V. POLICE APPEALS TRIBUNALS

5.12   On receipt of a notice of appeal it will be the responsibility of the police authority to appoint a Tribunal Chairman to consider any application from the appellant for an extension of the period allowed for the submission of the grounds of appeal; to consider any written or oral representations regarding the holding of an oral hearing of the appeal; to consider any application to amend the grounds of appeal; or to decide whether or not an 'out of time' appeal should be heard. It will also be the police authority's responsibility to appoint the remaining members of the Tribunal to consider and determine the appeal. Thereafter the police authority will be responsible for making any necessary arrangements for the Tribunal's consideration of the appeal.

5.13   The Tribunal appointed by the police authority will consist of a legally qualified Chairman drawn from a list maintained by the Home Office; a member of the police authority (ideally with relevant experience) nominated by the authority;[2] a serving or former chief officer (of a force other than that of the appellant) drawn from a list maintained by the Home Office; and a retired officer of appropriate rank, also drawn from a list supplied by the Home Office (where the appellant was a Superintendent this officer would be a retired Chief Superintendent or Superintendent and, in all other cases, a retired officer of the rank of Chief Inspector or below).

5.14   A Police Appeals Tribunal may decide to determine an appeal without a hearing, provided that there has been an opportunity for both parties to the appeal to make written or, if they wish, oral representations as to the holding of a hearing and that any such representations have been considered by the Chairman. A Tribunal may

[2 In Metropolitan Police cases the place of the police authority member will be filled by a member of the Metropolitan Police Committee.]

proceed to determine the appeal without further notice once representations have been considered or in the absence of such representations. Where an appeal hearing is held, or oral representations are made, the appellant and respondent will have a right to be legally represented or to be represented by a serving member of a police force. Where a hearing is held the procedure to be adopted at the hearing will be a matter for the Chairman of the Tribunal to decide, subject to the guidance contained in the following paragraphs.

5.15   Where a hearing is to be held, the Tribunal will give notice of the date of the hearing to the appellant and respondent not less than 28 days before that date. A shorter period of notice may be given with the agreement of both parties to the appeal. Appeals should be heard as soon as possible.

5.16   The Tribunal have discretion to proceed with the hearing in the absence of either party, whether represented or not, if it appears to be just and proper to do so. Where it is decided to proceed in the absence of either party the Tribunal will record its reasons for doing so. The Tribunal may adjourn the appeal as necessary.

5.17   Any hearing of an appeal, or of oral representations, will be held in private. The persons attending the hearing will normally be confined to the appellant and respondent, their representatives and any witnesses. Where the case under appeal arose originally as a result of a complaint from a member of the public, the complainant will be notified by the police authority of the date of the hearing and may be present throughout the hearing; provided that, if he or she is to be called as a witness, he or she should not be allowed to attend before this point. If the Chairman of the Tribunal considers it appropriate, the complainant and any witnesses may be accompanied by a friend or relative, to whose presence the same rules and restrictions will apply. A Tribunal will have discretion to allow other persons to attend the whole or part of the hearing if it considers this to be desirable. In addition, under the terms of the Tribunals and Inquiries Act 1992, a member of the Council on Tribunals may attend a hearing as part of the Council's supervisory function in respect of Police Appeals Tribunals.

5.18   Where, however, it appears to the Tribunal that evidence is to be given by a witness which might disclose information which ought not to be disclosed to a member of the public, the Tribunal may require any member of the public present to withdraw while that evidence is given. In particular, the Tribunal will normally require any member of the public present, including the complainant, to withdraw where evidence is to be given in mitigation (e.g. evidence relating to the appellant's character, service history or domestic circumstances).

5.19   Police Appeals Tribunals are not bound by strict rules of criminal procedure but must be conducted fairly. As regards evidence, particularly the admissibility of 'hearsay' evidence, they should follow the procedures described elsewhere in this guidance. A Tribunal will need to take account of all relevant evidence and background information in deciding an appeal, and may consider both written and oral evidence. Written evidence may be adduced only with the agreement of both parties but a Tribunal may nevertheless decide to call for the evidence to be given orally.

5.20   It is for the Tribunal to decide on the admissibility of any evidence, or to determine whether or not any question should or should not be put to a witness.

5.21   Any witnesses appearing before a Tribunal may be subject to examination and cross-examination. Under section 250 of the Local Government Act 1972 a Tribunal will have the power to require the attendance of witnesses or the production of documents.

5.22   A verbatim record of the proceedings will be taken and will be kept for seven years.

VI. DETERMINATION AND OUTCOME OF APPEAL

5.23   A Tribunal need not be unanimous in its determination of the appeal or of any other decision before it and may reach a decision based on majority voting. Where a Tribunal finds itself divided equally, the Chairman will have a second or casting vote.

5.24   In appeals against the findings of a hearing and the sanction imposed, the Tribunal will need to determine whether, on the basis of the evidence or material presented, it was reasonable for the hearing to conclude that the appellant's conduct or performance fell below the required standards and, if so, whether it was reasonable for the hearing to impose the sanction that it did. Where an appeal is against sanction only, the Tribunal will simply need to determine whether the sanction imposed could reasonably be considered to have been an appropriate response to the poor conduct or performance of the appellant. In misconduct appeals, when reaching their determination, the Tribunal will apply the appropriate standard of proof (see Section 3, paragraphs 3.66 and 3.67).

5.25   A Tribunal may dismiss or allow an appeal. Where an appeal against finding and sanction is allowed, a Tribunal will order the reinstatement of the officer in his or her force and/or former rank. Where an appeal against sanction only is allowed, a Tribunal may impose a sanction less severe than that which is the subject of the appeal, provided that such a sanction was available to the original hearing. Where an appeal is allowed, the order made by the Tribunal will replace the decision appealed against and will take effect from the date of the original decision.

5.26   The Chairman of a Tribunal is required to prepare a written statement of the Tribunal's determination of the appeal and the reasons for it. This statement will be sent, normally within four weeks of the conclusion of the appeal, to the police authority, who will copy it to the appellant and to the respondent. Where the decision appealed against arose from a case involving a complaint from a member of the public the police authority should notify the complainant of the outcome of the appeal, whether or not the complainant attended the hearing of the appeal. The notification to the complainant should simply consist of a statement to the effect that the appeal was either allowed or disallowed and, if relevant, whether there was a variation of sanction.

5.27   A Tribunal may direct that the whole or any part of the appellant's costs should be met by the police authority. It will normally do so where the appeal is allowed and, if it is not, where the appeal was soundly based and not frivolous or vexatious. Where no direction is given the appellant will pay the whole of his or her own costs. The respondent's costs, and any remuneration or expenses paid to Tribunal members, will be met by the police authority.

5.28   An officer ordered to be reinstated in his or her former force or rank will be deemed to have served in his or her force and/or rank continuously from the date of the original decision to the date of reinstatement. Where the Tribunal orders the reinstatement of an officer it may order the restoration of the officer's pay for this period, including London Weighting, and any allowances which have necessarily continued to be incurred (but not any allowances which might otherwise have been payable) and will normally do so in all such cases.

ANNEX A
APPOINTMENT OF AN INVESTIGATING OFFICER FROM ANOTHER FORCE

1.   Whether or not an investigating officer has already been appointed to conduct a formal misconduct investigation, the force (or the Police Complaints Authority) may request that an officer from another police force conduct the investigation. In

considering whether to call in an officer from another force, the force should take into account:

(a)   the seriousness of the allegations;

(b)   the rank of the officer or officers against whom they are made;

(c)   the interests of bringing greater independence to the investigation of complaints; and

(d)   the extent to which the incident giving rise to the complaint (or to concerns about an officer's conduct) has been or may be the subject of public concern or publicity.

2.   The procedure might be especially appropriate where, for example, a number of complaints allege widespread malpractice or where a particular incident leads to serious public concern. An investigating officer appointed from another force should have had no previous contact with the case nor recent contact with the requesting force which might give rise to doubts as to his or her impartiality.

Financial arrangements between forces

3.   Where an investigating officer is appointed from another force, provision of the investigating officer should not be regarded as mutual aid within the meaning of section 24 of the Police Act 1996, and arrangements made under section 24(4) therefore do not apply.

4.   As a general principle, outside investigation should not be so much more expensive than internal investigation that forces are deterred from seeking it in cases where it would clearly be appropriate. Conversely, the investigating force should not be put to extra expense as a result of undertaking the investigation. Subject to these general principles, any agreement between two forces to carry out investigations for one another on a 'knock-for-knock' basis, or under any other mutually agreed arrangement which cuts down on administration costs, is fully acceptable.

5.   More generally, it is for the two forces concerned to agree on what financial basis the investigation shall be undertaken. Clearly it is preferable, where possible, for an agreement to be in place between two forces in advance of need specifying the financial basis to be adopted, and it would normally be expected that any such agreement would conform to the principles set out below.

6.   It is considered to reflect the general community of interest, and also avoids work all round, for the force which supplies the investigating officer normally to make no claim on the requesting force, except for out-of-pocket expenses. In the case of most investigations these should amount to no more than the officers' travelling and subsistence expenses, plus any payment for overtime and rest day working, etc.

7.   However, where an investigation proves to be exceptionally long and complex, possibly involving provision of a team of officers, it would seem right for the investigating force to make a more substantial claim on the requesting force since the absence of so many officers over a prolonged period will have involved them in extra expense, e.g. for substitution and temporary promotion payments.

8.   It is therefore recommended, as a basis for agreement between forces, that the requesting force be prepared to pay all the additional expenses occasioned by the investigation. In the absence of any other specific agreement between the two forces concerned, this should be the expected basis for payment for a major investigation involving such additional expenses.

ANNEX B
NOTIFICATION OF INVESTIGATION TO OFFICER CONCERNED

1.   In misconduct cases, the notification of the investigation to the officer concerned must be in writing and must detail the nature of the complaint or concern that

is to be investigated. On being notified of the investigation the officer concerned should be advised that he or she has a right to seek advice from a staff association representative, if he or she has not already done so, and to be accompanied to any meeting, interview or hearing by a 'friend', who must be a serving police officer and not otherwise involved in the case. The officer concerned should at the same time also be given an opportunity to give his or her account of the conduct in question, if he or she wishes. At any meeting or interview the officer concerned should be advised that he or she is not obliged to say anything but may make a written or oral statement about the matter and that any such statement may be used in subsequent misconduct proceedings.

2.   The notification is the responsibility of the investigating officer, who may carry it out personally or arrange for it to be done by another officer on his or her behalf. In particular, the investigating officer is accountable for the timing of the notification.

3.   The investigating officer should consider at the outset of the investigation whether there is any reason why he or she should not inform the officer concerned that an alleged failure to meet the standards set out in the Code of Conduct is being investigated. Subject to the guidance contained in the following paragraphs, the presumption in all cases will be that the officer concerned should be informed.

4.   The officer concerned must be notified of the investigation as soon as is reasonably practicable. The investigating officer may first need to move to secure any evidence and to clarify details of the complaint or concern about the conduct in question. There may also be occasions where to inform the officer at the start of the investigation might prejudice it. It should be borne in mind, though, that the investigating officer may be called upon to justify any delay in notifying the officer concerned which might have been prejudicial to him or her.

5.   Where the investigating officer decides that it is necessary to delay notification this decision should be subject to regular scrutiny and review in order to avoid undue delay. Chief officers should ensure that they have satisfactory procedures in place for this scrutiny and review.

6.   Nothing in the preceding paragraphs is intended to change the practice whereby, if an officer is the subject of information (whether arising from a complaint or any other source) which suggests that he or she may have committed a criminal offence, a normal criminal investigation will take place; or to imply that, in such a case, the officer must immediately be informed of the allegations if this might impede investigation of the alleged criminal offence.

ANNEX C
WRITTEN WARNINGS IN COMPLAINTS CASES

1.   Written warnings from a Superintendent may be given only where the officer concerned admits the conduct in question and when a more serious sanction, following a hearing, is not considered appropriate. However, special considerations arise in cases involving the Police Complaints Authority (PCA).

2.   Where, following the investigation of a complaint, it is considered that a written warning would be an appropriate response (provided the officer concerned admits the conduct in question) the agreement of the PCA should be sought *before* any approach is made to the officer concerned about a written warning.

3.   The memorandum that is required to be sent to the PCA under section 75 of the 1996 Act should give the reasons for proposing not to hold a misconduct hearing and indicate that, provided the officer concerned admits the conduct complained of, it is proposed to deal with the matter by way of a written warning. The PCA may agree or disagree with this proposal.

4. Where the PCA *disagree* with the proposal to issue a written warning they may recommend or, if necessary, direct that a misconduct hearing be held. Where the PCA's recommendation is accepted, or a direction is issued, the officer concerned must appear before a hearing, even if he or she admits the conduct complained of.

5. Where the PCA *agree* with the proposal to issue a written warning they will notify the force and the complainant accordingly. At this point, and not before, the officer concerned may be informed that, if he or she admits the conduct complained of, it is proposed to give a written warning. If the officer concerned does admit the conduct in question arrangements may then be made for a written warning to be given. If the officer does not admit the conduct in question a written warning may not be given and the case will need to proceed to a hearing. The PCA should be informed accordingly.

ANNEX D
LEGAL REPRESENTATION

1. Section 84 of the 1996 Act provides that an officer may not be dismissed, required to resign or reduced in rank as a result of a hearing unless he or she has been given an opportunity to elect to be legally represented at the hearing. (Appeals to Police Appeals Tribunals carry an automatic right to legal representation.)

2. Accordingly, an officer who is to appear before an unsatisfactory performance hearing must be given the opportunity to elect to be legally represented at the hearing since it could result in the officer being required to resign or reduced in rank. In misconduct cases the consideration of this issue is less straightforward.

3. In misconduct cases there are two opposing considerations to be borne in mind. On the one hand, the outcomes available to the hearing will be limited to imposing a sanction no more severe than a fine if the officer concerned is not given an opportunity to elect to be legally represented. On the other hand, the number of occasions on which the right to elect for legal representation is offered should be kept to the minimum for the following reasons (among others):

(a) Such an offer is in effect a warning to the officer concerned that, if the misconduct is established, he or she is liable to receive one of the most severe sanctions; if it is given unnecessarily it is likely to cause the officer considerable needless anxiety;

(b) In such a situation the officer concerned may well feel that he or she ought to retain a lawyer rather than a police officer 'friend', which could be very expensive for the officer or relevant staff association; and

(c) Where the officer does elect to be legally represented the presenting officer's role at the hearing may be taken by a lawyer, which also has considerable cost implications.

4. It is therefore essential that the opportunity to elect to be legally represented at a misconduct hearing should be given if, and only if, there is a genuine prospect of the hearing considering a sanction of dismissal, requirement to resign or reduction in rank appropriate to the case.

Procedure

5. In misconduct cases the officer in charge of complaints and discipline, who will have decided that a hearing should be held, will be responsible for deciding whether or not the officer concerned should be given the opportunity to elect for legal representation. Where, in such a case, it is decided that legal representation should be offered, this must be done at the same time as the officer concerned is notified of the

decision to hold a hearing. In an unsatisfactory performance case, this must be done at the same time as the officer is notified of the date for the hearing or, if there is to be a delay in arranging a date for the hearing, at the time the officer is notified of the decision to hold a hearing.

6. The right conferred by the legislation is a right not to receive the most severe sanctions unless the offer has been made of legal representation at the officer's expense. If the officer gives notice that he or she does not wish to be so represented, or without reasonable cause fails within the time limit (see below) to give an indication of his or her wishes, the sanctions of loss of job or rank will be available to the hearing.

7. The officer concerned is required to indicate his or her decision on the matter of legal representation within 14 days of being notified of the decision to hold a misconduct hearing or of the date for an unsatisfactory performance hearing, or of receiving the copies of the papers for the hearing if this is later. If the officer fails within this period, without reasonable cause, to indicate his or her decision, this will be taken as a decision not to be legally represented at the hearing.

8. There may be cases in which two (or more) officers are to appear before a misconduct hearing in respect of the same matter where there is a reasonable likelihood that the sanction imposed on one will be loss of job or rank but on the other(s) a lesser sanction is more likely, perhaps because of differences of rank or in the perceived level of culpability. If it is decided that the cases should nonetheless be heard together, the right to elect legal representation should be offered to both officers.

ANNEX E
OFFICERS APPOINTED TO CONDUCT HEARINGS

1. This annex specifies the officers who will conduct unsatisfactory performance or misconduct hearings and sets out the considerations which should be borne in mind when appointing such officers.

2. Where the officer concerned is below the rank of Superintendent the hearing will be presided over by an Assistant Chief Constable with two officers of Superintendent rank acting as assessors. Where the officer concerned is a Superintendent the presiding officer will be an Assistant Chief Constable with two Assistant Chief Constables from outside the force (or Metropolitan Police Commanders) acting as assessors.

3. In the Metropolitan Police, hearings will be presided over by a Commander with two Superintendents acting as assessors or, where the officer concerned is a Superintendent, by a Commander from the same Area (where there is one) as the officer concerned with two Commanders from another Area (who have not had any supervisory responsibility for the officer concerned in the preceding two years) acting as assessors. In the City of London Police, hearings will be presided over by the Assistant Commissioner or Commander with two Superintendents acting as assessors or, where the officer concerned is a Superintendent, by a Commander or the Assistant Commissioner with two Assistant Chief Constables or Metropolitan Police Commanders acting as assessors.

4. None of the officers conducting a hearing should have earlier been involved in the case, nor should they have earlier been charged with the function of deciding that the proceedings should be held.

5. It is recognised that, in certain circumstances, the officer who would normally preside at a hearing will of necessity have at least some knowledge of a case while it is still under consideration. For example, in a misconduct case where the matters raised are *prima facie* serious and would amount to a substantial criticism of the force,

or where officers of higher rank are involved, the officer is likely to have kept him or herself informed as to the progress of the case. Such considerations might also arise in relation to unsatisfactory performance proceedings, particularly those concerning officers of higher rank. In such circumstances, it would normally be appropriate for another officer to preside over the hearing.

6.   If the officer who would normally preside over the hearing is interested in the case otherwise than in his or her capacity as a senior officer of the force, he or she should consider whether it would be more appropriate for another officer to preside over the hearing. It is not possible to define exactly the circumstances that would make such a decision necessary. They would, however, typically arise where the officer who would normally preside at the hearing had a connection with the officer concerned, or with someone connected with the case, which went so far beyond the purely professional that a suspicion of bias might arise. A family or close, out of office, social relationship are examples of such a connection. Any personal interest in the case which was insufficient to make it necessary for another officer to preside at the hearing should, nevertheless, be declared.

7.   Circumstances might arise where it would be more appropriate for an officer from another force to preside over a hearing. This could be because the officer who would normally preside had some involvement or connection with the case, or with the officer concerned, and either the same or similar considerations applied to the other senior officers in the force, or there was no alternative senior officer available. In such circumstances, consideration should be given to appointing an officer from another force to preside over the hearing.

8.   The principles outlined in the preceding paragraphs should be borne in mind in all cases. However, every effort should be made, consistent with the need for fairness towards the officer concerned, for the hearing to be presided over by an officer from the officer concerned's own force.

9.   The two officers to be appointed as assessors at the hearing should have no line management responsibility for the officer concerned, nor should they have a close connection (professional or otherwise) with the officer concerned, or with someone connected with the case, such as might give rise to a suspicion of bias. In the vast majority of cases it should be possible to avoid any potential difficulties by appointing as assessors officers from a division or unit other than that of the officer concerned. Where this is not possible, consideration should be given to appointing officers from another force to act as assessors. Every effort should be made, consistent with the need for fairness towards the officer concerned, for the assessors to be appointed from the same force as the officer concerned (unless he or she is a Superintendent, in which case the assessors will be officers from another force or, in the Metropolitan Police, from another area).

ANNEX F
EVIDENCE AT HEARINGS

1.   Hearings must be conducted fairly but need not be bound by the technical rules of evidence which apply in criminal proceedings. The officers conducting the hearing will be responsible for determining whether any particular piece of evidence is acceptable.

2.   It is neither expected nor desired that evidence should necessarily be collected or presented in the way which would be necessary for a criminal case, although evidence which has been collected in that way (in order to deal with any criminal allegation) will, of course, be acceptable. However, great care should be taken with

'hearsay' evidence, i.e. unsubstantiated statements offered by witnesses based upon what someone else has said and not upon personal knowledge or observation. Such statements should in general only be relied on if:

    (a)   there are reasons which make it impracticable to expect the original speaker to give evidence him or herself, for example because he or she has gone overseas for a protracted period; and

    (b)   the content is clearly relevant to the conduct at issue; and

    (c)   every effort has been made not only to test the reliability of what is reported, for example by comparing it with the available direct evidence, but also to assess the reliability of the witness, insofar as this is possible.

    3.   Even where these conditions are satisfied, and the hearsay material is put before the hearing, the officers taking the hearing should treat it with great caution and, in his or her account of the hearing, the presiding officer should specify the extent to which the hearing relied upon it.

Editing of statements

    4.   Statements taken from any person which include material not relevant to the issues before the hearing or not capable of proof should, as far as practicable, be edited to remove such material. The purpose of this is to avoid prejudicing the officers taking the hearing by the introduction of extraneous material. It should be borne in mind that blank spaces or over-markings in a copy of a statement can themselves indicate that possibly prejudicial material has been removed or hidden. The editing should therefore be done in such a way as not to reveal that it has taken place, for example by retyping the full, edited statement.

Rehabilitation of Offenders Act 1974

    5.   Evidence of criminal convictions which are 'spent' under the provisions of this Act may be given in misconduct proceedings, and questions may be asked to reveal any such convictions (paragraph 3 of Schedule 3 to the Rehabilitation of Offenders Act 1974 (Exceptions) Order 1975). However, it is suggested that the practice in misconduct proceedings should accord with that followed in the criminal courts in such circumstances. Therefore, if any of the parties at a misconduct hearing intends to refer to the 'spent' convictions of a witness, or ask questions about such convictions, he or she should first seek authority to do so, preferably at or before the beginning of the hearing, from the officer presiding over the hearing. Authority should be given only where it is considered that the interests of justice require the evidence to be admitted. The admission of evidence about 'spent' convictions does not automatically require the withdrawal from the proceedings of any members of the public present, such as the complainant in a complaints case.

Records of police officers' fingerprints

    6.   The Police Regulations provide for records to be kept of the fingerprints of all serving officers, but it should be clearly understood that this provision is made solely for the purpose of eliminating the fingerprints of officers at the scenes of crimes. This fingerprint collection is not to be used in order to provide evidence in any misconduct proceedings brought against a member of a police force. In the majority of cases where fingerprint evidence is desirable, it will probably follow a criminal investigation when fingerprints will have been taken as part of that enquiry and will be available as evidence.

    7.   The same principle applies to photographs held for official purposes.

ANNEX G
WITNESSES

1.   The following does not apply to fast track 'special case' hearings (see the Appendix to Section 3).

2.   In all other cases, an officer who is to appear before a hearing may call witnesses to speak on his or her behalf. Such witnesses may be in addition to any whose evidence is in dispute and who are therefore to be called to speak at the hearing (witnesses whose evidence is not in dispute need not be called).

3.   On being notified of the date for the hearing the officer concerned should be asked to indicate whether he or she wishes to call any witnesses and, if so, to provide their details. In some cases the officer concerned may not have decided at this stage whether to call witnesses, or may not be able to provide their details immediately. There is no objection to this, and the officer concerned should be allowed to give his or her response as soon as possible thereafter. The officer concerned may make his or her own arrangements for the attendance of witnesses, or may ask the case/presenting officer to make such arrangements on his or her behalf.

4.   All witnesses who are to be called to appear before a hearing should be warned in advance that they may be required on the day in question. Any police officer who is to appear as a witness will be ordered to attend the hearing. Any other person should be invited to indicate whether or not he or she is prepared to attend the hearing as a witness. Where such an individual indicates an unwillingness to attend, the chief officer may apply to the Crown Office of the Supreme Court for a *subpoena ad testificandum*, the service of which should be in accordance with the Rules of the Supreme Court. In cases where a witness fails to attend the hearing, the officers taking the hearing will need to decide whether it is reasonable to proceed with the hearing in the absence of the witness.

Interviewing witnesses

5.   Every effort should be made to assist the officer concerned, his or her 'friend' or legal representative to interview witnesses who might be called in the officer's defence. Cases may arise where the public interest in the protection of classified or otherwise sensitive information might require the presence of a senior officer of the force at interviews of this kind. Normally, however, the interviews should be permitted to take place in the absence of both the investigating officer and any other officer.

ANNEX H
OTHER PERSONS WHO MAY ATTEND A HEARING

1.   In addition to those individuals directly involved in a hearing it will sometimes be helpful, in the interests of gaining experience, for prospective presiding officers, presenting officers, assessors or 'friends' to attend hearings in their own force as observers. There is no objection to this, nor to such officers attending a hearing in a force other than their own, provided in all cases that the presiding officer gives permission and the officer concerned does not object. It must be made clear that such an officer is present simply as an observer and that he or she will take no part in the proceedings.

2.   Similarly, the attendance at hearings of a member or an official of the Police Complaints Authority (other than as an observer in a misconduct case where the proceedings follow a recommendation or direction from the Authority), an official of the Home Office or the Crown Prosecution Service, or a lawyer[1] may sometimes be

---

[1 It is recommended that a lawyer may be allowed to attend where the Police Federation or Superintendents' Association have indicated that he or she is likely to be used in the future to advise or represent their members at hearings or to appear before a Police Appeals Tribunal.]

acceptable, at the presiding officer's discretion and with the consent of the officer concerned. It must be made clear that such an individual is present simply as an observer and will take no part in the proceedings. In addition, the complainant or a witness may find it helpful to have a friend in attendance for support, particularly in cases of a sensitive or delicate nature, and it is within the presiding officer's discretion to allow this.

3. The preceding paragraphs provide examples of the individuals who, although not directly involved, may attend hearings. There may be others. The guiding principle in every case is that the attendance of any such persons is at the discretion of the presiding officer and, with the exception of a friend or relative attending to provide support to a complainant or witness, with the consent of the officer concerned.

ANNEX J
ILL-HEALTH AND ATTENDANCE AT HEARINGS

1. Attendance at an unsatisfactory performance or misconduct hearing is not subject to the same considerations as reporting for duty, and so the provisions of Regulation 35 (sick leave) of the Police Regulations 1995 do not apply. An illness or disability may render an officer unfit for duty without affecting his or her ability to attend a hearing.

2. A medical certificate stating merely that the officer concerned is suffering from a named illness or disability would not necessarily constitute sufficient reason to prevent the officer from attending the hearing. There will be some circumstances where hearing could still take place or be deferred for only a short while. For instance, where an officer was suffering a physical injury such that travelling was difficult, the hearing might be held at a more accessible location. Or, where an officer's health was expected to improve in a reasonable time, the hearing could be deferred.

3. Where there are doubts as to the ability of the officer to attend a hearing, the opinion of the force medical officer should be obtained. If there is a difference of opinion between the force medical officer and the officer's own doctor, it is open to the force to seek a second opinion from a medical practitioner who specialises in the particular field of medicine concerned. Failure on the part of the officer concerned to accept such a second opinion consultation will militate against any claim to be medically unfit to attend a hearing. It is thereafter for the presiding officer to determine, in the light of the medical evidence advanced, whether the officer's medical condition constitutes a good reason for the officer's non-appearance at the hearing or grounds for deferral of the hearing. Nothing in this paragraph should be taken as precluding the officer from seeking a second opinion, or the presiding officer from taking note of that second opinion, if invited to do so, as part of the determination of this issue.

4. In considering these issues, a statement that the officer will find the hearing distressing or that it might set back his or her recovery would not alone be a sufficiently good reason to justify failure to attend a hearing or, where appropriate, to demonstrate that the officer could not attend a hearing rearranged for a later date. On the other hand, a good reason would be established if the medical evidence as a whole demonstrated that attending such a hearing would be likely to damage permanently the officer's health or that the officer's condition fundamentally impaired his or her ability to prepare for a hearing and, where appropriate, to brief his or her 'friend' or legal representative.

5. If the officer's health is likely to improve sufficiently in the future to enable the officer to attend, the hearing may be adjourned to or rearranged for a date when the

officer would be able to attend, provided that, in a misconduct case, the delay between the incident or actions to be considered by the hearing and the date of the hearing is not likely to affect the reliability of any evidence given at the hearing. Where a hearing is to be deferred pending recovery from sickness chief officers will need to bear in mind the provisions of regulation 46 (pay during sick leave) of the Police Regulations 1995.

ANNEX K
ROLES OF HM INSPECTORS OF CONSTABULARY AND POLICE AUTHORITIES IN RELATION TO COMPLAINTS AND MISCONDUCT

1.   Police authorities are the disciplinary authority for officers above the rank of Superintendent and are thus responsible for dealing with complaints and misconduct proceedings in respect of such officers. Police authorities are responsible for the appointment of Police Appeals Tribunals in cases involving officers of Superintendent rank and below, and individual members of police authorities are appointed to sit on such Tribunals. Police authorities are not otherwise involved in individual misconduct cases.

2.   HM Inspectors of Constabulary may be called upon to serve as one of the members of a Police Appeals Tribunal where the appellant is a senior officer, that is, above the rank of Superintendent. HM Inspectors are not otherwise involved in individual misconduct cases.

3.   Clerks to police authorities and HM Inspectors may become involved in public interest disclosure cases, where a police officer wishes to report the conduct of a chief officer. Where this occurs the information is to be dealt with in accordance with the Police (Conduct) (Senior Officers) Regulations 1999.

4.   Both police authorities and HM Inspectors have a statutory function in respect of the operation of the complaints and misconduct procedures, as outlined in the following paragraphs.

5.   Section 77 of the 1996 Act requires both police authorities and HM Inspectors to keep themselves informed as to the working of the complaints and misconduct procedures. This is an aspect of their general duty to secure the maintenance of an efficient and effective police force and to exercise their statutory powers.

6.   Police authorities in particular are required to keep themselves informed about the way in which chief officers deal with complaints by members of the public against members of the force for which they are responsible. This responsibility is one of oversight, to ensure that the statutory procedures for the handling of complaints are being properly observed.

7.   The precise way in which police authorities act to discharge their statutory function may vary from one authority to another. However, common practice indicates that this is likely to be by way of a complaints panel, who may hold regular meetings with the police force and may regularly inspect the force's complaints register. Chief officers should make their complaints register available for scrutiny by members of the authority in such circumstances. Members of police authorities will, though, need to ensure that there is no conflict between the way in which they exercise this function and their possible membership of a Police Appeals Tribunal.

8.   Section 22(1) of the 1996 Act requires chief officers to submit a general report to the authority each year on the policing during that year of the area for which their forces are maintained. It is recommended that the report should include a section on complaints and misconduct. Section 22(3) of the Act requires chief officers, whenever required to do so by an authority, to submit a report on such matters as may be

specified by the authority. Clearly, such a report may be about both complaints and misconduct matters.

9. It is suggested that a statistical return of all complaints from members of the public against members of the force, indicating how they have been dealt with, including reference to any action by the Police Complaints Authority, be placed before the police authority at their meetings. It is further suggested that forces can most conveniently use the same form as is used for their return to the Home Secretary, although individual police authorities may have different requirements.

10. The force may wish to draw the police authority's attention to the following categories of case:

(a)   those in which an investigating officer has been appointed from another force;

(b)   those in which the investigation has been supervised by the Police Complaints Authority and in which the Authority have expressed dissatisfaction with the investigation;

(c)   those which have been referred to the Director of Public Prosecutions; and

(d)   those where the Police Complaints Authority have directed that misconduct proceedings be brought.

11. The Home Secretary expects chief officers and police authorities to discuss together what can be done to supplement the information provided to the authority with further information which may be of assistance to them in the exercise of their function of general oversight of the handling of complaints. For instance, it may be helpful to the authority, particularly in cases which have aroused local concern, to know something of the background to a case. It will also be useful to the authority to be provided with information, beyond that referred to above, about the general pattern of complaints in the force area.

12. HM Inspectors will, as part of their annual inspection of individual forces, consider the handling of complaints and misconduct within forces, and chief officers should make available all papers and records relating to complaints and misconduct issues for this purpose. It is anticipated that details from the annual statistical returns to the Home Secretary of all complaints, which are copied to HM Chief Inspector of Constabulary and to the Regional Inspector, will form the basis of whatever comments HM Chief Inspector of Constabulary may make on complaints and misconduct in his or her annual report.

13. Oversight of the procedure for dealing with less serious complaints by way of informal resolution will fall to police authorities and HM Inspectors, as part of their function under section 77 of the 1996 Act, and they will be expected to pay particular attention to this area. It will not be their function to intervene in cases already being dealt with or completed. They should, however, be able to form a view as to the appropriateness of informal resolution for the complaint in question and of the means by which it was conducted.

14. Chief officers are required to include in the register of complaints those complaints which are settled by informal resolution. The register should be made available for inspection by police authorities and HIM Inspectors. It is therefore important that cases dealt with by way of informal resolution should easily be found in the register and that the register should be sufficiently complete to enable a person inspecting it to form a view as to the appropriateness and manner of informal resolution in such cases.

15. As noted above, a police authority may require a chief officer to submit a report to them on such matters as may be specified by the authority. Such a requirement may, of course, relate to complaints and misconduct matters. Chief

officers are obliged to comply with such a requirement. However, if it appears to the chief officer that a report required by the authority would contain information which ought not to be disclosed in the public interest, or which is not needed by the authority for the proper discharge of their functions, he or she may, under section 22(5) of the 1996 Act, ask the authority to refer the requirement to the Home Secretary. The requirement will have no effect unless confirmed by the Home Secretary.

16.   It is considered that the same principle should apply to any request by the authority to see the completed files, or material from such files, on individual cases. If the chief officer feels that disclosure of information concerning a complaint may involve a breach of confidentiality, or that disclosure would in any way be improper, he or she should direct the authority to refer their requirement to the Home Secretary.

17.   Both HM Inspectors and police authorities will be entitled to receive information on the part played by the Police Complaints Authority in the handling of complaints. The normal channel for such information will be the chief officer. It is for this reason that it is suggested that information on this aspect of the handling of complaints should form part of the regular return by the chief officer to the police authority. HM Inspectorate will receive this information in their copy of the chief officer's statistical return to the Home Secretary.

ANNEX L
OFFICERS SECONDED UNDER SECTION 97 OF THE POLICE ACT 1996

1.   This guidance sets out the procedures which have been agreed for applying the provisions which have been set out in this Guidance in sections 1, 2 and 3 to those officers on central service or serving temporarily with the National Criminal Intelligence Service (NCIS) and the National Crime Squad (NCS). (Separate arrangements apply to senior, permanent police members of NCIS and the NCS, referred to in section 6 of this Guidance.)

Unsatisfactory performance procedures
2.   It is recognised that the public is entitled to expect the highest standards of performance of police duties from all seconded officers. Similarly, police managers need a management system which both supports officers performing their tasks and reinforces the aims of the service.

3.   Unlike the broad policing functions performed by police forces throughout England and Wales, the nature and range of the tasks carried out by Central Service Units (CSUs), NCIS and NCS are specific and, by their nature, narrow. It follows that the scope for dealing fairly with a seconded officer whose performance is giving rise to concern is limited. The following procedure is designed to deal fairly and effectively with a seconded officer whose performance, or part of whose performance, is not meeting the needs of the organisation. It recognises that, unlike in police forces, an officer having difficulty in his or her role cannot be given the opportunity elsewhere within the CSU/NCIS/NCS to show his or her worth in performing different tasks. Such officers will therefore have to be returned to his or her parent force so that development can continue to and, as appropriate, opportunities provided to raise the level of performance. This course of action would not in itself preclude an officer from re-applying to the CSU/NCIS/NCS in due course and, if successful, be welcomed back.

4.   Where a pattern of performance by a seconded officer is giving rise to concern, managers should follow the guidance on initial action in Section 1, paragraphs 1.8 to

1.10. If, though, there is no or insufficient improvement, the seconded officer's line manager should prepare a written report which details the nature of the unsatisfactory performance, the remedial and other measures taken, and recommending that the officer be returned to his or her parent force. The manager should forward this report to the Superintendent (or Assistant Chief Officer where the officer concerned is a Chief Inspector or above) and copy it to the officer concerned.

5.   Not later than two weeks after receipt of the report, the Superintendent/ACC should determine whether to accept or reject the recommendation, and notify the officer concerned of the outcome. If the recommendation has been accepted, the officer concerned will be informed of his or her right to an interview with the deputy head of the Unit (Deputy Director General, in the case of NCIS and NCS), and asked to decide within two weeks whether he or she wishes to exercise this right. The interview should take place within one week of the request by the officer concerned being lodged. This interview is not a right of appeal. However, as noted above, any officer returned to his or her parent force on the grounds of unsatisfactory performance may (re-)apply for a period of secondment to the CSU, NCIS or NCS.

6.   It is hoped that an officer who has been returned to his or her parent force under this procedure will be able to resume performing duties satisfactorily. If, though, the same pattern of poor performance continues once the officer is back in his or her parent force, the performance on secondment may be taken into account, under the provisions of section 97 of the Police Act 1996.

Complaints procedures

7.   Attention is drawn to the benefits to be gained in early resolution of problems and averting complaints being made. This includes the facility, where appropriate, to offer apologies and to make ex gratia payments in compensation for losses incurred. (See Section 2 paragraph 2.1.)

8.   When a complaint about the conduct of a seconded officer is received by a parent force, steps should be taken to ensure that the head (Chairman/Director/ Director General as appropriate) of the CSU/NCIS/NCS is informed without delay. Equally, when such a complaint is received by a CSU or NCIS/NCS, the Chief Constable of the parent force should be informed without delay.

9.   Where a complaint is made against an officer serving with a CSU/NCIS/NCS, an officer of the officer concerned's parent force should be appointed to investigate it. If for any reason an investigating officer from another force is appointed to investigate the complaint, the officer's parent force should nevertheless be informed of the position. It will not automatically be necessary to return the officer concerned to his or her parent force during the course of the investigation; each case should be decided on its merits.

10.   Under the provisions of the NCIS (Complaints) (Amendment) Regulations 1999 and the National Crime Squad (Complaints) (Amendment) Regulations 1999, a complaint made against an officer serving temporarily with NCIS/NCS will be recorded and dealt with by the appropriate Director General in accordance with those provisions, the investigation being carried out by an officer appointed by the Director General, with the consent of the officer concerned's parent force. The investigating officer will normally be a member of the officer's parent force but, where it is not, the parent force should be notified of the position.

11.   The head of the CSU or the Director General, as appropriate, should refer a complaint to the Police Complaints Authority for supervision of the investigation where this is required (in the case of NCIS/NCS, by the Regulations) or where he or she considers it appropriate. The principles set out in Section 2 of this guidance

should be followed. If, on completion of the investigation, it is decided by the Head of the CSU in association with the Chief Constable of the parent force (or, in the case of an officer serving with NCIS/NCS, the Director General) and the PCA that misconduct proceedings need to be taken against the officer, he or she must be returned to the parent force without delay (see below). For this reason, it is important to establish and maintain effective systems of communication between the departments responsible for complaints and discipline in parent forces and their counterparts in the CSU and in NCIS/NCS.

Misconduct procedures

12.   The public is entitled to expect the highest standards of integrity, ability and commitment of police officers. Those serving on secondment with a CSU/NCIS/NCS are expected to act in accordance with the Code of Conduct (pages ii – iv at the front of this Guidance).

13.   Paragraphs 3.1 to 3.6 of Section 3 of this Guidance set out the general principles which apply in misconduct cases. Paragraphs 3.10 to 3.12 should be followed in respect of non-complaints cases. (For guidance on complaints cases, see above.) This allows for less serious matters to be dealt with locally in the CSU/NCIS/NCS. However, where an alleged breach of the Code of Conduct is such that the matter should be referred for investigation, an investigating officer should be appointed, normally from the officer concerned's parent force. The officer concerned should be warned of the nature of the report, allegation or complaint and invited to make a statement if s/he wishes, though s/he is not obliged to do so.

14.   On conclusion of the investigation, if it is decided that formal discipline should result, the officer should be returned to his or her parent force, where the guidance set out in Section 3 — paragraph 3.23 onwards — should be followed, starting with the service of a regulation 9 notice. Although the procedures which had been followed whilst the officer remained on secondment do not constitute the formal procedures provided for in the misconduct regulations, the material which had been obtained in the course of the inquiry may be subsumed/relied upon in the proceedings being followed in the parent force. The matter may then be brought to a hearing, as set out in Section 3 part IV, without undue delay.

ANNEX M

FORMS FOR USE WITH THE POLICE UNSATISFACTORY
PERFORMANCE, COMPLAINTS AND MISCONDUCT PROCEDURES

NOTE: These forms have been produced to assist police managers and others with the implementation of the procedures covered in the Guidance on police unsatisfactory performance, complaints and misconduct procedures. There is no obligation to use them or rely on them, but they may provide a useful prompt to the actions necessary to carry out the procedures correctly, including the need to make a record at each significant stage.

INDEX TO FORMS

Second stage interview
Notice of formal hearing
Unsatisfactory performance hearing

Annex M2   **Notice of misconduct report, allegation or complaint (Regulation 9 notice)**

Annex M3   **Forms relating to misconduct procedures**
Matters being put to a hearing
Questions to be answered by officer
Misconduct hearing

Annex M4   **Forms relating to Chief Constable's Review**
Request for review

Annex M5   **Forms relating to Appeal to Police Appeals Tribunal**
Notice of appeal
Grounds of appeal

UNSATISFACTORY PERFORMANCE PROCEDURES

Initial action stage

Officer's name..Area/Department....................

Force number..Rank...................... Role........................

Record below brief minutes of the meeting between the officer concerned and the reporting officer (supervisor):

Please turn over ...

Record below any agreed objectives and timescale for improvement:

Follow up action:

Action	✔ Course of action to be followed	Date actioned
Improved performance — no further action		
Further review necessary		
Refer to Personnel for consideration of posting to another role		
Move to first stage interview		
Refer to Welfare and Counselling Services		
Refer to Occupational Health		
Other (specify)		

Reporting officer: Name .... Rank ....

Force number .... Area/Department ....

Signature of reporting officer .... Date ....

Signature of officer .... Date ....

Turn to next page ...

Comments by officer concerned

UNSATISFACTORY PERFORMANCE PROCEDURES

NOTICE OF FIRST STAGE INTERVIEW

OFFICER'S PARTICULARS	
Name:	Rank:
No:	Current Duty:

1.   You are required to attend an interview at .... hrs on .... (not less than 14 days' notice) at .... about the unsatisfactory aspect(s) of your work performance as detailed in section 2 below. I will conduct the interview unless you complete section 3 overleaf asking that the interview be conducted by .... (Countersigning Officer) and return this notice to me by .... (no later than 7 days from the date of this notice). You will be expected to answer all questions put to you about your performance of police duties. You have the right to be accompanied by a colleague who is a serving police officer. Any colleague accompanying you may advise, assist and speak in your support. You may wish to seek advice from your staff association before the interview.

At the interview you will be given full opportunity to make representations about the matters set out at 2 below. You may also provide written comments, using the space at 4 overleaf, and return it to me by .... (no later than 7 days from the date of this notice).

2.   **Reasons for interview:**

Please turn over ...

3. I ask that the interview be conducted by .... (Countersigning Officer).

Signature of officer concerned .... Date ....

4. **Comments by officer concerned:**

Name of officer concerned .... Date of interview ....

Signed .... Date ....

Received by Reporting Officer

Name .... Date ....

Signature of Reporting Officer ....

FIRST STAGE INTERVIEW

Officer's name... Area/Department...................................

Force number.................. Rank......................... Role...

Record below brief minutes of the interview of the member concerned by the reporting officer and, if present, the countersigning officer:

Please turn over ...

Record below any agreed objectives and timescale for improvement:

Follow up action:

Action	✔ Course of action to be followed	Date actioned
Improved performance — no further action		
Further review necessary		
Refer to Personnel for consideration of posting to another role		
Move to second stage interview		
Refer to Welfare and Counselling Services		
Refer to Occupational Health		
Other (specify)		

Reporting officer: Name .... Rank ....

Force number .... Area/Department ....

Signature of reporting officer .... Date ....

Countersigning officer: Name .... Rank ....

Force number .... Area/Department ....

Signature of countersigning officer .... Date ....

Signature of officer interviewed... Date ....

Turn to next page ...

Comments by officer concerned

UNSATISFACTORY PERFORMANCE PROCEDURES

NOTICE OF SECOND STAGE INTERVIEW

OFFICER'S PARTICULARS	
Name:	Rank:
No:	Current Duty:

1. You are required to attend an interview at .... hrs on .... (not less than 14 days' notice) at .... about the unsatisfactory aspect(s) of your work performance as detailed in section 2 below, and to consider whether it is in the force's interests to retain your services. The interview will be conducted by .... and .... You will be expected to answer all questions put to you about your performance of police duties. You have the right to be accompanied by a colleague who is a serving police officer. Any colleague accompanying you may advise, assist and speak in your support. You may wish to seek advice from your staff association before the interview.

At the interview you will be given full opportunity to make representations about the matters set out at 2 below. You may also provide written comments, using the space at 3 overleaf, and return it to me by .... (no later than 7 days from the date of this notice).

2. **Reasons for interview:**

Please turn to next page ...

3.   **Comments by officer concerned:**

Name of officer concerned .... Date of interview ....

Signed .... Date ....

Received by Countersigning Officer

Name .... Date ....

Signature of Countersigning Officer ....

SECOND STAGE INTERVIEW

Officer's name.. Area/Department...........................

Force number...............................Rank...................... Role...............................

Record below brief minutes of the interview of the officer concerned by the reporting officer, the countersigning officer and the personnel representative:

Please turn over ...

2. *Record below any agreed objectives and timescale for improvement:*

3. *Follow up action:*

Action	✔ Course of action to be followed	Date actioned
Improved performance — no further action		
Written warning issued		
Further review necessary		
Refer to Personnel for consideration of posting to another role		
Move to formal hearing		
Refer to Welfare and Counselling Services		
Refer to Occupational Health		
Other (specify)		

Reporting officer: Name .... Rank ....

Force number .... Area/Department ....

Signature of reporting officer .... Date ....

Countersigning officer: Name .... Rank ....

Force number .... Area/Department ....

Signature of countersigning officer .... Date ....

Officer from Personnel Department: Name .... Grade/rank ....

Signature of Personnel representative... Date ....

Signature of officer interviewed... Date ....

Turn to next page ...

Comments by officer concerned

UNSATISFACTORY PERFORMANCE PROCEDURE

NOTICE OF FORMAL HEARING

OFFICER'S PARTICULARS	
Name:	Rank:
No:	Current Duty:

1.   Your performance of police duties following the second interview remains unsatisfactory. You are therefore required to attend an Unsatisfactory Performance hearing:

(a)   at .... hrs on .... (date) at .... (place)

OR

(b)   at a time, date and place to be notified*

Note: At least 21 days' notice must be given.

2.   The hearing will have the authority to require you to resign or reduce you in rank. You have the right to be legally represented at the hearing but you must indicate whether you wish to be legally represented within 14 days of the date of this notice.

3.   You may be accompanied to the hearing by a 'friend' (who must be a serving police officer and may be a Police Federation of Superintendents' Association representative). If you have not already done so you are strongly advised to seek assistance from your staff association. A 'friend' or legal representative may speak on your behalf, call witnesses and produce documentary or other evidence.

4.   The attached papers/papers not attached will be supplied to you at least 21 days before the hearing* will be supplied to the members of the Unsatisfactory Performance hearing and will form the basis for considering your future service.

5.   If you wish to call any witnesses to speak on your behalf please provide their names and addresses on the form attached, or supply them in advance of the date of the hearing.

*delete as appropriate

Turn to next page ...

To be returned to .... by .... (date)

To be completed by the officer concerned

1. I do/do not* wish to be legally represented at the hearing/I will inform you within 14 days whether I wish to be legally represented at the hearing*

Details (if known) ....

....

2. I do/do not* wish to nominate a serving officer to act as 'friend'/I will inform you before the hearing whether I wish to have a 'friend'*

Details (if known) ....

....

3. I wish the following witnesses to attend the hearing:

Witness 1: ....

Witness 2: ....

Witness 3: ....
(continue on a separate sheet if necessary)

4. I acknowledge service of this notice/and attached papers*

Signed .... Date ....

To be completed by officer serving papers:

5. Papers served as shown above

Signed .... Date ....

*delete as appropriate

Completed form received on .... (date)

Signed .... Name ....

UNSATISFACTORY PERFORMANCE HEARING

Officer's name..Area/Department....................

Force number...Rank...................... Role........................

Record below minutes of the hearing relating to the officer concerned before the reporting officer, the countersigning officer, the personnel representative and the Superintendent chairing the hearing. The hearing should be tape- or stenographer-recorded.

Please turn over ...

Record below the outcome of the hearing:

Officers in attendance at the hearing:

Name & rank/grade	Role	Force number	Signature
	Presiding officer		
	Panel member		
	Panel member		
	Presenting officer		
	Personnel representative		
	Officer concerned 'Friend'/Federation representative		
	Legal representative		

FOR INTERNAL USE ONLY

1. <u>Initial action stage</u> completed and signed off.

Signed .... Date ....

<u>First stage interview</u>
2.   Officer concerned notified of the date etc of the interview with a full explanation of what this entails.

Signed .... Date notified ....

3.   Record of interview completed, with objectives recorded and any necessary follow up action noted and, where applicable, actioned.

Signed .... Date record completed ....

<u>Second stage interview</u>
4.   Officer concerned notified of the date etc of the interview with a full explanation of what this entails.

Signed .... Date notified ....

5.   Record of interview completed, with objectives recorded and any necessary follow up action noted and, where applicable, actioned.

Signed .... Date record completed ....

<u>Formal hearing</u>
6.   Officer concerned notified of the date etc of the hearing with a full explanation of what this entails.

Signed .... Date notified ....

7.   Officers appointed to board: (1) ....(chairman)
                                     (2) ....
                                     (3) ....

8.   Date on which the accused officer responded as to whether s/he intended to be legally represented at the hearing.

Signed .... Date of response ....

9.   Date of letter to witnesses.

Signed .... Date ....

10.   Record of meeting made and outcome actioned.

Signed .... Date ....

NOTICE OF MISCONDUCT REPORT, ALLEGATION OR COMPLAINT

RANK	NUMBER	NAME

NAME & ADDRESS OF COMPLAINANT (if applicable)

Details of report/allegation/complaint (delete as appropriate):

1. You are not obliged to respond to this notice immediately, but you may do so if you wish. No inference may be drawn should you decide not to respond at this stage. However, any such response whether oral or in writing may be admissible at a future misconduct hearing.
2. You have the right to seek advice from a staff association representative and to be accompanied to any meeting, interview or hearing by a 'friend', who must be a serving police officer.
3. This notice has been served in accordance with regulation 9 of the Police (Misconduct) Regulations 1999 to inform you at the earliest possible stage that an allegation has been made. It does not necessarily imply that misconduct proceedings will be taken but is served to safeguard your interests.
4. You may be interviewed by the investigating officer at a later stage of the enquiry. At that interview you will be informed that you are not obliged to answer questions.

You are reminded that you may be accompanied to any interview by a Federation Representative, or other serving officer acting as 'friend'.

Served by:
Date .... Signed ....
Rank .... Number .... Name ....

Investigating Officer (if different from above)
Rank .... Number .... Name ....

I acknowledge that I have been served with a copy of this notice and that the notes above have been explained to me.

Signed ....

NB You will be informed of the outcome of this enquiry and of any undue delay.

MISCONDUCT PROCEDURES

Officer's name .... Force no. ....

Area/Department ....Rank .... Rate of pay ....

Matter(s) being put to a hearing (note any being brought on the direction of the PCA). *In each case please give details of the relevant part of the Code of Conduct, the particulars of the alleged breach, including time(s), date(s) and place(s), and names of addresses of witnesses. Continue on a separate sheet if necessary.*

1

2

3

Please turn over ...

Questions to be answered by the officer concerned:

1. Do you admit or deny the breach(es)? (You must answer on each.)

1. ....   2. ....   3. ....

2. Do you want a member of a police force (a 'friend') to help you in preparing your case? **YES/NO**

If yes, please provide the name, rank and name of force:

....

3. Do you want the force to arrange for the attendance of any witnesses on your behalf at the hearing of the case? **YES/NO**

If yes, please give their names and addresses (continue on a separate sheet if necessary):

....
....

4. Do you intend to make your own arrangement for any other witnesses (not members of a police force) to attend? **YES/NO**

If yes, it would help in arranging waiting facilities and timing for you to indicate how many witnesses are involved.
Number of further witnesses: ....

NB You must answer the questions above within fourteen days of the service of this form.

Date of misconduct hearing

5. You will be notified in writing, as soon as possible and at least 21 days before, of the date of the hearing and the names of those who will be conducting the hearing.

6. If you are found guilty of any of the above breaches, the officers conducting the hearing will wish to have the full range of sanctions available, including dismissal, requirement to resign and reduction in rank. You are therefore entitled to be legally represented at the hearing[1] and should indicate below whether you intend to be so represented. (Your 'friend' may attend whether or not you are legally represented.)

I do/do not intend to be legally represented at the misconduct hearing.

Signature of officer concerned .... Date ....

[1 You may forfeit your right to legal representation if you fail to answer the above questions and provide the information requested within fourteen days of the date of service of this form. If you do forfeit your right to legal representation, the full range of sanctions will remain available if you are found guilty.]

MISCONDUCT HEARING

The hearing will be conducted by an Assistant Chief Constable and two Superintendents (or two further Assistant Chief Constables where the accused officer is a Superintendent).

Date .... Time .... Place ....

and by adjournment on

Date .... Time .... Place ....

The above information was given to the officer concerned on .... *(date)*

Name .... Signed .... Date ....

Where applicable, any subsequent hearing solely to consider the sanction to be imposed will be held on:

Date .... Time .... Place ....

The above information was given to the officer concerned on ....*(date)*

Name .... Signed .... Date ....

Decisions on finding(s) and sanction(s)

Breach alleged	Finding	Sanction imposed (if breach proved)
1	Proved/Not proved	....
2	Proved/Not proved	....
3	Proved/Not proved	....

I confirm that the finding and sanction on each of the above alleged breaches are correctly recorded. I also confirm that the officer's personal record was seen and considered before a decision was reached on any of the sanctions to be imposed.

Signed .... (Chairman of tribunal) Date ....

Notification of finding(s) and sanction(s)

I confirm I have been notified of the decisions of the misconduct hearing as set out above.

Signed .... (Officer concerned) Date ....

FOR INTERNAL USE ONLY

1. Copy of misconduct form served on the officer concerned.

Signed .... Date of service ....

2. Officer concerned notified of the nature of the hearing with full explanation of what this entails.

Signed .... Date of notification ....

3. Date on which the officer concerned was provided with a copy of the relevant documents.

Signed .... Date of issue of documents ....

4. (If applicable) Date on which the officer concerned responded as to whether s/he intended to be legally represented at the hearing.

Signed .... Date of response ....

5. (If misconduct admitted) Date on which officer concerned was provided with a summary of the facts of the case (at least two weeks before the date of the hearing).

Signed .... Date of issue of summary ....

6. Date members of board appointed.

Signed .... Date board appointed ....

7. Officers appointed to board: (1) ....(chairman)
                                   (2) ....
                                   (3) ....

8. Date of letter to witnesses.

Signed .... Date letter sent ....

9. (If applicable) Case entered in Complaints Register.

Signed .... Date entered ....

10. Case entered in Misconduct Book.

Signed .... Date entered ....

CHIEF OFFICER'S REVIEW

Request for review   (This must be submitted within fourteen days of receipt of the notification of the outcome of the hearing.)

Officer's name .... Force no. ....

Area/Department .... Rank .... Rate of pay ....

1. Nature of action on which a review is sought:
    Unsatisfactory performance ☐
    Misconduct   ☐

2. Name of personnel officer/presenting officer ....

3. Name of presiding officer .... Date of hearing ....

4. Outcome(s) of the hearing:

```



```

5. **Particulars of those aspects on which the review is sought:**

```




```

6. Whether the officer seeking the review wants a personal hearing.   **YES/NO**

7. Whether the officer will be accompanied by a 'friend'.   **YES/NO**

8. Whether the officer will be legally represented (where s/he was entitled to be so represented at the hearing).   **YES/NO**

FOR INTERNAL USE ONLY

1. Notice of request for review received.

Signed .... Date ....

2. Nature of hearing: **unsatisfactory performance/misconduct**.

3. Whether a personal interview was requested: **YES/NO**.

4. Whether the officer was accompanied by a 'friend': **YES/NO**.

5. Whether the officer was legally represented: **YES/NO**.

6. Outcome of review:

```



```

Signed .... Date ....

Name and rank ....

ANNEX M5

APPEAL TO POLICE APPEALS TRIBUNAL[2]

Notice of appeal   (This must be submitted within 21 days[3] of the date on which the officer was notified in writing of the outcome of the Chief Constable's Review.)

Appellant's name .... Force no. ....

Area/Department .... Rank .... Rate of pay ....

1. Nature of action on which a review is sought:
    Unsatisfactory performance ☐
    Misconduct   ☐

2. Name of personnel officer/presenting officer ....

3. Name of presiding officer .... Date of hearing ....

4. Outcome of the hearing:

5. Date of Chief Constable's Review ....

6. Outcome of Chief Constable's Review:

7. Notice is hereby given of the exercise of the right to a Police Appeals Tribunal against the decision by the Chief Constable. A copy of the transcript of the unsatisfactory performance/misconduct hearing held on .... at .... is now requested.

Signed .... Date ....

Name and address to which correspondence for the appellant should be sent:
....
....

[2 Available only to officers against whom a sanction of dismissal, requirement to resign or reduction in rank was imposed.]
[3 Unless a Tribunal Chairman has agreed that an 'out of time' appeal should be heard.]

GROUNDS OF APPEAL TO POLICE APPEALS TRIBUNAL

Appellant's name... Force no. ....

Area/Department .... Rank .... Rate of pay ....

1. *Full statement of the grounds on which the appeal is based:*

2. *List of supporting statements attached:*

Please turn over ...

3. Whether the appellant wants an oral hearing. **YES/NO**

4. Whether the appellant or his or her representative wishes to make oral representations to the Chairman for the holding of a hearing. **YES/NO**

OR

5. *Written representations in support of any oral hearing requested:*

6. Witnesses the appellant wishes to call in support of the appeal (continue on a separate sheet if necessary):

(a) ....

(b) ....

(c) ....

(d) ....

7. At the time the sanction was imposed/varied on Review the appellant was in receipt of pay at the rate of .... per year.

8. The appellant was suspended on .... (date) and was still suspended immediately before the sanction was imposed.

9. A copy of this notice has been sent to the Chief Constable of the force concerned.

Signed .... Date ....

Name and address to which correspondence for the appellant should be addressed:

....

....

FOR INTERNAL USE ONLY

1. Notice of appeal received.

Signed .... Date received .... Date of notice ....

2. Transcript ordered and despatched.

Ordered on .... (date) Despatched ....(date)

Signed .... Date ....

3. Copy of the report of the decisions of the hearing and the note of the Chief Constable's review received.

Signed .... Date documents received ....

4. Grounds of appeal received.

Signed .... Date received ....

5. Chief Constable's response received.

Signed .... Date received ....

6. Tribunal members appointed:

Chairman:	Member of police authority:
....	....
(Former) Chief Officer:	Retired officer of appropriate rank:
....	....

Signed .... Date appointment letters sent ....

Please turn over ...

7. Date, time and place of oral representations (if applicable):

....

8. Date, time and place of hearing:

....

9. Appellant, respondent, complainant (if applicable) and witnesses notified of date etc of hearing.

Signed .... Letters sent ....

10. Tribunal report received.

Signed .... Date report received ....

11. Appellant and respondent informed of outcome of appeal.

Signed .... Date notification sent ....

12. Complainant notified of outcome.

Signed .... Date notification sent ....

13. Outcome of appeal implemented.

Signed .... Date of implementation ....

14. Expenses claims by tribunal members received.

Chairman ....(date)   Police Authority member ....(date)

Chief Officer ....(date)   Fourth member ....(date)

15. Expenses claims approved and passed for payment.

Signed .... Date of action ....

16. Appellants' costs checked and passed for payment (if awarded).

Signed .... Date of action ....

Appendix 2   The Police (Efficiency) Regulations 1999 (SI 1999 No. 732)

The Secretary of State, in exercise of the powers conferred on him by sections 50 and 84 of the Police Act 1996, and after complying with the requirements of section 63(3) of that Act, hereby makes the following Regulations:

1.   Citation and commencement
These Regulations may be cited as the Police (Efficiency) Regulations 1999 and shall come into force on 1st April 1999.

2.   Application
These Regulations shall not apply in relation to—
    (a)   a chief constable or other officer above the rank of superintendent;
    (b)   an officer of the rank of constable who has not completed his period of probation.

3.   Interpretation
  (1)   In these Regulations, unless the context otherwise requires—
    'countersigning officer' means a member of the police force concerned having supervisory responsibility and who is senior in rank to the reporting officer;
    'first interview' has the meaning assigned to it by regulation 4;
    'inefficiency hearing' has the meaning assigned to it by regulation 12(2);
    'interviewing officer' means the officer who conducts a first interview;
    'member concerned' means the member of a police force in respect of whom proceedings under these Regulations are, or are proposed to be, taken;
    'personnel officer' means a person employed under section 15 of the 1996 Act or a member of a police force who, in either case, has responsibility for personnel matters relating to members of the police force concerned;
    'police force concerned' means the police force of which the member concerned is a member;
    'reporting officer' means the member of the police force concerned who has the immediate supervisory responsibility for the member concerned;
    'second interview' has the meaning assigned to it by regulation 8(2);
    'senior manager' means—

(a)   the officer who is for the time being the supervisory officer of the person who is, in relation to the member concerned, the countersigning officer; or

(b)   where the member concerned is of the rank of superintendent, his supervising officer;

'the 1996 Act' means the Police Act 1996.

(2)   In these Regulations, unless the context otherwise requires, any reference to a regulation shall be construed as a reference to a regulation contained in these Regulations.

4.   Circumstances in which a first interview may be required

Where the reporting officer for a member of a police force is of the opinion that the performance of that member is unsatisfactory, he may require the member concerned to attend an interview (in these Regulations referred to as a first interview) to discuss the performance of the member concerned.

5.   Arrangement of first interview

(1)   If the reporting officer decides to require a member of a police force to attend a first interview, he shall—

(a)   send a notice in writing to the member concerned—

(i)   requiring him to attend, at a specified time and place, an interview with the reporting officer or, if the member concerned so requests, the countersigning officer;

(ii)   stating the reasons why his performance is considered unsatisfactory;

(iii)   informing him that he may seek advice from a representative of his staff association and be accompanied at the interview by a member of a police force selected by him; and

(b)   send a copy of the notice to the countersigning officer.

(2)   A member of a police force who receives a notice pursuant to paragraph (1) may, not later than 7 days (or such longer period as the reporting officer may permit when sending the notice under paragraph (1)(a)) after the date on which the notice was received by him, request by notice in writing that the interview be conducted by the countersigning officer; and if the member concerned so requests the interview shall be conducted by the countersigning officer.

6.   Procedure at first interview

(1)   The following provisions of this regulation apply to the procedure to be followed at the first interview.

(2)   The interviewing officer shall—

(a)   explain to the member concerned the reasons why the reporting officer is of the opinion that the performance of that member is unsatisfactory; and

(b)   provide the member concerned, or the member of a police force who has accompanied him to the interview, or both of them, with an opportunity to make representations in response.

(3)   If, after considering any representations made in accordance with paragraph (2)(b), the interviewing officer is satisfied that the performance of the member concerned has been unsatisfactory, he shall—

(a)   inform the member concerned in what respect his performance is considered unsatisfactory;

(b)   warn the member concerned of any specific action which he is required to take to achieve an improvement in his performance; and

(c)   warn the member concerned that, if a sufficient improvement is not made within such reasonable period as the interviewing officer shall specify, he may be required to attend a second interview in accordance with regulation 9.

(4)   The interviewing officer may, if he considers it appropriate, recommend that the member concerned seek assistance in relation to any matter affecting his health or welfare.

(5)   The interviewing officer may adjourn the interview to a specified later time or date if it appears to him necessary or expedient to do so.

7. Procedure following first interview

(1)   The interviewing officer shall, not later than 7 days after the date of the conclusion of the first interview—

(a)   cause to be prepared a written record of the substance of the matters discussed at the interview; and

(b)   send one copy or, where the member concerned was accompanied at the interview by a member of a police force selected by him, two copies of that record to the member concerned together with a notice in writing informing him that he may submit written comments, or indicate that he has no comment to make, not later than 7 days after the date on which the copy is received by him.

(2)   Subject to paragraph (3), the member concerned shall be entitled to submit written comments in relation to the record of the interview to the interviewing officer not later than 7 days after the date on which the copy is received by him.

(3)   The interviewing officer may, on the application of the member concerned, extend the period specified in paragraph (2) if he is satisfied that it is appropriate to do so.

(4)   The interviewing officer shall send a copy of the record of the interview, and of any written comments of the member concerned, to—

(a)   the senior manager;

(b)   the personnel officer; and

(c)(i)   if the interview was conducted by the reporting officer, the countersigning officer; or

(ii)   if the interview was conducted by the countersigning officer, the reporting officer.

(5)   If the interviewing officer receives any written comments under paragraph (2), he shall ensure that they are retained with the record of the interview.

8. Circumstances in which a second interview may be required

(1)   Where the reporting officer is of the opinion that a member of a police force who was warned under regulation 6(3)(b) that he was required to improve his performance has, at the end of the period specified by the interviewing officer under regulation 6(3)(c), failed to make a sufficient improvement in his performance, he may refer the case to the countersigning officer.

(2)   Where a case is referred under paragraph (1), the countersigning officer may, after consulting with the personnel officer, require the member concerned to attend a further interview (in these Regulations referred to as a second interview) to discuss the performance of the member concerned.

9. Arrangement of second interview

If the countersigning officer decides to require a member of a police force to attend a second interview, he shall—

(a)   send a notice in writing to the member concerned—

(i)   requiring him to attend, at a specified time and place, an interview with the countersigning officer and the personnel officer;

(ii)   stating the reasons why his performance is considered unsatisfactory and that further action will be considered in the light of the interview; and

(iii)   informing him that he may seek advice from a representative of his staff association and be accompanied at the interview by a member of a police force selected by him; and

(b)   send a copy of the notice to the reporting officer, the senior manager and the personnel officer.

10.   Procedure at second interview

(1)   The following provisions of this Regulation shall apply to the procedure to be followed at a second interview.

(2)   The interview shall be conducted by the countersigning officer and the personnel officer.

(3)   The countersigning officer shall—

(a)   explain to the member concerned the reasons why the reporting officer is of the opinion that the member concerned has failed to make a sufficient improvement in his performance or, as the case may be, that his performance is unsatisfactory and the conditions specified in regulation 8(2) are satisfied; and

(b)   provide the member concerned, or the member of a police force who has accompanied him to the interview, or both of them, with an opportunity to make representations in response.

(4)   If, after considering any representations made under paragraph (3), the countersigning officer is satisfied that the performance of the member concerned has been unsatisfactory during the period specified by the interviewing officer under regulation 6(3)(c) or, as the case may be, the period specified in regulation 8(2), he shall—

(a)   inform the member concerned in what respect his performance is considered unsatisfactory;

(b)   warn the member concerned that he is required to improve his performance in any such respect;

(c)   inform the member concerned of any specific action which he is required to take to achieve such an improvement; and

(d)   warn the member concerned that, if a sufficient improvement is not made within such reasonable period as the countersigning officer shall specify, he may be required to attend an inefficiency hearing at which the officers conducting the hearing will have the power, if appropriate, to require the member concerned to resign from the force or to order reduction in rank.

(5)   The countersigning officer may adjourn the interview to a specified later time or date if it appears to him necessary or expedient to do so.

11.   Procedure following second interview

(1)   The countersigning officer shall, not later than 7 days after the conclusion of the second interview—

(a)   in consultation with the personnel officer, prepare a written record of the substance of the matters discussed during the interview; and

(b)   send one copy or, where the member concerned was accompanied at the interview by a member of a police force selected by him, two copies of that record to the member concerned together with a notice in writing—

(i)   if a warning was given under regulation 10(4), confirming the terms of that warning; and

(ii)   informing him that he may submit written comments, or indicate that he has no such comments, not later than 7 days after the date on which the copy is received by him.

(2)   Subject to paragraph (3), the member concerned shall be entitled to submit written comments in relation to the record of the interview to the countersigning officer not later than 7 days after the date on which it was received by him.

(3)   The countersigning officer may, on the application of the member concerned, extend the period specified in paragraph (2) if he is satisfied that it is appropriate to do so.

(4)   If the countersigning officer receives any written comments under paragraph (2), he shall ensure that they are retained with the record of the interview.

(5)   The countersigning officer shall send a copy of the record of the interview, and of any written comments by the member concerned, to the reporting officer, the personnel officer and the senior manager.

12.   Assessment of performance following second interview

(1)   Not later than 14 days after the date on which the period specified under regulation 10(4)(d) ends—

(a)   the countersigning officer shall, in consultation with the reporting officer, assess the performance of the member concerned during that period; and

(b)   the countersigning officer shall inform the member concerned in writing whether the reporting officer and the countersigning officer are of the opinion that there has been a sufficient improvement in performance during that period.

(2)   If the countersigning officer is of the opinion that there has been an insufficient improvement, the member concerned shall also, within the period of 14 days mentioned in paragraph (1), be informed in writing that he may be required to attend, at a time (being not sooner than 21 days, but not later than 56 days, after the date on which the notification under this paragraph is received by him) to be notified separately, a hearing (in these Regulations referred to as an inefficiency hearing) to consider his performance.

(3)   The countersigning officer shall refer any case in which the member concerned has been informed in accordance with paragraph (2) to the senior manager, who shall, if he thinks it appropriate to do so, direct that an inefficiency hearing be arranged under regulation 13.

13.   Arrangement of an inefficiency hearing

(1)   The personnel officer shall, not less than 21 days before the date fixed for the hearing, send a notice in writing to the member concerned—

(a)   requiring him to attend an inefficiency hearing at a specified time and place;

(b)   stating the reasons why his performance is considered unsatisfactory;

(c)   informing him that he may be represented at the hearing—

(i)   either by counsel or a solicitor; or

(ii)   by a member of a police force selected by him; and

(d)   warning him of the powers under regulation 17 which are available to the officers conducting the inefficiency hearing in the event that they find that the performance of the member concerned has been unsatisfactory.

(2)   If the member concerned wishes to call any witnesses other than the person representing him at the inefficiency hearing, he shall, not later than seven days before the hearing, give notice in writing to the personnel officer of the names and addresses of those witnesses.

(3)   In paragraph (2), the reference to the hearing includes a reference to any hearing under regulation 15; and in relation to such a hearing the period within which notice is to be given under that paragraph shall be such period as the chairman of the hearing may direct when he postpones or, as the case may be, adjourns the hearing.

14. Procedure at an inefficiency hearing

(1)   The inefficiency hearing shall be conducted by three officers appointed by the chief officer of police one of whom shall—

(a)   where the member concerned is a member of a police force maintained under section 2 of the 1996 Act, be a member of such a police force holding the rank of assistant chief constable;

(b)   where the member concerned is a member of the metropolitan police force, be a member of that police force holding the rank of commander; and

(c)   where the member concerned is a member of the City of London police force, be an assistant commissioner or a member of that police force holding the rank of commander,

(referred to in these Regulations as the chairman of the inefficiency hearing).

(2)   The chairman and any assessor assisting him under paragraph (3) shall be a person who has neither attended nor otherwise been involved with the first interview or the second interview held in relation to the member concerned.

(3)   The chairman shall be assisted by two assessors who shall be—

(a)   in a case falling within paragraph (1)(a) or (c)—

(i)   where the member concerned is of the rank of superintendent, members of a police force other than the police force concerned who hold the rank of assistant chief constable or commander in the metropolitan police force, and

(ii)   where the member concerned is below the rank of superintendent, members of a police force who hold the rank of superintendent; and

(b)   in a case falling within paragraph (1)(b)—

(i)   where the member concerned is of the rank of superintendent, members of the metropolitan police force who hold the rank of commander, and

(ii)   where the member concerned is below the rank of superintendent, members of the metropolitan police force who hold the rank of superintendent.

(4)   As soon as the chief officer of police has appointed the chairman, the personnel officer shall arrange for a copy of any document—

(a)   which was available to the interviewing officer in relation to the first interview;

(b)   which was available to the countersigning officer in relation to the second interview; or

(c)   which was prepared or submitted under regulation 11, 12 or 13,

to be made available to the chairman; and a copy of any such document shall be sent to the member concerned.

(5)   Subject to the provisions of this regulation, the procedure at the inefficiency hearing shall be such as the chairman may determine.

(6)   The inefficiency hearing shall be held in private unless the chairman, with the consent of the member concerned, decides otherwise.

(7)   The chairman shall afford the member concerned an opportunity to make representations in relation to the matters referred to in the notice sent under regulation 13(1) and to call any witness in respect of whom notice has been given under regulation 13(2).

(8)   A verbatim record of the proceedings at the inefficiency hearing shall be taken and, if the member concerned so requests within the time limit for any appeal and after he has lodged notice of appeal in accordance with rules made under section 85 of the 1996 Act, a transcript of the record or a copy thereof shall be supplied to him by the chairman.

(9)   Subject to regulation 15(1), if the member concerned does not attend the inefficiency hearing or at any adjournment thereof, the hearing may be proceeded with and concluded in his absence if it appears to the chairman just and proper to do so.

(10)   Where, owing to the absence of the member concerned, it is not possible to comply with the whole or any part of the procedure described in this regulation or regulation 15, the case may be proceeded with as if that procedure had been complied with.

15.   Postponement or adjournment of an inefficiency hearing

(1)   If the member concerned intimates to the chairman that he will be unable to attend the inefficiency hearing, or in the absence of such intimation does not attend the hearing, and the chairman is satisfied that a good reason for such non-attendance is given by, or on behalf of, the member concerned, he shall postpone, or as the case may be adjourn, the hearing.

(2)   The chairman may also adjourn the inefficiency hearing if, having given the member concerned the opportunity of making representations under regulation 14(7), he considers it appropriate to allow a further period for assessment of the performance of the member concerned.

(3)   Where the chairman adjourns the inefficiency hearing for the purposes of paragraph (2), he shall—

(a)   specify a period (not exceeding 3 months) during which the reporting officer and the countersigning officer shall assess the performance of the member concerned;

(b)   fix a date on which the hearing shall resume; and

(c)   require the member concerned to attend on that date at a specified place.

(4)   Not later than 14 days after the date on which the period for further assessment specified by the chairman under paragraph (3)(a) ends—

(a)   the reporting officer and the countersigning officer shall prepare a report containing their assessment of the performance of the member concerned during that period; and

(b)   the countersigning officer shall send the report to the chairman of the inefficiency hearing and a copy of the report to the member concerned.

(5)   At the continuation of the inefficiency hearing the chairman shall afford the member concerned an opportunity to make representations in relation to the matters referred to in the report mentioned in paragraph (4) and to call any witnesses in respect of whom notice was given under regulation 13(2).

(6)   Where at the time the report mentioned in paragraph (4) is sent under paragraph (4)(b) the chairman of the inefficiency hearing is absent, incapacitated or suspended from duty and it is likely that his absence, incapacity or suspension will continue for a period of more than 28 days, the chief officer of police shall arrange for another member of a police force, being a person who would have been eligible for appointment as chairman of the inefficiency hearing under regulation 14(1) and (2) in relation to the hearing in question, to carry out in relation to the member concerned the functions of the chairman of the inefficiency hearing specified in paragraph (5) and in regulations 16 and 17.

(7)   The chairman of an inefficiency hearing may adjourn the hearing to a specified later time or date if it appears to him necessary or expedient to do so.

16.   Finding

(1)   Subject to paragraph (2), at the conclusion of the inefficiency hearing, the officers conducting the hearing shall reach a decision whether the performance of the member concerned—

(a)   in the period referred to in regulation 10(4)(d); or

(b)   where the hearing was adjourned under regulation 15(2), over the whole of the period comprising the period referred to in regulation 10(4)(d) and the further period specified by the chairman under regulation 15(3)(a),

has been satisfactory or not.

(2)   The chairman may, at the conclusion of the hearing, defer reaching a decision until a later time or date if it appears necessary or expedient to do so.

(3)   The decision of the officers conducting the hearing shall state the finding and, where they have found that the performance of the member concerned has not been satisfactory, their reasons as well as any sanction which they impose under regulation 17.

(4)   The chairman shall record the decision in writing, and shall, not later than three days after the finding is stated under paragraph (3), send a copy of it to—

   (a)   the member concerned;
   (b)   the senior manager; and
   (c)   the personnel officer;

and the copy sent to the member concerned shall be accompanied by a notice in writing informing him of his right to request a review under regulation 19.

(5)   Any decision of the officers conducting the hearing under this regulation or regulation 17 shall be based on a simple majority, but shall not indicate whether it was taken unanimously or by a majority.

17.   Sanctions

(1)   If the officers conducting the inefficiency hearing make a finding that the performance of the member concerned during the relevant period has been unsatisfactory, they may—

   (a)   require the member concerned to resign from the force either one month after the date on which a copy of the decision sent under regulation 16(4) is received by him or on such later date as may be specified;

   (b)   order reduction in his rank with immediate effect and issue a written warning to the member concerned that unless a sufficient improvement in his performance is made within such period as the chairman shall specify, he may, following consideration of his performance during that period in accordance with regulation 18, be required to attend a first interview in respect of that performance; or

   (c)   issue such a written warning as is mentioned in sub-paragraph (b).

(2)   Where the sanction under paragraph (1)(a) is imposed and where the member concerned has not resigned from the force in accordance with the requirement, then the effect of the decision shall be to dismiss the member concerned from the force as from the time referred to in that paragraph.

18.   Assessment of performance following inefficiency hearing

(1)   This regulation applies where the member concerned has been given a written warning under paragraph (1)(b) or (c) of regulation 17.

(2)   Not later than 14 days after the end of the period specified in the warning, the reporting officer shall—

   (a)   assess the performance of the member concerned during that period;
   (b)   cause to be prepared a report on the performance; and
   (c)   send a copy of the report to the member concerned.

(3)   Where the report prepared under paragraph (2)(b) concludes that the performance of the member concerned has been satisfactory during the period specified in the warning, no further action shall be taken in respect of that performance during that period.

(4)   Where the report prepared under paragraph (2)(b) concludes that, in the opinion of the reporting officer, the performance of the member concerned has been unsatisfactory during that period, the reporting officer shall request the member concerned to attend a first interview in accordance with regulation 4; and these Regulations shall have effect for the purposes of the performance of the member

concerned during that period as if he had been invited to a first interview under regulation 4.

19. Request for a review

(1)   Where the officers conducting the inefficiency hearing have imposed a sanction under regulation 17, the member concerned shall be entitled to request the chief officer of the police force concerned, or where the member concerned is a member of the metropolitan police force an assistant commissioner, ('the reviewing officer') to review the finding or the sanction imposed, or both the finding and the sanction.

(2)   A request for a review must be made to the reviewing officer in writing within 14 days of the date on which a copy of the decision sent under regulation 16(4) is received by the member concerned unless this period is extended by the reviewing officer.

(3)   The request for a review shall state the grounds on which the review is requested and whether a meeting is requested.

20. Conduct of the review

(1)   The reviewing officer shall hold a meeting with the member concerned if requested to do so.

(2)   Where a meeting is held, the member concerned may be accompanied by a member of a police force and by counsel or a solicitor.

21. Finding of the review

(1)   The member concerned shall be informed of the finding of the reviewing officer in writing within three days of completion of the review.

(2)   The reviewing officer may confirm the decision of the hearing or he may impose a different sanction but he may not impose a sanction greater than that imposed at the hearing.

(3)   The decision of the reviewing officer shall take effect by way of substitution for the decision of the hearing and as from the date of that hearing.

(4)   Where as a result of the decision of the reviewing officer the member concerned is required to resign or reduced in rank he shall be notified in writing of his right of appeal to a Police Appeals Tribunal.

22. Hearing of review in absence of chief officer

(1)   Subject to paragraphs (2) to (4), where the chief officer is an interested party or the circumstances in section 12(4)(a) or (b) of the 1996 Act apply, the review shall be conducted by the assistant chief constable designated under section 12(4) of the 1996 Act.

(2)   Where the designated assistant chief constable is absent or an interested party, the review shall be conducted by the chief officer of another force who has agreed to act in that capacity.

(3)   Where the member concerned is a member of the metropolitan police force, the review shall be conducted by an assistant commissioner who is not an interested party.

(4)   Where the member concerned is a member of the City of London police force, the review shall be conducted by the Commissioner or, if he is absent or an interested party, by a chief officer of another force who has agreed to act in that capacity or an assistant commissioner of the metropolitan police force who has agreed to act in that capacity.

23. Amendment of Police Regulations 1995

(1)   In regulation 17(2) of the Police Regulations 1995—

(a)   in sub-paragraph (g), for the words 'punishments other than cautions,' there shall be substituted the words 'sanctions other than cautions imposed under regulation 31 of the Police (Conduct) Regulations 1999 or under regulation 17 of the Police (Efficiency) Regulations 1999'; and

(b)   in the proviso—

(i)   for the word 'punishment' wherever it occurs there shall be substituted the word 'sanction'; and

(ii)   after paragraph (ii) there shall be inserted the following paragraph:

'(iii)   a sanction under regulation 17 of the Police (Efficiency) Regulations 1999 shall be expunged after 2 years free from any such sanction;'.

(2)   After regulation 17(2) there shall be inserted the following paragraph:

'(2A)   Where following a review of a sanction imposed under regulation 31 of the Police (Conduct) Regulations 1999 or under regulation 17 of the Police (Efficiency) Regulations 1999 the reviewing officer substitutes for the decision of the conduct hearing or, as the case may be, inefficiency hearing a decision that the member concerned had not failed to meet the appropriate standard or, as the case may be, that the performance of the member concerned was not unsatisfactory, the sanction imposed by that hearing shall be expunged forthwith.'.

EXPLANATORY NOTE

(This note is not part of the Regulations)

These Regulations, made in pursuance of section 50 of the Police Act 1996 ('the Act'), make provision with respect to the efficiency of members of police forces and establish procedures for cases in which members of a police force may be dealt with by requirement to resign or reduction in rank. The Regulations, by virtue of regulation 2, do not apply to officers above the rank of superintendent or probationers.

Regulations 4 to 7 provide for a first interview to be held in respect of a member of a police force whose performance is considered to be unsatisfactory, and lay down the arrangements concerning and the procedure at and following such an interview. Regulations 8 to 12 make similar provision in respect of second interviews, which may be held where the performance of a member of a police force continues to be, or again becomes, unsatisfactory.

Regulations 13 to 18 provide for an inefficiency hearing to be held in respect of a member of a police force whose performance following a second interview has remained unsatisfactory and for the procedure and findings of such a hearing. Regulations 19 to 22 provide for the review of the decision of an inefficiency hearing by the chief officer or another senior officer and regulation 23 makes consequential amendments to the Police Regulations 1995 (which have effect as if made under section 50 of the Act).

Appendix 3   The Police (Conduct) Regulations 1999 (SI 1999 No. 730)

ARRANGEMENT OF REGULATIONS

SCHEDULES

The Secretary of State, in exercise of the powers conferred on him by sections 50 and 84 of the Police Act 1996, and after complying with the requirements of section 63(3) of that Act, hereby makes the following Regulations:

1. Citation and commencement

These Regulations may be cited as the Police (Conduct) Regulations 1999 and shall come into force on 1st April 1999.

2. Revocations and transitional provisions

(1) Subject to the following provisions of this regulation, the Police (Discipline) Regulations 1985 ('the 1985 Regulations'), the Police (Discipline) (Amendment) Regulations 1991, the Police (Discipline) (Amendment) Regulations 1995 and the Police (Discipline) (Amendment No. 2) Regulations 1995 are hereby revoked.

(2) Subject to paragraph (3), where a report, complaint or allegation has been or is received in respect of conduct by a member of a police force which occurred or commenced before 1st April 1999—

(a) nothing in these Regulations shall apply, and

(b) the 1985 Regulations shall, as far as applicable, continue to have effect.

(3) In the case of a report, complaint or allegation which—

(a) relates to conduct by a member of a police force which occurred or commenced before 1st April 1999, but

(b) is received on or after 1st April 2000,

the conduct shall be treated, for the purposes of this regulation, as having occurred or, as the case may be, commenced on 1st April 1999.

3. Regulations not to apply in the case of senior officers

These Regulations shall not apply in relation to the conduct of a chief constable or other officer holding a rank above that of superintendent.

4. Interpretation

(1) In these Regulations, unless the context otherwise requires—

'the appropriate officer' means—

(a) where the member concerned is a member of the metropolitan police force or the City of London police force, an assistant commissioner in that police force;

(b) in any other case, an assistant chief constable;

'appropriate standard' means the standard set out in the Code of Conduct;

'Authority' means the Police Complaints Authority;

'Code of Conduct' means the code of conduct contained in Schedule 1;

'complaint' has the meaning assigned to it by section 65 of the 1996 Act;

'an interested party' means a witness or any person involved in the conduct which is the subject of the case or who otherwise has a direct interest in the case;

'member concerned' means the officer in relation to whose conduct there has been a report, complaint or allegation;

'police force concerned' means, in relation to a person whose conduct is the subject of a report, complaint or allegation, the police force of which he is a member; and any reference to the chief officer concerned is a reference to the chief officer of that force;

'supervising officer' means the officer appointed under regulation 7 to supervise the investigation of the case; and

'the 1996 Act' means the Police Act 1996.

(2)   In these Regulations, unless the context otherwise requires, any reference to a regulation or Schedule shall be construed as a reference to a regulation or Schedule contained in these Regulations.

5.   Suspension

(1)   Where there has been a report, complaint or allegation which indicates that the conduct of a member of a police force does not meet the appropriate standard the chief officer of the force may suspend the member concerned from membership of the force and from his office of constable whether or not the matter has been investigated.

(2)   The chief officer concerned may exercise the power to suspend the member concerned under this regulation at any time from the time of the receipt of the report, complaint or allegation until—

(a)   the supervising officer decides not to refer the case to a hearing,

(b)   the notification of a finding that the conduct of the member concerned did not fail to meet the appropriate standard,

(c)   the time limit under regulation 34 for giving notice of intention to seek a review has expired, or

(d)   any review under regulation 35 has been completed.

(3)   Where the member concerned is suspended under this regulation, he shall be suspended until there occurs any of the events mentioned in paragraph (2)(a) to (d), or until the chief officer decides he shall cease to be suspended, whichever first occurs.

(4)   Where the member concerned who is suspended is required to resign under regulation 31, he shall remain suspended during the period of his notice.

(5)   The chief officer concerned may delegate his powers under this regulation to an officer of at least the rank of assistant chief constable or, where the member concerned is a member of the City of London or metropolitan police force, to an officer of at least the rank of commander.

6.   Conduct of investigations where there are outstanding criminal proceedings

Where there are criminal proceedings outstanding against the member concerned, proceedings under these Regulations, other than exercise of the power to suspend under regulation 5, shall not take place unless the chief officer concerned believes that in the exceptional circumstances of the case it would be appropriate for them to do so.

7.   Investigation procedure

(1)   Subject to paragraph (2), where a report, complaint or allegation is received by the chief officer which indicates that the conduct of a member of a police force did

not meet the appropriate standard, the case may be referred by him to an officer, who shall satisfy the conditions in paragraph (3), to supervise the investigation of the case.

(2)   Paragraph (1) shall not apply where the case arises from a complaint to which section 72 of the 1996 Act applies.

(3)   The supervising officer shall be—
(a)   at least one rank above that of the member concerned;
(b)   of at least the rank of superintendent;
(c)   a member of the same force as the member concerned; and
(d)   not an interested party.

8.   Appointment of investigating officer

(1)   The supervising officer may appoint an investigating officer to investigate the case.

(2)   The investigating officer shall be—
(a)   a member of the same police force as the member concerned or, if at the request of the supervising officer the chief officer of some other force agrees to provide an investigating officer, a member of that other force;
(b)   of at least the rank of inspector or, if the member concerned is a superintendent, of at least the rank of assistant chief constable or, if the investigating officer is a member of the City of London or metropolitan police force, of at least the rank of commander;
(c)   of at least the same rank as the member concerned; and
(d)   not an interested party.

(3)   The provisions of this regulation are without prejudice to the powers of the Authority with regard to the approval of the investigating officer under section 72(3)(a) and (b) of the 1996 Act in a case where the Authority are required, or have determined, to supervise the investigation of a complaint or other matter under that section.

9.   Notice of investigation

The investigating officer shall as soon as is practicable (without prejudicing his or any other investigation of the matter) cause the member concerned to be given written notice—
(a)   that there is to be an investigation into the case;
(b)   of the nature of the report, complaint or allegation;
(c)   informing him that he is not obliged to say anything concerning the matter, but that he may, if he so desires, make a written or oral statement concerning the matter to the investigating officer or to the chief officer concerned;
(d)   informing him that if he makes such a statement it may be used in any subsequent proceedings under these Regulations;
(e)   informing him that he has the right to seek advice from his staff association, and
(f)   informing him that he has the right to be accompanied by a member of a police force, who shall not be an interested party, to any meeting, interview or hearing.

10.   Investigating officer's report

(1)   At the end of his investigation the investigating officer shall submit a written report on the case to the supervising officer and, if the Authority are supervising the investigation, also to the Authority.

(2)   If at any time during his investigation it appears to the investigating officer that the case is one in respect of which the conditions specified in Part I of Schedule 2 are likely to be satisfied, he shall, whether or not the investigation is at an end, submit to the supervising officer—

    (a)   a statement of his belief that the case may be one to which regulation 39 applies and the grounds for that belief; and

    (b)   a written report on the case so far as it has then been investigated.

11.   Procedure on receipt of investigating officer's report

    (1)   Subject to paragraphs (2) and (3), on receipt of the investigating officer's report the supervising officer may refer the case to a hearing.

    (2)   Where—

    (a)   the chief officer has a duty to proceed under section 75(7) or 76(2) or (5) of the 1996 Act; or

    (b)   the member concerned has received two written warnings about his conduct within the previous twelve months and has in a statement made under regulation 9 admitted that his conduct failed to meet the appropriate standard,
the supervising officer shall refer the case to a hearing.

    (3)   Where the supervising officer, on receipt of a report submitted by the investigating officer under paragraph (2) of regulation 10, is of the opinion that the case is one in respect of which the conditions specified in Part I of Schedule 2 are likely to be satisfied, he shall refer the case to the appropriate officer, who shall—

    (a)   if the conditions specified in Part I of Schedule 2 are not satisfied, return the case to the supervising officer;

    (b)   if the conditions specified in Part I of Schedule 2 are satisfied—

       (i)   certify the case as a special case and refer it to a hearing, or

       (ii)   if the circumstances are such as, in his opinion, make such certification inappropriate, return the case to the supervising officer.

    (4)   Where a case is not referred to a hearing no reference to it shall be made on the member concerned's personal record.

    (5)   Proceedings at or in connection with a hearing to which a case is referred under this regulation shall, for the purposes of section 65 of the 1996 Act (interpretation of Chapter I of Part IV), be disciplinary proceedings.

12.   Withdrawal of case

    (1)   At any time before the beginning of the hearing the supervising officer may direct that the case be withdrawn, unless the chief officer has a duty to proceed under section 75(7) or 76(2) or (5) of the 1996 Act.

    (2)   Where a case is withdrawn it shall be treated as if the supervising officer had decided not to refer it to a hearing.

13.   Notice of decision to refer case to a hearing

    (1)   The supervising officer shall ensure that, as soon as practicable, the member concerned is given written notice of a decision to refer the case to a hearing and that, not less than 21 days before the date of hearing, the member concerned is supplied with copies of—

    (a)   any statement he may have made to the investigating officer; and

    (b)   any relevant statement, document or other material obtained during the course of the investigation.

    (2)   The notice given under paragraph (1) shall specify the conduct of the member concerned which it is alleged failed to meet the appropriate standard and the paragraph of the Code of Conduct in respect of which the appropriate standard is alleged not to have been met.

    (3)   In this regulation any reference to a copy of a statement shall, where it was not made in writing, be construed as a reference to a copy of an account thereof.

14. Limitation on sanctions

No sanction may be imposed under regulation 31 unless the case has been referred to a hearing.

15. Notice of hearing

(1)   The supervising officer shall ensure that at least 21 days in advance the member concerned is notified of the time, date and place of the hearing.

(2)   In a case to which this paragraph applies the hearing may, if the supervising officer considers it appropriate in the circumstances, take place before the expiry of the 21 days referred to in paragraph (1).

(3)   Paragraph (2) applies where the member concerned is given a written notice under regulation 13(1) of a decision to refer the case to a hearing and—

(a)   at the time he receives such a notice he is detained in pursuance of the sentence of a court in a prison or other institution to which the Prison Act 1952 applies, or has received a suspended sentence of imprisonment; and

(b)   having been supplied under regulation 13 with the documents therein mentioned he does not elect to be legally represented at the hearing.

16. Legal representation

If the supervising officer is of the opinion that the hearing should have available the sanctions of dismissal, requirement to resign or reduction in rank, he shall cause the member concerned to be given notice in writing, at the same time as he is given notice of the hearing under regulation 15, of the opportunity to elect to be legally represented at the hearing and of the effect of section 84(1) to (3) of the 1996 Act.

17. Procedure on receipt of notice

(1)   The member concerned shall be invited to state in writing, within 14 days of the date on which he is notified that the last of the documents required by regulation 13(1) to be supplied to him have been so supplied—

(a)   whether or not he accepts that his conduct did not meet the appropriate standard;

(b)   in a case where regulation 16 applies, whether he wishes to be legally represented at the hearing;

(c)   whether he proposes to call any witnesses to relevant facts at the hearing and the names and addresses of any such witnesses whose attendance he wishes the supervising officer to take steps to secure.

(2)   Any witness whose attendance the member concerned wishes the supervising officer to take steps to secure who is a member of a police force shall be ordered to attend at the hearing of the case, and the supervising officer, where so requested, shall cause any other such witnesses to be given due notice that their attendance is desired and of the time and place of the hearing.

(3)   Nothing in this regulation shall require a hearing to be adjourned where a witness is unable or unwilling to attend the hearing.

18. Officers conducting the hearing

(1)   Where a case is referred to a hearing it shall be heard by three officers appointed by the chief officer concerned who shall not be interested parties.

(2)   Subject to regulation 29, one such officer shall be of the rank of assistant chief constable or, where the member concerned is a member of the City of London or metropolitan police force of at least the rank of commander, who shall be the presiding officer.

(3)   Subject to paragraph (4), the presiding officer shall be assisted by two officers of at least the rank of superintendent who shall be from the same force as the member concerned.

(4)   Where the member concerned is a superintendent, the presiding officer shall be assisted by two officers of the rank of assistant chief constable or, if the assisting officers are members of the City of London or metropolitan police force, of at least the rank of commander, who shall be from a different force or forces from the member concerned.

19.   Documents to be supplied to the member concerned

(1)   Where the member concerned accepts, in accordance with regulation 17, that his conduct fell short of the appropriate standard a summary of the facts of the case shall be prepared, a copy of which shall be supplied to the member concerned at least 14 days before the hearing.

(2)   If the member concerned does not agree with the summary of facts he may submit a response within 7 days of receipt of the summary.

(3)   Where the member concerned does not accept that his conduct fell short of the appropriate standard no summary of facts shall be prepared.

20.   Documents to be supplied to officers conducting the hearing

There shall be supplied to the officers conducting the hearing—

(a)   a copy of the notice given under regulation 13; and

(b)   where a summary of facts has been prepared under regulation 19, a copy of that summary and of any response from the member concerned.

21.   Representation

(1)   Unless the member concerned has given notice in accordance with regulation 17 that he wishes to be legally represented, the supervising officer shall appoint a member of a police force to present the case.

(2)   The member concerned may conduct his case either in person or by a member of a police force selected by him or, if he has given notice in accordance with regulation 17 that he wishes to be legally represented, by counsel or a solicitor.

22.   Conduct of hearing

(1)   The officers conducting the hearing may from time to time adjourn if it appears to them to be necessary or expedient to do so for the due hearing of the case.

(2)   Any decision of the officers conducting the hearing shall be based on a simple majority, but shall not indicate whether it was taken unanimously or by a majority.

23.   Procedure at hearing

(1)   Subject to the provisions of these Regulations, the officers conducting the hearing shall determine their own procedure.

(2)   The officers conducting the hearing shall review the facts of the case and decide whether or not the conduct of the member concerned met the appropriate standard and, if it did not, whether in all the circumstances it would be reasonable to impose any, and if so which, sanction.

(3)   The officers conducting the hearing shall not find that the conduct of the member concerned failed to meet the appropriate standard unless the conduct is—

(a)   admitted by the member concerned; or

(b)   proved by the person presenting the case on the balance of probabilities, to have failed to meet that standard.

24.   Attendance of member concerned at hearing

(1)   The member concerned shall be ordered to attend the hearing.

(2)   If the member concerned fails to attend the hearing, it may be proceeded with and concluded in his absence.

(3)   Where the member concerned informs the presiding officer in advance that he is unable to attend due to ill-health or some other unavoidable reason, the hearing may be adjourned.

(4)   Where, owing to the absence of the member concerned, it is impossible to comply with any of the procedures set out in these Regulations, that procedure shall be dispensed with.

25.   Attendance of complainant at hearing

(1)   This regulation shall apply where there has been a complaint against the member concerned.

(2)   Notwithstanding anything in regulation 26(1), but subject to paragraphs (3) and (5), the complainant shall be allowed to attend the hearing while witnesses are being examined, or cross-examined, and may at the discretion of the presiding officer be accompanied by a friend or relative.

(3)   Where the complainant or any person allowed to accompany him is to be called as a witness at the hearing, he and any person allowed to accompany him shall not be allowed to attend before he gives his evidence.

(4)   Where the member concerned gives evidence, then, after the presenting officer has had an opportunity of cross-examining him, the presiding officer shall put to him any questions which the complainant requests should be so put and might have been properly so put by the presenting officer or, at the presiding officer's discretion, may allow the complainant to put such questions to the member concerned.

(5)   Subject as aforesaid, the complainant and any person allowed to accompany him shall neither intervene in, nor interrupt, the hearing; and if he or such a person shall behave in a disorderly or abusive manner, or otherwise misconduct himself, the presiding officer may exclude him from the remainder of the hearing.

(6)   In this regulation a reference to the complainant is a reference to the originator of the complaint notwithstanding that it was transmitted to the chief officer concerned by some other person or by the Authority or some other body.

26.   Attendance of others at hearing

(1)   Subject to regulation 25 and paragraphs (2) and (3), the hearing shall be in private:

Provided that it shall be within the discretion of the presiding officer to allow any solicitor or any such other persons as he considers desirable to attend the whole or such part of the hearing as he may think fit, subject to the consent of all parties to the hearing.

(2)   Any member of the Authority shall be entitled to attend the hearing in a case to which regulation 25 applies or which arises from a matter to which section 72 of the 1996 Act applies.

(3)   The member concerned may be accompanied at the hearing by a member of a police force.

(4)   The presiding officer may allow witnesses to be accompanied at the hearing by a friend or relative.

27.   Exclusion of public from hearing

Where it appears to the presiding officer that a witness may, in giving evidence, disclose information which, in the public interest, ought not to be disclosed to a member of the public he shall require any member of the public including the complainant and any person allowed to accompany the complainant or any witness to withdraw while the evidence is given.

28. Statements in lieu of oral evidence

(1) Any question as to whether any evidence is admissible, or whether any question should or should not be put to a witness, shall be determined by the presiding officer.

(2) With the consent of the member concerned the presiding officer may allow any document to be adduced in evidence during the hearing notwithstanding that a copy thereof has not been supplied to the member concerned in accordance with regulation 13(1).

29. Remission of cases

(1) The hearing of the case—
  (a) shall, in the circumstances mentioned in paragraph (2); or
  (b) may, in the circumstances mentioned in paragraph (5),
be remitted by the presiding officer concerned to an officer of equivalent rank in the force concerned or to an officer of equivalent rank in another force who, at the presiding officer's request, has agreed to act as the presiding officer in the matter.

(2) A case shall be so remitted if—
  (a) the presiding officer is an interested party otherwise than in his capacity as such; or
  (b) there would not, because the member concerned was not given notice under regulation 16 of the opportunity to elect to be legally represented at the hearing, be available on a finding against him any of the sanctions referred to in that regulation, and it appears to the presiding officer concerned that those sanctions ought to be so available and that accordingly it would be desirable for there to be another hearing at which the member concerned could, if he so wished, be so represented.

(3) Where a case is remitted to another officer under paragraph (2)(b) notice in writing shall be served on the member concerned inviting him to elect, within 14 days of the receipt thereof, to be legally represented at the hearing before that officer.

(4) An officer remitting a case under paragraph (2)(b) shall not give to the officer to whom the case has been remitted any indication of his assessment of the case or of the sanction which might be imposed.

(5) A case not falling within paragraph (2) may be remitted by the presiding officer in accordance with paragraph (1) if, either before or during the hearing, the presiding officer concerned considers remission appropriate.

30. Record of hearing

A verbatim record of the proceedings at the hearing shall be taken and, if the member concerned so requests within the time limit for any appeal and after he has lodged notice of appeal in accordance with rules made under section 85 of the Police Act 1996, a transcript of the record or a copy thereof shall be supplied to him by the presiding officer.

31. Sanctions

(1) Subject to section 84(1) of the 1996 Act, the officers conducting the hearing may impose any of the following sanctions, namely—
  (a) dismissal from the force;
  (b) requirement to resign from the force as an alternative to dismissal taking effect either forthwith or on such date as may be specified in the decision;
  (c) reduction in rank;
  (d) fine;
  (e) reprimand;
  (f) caution.

(2)   Any sanction imposed under paragraph (1), except a requirement to resign, shall have immediate effect.

(3)   A fine imposed under paragraph (1) shall be such that, if it were recovered by way of deductions from the pay of the member concerned during the period of thirteen weeks following the imposition of the sanction, the aggregate sum which might be so deducted in respect of any one week (whether on account of one or more fines) would not exceed one seventh of his weekly pay.

32.   Personal record to be considered before sanction imposed

Where the question of the sanction to be imposed is being considered, the officers conducting the hearing—

(a)   shall have regard to the record of police service of the member concerned as shown on his personal record and may receive evidence from any witness whose evidence would, in the opinion of the officers conducting the hearing or member concerned, assist in determining the question; and

(b)   the member concerned, or his representative, shall be afforded an opportunity to make oral or, if appropriate, written representations as respects the question or to adduce evidence relevant thereto.

33.   Notification of finding

The member concerned shall be informed orally of the finding and of any sanction imposed at the conclusion of the hearing and shall be provided with a written notification and summary of the reasons within three days.

34.   Request for a review

(1)   Where a sanction is imposed under regulation 31, the member concerned shall be entitled to request the chief officer of the force concerned or, where the member concerned is a member of the metropolitan police force, an assistant commissioner ('the reviewing officer'), to review the finding or the sanction imposed or both the finding and the sanction.

(2)   A request for a review must be made to the reviewing officer in writing within 14 days of receipt of the written summary of reasons given in accordance with regulation 33 unless this period is extended by the reviewing officer.

(3)   The request for a review shall state the grounds on which the review is requested and whether a meeting is requested.

35.   Conduct of the review

(1)   The reviewing officer shall hold a meeting with the member concerned if requested to do so.

(2)   Where a meeting is held the member concerned may be accompanied by a member of a police force and, in a case where regulation 16 applies, by counsel or a solicitor.

36.   Finding of the review

(1)   The member concerned shall be informed of the finding of the reviewing officer in writing within three days of completion of the review.

(2)   The reviewing officer may confirm the decision of the hearing or he may impose a different sanction which is specified in regulation 31(1) but he may not impose a sanction greater than that imposed at the hearing.

(3)   The decision of the reviewing officer shall take effect by way of substitution for the decision of the hearing and as from the date of that hearing.

(4)   Where as a result of the decision of the reviewing officer the member concerned is dismissed, required to resign or reduced in rank he shall be notified in writing of his right of appeal to a Police Appeals Tribunal.

37. Hearing of review in absence of chief officer

(1)   Subject to paragraphs (2) to (4), where the chief officer is an interested party or the circumstances in section 12(4)(a) or (b) of the 1996 Act apply, the review shall be conducted by the assistant chief constable designated under section 12(4) of the 1996 Act.

(2)   Where the designated assistant chief constable is absent or an interested party, the review shall be conducted by the chief officer of another force who has agreed to act in that capacity.

(3)   Where the member concerned is a member of the metropolitan police force the review shall be conducted by an assistant commissioner who is not an interested party.

(4)   Where the member concerned is a member of the City of London police force, the review shall be conducted by the Commissioner or, if he is absent or an interested party, by the chief officer of another force who has agreed to act in that capacity or an assistant commissioner of the metropolitan police force who has agreed to act in that capacity.

38. Record of conduct proceedings

The chief officer concerned shall cause a book of record to be kept in which shall be entered every case brought against a member of the police force, together with the finding thereon and a record of the decision in any further proceedings in connection therewith.

39. Special cases

(1)   This regulation applies to any case in which a report, complaint or allegation is made which indicates that the conduct of a member of a police force did not meet the appropriate standard and in respect of which the conditions specified in Part I of Schedule 2 are satisfied and his appropriate officer has issued a certificate under regulation 11(3)(b)(i).

(2)   In the application of these Regulations to a case to which this regulation applies, regulations 12 to 37 shall, subject to paragraph (3), have effect subject to the modifications specified in Part II of Schedule 2.

(3)   Where the case is one to which this regulation applies but has been returned to the supervising officer in pursuance of any provision of these Regulations as modified by Part II of Schedule 2, the provisions referred to in paragraph (2) shall thereafter have effect in relation to the case without modification.

(4)   In Part II of Schedule 2, any reference to a provision in these Regulations shall, unless the contrary intention appears, be construed as a reference to that provision as modified by that Part.

Regulation 4(1)   SCHEDULE 1
                                   CODE OF CONDUCT

1. Honesty and integrity

It is of paramount importance that the public has faith in the honesty and integrity of police officers. Officers should therefore be open and truthful in their dealings; avoid being improperly beholden to any person or institution; and discharge their duties with integrity.

2. Fairness and impartiality

Police officers have a particular responsibility to act with fairness and impartiality in all their dealings with the public and their colleagues.

3. Politeness and tolerance
Officers should treat members of the public and colleagues with courtesy and respect, avoiding abusive or deriding attitudes or behaviour. In particular, officers must avoid: favouritism of an individual or group; all forms of harassment, victimisation or unreasonable discrimination; and overbearing conduct to a colleague, particularly to one junior in rank or service.

4. Use of force and abuse of authority
Officers must never knowingly use more force than is reasonable, nor should they abuse their authority.

5. Performance of duties
Officers should be conscientious and diligent in the performance of their duties. Officers should attend work promptly when rostered for duty. If absent through sickness or injury, they should avoid activities likely to retard their return to duty.

6. Lawful orders
The police service is a disciplined body. Unless there is good and sufficient cause to do otherwise, officers must obey all lawful orders and abide by the provisions of Police Regulations. Officers should support their colleagues in the execution of their lawful duties, and oppose any improper behaviour, reporting it where appropriate.

7. Confidentiality
Information which comes into the possession of the police should be treated as confidential. It should not be used for personal benefit and nor should it be divulged to other parties except in the proper course of police duty. Similarly, officers should respect, as confidential, information about force policy and operations unless authorised to disclose it in the course of their duties.

8. Criminal offences
Officers must report any proceedings for a criminal offence taken against them. Conviction of a criminal offence may of itself result in further action being taken.

9. Property
Officers must exercise reasonable care to prevent loss or damage to property (excluding their own personal property but including police property).

10. Sobriety
Whilst on duty officers must be sober. Officers should not consume alcohol when on duty unless specifically authorised to do so or it becomes necessary for the proper discharge of police duty.

11. Appearance
Unless on duties which dictate otherwise, officers should always be well turned out, clean and tidy whilst on duty in uniform or in plain clothes.

12. General conduct
Whether on or off duty, police officers should not behave in a way which is likely to bring discredit upon the police service.

Notes
(a) The primary duties of those who hold the office of constable are the protection of life and property, the preservation of the Queen's peace, and the prevention and detection of criminal offences. To fulfil these duties they are granted extraordinary powers; the public and the police service therefore have the right to expect the highest standards of conduct from them.

(b)   This Code sets out the principles which guide police officers' conduct. It does not seek to restrict officers' discretion: rather it aims to define the parameters of conduct within which that discretion should be exercised. However, it is important to note that any breach of the principles in this Code may result in action being taken by the organisation, which, in serious cases, could involve dismissal.

(c)   This Code applies to the conduct of police officers in all ranks whilst on duty, or whilst off duty if the conduct is serious enough to indicate that an officer is not fit to be a police officer. It will be applied in a reasonable and objective manner. Due regard will be paid to the degree of negligence or deliberate fault and to the nature and circumstances of an officer's conduct. Where off duty conduct is in question, this will be measured against the generally accepted standards of the day.

[. . .]

EXPLANATORY NOTE
(This note is not part of the Regulations)

These Regulations make provision, in pursuance of section 50 of the Police Act 1996, with respect to the conduct of members of police forces and the maintenance of discipline and establish procedures for cases in which a member of a police force may be dealt with by dismissal, requirement to resign, reduction in rank, fine, reprimand or caution. The Regulations, by virtue of regulation 3, do not apply to senior officers.

The Regulations revoke (with savings) the Police (Discipline) Regulations 1985 and provide new procedures for dealing with conduct which fails to meet the standard set out in the Code of Conduct contained in Schedule 1 to the Regulations.

Regulation 5 enables a chief officer of police to suspend a member of his force in respect of whose conduct a report, complaint or allegation has indicated failure to meet the appropriate standard. Regulation 6 precludes proceedings (except suspension) being taken under the Regulations while criminal proceedings are outstanding, unless there are exceptional circumstances.

Regulations 7 to 10 provide for an investigation of the case and a report to a supervising officer who may then refer the case to a hearing under regulation 11. Regulations 12 to 20 deal with the preliminary stages prior to a hearing and regulations 21 to 28 with representation, procedure and attendance at the hearing. Regulation 29 allows (and in certain cases requires) a hearing to be remitted to another presiding officer. Regulation 30 requires a record to be kept and regulations 31 and 32 deal with the imposition of sanctions.

Regulations 33 to 37 deal with the procedure following a hearing, including review at the request of the member concerned by the chief officer of his force or another senior officer. Regulation 38 requires a record book to be kept by each chief officer recording all proceedings under the Regulations against members of his force.

Regulation 39 and Schedule 2 provide for the Regulations to be modified in the case of special cases of serious conduct of a criminal nature.

Appendix 4 The Police (Conduct) Regulations 1999 (SI 1999 No. 730) as modified by Schedule 2

SPECIAL CASES

PART I   CONDITIONS

1.—(1)   The conditions referred to in regulation 39 are—

(a)   the report, complaint or allegation indicates that the conduct of the member concerned is of a serious nature and that an imprisonable offence may have been committed by the member concerned; and

(b)   the conduct is such that, were the case to be referred to a hearing under regulation 11 and the officers conducting that hearing were to find that the conduct failed to meet the appropriate standard, they would in the opinion of the appropriate officer be likely to impose the sanction specified in regulation 31(1)(a) (dismissal from the force); and

(c)   the report, complaint or allegation is supported by written statements, documents or other material which is, in the opinion of the appropriate officer, sufficient without further evidence to establish on the balance of probabilities that the conduct of the member concerned did not meet the appropriate standard; and

(d)   the appropriate officer is of the opinion that it is in the public interest for the member concerned to cease to be a member of a police force without delay.

(2)   In this paragraph an 'imprisonable offence' means an offence which is punishable with imprisonment in the case of a person aged 21 or over.

PART II   MODIFICATIONS

1.   Citation and commencement

These Regulations may be cited as the Police (Conduct) Regulations 1999 and shall come into force on 1st April 1999.

2.   Revocations and transitional provisions

(1)   Subject to the following provisions of this regulation, the Police (Discipline) Regulations 1985 ('the 1985 Regulations'), the Police (Discipline) (Amendment)

Regulations 1991, the Police (Discipline) (Amendment) Regulations 1995 and the Police (Discipline) (Amendment No. 2) Regulations 1995 are hereby revoked.

(2)   Subject to paragraph (3), where a report, complaint or allegation has been or is received in respect of conduct by a member of a police force which occurred or commenced before 1st April 1999—

(a)   nothing in these Regulations shall apply, and

(b)   the 1985 Regulations shall, as far as applicable, continue to have effect.

(3)   In the case of a report, complaint or allegation which—

(a)   relates to conduct by a member of a police force which occurred or commenced before 1st April 1999, but

(b)   is received on or after 1st April 2000,

the conduct shall be treated, for the purposes of this regulation, as having occurred or, as the case may be, commenced on 1st April 1999.

3.   Regulations not to apply in the case of senior officers

These Regulations shall not apply in relation to the conduct of a chief constable or other officer holding a rank above that of superintendent.

4.   Interpretation

(1)   In these Regulations, unless the context otherwise requires—

'the appropriate officer' means—

(a)   where the member concerned is a member of the metropolitan police force or the City of London police force, an assistant commissioner in that police force;

(b)   in any other case, an assistant chief constable;

'appropriate standard' means the standard set out in the Code of Conduct;

'Authority' means the Police Complaints Authority;

'Code of Conduct' means the code of conduct contained in Schedule 1;

'complaint' has the meaning assigned to it by section 65 of the 1996 Act;

'an interested party' means a witness or any person involved in the conduct which is the subject of the case or who otherwise has a direct interest in the case;

'member concerned' means the officer in relation to whose conduct there has been a report, complaint or allegation;

'police force concerned' means, in relation to a person whose conduct is the subject of a report, complaint or allegation, the police force of which he is a member; and any reference to the chief officer concerned is a reference to the chief officer of that force;

'supervising officer' means the officer appointed under regulation 7 to supervise the investigation of the case; and

'the 1996 Act' means the Police Act 1996.

(2)   In these Regulations, unless the context otherwise requires, any reference to a regulation or Schedule shall be construed as a reference to a regulation or Schedule contained in these Regulations.

5.   Suspension

(1)   Where there has been a report, complaint or allegation which indicates that the conduct of a member of a police force does not meet the appropriate standard the chief officer of the force concerned may suspend the member concerned from membership of the force and from his office of constable whether or not the matter has been investigated.

(2)   The chief officer concerned may exercise the power to suspend the member concerned under this regulation at any time from the time of the receipt of the report, complaint or allegation until—

(a) the supervising officer decides not to refer the case to a hearing,

(b) the notification of a finding that the conduct of the member concerned did not fail to meet the appropriate standard,

(c) the time limit under regulation 34 for giving notice of intention to seek a review has expired, or

(d) any review under regulation 35 has been completed.

(3) Where the member concerned is suspended under this regulation, he shall be suspended until there occurs any of the events mentioned in paragraph (2)(i) to (iv), or until the chief officer decides he shall cease to be suspended, whichever first occurs.

(4) Where the member concerned who is suspended is required to resign under regulation 31, he shall remain suspended during the period of his notice.

(5) The chief officer concerned may delegate his powers under this regulation to an officer of at least the rank of assistant chief constable or, where the member concerned is a member of the City of London or metropolitan police force, to an officer of at least the rank of commander.

6. Conduct of investigations where there are outstanding criminal proceedings

Where there are criminal proceedings outstanding against the member concerned, proceedings under these Regulations, other than exercise of the power to suspend under regulation 5, shall not take place unless the chief officer concerned believes that in the exceptional circumstances of the case it would be appropriate for them to do so.

7. Investigation procedure

(1) Subject to paragraph (2), where a report, complaint or allegation is received by the chief officer which indicates that the conduct of a member of a police force did not meet the appropriate standard, the case may be referred by him to an officer, who shall satisfy the conditions in paragraph (3), to supervise the investigation of the case.

(2) Paragraph (1) shall not apply where the case arises from a complaint to which section 72 of the 1996 Act applies.

(3) The supervising officer shall be—

(a) at least one rank above that of the member concerned;

(b) of at least the rank of superintendent;

(c) a member of the same force as the member concerned; and

(d) not an interested party.

8. Appointment of investigating officer

(1) The supervising officer may appoint an investigating officer to investigate the case.

(2) The investigating officer shall be—

(a) a member of the same police force as the member concerned or, if at the request of the supervising officer the chief officer of some other force agrees to provide an investigating officer, a member of that other force;

(b) of at least the rank of inspector or, if the member concerned is a superintendent, of at least the rank of assistant chief constable or, if the investigating officer is a member of the City of London or metropolitan police force, of at least the rank of commander;

(c) of at least the same rank as the member concerned; and

(d) not an interested party.

(3) The provisions of this regulation are without prejudice to the powers of the Authority with regard to the approval of the investigating officer under section 72(3)(a) and (b) of the 1996 Act in a case where the Authority are required, or have

determined, to supervise the investigation of a complaint or other matter under that section.

9.   Notice of investigation

The investigating officer shall as soon as is practicable (without prejudicing his or any other investigation of the matter) cause the member concerned to be given written notice—

(a)   that there is to be an investigation into the case;

(b)   of the nature of the report, complaint or allegation;

(c)   informing him that he is not obliged to say anything concerning the matter, but that he may, if he so desires, make a written or oral statement concerning the matter to the investigating officer or to the chief officer concerned;

(d)   informing him that if he makes such a statement it may be used in any subsequent proceedings under these Regulations;

(e)   informing him that he has the right to seek advice from his staff association, and

(f)   informing him that he has the right to be accompanied by a member of a police force, who shall not be an interested party, to any meeting, interview or hearing.

10.   Investigating officer's report

(1)   At the end of his investigation the investigating officer shall submit a written report on the case to the supervising officer and, if the Authority are supervising the investigation, also to the Authority.

(2)   If at any time during his investigation it appears to the investigating officer that the case is one in respect of which the conditions specified in Part I of Schedule 2 are likely to be satisfied, he shall, whether or not the investigation is at an end, submit to the supervising officer—

(a)   a statement of his belief that the case may be one to which regulation 39 applies and the grounds for that belief; and

(b)   a written report on the case so far as it has then been investigated.

11.   Procedure on receipt of investigating officer's report

(1)   Subject to paragraphs (2) and (3), on receipt of the investigating officer's report the supervising officer may refer the case to a hearing.

(2)   Where—

(a)   the chief officer has a duty to proceed under section 75(7) or 76(2) or (5) of the 1996 Act; or

(b)   the member concerned has received two written warnings about his conduct within the previous twelve months and has in a statement made under regulation 9 admitted that his conduct failed to meet the appropriate standard, the supervising officer shall refer the case to a hearing.

(3)   Where the supervising officer, on receipt of a report submitted by the investigating officer under paragraph (2) of regulation 10, is of the opinion that the case is one in respect of which the conditions specified in Part I of Schedule 2 are likely to be satisfied, he shall refer the case to the appropriate officer, who shall—

(a)   if the conditions specified in Part I of Schedule 2 are not satisfied, return the case to the supervising officer;

(b)   if the conditions specified in Part I of Schedule 2 are satisfied—

(i)   certify the case as a special case and refer it to a hearing, or

(ii)   if the circumstances are such as, in his opinion, make such certification inappropriate, return the case to the supervising officer.

(4)   Where a case is not referred to a hearing no reference to it shall be made on the member concerned's personal record.

(5)   Proceedings at or in connection with a hearing to which a case is referred under this regulation shall, for the purposes of section 65 of the 1996 Act (interpretation of Chapter I of Part IV), be disciplinary proceedings.

12.   Withdrawal of case
At any time before the beginning of the hearing the appropriate officer may direct that the case be returned to the supervising officer.

13.   Notice of decision to refer case to a hearing
(1)   The appropriate officer shall ensure that, as soon as practicable, the member concerned is invited to an interview with the appropriate officer at which he shall be given written notice of the decision to refer the case to a hearing and supplied with copies of—

   (a)   the certificate issued under regulation 11(3)(b)(i);

   (b)   any statement he may have made to the investigating officer; and

   (c)   any relevant statement, document or other material obtained during the course of the investigation.

(2)   The notice given under paragraph (1) shall specify the conduct of the member concerned which it is alleged failed to meet the appropriate standard and the paragraph of the Code of Conduct in respect of which the appropriate standard is alleged not to have been met.

(3)   In this regulation any reference to a copy of a statement shall, where it was not made in writing, be construed as a reference to a copy of an account thereof.

(4)   Where the member concerned fails or is unable to attend the interview referred to in paragraph (1), the notice and copy document referred to in that paragraph shall be—

   (a)   delivered to the member concerned personally, or

   (b)   left with some person at, or sent by recorded delivery to, the address at which he is, with the approval of the chief constable, residing.

14.   Limitation on sanctions
No sanction may be imposed under regulation 31 unless the case has been referred to a hearing.

15.   Notice of hearing
The appropriate officer shall fix a date for the hearing which shall be not less than 21 and not more than 28 days from the date on which notice is given under regulation 13 and shall ensure that the member concerned is forthwith notified of the time, date and place of the hearing.

16.   Legal representation
The appropriate officer shall cause the member concerned to be given notice in writing, at the same time as he is given notice of the hearing under regulation 15, of the opportunity to elect to be legally represented at the hearing and of the effect of section 84(1) to (3) of the 1996 Act.

17.   Procedure on receipt of notice
(1)   The member concerned shall be invited to state in writing, within 14 days of the date on which he receives the documents referred to in regulation 13—

   (a)   whether or not he accepts that his conduct did not meet the appropriate standard; and

   (b)   whether he wishes to be legally represented at the hearing; and

   (c)   whether he proposes to call any witnesses to relevant facts at the hearing and the names and addresses of any such witnesses whose attendance he wishes the supervising officer to take steps to secure.

18.   Officers conducting the hearing

(1)   Subject to paragraph (2), a case which is referred to a hearing under regulation 11(3)(b)(i) shall be heard by the chief officer concerned.

(2)   Where the chief officer concerned is an interested party, the case shall be heard by the chief officer of another force who has agreed to act in that capacity.

19.   (omitted)

20.   Documents to be supplied to officers conducting the hearing

There shall be supplied to the officer conducting the hearing a copy of the notice given, and of any documents provided to the member concerned, under regulation 13.

21.   Representation

(1)   Unless the member concerned has given notice in accordance with regulation 17 that he wishes to be legally represented, the appropriate officer shall appoint a member of a police force to present the case.

(2)   The member concerned may conduct his case either in person or by a member of a police force selected by him or, if he has given notice in accordance with regulation 17 that he wishes to be legally represented, by counsel or a solicitor.

22.   Conduct of hearing

The officer conducting the hearing may adjourn if it appears to him to be necessary or expedient to do so; but

(a)   shall not exercise the power to adjourn more than once; and

(b)   shall not adjourn for longer than a period of one week or, on application by the member concerned, 4 weeks.

23.   Procedure at hearing

(1)   Subject to the provisions of these Regulations, the officer conducting the hearing shall determine his own procedure.

(2)   The officer conducting the hearing shall review the facts of the case and decide whether or not the conduct of the member concerned met the appropriate standard and, if it did not, whether in all the circumstances it would be reasonable to impose any, and if so which, sanction.

(3)   The officer conducting the hearing shall not find that the conduct of the member concerned failed to meet the appropriate standard unless the conduct is—

(a)   admitted by the member concerned; or

(b)   proved by the person presenting the case on the balance of probabilities, to have failed to meet that standard.

24.   Attendance of member concerned at hearing

(1)   The member concerned shall be ordered to attend the hearing.

(2)   If the member concerned fails to attend the hearing, it may be proceeded with and concluded in his absence.

(3)   Where the member concerned informs the presiding officer in advance that he is unable to attend due to ill-health or some other unavoidable reason, the hearing may be adjourned.

(4)   Where, owing to the absence of the member concerned, it is impossible to comply with any of the procedures set out in these Regulations, that procedure shall be dispensed with.

25.   Attendance of complainant at hearing

(1)   This regulation shall apply where there has been a complaint against the member concerned.

(2)   Notwithstanding anything in regulation 26(1), but subject to paragraph 5 the complainant shall be allowed to attend the hearing and may at the discretion of the officer conducting the hearing be accompanied by a friend or relative.

(3)   (omitted)

(4)   (omitted)

(5)   The complainant and any person allowed to accompany him shall neither intervene in, nor interrupt, the hearing; and if he or such a person shall behave in a disorderly or abusive manner, or otherwise misconduct himself, the officer conducting the hearing may exclude him from the remainder of the hearing.

(6)   In this regulation a reference to the complainant is a reference to the originator of the complaint notwithstanding that it was transmitted to the chief officer concerned by some other person or by the Authority or some other body.

26.   Attendance of others at hearing

(1)   Subject to regulation 25 and paragraphs (2) and (3), the hearing shall be in private: Provided that it shall be within the discretion of the officer conducting the hearing to allow any solicitor or any such other persons as he considers desirable to attend the whole or such part of the hearing as he may think fit, subject to the consent of all parties to the hearing.

(2)   Any member of the Authority shall be entitled to attend the hearing in a case to which regulation 25 applies or which arises from a matter to which section 72 of the 1996 Act applies.

(3)   The member concerned may be accompanied at the hearing by a member of a police force.

(4)   (omitted)

27.   (omitted)

28.   Statements in lieu of oral evidence

(1)   Any question as to whether any evidence is admissible shall be determined by the officer conducting the hearing.

(2)   With the consent of the member concerned the officer conducting the hearing may allow any document to be adduced in evidence during the hearing notwithstanding that a copy thereof has not been supplied to the member concerned in accordance with regulation 13(1) or (4).

(3)   No witnesses shall be called by either party to the case.

29.   Remission of cases

(1)   The hearing of the case—

(a)   shall, in the circumstances mentioned in paragraph (2);

(b)   may, in the circumstances mentioned in paragraph (5),

be remitted by the officer conducting the hearing concerned to an officer of equivalent rank in the force concerned or to an officer of equivalent rank in another force who, as the officer conducting the hearing request, has agreed to act as the officer conducting the hearing in the matter.—

(2)   A case shall be so remitted if—

(a)   the officer conducting the hearing is an interested party otherwise than in his capacity as such; or

(b)   (omitted)

(3)   (omitted)

(4)   (omitted)

(5)   A case not falling within paragraph (2) may be remitted by the officer conducting the hearing in accordance with paragraph (1) if, either before or during

the hearing, the officer conducting the hearing concerned considers remission appropriate.

(6) The officer conducting the hearing may return the case to the supervising officer if, either before or during the hearing, the officer conducting the hearing considers it appropriate to do so.

30. Record of hearing

A verbatim record of the proceedings at the hearing shall be taken and, if the member concerned so requests within the time limit for any appeal and after he has lodged notice of appeal in accordance with rules made under section 85 of the Police Act 1996, a transcript of the record or a copy thereof shall be supplied to him by the officer conducting the hearing.

31. Sanctions

(1) Subject to section 84(1) of the 1996 Act, the officer conducting the hearing may impose any of the following sanctions, namely—

(a) dismissal from the force;

(b) requirement to resign from the force as an alternative to dismissal taking effect either forthwith or on such date as may be specified in the decision;

(c) reduction in rank;

(d) fine;

(e) reprimand;

(f) caution.

(2) Any sanction imposed under paragraph (1), except a requirement to resign, shall have immediate effect.

(3) A fine imposed under paragraph (1) shall be such that, if it were recovered by way of deductions from the pay of the member concerned during the period of thirteen weeks following the imposition of the sanction, the aggregate sum which might be so deducted in respect of any one week (whether on account of one or more fines) would not exceed one seventh of his weekly pay.

32. Personal record to be considered before sanction imposed

Where the question of the sanction to be imposed is being considered, the officer conducting the hearing—

(a) shall have regard to the record of police service of the member concerned as shown on his personal record and may admit such documentary evidence as would in the opinion of the officer conducting the hearing or member concerned, assist in determining the question; and

(b) the member concerned, or his representative, shall be afforded an opportunity to make oral or, if appropriate, written representations as respects the question or to adduce documentary evidence relevant thereto.

33. Notification of finding

The member concerned shall be informed orally of the finding and of any sanction imposed at the conclusion of the hearing and shall be provided with a written notification and summary of the reasons within 24 hours.

34. Request for a review

(1) Where a sanction is imposed under regulation 31, the member concerned shall be entitled to request the chief officer concerned to refer the case to the chief officer of another force who has agreed to act in that capacity ('the reviewing officer') to review the finding or the sanction imposed or both the finding and the sanction.

(2)   A request for a review must be made to the chief officer concerned in writing within 14 days of receipt of the written summary of reasons given in accordance with regulation 33.

35.   Conduct of the review

(1)   The reviewing officer shall hold a meeting with the member concerned if requested to do so.

(2)   Where a meeting is held the member concerned may be accompanied by a member of a police force and, in a case where regulation 16 applies, by counsel or a solicitor.

36.   Finding of the review

(1)   The member concerned shall be informed of the finding of the reviewing officer in writing within 24 hours of completion of the review.

(2)   The reviewing officer may confirm the decision of the hearing or he may impose a different sanction which is specified in regulation 31(1) but he may not impose a sanction greater than that imposed at the hearing.

(3)   The decision of the reviewing officer shall take effect by way of substitution for the decision of the hearing and as from the date of that hearing.

(4)   Where as a result of the decision of the reviewing officer the member concerned is dismissed, required to resign or reduced in rank he shall be notified in writing of his right of appeal to a Police Appeals Tribunal.

(5)   Where the reviewing officer considers that the officer conducting the hearing should have returned the case to the supervising officer under regulation 29(6), he shall so return the case and the case shall thereafter be deemed to have been returned under that paragraph.

37.   (omitted)

38.   Record of conduct proceedings

The chief officer concerned shall cause a book of record to be kept in which shall be entered every case brought against a member of the police force, together with the finding thereon and a record of the decision in any further proceedings in connection therewith.

39.   . . .

Appendix 5 Police: The NCIS (Complaints) (Amendment) Regulations 1999 (SI 1999 No. 1273)

Made	*29th April 1999*
Laid before Parliament	*11th May 1999*
Coming into force	*1st June 1999*

The Secretary of State, in exercise of the powers conferred upon him by section 39 of the Police Act 1997, and after complying with the requirements of section 63(3) of the Police Act 1996, hereby makes the following Regulations:

1. These Regulations may be cited as the NCIS (Complaints) (Amendment) Regulations 1999 and shall come into force on 1st June 1999.

2. The NCIS (Complaints) Regulations 1998 shall be amended in accordance with the following provisions of these Regulations.

3. In regulation 2—

(a) after the words 'In these Regulations' there shall be inserted 'unless the context otherwise requires';

(b) in the definition of 'complaint', the words ', other than a police member engaged with NCIS on a period of temporary service under section 97 of the Police Act 1996,' shall be omitted;

(c) in the definition of 'disciplinary proceedings' at the end there shall be added the words 'or, in the case of a seconded police member, section 50 of the Police Act 1996 or any corresponding provision for the time being in force in Scotland or Northern Ireland';

(d) after the definition of 'disciplinary proceedings' there shall be inserted the following definition:

'"interested party" means any person involved in the conduct which is the subject of the complaint or who otherwise has a direct interest in the investigation;'; and

(e) for the definition of 'police force' there shall be substituted the following definition:

'"seconded police member" means a police member appointed under section 9(2)(b) of the 1997 Act.'.

4.—(1) In Part I, for the words 'these Regulations' wherever they occur there shall be substituted 'this Part of these Regulations'.

(2) For regulation 10(4) there shall be substituted the following paragraph:

'(4) The PCA shall send to the NCIS Service Authority—

(a) a copy of every report made under subsection (4) of section 79 of the Police Act 1996; and

(b) any statistical or other general information which relates to the year dealt with by the report and which the PCA consider should be brought to the NCIS Service Authority's attention in connection with its functions under section 40 of the 1997 Act.'.

5. After Part II, there shall be inserted the following provisions:

'PART III   PROCEDURE FOR HANDLING COMPLAINTS RELATING TO THE CONDUCT OF SECONDED POLICE MEMBERS OF NCIS

18. Preliminary
Where a complaint regarding the conduct of a seconded police member of NCIS is submitted to the Director General, he shall take any steps that appear to him to be desirable for the purpose of obtaining or preserving evidence relating to the conduct complained of and shall record the complaint.

19. Investigation of complaint
(1) After recording a complaint under regulation 18, the Director General shall consider whether the complaint is suitable for informal resolution and may appoint a member of NCIS to assist him.

(2) A complaint is not suitable for informal resolution unless—

(a) the member of the public concerned gives his consent, and

(b) the Director General is satisfied that the conduct complained of, even if proved, would not justify criminal or disciplinary proceedings.

(3) If it appears to the Director General that the complaint is suitable for informal resolution, he shall seek to resolve it informally and may appoint a member of NCIS to do so on his behalf.

(4) If it appears to the Director General that the complaint is not suitable for informal resolution, he shall appoint a member of NCIS or a member of the National Crime Squad or of a police force to investigate it formally.

(5) If, after attempts have been made to resolve a complaint informally, it appears to the Director General—

(a) that informal resolution of the complaint is impossible, or

(b) that the complaint is for any other reason not suitable for informal resolution,

he shall appoint a member of NCIS or a member of the National Crime Squad or of a police force to investigate it formally.

(6) If the Director General requests the chief officer of a police force or the Director General of the National Crime Squad to provide a member of that force or, as the case may be, of the National Crime Squad for appointment under paragraph (4) or (5), the chief officer or Director General to whom the request is made shall comply with that request.

(7) No member of NCIS or of the National Crime Squad or of a police force of a rank lower than inspector, or of a rank lower than that of the member whose conduct is the subject of the complaint, may be appointed under paragraph (4) or (5).

(8) As soon as practicable after appointing an investigating officer under paragraph (4) or (5), the Director General shall ensure that the seconded police member whose conduct is the subject of the investigation is given written notice of the nature of the complaint and informed—

(a) that he is not obliged to say anything concerning the matter, but that he may, if he so desires, make a written or oral statement concerning the matter to the investigating officer or to the Director General,

(b) that if he makes such a statement it may be used in any subsequent disciplinary proceedings,

(c) that he has the right to seek advice from his staff association, and

(d) that he has the right to be accompanied by a member of NCIS or a member of the National Crime Squad or of a police force, who shall not be an interested party, to any meeting or interview.

(9) Unless an investigation under this regulation is supervised by the PCA under regulation 22, the investigating officer shall submit his report on it to the Director General.

(10) The Director General shall inform the chief officer of police with whose consent the member whose conduct is the subject of the complaint is engaged with NCIS—

(a) of the appointment of an investigating officer under paragraph (4) or (5); and

(b) of the outcome of the investigation.

20. References of complaints to the PCA

(1) The Director General—

(a) shall refer to the PCA—

(i) any complaint regarding a seconded police member of NCIS alleging that the conduct complained of resulted in the death of, or serious injury to, some other person, and

(ii) any complaint regarding a seconded police member of NCIS which is of the same description as a complaint specified in regulations made by the Secretary of State for the purposes of section 70 of the Police Act 1996, and

(b) may refer to the PCA any complaint which is not required to be referred to them.

(2) The PCA may require the submission to them for consideration of any complaint regarding the conduct of a seconded police member of NCIS not referred to them by the Director General; and the Director General shall comply with any such requirement not later than the end of the specified period.

(3) For the purposes of paragraph (2) the specified period shall be the period which is specified in regulations made by the Secretary of State for the purpose of subsection (2) of section 70 of the Police Act 1996.

(4) Where a complaint falls to be referred to the PCA under paragraph (1)(a), it shall be the duty of the Director General to refer it to them not later than the end of the period specified for the purpose of subsection (1) of section 70 of the Police Act 1996 in regulations made by the Secretary of State.

21. Reference of other matters to the PCA

(1) The Director General may refer to the PCA any matter to which this regulation applies, if it appears to the Director General that the matter ought to be referred by reason—

(a) of its gravity, or

(b) of its exceptional circumstances.

(2)   This regulation applies to any matter which—

(a)   appears to the Director General to indicate that a seconded police member of NCIS may have committed a criminal offence or behaved in a manner which would justify disciplinary proceedings, and

(b)   is not the subject of a complaint.

22.   Supervision of investigation by PCA

(1)   The PCA shall supervise the investigation of—

(a)   any complaint alleging that the conduct of a seconded police member of NCIS resulted in the death of, or serious injury to, some other person,

(b)   any other complaint which is of the same description as a complaint specified for the purposes of section 72 of the Police Act 1996 in regulations made by the Secretary of State under that Act, and

(c)   any complaint which is not within paragraph (a) or (b) and any matter referred to the PCA under regulation 21, if the PCA determine that it is desirable in the public interest that they should do so.

(2)   Where the PCA have made a determination under paragraph (1)(c), they shall notify it to the Director General.

(3)   Where an investigation is to be supervised by the PCA, they may require—

(a)   that no appointment is made under regulation 19(4) or (5) unless they have given notice to the Director General that they approve the person he proposes to appoint, or

(b)   if such an appointment has already been made and the PCA are not satisfied with the person appointed, that—

(i)   the Director General, as soon as reasonably practicable, appoint another member of NCIS or of the National Crime Squad or of a police force and notify the PCA that he proposes to appoint him, and

(ii)   the appointment is not made unless the PCA give notice to the Director General that they approve that person.

(4)   Where the Secretary of State, by regulations made under section 72(4) of the Police Act 1996, authorises the PCA to impose requirements as to a particular investigation additional to any requirement imposed by subsection (3) of that section then, in addition to any requirement imposed by paragraph (3) above, the PCA may impose the like additional requirements, subject to any restrictions or conditions specified in those regulations, in relation to any investigation under this Part of these Regulations.

(5)   A member of NCIS or of the National Crime Squad or of a police force shall comply with any requirement imposed upon him by virtue of the application of paragraph (4).

23.   Reports on investigations etc.

(1)   At the end of an investigation which the PCA have supervised, the investigating officer shall—

(a)   submit a report on the investigation to the PCA, and

(b)   send a copy of the report to the Director General.

(2)   After consideration of a report submitted to them under paragraph (1) the PCA shall submit an appropriate statement to the Director General.

(3)   If it is practicable to do so, the PCA, when submitting the appropriate statement under paragraph (2), shall send a copy of it to the seconded police member of NCIS whose conduct has been investigated.

(4)   If—

(a)   the investigation related to a complaint, and

(b)   it is practicable to do so,
the PCA shall also send a copy of the appropriate statement to the person by or on behalf of whom the complaint was submitted.

(5)   The power to issue an appropriate statement includes power to issue separate statements in respect of the disciplinary and criminal aspects of the investigation.

(6)   No disciplinary proceedings shall be brought before the appropriate statement is submitted to the Director General.

(7)   Subject to paragraph (8), neither the Director General nor the Director of Public Prosecutions shall bring criminal proceedings before the appropriate statement is submitted to the Director General.

(8)   The restriction imposed by paragraph (7) does not apply if it appears to the Director of Public Prosecutions that there are exceptional circumstances which make it undesirable to wait for the submission of the appropriate statement.

(9)   In this regulation "appropriate statement" means a statement—

(a)   as to whether the investigation was or was not conducted to the PCA's satisfaction,

(b)   specifying any respect in which it was not so conducted, and

(c)   dealing with any other matters which are matters of the kind provided for in regulations made under section 72 of the Police Act 1996 for the purposes of that section.

24.   Steps to be taken after investigation

(1)   On receiving—

(a)   a report concerning the conduct of a seconded police member of NCIS which is submitted to him under regulation 19(9), or

(b)   a copy of a report concerning the conduct of such a member which is sent to him under regulation 23(1)(b),
the Director General shall determine whether the report indicates that a criminal offence may have been committed by a seconded police member of NCIS.

(2)   If the Director General determines that the report indicates that a criminal offence may have been committed by a seconded police member of NCIS, he shall send a copy of the report to the Director of Public Prosecutions.

(3)   After the Director of Public Prosecutions has dealt with the question of criminal proceedings, the Director General shall send the PCA a memorandum which—

(a)   is signed by the Director General,

(b)   states whether he considers that disciplinary proceedings should be brought in pursuance of section 97(6)(a) of the Police Act 1996 or any corresponding provision for the time being in force in Scotland or Northern Ireland in respect of the conduct which was the subject of the investigation, and

(c)   if he does not consider that such proceedings should be brought, gives his reasons.

(4)   If the Director General considers that the report does not indicate that a criminal offence may have been committed by a seconded police member of NCIS, he shall send the PCA a memorandum to that effect which—

(a)   is signed by the Director General,

(b)   states whether he considers that disciplinary proceedings should be brought in pursuance of section 97(6)(a) of the Police Act 1996 or any corresponding provision for the time being in force in Scotland or Northern Ireland in respect of the conduct which was the subject of the investigation, and

(c)   if he does not consider that such proceedings should be brought, gives his reasons.

(5)   Where the investigation—

(a)   related to conduct which was the subject of a complaint, and

(b)   was not supervised by the PCA,

the Director General shall, at the same time as he sends the PCA a memorandum under paragraph (3) or (4), send them a copy of the complaint, or of the record of the complaint, and a copy of the report of the investigation.

(6)   Where the Director General has sent a memorandum to the PCA under paragraph (3) or (4) which states that he considers that disciplinary proceedings should be brought—

(a)   he shall take steps to ensure that the temporary service with NCIS of the seconded police member whose conduct was the subject of the investigation is completed as soon as is practicable, and

(b)   he shall inform the chief officer of police with whose consent that member was engaged on such service that he considers that disciplinary proceedings should be brought in pursuance of section 97(6)(a) of the Police Act 1996 or any corresponding provision for the time being in force in Scotland or Northern Ireland in respect of that member's conduct.

25.   Powers of PCA as to disciplinary proceedings

(1)   Where a memorandum under regulation 24 states that the Director General does not consider that disciplinary proceedings should be brought in pursuance of section 97(6)(a) of the Police Act 1996 or any corresponding provision for the time being in force in Scotland or Northern Ireland, the PCA may recommend him to take such steps as are referred to in paragraph (6)(a), and inform the chief officer of police in accordance with paragraph (6)(b), of that regulation.

(2)   If after the PCA have made a recommendation under this regulation and consulted the Director General he is still unwilling to proceed in accordance with regulation 24(6)(a) and (b), they may direct him to do so.

(3)   Where the PCA gives the Director General a direction under this regulation, they shall supply him with a written statement of their reasons for doing so.

(4)   Subject to paragraph (5), it shall be the duty of the Director General to comply with such a direction.

(5)   The PCA may withdraw a direction given under this regulation.

(6)   The Director General shall—

(a)   advise the PCA and the chief officer of police referred to in regulation 24(6)(b) of what action he has taken in response to a recommendation or direction under this regulation, and

(b)   supply the PCA with such other information as they may reasonably require for the purposes of discharging their functions under this regulation.

26.   Reports by PCA

(1)   The PCA may make a report to the Secretary of State on any matters coming to their notice under these Regulations to which they consider that his attention should be drawn by reason of their gravity or of other exceptional circumstances.

(2)   The PCA shall send a copy of any report under paragraph (1) to the NCIS Service Authority and the Director General.

(3)   The Secretary of State shall lay before Parliament a copy of every report received by him under this regulation and shall cause every such report to be published.

(4)   The PCA shall send to the NCIS Service Authority—
(a)   a copy of every report made under subsection (4) of section 79 of the Police Act 1996, and
(b)   any statistical or other general information which relates to the year dealt with by the report and which the PCA consider should be brought to the NCIS Service Authority's attention in connection with its functions under section 40 of the 1997 Act.

27.   Restriction on disclosure of information

(1)   No information received by the PCA in connection with any of their functions under this part of these Regulations shall be disclosed by any person who is or has been a member, officer or servant of the PCA except—
(a)   to the Secretary of State or to a member, officer or servant of the PCA or, so far as may be necessary for the proper discharge of the functions of the PCA, to other persons,
(b)   for the purposes of any criminal, civil or disciplinary proceedings, or
(c)   in the form of a summary or other general statement made by the PCA which does not identify the person from whom the information was received or any person to whom it relates.
(2)   Any person who discloses information in contravention of this regulation shall be guilty of an offence and liable on summary conviction to a fine of an amount not exceeding level 5 on the standard scale.

28.   Regulations

Where the Secretary of State makes regulations under section 81 of the Police Act 1996 as to the procedure to be followed under Chapter I of Part IV of that Act then the procedures provided for by those regulations shall be the procedures to be followed under this Part of these Regulations with the following modifications—
(i)   references to "appropriate authority" and "chief officer" shall be interpreted as references to the Director General;
(ii)   references to a "complaint" shall be interpreted as references to a complaint under this Part of these Regulations, and references to a complainant shall be construed accordingly;
(iii)   references to a "member of a police force" shall be interpreted as references to a seconded police member of NCIS;
(iv)   references to provisions of the Police Act 1996 shall be interpreted as references to the equivalent provisions in this Part of these Regulations.

29.   Admissibility of statements in subsequent proceedings

(1)   Subject to paragraph (2), no statement made by a person for the purpose of the informal resolution of a complaint shall be admissible in any subsequent criminal, civil or disciplinary proceedings.
(2)   A statement is not rendered inadmissible by paragraph (1) if it consists of or includes an admission relating to a matter which does not fall to be resolved informally.'.

EXPLANATORY NOTE
(This note is not part of the Regulations)

These Regulations amend the NCIS (Complaints) Regulations 1998 (the 1998 Regulations) in relation to complaints against seconded police members.
Regulation 3 amends and inserts certain definitions in regulation 2 of the 1998 Regulations. Regulation 5 inserts a new Part III in the 1998 Regulations which makes

provision for the procedures for handling complaints relating to the conduct of police members of NCIS who are engaged on temporary service under section 97 of the Police Act 1996 ('seconded police members'). Part III generally mirrors Chapter I of Part IV of that Act in its application to members of police forces other than senior officers. Regulation 4 makes minor and consequential amendments to Part I of the 1998 Regulations.

Appendix 6 Police: The National Crime Squad (Complaints) (Amendment) Regulations 1999 (SI 1999 No. 1266)

Made	*29th April 1999*
Laid before Parliament	*11th May 1999*
Coming into force	*1st June 1999*

The Secretary of State, in exercise of the powers conferred upon him by section 83 of the Police Act 1997, and after complying with the requirements of section 63(3) of the Police Act 1996, hereby makes the following Regulations:

1. These Regulations maybe cited as the National Crime Squad (Complaints) (Amendment) Regulations 1999 and shall come into force on 1st June 1999.

2. The National Crime Squad (Complaints) Regulations 1998 shall be amended in accordance with the following provisions of these Regulations.

3. In regulation 2—

(a) after the words 'In these Regulations' there shall be inserted 'unless the context otherwise requires';

(b) in the definition of 'complaint', the words ', other than a police member engaged with the National Crime Squad on a period of temporary service under section 97 of the Police Act 1996,' shall be omitted;

(c) in the definition of 'disciplinary proceedings' at the end there shall be added the words 'or, in the case of a seconded police member, section 50 of the Police Act 1996';

(d) after the definition of 'disciplinary proceedings' there shall be inserted the following definition:

"'interested party" means any person involved in the conduct which is the subject of the complaint or who otherwise has a direct interest in the investigation;'; and

(e) for the definition of 'police force' there shall be substituted the following definition:

"'seconded police member" means a police member appointed under section 55(2)(b) of the 1997 Act.'.

4.—(1)   In Part I, for the words 'these Regulations' wherever they occur there shall be substituted 'this Part of these Regulations'.

(2)   For regulation 10(4) there shall be substituted the following paragraph:

'(4)   The PCA shall send to the NCS Service Authority—

(a)   a copy of every report made under subsection (4) of section 79 of the Police Act 1996, and

(b)   any statistical or any other general information which relates to the year dealt with by the report and which the PCA consider should be brought to the NCS Service Authority's attention in connection with its functions under section 84 of the 1997 Act.'.

5.   After Part II, there shall be inserted the following provisions:

'PART III   PROCEDURE FOR HANDLING COMPLAINTS RELATING TO THE CONDUCT OF SECONDED POLICE MEMBERS OF THE NATIONAL CRIME SQUAD

18. Preliminary

Where a complaint regarding the conduct of a seconded police member of the National Crime Squad is submitted to the Director General, he shall take any steps that appear to him to be desirable for the purpose of obtaining or preserving evidence relating to the conduct complained of and shall record the complaint.

19. Investigation of complaint

(1)   After recording a complaint under regulation 18, the Director General shall consider whether the complaint is suitable for informal resolution and may appoint a member of the National Crime Squad to assist him.

(2)   A complaint is not suitable for informal resolution unless—

(a)   the member of the public concerned gives his consent, and

(b)   the Director General is satisfied that the conduct complained of, even if proved, would not justify criminal or disciplinary proceedings.

(3)   If it appears to the Director General that the complaint is suitable for informal resolution, he shall seek to resolve it informally and may appoint a member of the National Crime Squad to do so on his behalf.

(4)   If it appears to the Director General that the complaint is not suitable for informal resolution, he shall appoint a member of the National Crime Squad or a member of NCIS or of a police force to investigate it formally.

(5)   If, after attempts have been made to resolve a complaint informally, it appears to the Director General—

(a)   that informal resolution of the complaint is impossible, or

(b)   that the complaint is for any other reason not suitable for informal resolution,

he shall appoint a member of the National Crime Squad or a member of NCIS or of a police force to investigate it formally.

(6)   If the Director General requests the chief officer of a police force or the Director General of NCIS to provide a member of that force or, as the case may be, of NCIS for appointment under paragraph (4) or (5), the chief officer or Director General to whom the request is made shall comply with that request.

(7)   No member of the National Crime Squad or of NCIS or of a police force of a rank lower than inspector, or of a rank lower than that of the member whose conduct is the subject of the complaint, may be appointed under paragraph (4) or (5).

(8)   As soon as practicable after appointing an investigating officer under paragraph (4) or (5), the Director General shall ensure that the seconded police

member whose conduct is the subject of the investigation is given written notice of the nature of the complaint and informed—

(a)   that he is not obliged to say anything concerning the matter, but that he may, if he so desires, make a written or oral statement concerning the matter to the investigating officer or to the Director General,

(b)   that if he makes such a statement it may be used in any subsequent disciplinary proceedings,

(c)   that he has the right to seek advice from his staff association, and

(d)   that he has the right to be accompanied by a member of the National Crime Squad or a member of NCIS or of a police force, who shall not be an interested party, to any meeting or interview.

(9)   Unless an investigation under this regulation is supervised by the PCA under regulation 22, the investigating officer shall submit his report on it to the Director General.

(10)   The Director General shall inform the chief officer of police with whose consent the member whose conduct is the subject of the complaint is engaged with the National Crime Squad—

(a)   of the appointment of an investigating officer under paragraph (4) or (5); and

(b)   of the outcome of the investigation.

20.   References of complaints to the PCA

(1)   The Director General—

(a)   shall refer to the PCA—

(i)   any complaint regarding a seconded police member of the National Crime Squad alleging that the conduct complained of resulted in the death of, or serious injury to, some other person, and

(ii)   any complaint regarding a seconded police member of the National Crime Squad which is of the same description as a complaint specified in regulations made by the Secretary of State for the purposes of section 70 of the Police Act 1996, and

(b)   may refer to the PCA any complaint which is not required to be referred to them.

(2)   The PCA may require the submission to them for consideration of any complaint regarding the conduct of a seconded police member of the National Crime Squad not referred to them by the Director General; and the Director General shall comply with any such requirement not later than the end of the specified period.

(3)   For the purposes of paragraph (2) the specified period shall be the period which is specified in regulations made by the Secretary of State for the purpose of subsection (2) of section 70 of the Police Act 1996.

(4)   Where a complaint falls to be referred to the PCA under paragraph (1)(a), it shall be the duty of the Director General to refer it to them not later than the end of the period specified for the purpose of subsection (1) of section 70 of the Police Act 1996 in regulations made by the Secretary of State.

21.   Reference of other matters to the PCA

(1)   The Director General may refer to the PCA any matter to which this regulation applies, if it appears to the Director General that the matter ought to be referred by reason—

(a)   of its gravity, or

(b)   of its exceptional circumstances.

(2)   This regulation applies to any matter which—

(a)   appears to the Director General to indicate that a seconded police member of the National Crime Squad may have committed a criminal offence or behaved in a manner which would justify disciplinary proceedings, and

(b)   is not the subject of a complaint.

22.   Supervision of investigation by PCA

(1)   The PCA shall supervise the investigation of—

(a)   any complaint alleging that the conduct of a seconded police member of the National Crime Squad resulted in the death of, or serious injury to, some other person,

(b)   any other complaint which is of the same description as a complaint specified for the purposes of section 72 of the Police Act 1996 in regulations made by the Secretary of State under that Act, and

(c)   any complaint which is not within paragraph (a) or (b) and any matter referred to the PCA under regulation 21, if the PCA determine that it is desirable in the public interest that they should do so.

(2)   Where the PCA have made a determination under paragraph (1)(c), they shall notify it to the Director General.

(3)   Where an investigation is to be supervised by the PCA, they may require—

(a)   that no appointment is made under regulation 19(4) or (5) unless they have given notice to the Director General that they approve the person he proposes to appoint, or

(b)   if such an appointment has already been made and the PCA are not satisfied with the person appointed, that—

(i)   the Director General, as soon as reasonably practicable, appoint another member of the National Crime Squad or of NCIS or of a police force and notify the PCA that he proposes to appoint him, and

(ii)   the appointment is not made unless the PCA give notice to the Director General that they approve that person.

(4)   Where the Secretary of State, by regulations made under section 72(4) of the Police Act 1996, authorises the PCA to impose requirements as to a particular investigation additional to any requirement imposed by subsection (3) of that section then, in addition to any requirement imposed by paragraph (3) above, the PCA may impose the like additional requirements, subject to any restrictions or conditions specified in those regulations, in relation to any investigation under this Part of these Regulations.

(5)   A member of the National Crime Squad or of NCIS or of a police force shall comply with any requirement imposed upon him by virtue of the application of paragraph (4).

23.   Reports on investigations etc.

(1)   At the end of an investigation which the PCA have supervised, the investigating officer shall—

(a)   submit a report on the investigation to the PCA, and

(b)   send a copy of the report to the Director General.

(2)   After consideration of a report submitted to them under paragraph (1) the PCA shall submit an appropriate statement to the Director General.

(3)   If it is practicable to do so, the PCA, when submitting the appropriate statement under paragraph (2), shall send a copy of it to the seconded police member of the National Crime Squad whose conduct has been investigated.

(4)   If—

(a)   the investigation related to a complaint, and

(b)   it is practicable to do so,

the PCA shall also send a copy of the appropriate statement to the person by or on behalf of whom the complaint was submitted.

(5)   The power to issue an appropriate statement includes power to issue separate statements in respect of the disciplinary and criminal aspects of the investigation.

(6)   No disciplinary proceedings shall be brought before the appropriate statement is submitted to the Director General.

(7)   Subject to paragraph (8), neither the Director General nor the Director of Public Prosecutions shall bring criminal proceedings before the appropriate statement is submitted to the Director General.

(8)   The restriction imposed by paragraph (7) does not apply if it appears to the Director of Public Prosecutions that there are exceptional circumstances which make it undesirable to wait for the submission of the appropriate statement.

(9)   In this regulation "appropriate statement" means a statement—

(a)   as to whether the investigation was or was not conducted to the PCA's satisfaction,

(b)   specifying any respect in which it was not so conducted, and

(c)   dealing with any other matters which are matters of the kind provided for in regulations made under section 72 of the Police Act 1996 for the purposes of that section.

24.   Steps to be taken after investigation

(1)   On receiving—

(a)   a report concerning the conduct of a seconded police member of the National Crime Squad which is submitted to him under regulation 19(9), or

(b)   a copy of a report concerning the conduct of such a member which is sent to him under regulation 23(1)(b),

the Director General shall determine whether the report indicates that a criminal offence may have been committed by a seconded police member of the National Crime Squad.

(2)   If the Director General determines that the report indicates that a criminal offence may have been committed by a seconded police member of the National Crime Squad, he shall send a copy of the report to the Director of Public Prosecutions.

(3)   After the Director of Public Prosecutions has dealt with the question of criminal proceedings, the Director General shall send the PCA a memorandum which—

(a)   is signed by the Director General,

(b)   states whether he considers that disciplinary proceedings should be brought in pursuance of section 97(6)(a) of the Police Act 1996 in respect of the conduct which was the subject of the investigation, and

(c)   if he does not consider that such proceedings should be brought, gives his reasons.

(4)   If the Director General considers that the report does not indicate that a criminal offence may have been committed by a seconded police member of the National Crime Squad, he shall send the PCA a memorandum to that effect which—

(a)   is signed by the Director General,

(b)   states whether he considers that disciplinary proceedings should be brought in pursuance of section 97(6)(a) of the Police Act 1996 in respect of the conduct which was the subject of the investigation, and

(c)   if he does not consider that such proceedings should be brought, gives his reasons.

(5)   Where the investigation—

(a)   related to conduct which was the subject of a complaint, and

(b)   was not supervised by the PCA,

the Director General shall, at the same time as he sends the PCA a memorandum under paragraph (3) or (4), send them a copy of the complaint, or of the record of the complaint, and a copy of the report of the investigation.

(6)   Where the Director General has sent a memorandum to the PCA under paragraph (3) or (4) which states that he considers that disciplinary proceedings should be brought—

(a)   he shall take steps to ensure that the temporary service with the National Crime Squad of the seconded police member whose conduct was the subject of the investigation is completed as soon as is practicable, and

(b)   he shall inform the chief officer of police with whose consent that member was engaged on such service that he considers that disciplinary proceedings should be brought in pursuance of section 97(6)(a) of the Police Act 1996 in respect of that member's conduct.

25. Powers of PCA as to disciplinary proceedings

(1)   Where a memorandum under regulation 24 states that the Director General does not consider that disciplinary proceedings should be brought in pursuance of section 97(6)(a) of the Police Act 1996, the PCA may recommend him to take such steps as are referred to in paragraph (6)(a), and inform the chief officer of police in accordance with paragraph (6)(b), of that regulation.

(2)   If after the PCA have made a recommendation under this regulation and consulted the Director General he is still unwilling to proceed in accordance with regulation 24(6)(a) and (b), they may direct him to do so.

(3)   Where the PCA gives the Director General a direction under this regulation, they shall supply him with a written statement of their reasons for doing so.

(4)   Subject to paragraph (5), it shall be the duty of the Director General to comply with such a direction.

(5)   The PCA may withdraw a direction given under this regulation.

(6)   The Director General shall—

(a)   advise the PCA and the chief officer of police referred to in regulation 24(6)(b) of what action he has taken in response to a recommendation or direction under this regulation, and

(b)   supply the PCA with such other information as they may reasonably require for the purposes of discharging their functions under this regulation.

26. Reports by PCA

(1)   The PCA may make a report to the Secretary of State on any matters coming to their notice under these Regulations to which they consider that his attention should be drawn by reason of their gravity or of other exceptional circumstances.

(2)   The PCA shall send a copy of any report under paragraph (1) to the NCS Service Authority and the Director General.

(3)   The Secretary of State shall lay before Parliament a copy of every report received by him under this regulation and shall cause every such report to be published.

(4)   The PCA shall send to the NCS Service Authority—

(a)   a copy of every report made under subsection (4) of section 79 of the Police Act 1996, and

(b)   any statistical or other general information which relates to the year dealt with by the report and which the PCA consider should be brought to the NCS Service Authority's attention in connection with its functions under section 84 of the 1997 Act.

27.   Restriction on disclosure of information

(1)   No information received by the PCA in connection with any of their functions under this part of these Regulations shall be disclosed by any person who is or has been a member, officer or servant of the PCA except—

(a)   to the Secretary of State or to a member, officer or servant of the PCA or, so far as may be necessary for the proper discharge of the functions of the PCA, to other persons,

(b)   for the purposes of any criminal, civil or disciplinary proceedings, or

(c)   in the form of a summary or other general statement made by the PCA which does not identify the person from whom the information was received or any person to whom it relates.

(2)   Any person who discloses information in contravention of this regulation shall be guilty of an offence and liable on summary conviction to a fine of an amount not exceeding level 5 on the standard scale.

28.   Regulations

Where the Secretary of State makes regulations under section 81 of the Police Act 1996 as to the procedure to be followed under Chapter I of Part IV of that Act then the procedures provided for by those regulations shall be the procedures to be followed under this Part of these Regulations with the following modifications—

(i)   references to "appropriate authority" and "chief officer" shall be interpreted as references to the Director General;

(ii)   references to a "complaint" shall be interpreted as references to a complaint under this Part of these Regulations, and references to a complainant shall be construed accordingly;

(iii)   references to a "member of a police force" shall be interpreted as references to a seconded police member of the National Crime Squad;

(iv)   references to provisions of the Police Act 1996 shall be interpreted as references to the equivalent provisions in this Part of these Regulations.

29.   Admissibility of statements in subsequent proceedings

(1)   Subject to paragraph (2), no statement made by a person for the purpose of the informal resolution of a complaint shall be admissible in any subsequent criminal, civil or disciplinary proceedings.

(2)   A statement is not rendered inadmissible by paragraph (1) if it consists of or includes an admission relating to a matter which does not fall to be resolved informally.'.

EXPLANATORY NOTE
(This note is not part of the Regulations)

These Regulations amend the National Crime Squad (Complaints) Regulations 1998 (the 1998 Regulations) in relation to complaints against seconded police members.

Regulation 3 amends and inserts certain definitions in regulation 2 of the 1998 Regulations. Regulation 5 inserts a new Part III in the 1998 Regulations which makes provision for the procedures for handling complaints relating to the conduct of police members of the National Crime Squad who are engaged on temporary service under section 97 of the Police Act 1996 ('seconded police members'). Part III generally mirrors Chapter I of Part IV of that Act in its application to members of police forces other than senior officers. Regulation 4 makes minor and consequential amendments to Part I of the 1998 Regulations.

Appendix 7　Police Forces: England and Wales

AVON & SOMERSET Constabulary, P.O. Box 37, Portishead Bristol, Avon BS20 8QJ (01275) 818181

BEDFORDSHIRE Police, Woburn Road, Kempston, Bedford MK43 9AX (01234) 841212

CAMBRIDGESHIRE Constabulary, Hinchingbrooke Park, Huntingdon PE18 8NP (01480) 456111

CHESHIRE Constabulary, Castle Esplanade, Chester CH1 2PP (01244) 350000

CLEVELAND Police, P.O. Box 70, Ladgate Lane, Middlesbrough TS8 9EH (01642) 326326

CUMBRIA Constabulary, Carleton Hall, Penrith CA10 2AU (01768) 891999

DERBYSHIRE Constabulary, Butterley Hall, Ripley, Derby DE5 3RS (01773) 570100

DEVON & CORNWALL Constabulary, Middlemoor, Exeter EX2 7HQ (0990) 777444

DORSET Police, Winfrith, Dorchester DT2 8DZ (01929) 462727

DURHAM Constabulary, Aykley Heads, Durham DH1 5TT (0191) 386 4929

DYFED-POWYS Police, P.O. Box 99, Llangunnor, Carmarthen SA31 2PF (01267) 222020

ESSEX Police, P.O. Box 2, Springfield, Chelmsford CM2 6DA (01245) 491491

GLOUCESTERSHIRE Constabulary, Holland House, Lansdown Road, Cheltenham GL51 6QH (01242) 521321

GREATER MANCHESTER Police, P.O. Box 22 (S. West PDO), Chester House, Boyer Street, Manchester M16 0RE (0161) 872 5050

GWENT Police, Croesyceiliog, Cwmbran NP44 2XJ (01633) 838111

HAMPSHIRE Constabulary, West Hill, Winchester SO22 5DB (01962) 841500

HERTFORDSHIRE Constabulary, Stanborough Road, Welwyn Garden City AL8 6XF (01707) 354200

HUMBERSIDE Police, Queens Gardens, Kingston upon Hull HU1 3DJ (01482) 326111

KENT County Constabulary, Sutton Road, Maidstone ME15 9BZ (01622) 690690

LANCASHIRE Constabulary, P.O. Box 77, Hutton, Nr. Preston PR4 5SB (01772) 614444

LEICESTERSHIRE Constabulary, P.O. Box 999, Leicester LE99 1AZ (0116) 222 2222

LINCOLNSHIRE Police, P.O. Box 999, Lincoln LN5 7PH (01522) 532222

LONDON, METROPOLITAN Police, New Scotland Yard, Broadway, London SW1H 0BG (020) 7230 1212

LONDON, CITY OF Police, 26 Old Jewry, London EC2R 8DJ (020) 7601 2222

MERSEYSIDE Police, P.O. Box 59, Liverpool L69 1JD (0151) 709 6010

NORFOLK Constabulary, Martineau Lane, Norwich NR1 2DJ (01603) 768769

NORTHAMPTONSHIRE Police, Wootton Hall, Northampton NN4 0JQ (01604) 700700

NORTHUMBRIA Police, Ponteland, Newcastle upon Tyne NE20 0BL (01661) 872555

NORTH WALES Police, Colwyn Bay LL29 8AW (01492) 517171

NORTH YORKSHIRE Police, Newby Wiske Hall, Northallerton DL7 9HA (01609) 783131

NOTTINGHAMSHIRE Police, Sherwood Lodge, Arnold, Nottingham NG5 8PP (0115) 967 0999

SOUTH WALES Police, Bridgend CF31 3SU (01656) 655555

SOUTH YORKSHIRE Police, Sheffield S3 8LY (0114) 220 2020

STAFFORDSHIRE Police, Cannock Road, Stafford ST17 0QG (01785) 257717

SUFFOLK Constabulary, Martlesham Heath, Ipswich IP5 7QS (01473) 613500

SURREY Police, Mount Browne, Sandy Lane, Guildford GU3 1HG (01483) 571212

SUSSEX Police, Malling House, Lewes BN7 2DZ (01273) 475432

THAMES VALLEY Police, Kidlington, Oxon OX5 2NX (01865) 846000

WARWICKSHIRE Constabulary, P.O. Box 4, Leek Wootton, Warwick CV35 7QB (01926) 415000

WEST MERCIA Constabulary, Hindlip Hall, Hindlip, P.O. Box 55, Worcester WR3 8SP (01905) 723000

WEST MIDLANDS Police, P.O. Box 52, Lloyd House, Colmore Circus Queensway, Birmingham B4 6NQ (0121) 626 5000.

WEST YORKSHIRE Police, P.O. Box 9, Wakefield WF1 3QP (01924) 375222

WILTSHIRE Constabulary, London Road, Devizes SN10 2DN (01380) 722341

Non-Home Office Police Forces

BRITISH TRANSPORT POLICE, P.O. Box 260, Tavistock Place, London WC1H 9SJ (020) 7388 7541

ISLE OF MAN Constabulary, Glencrutchery Road, Douglas, Isle of Man 1M2 4RG (01624) 631212

MINISTRY OF DEFENCE Police, MDP Weathersfield, Braintree, Essex CM7 4AZ (01371) 854000

ROYAL PARKS Constabulary, The Old Police House, Hyde Park, London W2 2UH (020) 7298 2000

Other Relevant Agencies and Organisations

ASSOCIATION OF CHIEF POLICE OFFICERS OF ENGLAND & WALES, 25 Victoria Street, London SW1H 0EX (020) 7227 3434

CROWN PROSECUTION SERVICE 50, Ludgate Hill, London EC4M 7EX (020) 7796 8000

HM CUSTOMS & EXCISE NATIONAL INVESTIGATION SERVICE, Custom House, Lower Thames Street, London EC3R 6EE (020) 7283 5353

HOME OFFICE, 50, Queen Anne's Gate, London SW1H 9AT (020) 7273 4000

NATIONAL CRIME SQUAD, P.O. Box 2500, London SW1V 2WF (020) 7238 2500

NATIONAL CRIMINAL INTELLIGENCE SERVICE, P.O. Box 8000, London SE11 5EN (020) 7238 2600

NATIONAL IDENTIFICATION SERVICE, New Scotland Yard, Broadway, London SW1H 0BG (020) 7230 4458

NATIONAL POLICE TRAINING, Bramshill House, Hook, Hampshire RG27 0JW (01256) 602100

POLICE COMPLAINTS AUTHORITY, 10 Great George Street, London SW1P 3AE (020) 7273 6450

POLICE FEDERATION OF ENGLAND & WALES, 15–17 Langley Road, Surbiton, Surrey KT6 6LP (020) 8399 2224

POLICE SUPERINTENDENTS' ASSOCIATION OF ENGLAND & WALES, 67A Reading Road, Pangbourne, Berkshire RG8 7JD (0118) 9844005

SERIOUS FRAUD OFFICE, Elm House, 10–16 Elm Street, London WC1X 0BJ (020) 7239 7272

Appendix 8   The Police (Complaints) (Informal Resolution) Regulations 1985 (SI 1985 No. 671)

Whereas a draft of these Regulations has been approved by resolution of each House of Parliament:

Now, therefore, in exercise of the powers conferred on me by section 99(2)(b) of the Police and Criminal Evidence Act 1984, and after furnishing the Police Advisory Board for England and Wales with a draft of the Regulations and taking into consideration the representations of the said Board thereon in accordance with section 100(2) of the said Act of 1984, I hereby make the following Regulations:—

1.   Citation and commencement
These Regulations may be cited as the Police (Complaints) (Informal Resolution) Regulations 1985 and shall come into operation on 29th April 1985.

2.   Interpretation
In these Regulations the following expressions have the meanings respectively assigned to them, that is to say:—

'the Act of 1984' means the Police and Criminal Evidence Act 1984;

'the appointed officer' means the officer appointed for the informal resolution of complaints under section 85(4) of the Act of 1984;

'the Authority' means the Police Complaints Authority established under section 83(1) of the Act of 1984;

'chief officer' shall be construed as including a reference to a person discharging the functions of a chief officer and 'chief officer concerned' means, in relation to a complaint about the conduct of a member of a police force, the chief officer of the force of which he is a member;

'complaint' means a complaint to which Part IX of the Act of 1984 applies;

'complainant' means the person by whom or on whose behalf a complaint is submitted to the chief officer concerned;

'member concerned', in relation to a complaint, means the member about whose conduct the complaint is made;

'senior officer' means a police officer of the rank of chief constable, deputy chief constable or assistant chief constable or, in the case of the City of London and metropolitan police forces, a member of the force in question of, or above, the rank of commander.

3. Application of Regulations

(1)   Subject to the following provisions of this Regulation, these Regulations apply to a complaint received by the chief officer concerned on or after 29th April 1985, being a complaint which he considers to be suitable for informal resolution.

(2)   Nothing in these Regulations applies in the case of a complaint against a senior officer.

(3)   Where under Part IX of the Act of 1984 the Authority are required or determine to supervise the investigation of a complaint it shall not be dealt with or, as the case may be, continue to be dealt with by way of informal resolution.

4. Procedure for informal resolution of complaints

(1)   Subject to paragraph (2) below, for the purpose of informally resolving a complaint to which these Regulations apply about the conduct of a member of his force, the appointed officer shall as soon as practicable—

(a)   seek the views of the complainant and the member concerned about the matter; and

(b)   take such other steps as appear to him appropriate,

and, without prejudice to the foregoing, where it appears to the appointed officer that the complaint had in fact already been satisfactorily dealt with at the time it was brought to his notice, he may, subject to any representation made by the complainant, treat it as having been informally resolved.

(2)   The appointed officer shall not, for the purpose of informally resolving a complaint, tender on behalf of the member concerned an apology for his conduct unless he has admitted the conduct in question.

5. Records

When a complaint is dealt with by way of informal resolution under these Regulations a record shall be made of the outcome of the procedure and a complainant shall be entitled to obtain a copy thereof from the chief officer concerned if he applies for such a copy not later than the end of 3 months from the day on which—

(a)   the informal resolution of his complaint was achieved; or

(b)   for whatever other reason, it was determined that the complaint should no longer be subject to the said procedure.

EXPLANATORY NOTE

(This Note is not part of the Regulations.)

These Regulations provide for the informal resolution of complaints against police officers in accordance with section 85 of the Police and Criminal Evidence Act 1984.

By Regulation 3 the Regulations apply only to complaints received by the chief officer of police on or after 29th April 1985. They do not apply in the case of senior officers (officers above the rank of chief superintendent).

Regulation 4 sets out the procedure for informal resolution. Regulation 5 requires a record to be kept of the outcome of the procedure and enables the complainant to obtain a copy of the record.

Appendix 9 The Police Act 1996, Schedule 5

Section 66 SCHEDULE 5
THE POLICE COMPLAINTS AUTHORITY

Constitution of Authority

1.—(1) The Police Complaints Authority shall consist of a chairman and not less than eight other members.

(2) The chairman shall be appointed by Her Majesty.

(3) The other members shall be appointed by the Secretary of State.

(4) The members of the Authority shall not include any person who is or has been a constable in any part of the United Kingdom.

(5) Persons may be appointed as whole-time or part-time members of the Authority.

(6) The Secretary of State may appoint not more than two of the members of the Authority to be deputy chairmen.

Status of Authority

2.—The Authority shall not be regarded as the servant or agent of the Crown or as enjoying any status, privilege or immunity of the Crown; and the Authority's property shall not be regarded as property of or property held on behalf of the Crown.

Members

3.—(1) Subject to the following provisions of this Schedule, a person shall hold an office to which he is appointed under paragraph 1(2), (3) or (6) in accordance with the terms of his appointment.

(2) A person shall not be appointed to such an office for more than three years at a time.

(3) A person may at any time resign such an office.

(4) The Secretary of State may at any time remove a person from such an office if satisfied that—

(a) he has without reasonable excuse failed to carry out his duties for a continuous period of three months beginning not earlier than six months before that time;

    (b)   he has been convicted of a criminal offence;

    (c)   he has become bankrupt or made an arrangement with his creditors;

    (d)   he is incapacitated by physical or mental illness;

    (e)   he has acted improperly in relation to his duties; or

    (f)   he is otherwise unable or unfit to perform his duties.

4.—The Secretary of State may pay, or make such payments towards the provision of, such remuneration, pensions, allowances or gratuities to or in respect of persons appointed to office under paragraph 1(2), (3) or (6) or any of them as he may, with the consent of the Treasury, determine.

5.—Where a person ceases to hold such an office otherwise than on the expiry of his term of office, and it appears to the Secretary of State that there are special circumstances which make it right for that person to receive compensation, the Secretary of State may, with the consent of the Treasury, direct the Authority to make to the person a payment of such amount as the Secretary of State may, with the consent of the Treasury, determine.

Staff

6.—The Authority may, after consultation with the Secretary of State, appoint such officers and servants as appear to the Authority to be appropriate, subject to the approval of the Treasury as to numbers and as to remuneration and other terms and conditions of service.

7.—Where a person who is employed by the Authority and is by reference to that employment a participant in a scheme under section 1 of the Superannuation Act 1972 is appointed to an office under paragraph 1(2), (3) or (6), the Treasury may determine that his service in that office shall be treated for the purposes of the scheme as service as an employee of the Authority; and his rights under the scheme shall not be affected by paragraph 4.

8.—The Employers' Liability (Compulsory Insurance) Act 1969 shall not require insurance to be effected by the Authority.

Power of Authority to set up regional offices

9.—(1) If it appears to the Authority that it is necessary to do so in order to discharge their duties efficiently, the Authority may, with the consent of the Secretary of State and the Treasury, set up a regional office in any place in England and Wales.

    (2) The Authority may delegate any of their functions to a regional office.

Proceedings

10.—(1) Subject to the provisions of Chapter I of Part IV and section 87, the arrangements for the proceedings of the Authority (including the quorum for meetings) shall be such as the Authority may determine.

    (2) The arrangements may, with the approval of the Secretary of State, provide for the discharge, under the general direction of the Authority, of any of the Authority's functions by a committee or by one or more of the members, officers or servants of the Authority.

11.—The validity of any proceedings of the Authority shall not be affected by—

    (a)   any defect in the appointment of the chairman or any other member, or

    (b)   any vacancy in the office of chairman or among the other members.

Finance

12.—The Secretary of State—

    (a)   shall pay to the Authority expenses incurred or to be incurred by the Authority under paragraphs 5 and 6, and

    (b)   shall, with the consent of the Treasury, pay to the Authority such sums as appear to the Secretary of State to be appropriate for enabling the Authority to meet other expenses.

13.—(1)   The Authority shall—

    (a)   keep proper accounts and proper records in relation to the accounts,

    (b)   prepare in respect of each financial year of the Authority a statement of accounts in such form as the Secretary of State may, with the approval of the Treasury, direct, and

    (c)   send copies of the statement to the Secretary of State and the Comptroller and Auditor General before the end of the month of August next following the financial year to which the statement relates.

    (2)   The Comptroller and Auditor General shall examine, certify and report on each statement received by him in pursuance of this paragraph and shall lay copies of each statement and of his report before Parliament.

    (3)   The financial year of the Authority shall be the twelve months ending on 31st March.

Appendix 10 The Police (Dispensation from Requirement to Investigate Complaints) Regulations 1985 (SI 1985 No. 672)

1. These Regulations may be cited as the Police (Dispensation from Requirement to Investigate Complaints) Regulations 1985 and shall come into operation on 29th April 1985.

2.—(1) In these Regulations, unless the context otherwise requires, the following expressions have the meanings respectively assigned to them, that is to say:—
'the Act of 1984' means the Police and Criminal Evidence Act 1984;
'the appropriate authority' means the appropriate authority within the meaning of section 84(4) of the Act of 1984;
'the Authority' means the Police Complaints Authority established under section 83(1) of the Act of 1984;
'the Board' means the Police Complaints Board established under section 1 of the Police Act 1976;
'complaint' means a complaint made on or after 29th April 1985 to which Part IX of the Act of 1984 applies; and 'copy of a complaint', in the case of a complaint made orally, shall include a copy of the record of the complaint;
'complainant' means the member of the public by or on whose behalf a complaint is submitted.
(2) In these Regulations, unless the context otherwise requires, any reference to a Regulation shall be construed as a reference to a Regulation contained in these Regulations, any reference in a Regulation, or in the Schedule to these Regulations, to a paragraph shall be construed as a reference to a paragraph of that Regulation, or of that Schedule, and any reference in a paragraph to a sub-paragraph shall be construed as a reference to a sub-paragraph of that paragraph.

3.—(1) Where the appropriate authority is of the opinion—
(a) that a complaint is an anonymous or a repetitious one within the meaning of paragraph 2 or 3 of the Schedule to these Regulations, or that it is not reasonably

practicable to complete the investigation of a complaint, within the meaning of paragraph 4 thereof, and

(b)   that, in all the circumstances, the requirements of Part IX of the Act of 1984 (to the extent that they have not already been satisfied) should be dispensed with, the appropriate authority may, in accordance with this Regulation, request the Authority to dispense with the said requirements as respects the complaint.

(2)   The request, which shall be made in writing, shall be accompanied by—

(a)   a copy of the complaint;

(b)   a memorandum from the appropriate authority explaining the reasons for being of the opinion mentioned in paragraph (1); and

(c)   where the appropriate authority is of the opinion that the complaint is a repetitious complaint and, as respects the previous complaint, the person then the complainant gave such notification as is mentioned in Regulation 3 of the Police (Withdrawn, Anonymous Etc. Complaints) Regulations 1977 or Regulation 11 of the Police (Complaints) (General) Regulations 1985, a copy of that notification unless it has previously been sent to the Board or, as the case may be, the Authority in pursuance of that Regulation.

(3)   If, after considering a request under this Regulation, the Authority share the opinion of the appropriate authority, they may dispense with the requirements mentioned in paragraph (1) but they shall not reject such a request except after consultation with the appropriate authority.

(4)   The Authority shall, as soon as may be, notify the appropriate authority, in writing, of their decision on such a request and, where they dispense with the requirements mentioned in paragraph (1), shall inform the complainant of their action unless the complaint is an anonymous one or it otherwise appears to them to be not reasonably practicable so to inform him within a period which is reasonable in all the circumstances of the case.

Regulation 3(1)   SCHEDULE

COMPLAINTS WHICH ARE ANONYMOUS, REPETITIOUS OR INCAPABLE OF INVESTIGATION

1.—(1)   In this Schedule any reference to an injured person other than the complainant shall have effect only in the case of a complaint against a member of a police force in respect of his conduct towards a person other than the complainant; and, in such a case, any such reference is a reference to that other person.

(2)   In this Schedule any reference to action not being reasonably practicable shall include a reference to action which it does not appear reasonably practicable to take within a period which is reasonable in all the circumstances of the case.

2.   For the purposes of Regulation 3 a complaint is an anonymous one if, and only if, it discloses (or purports to disclose) neither the name and address of the complainant nor that of any other injured person and it is not reasonably practicable to ascertain such a name and address.

3.—(1)   For the purposes of Regulation 3 a complaint is a repetitious one if, and only if—

(a)   it is substantially the same as a previous complaint (whether made by or on behalf of the same or a different complainant);

(b)   it contains no fresh allegations which significantly affect the account of the conduct complained of;

(c)   no fresh evidence, being evidence which was not reasonably available at the time the previous complaint was made, is tendered in support of it; and

(d)   such action as is referred to in sub-paragraph (2) has been taken as respects the previous complaint.

(2)   The condition in sub-paragraph (1)(d) shall be satisfied if, as respects the previous complaint, either—

(a)   the requirements of section 90(5), (6) and (7) of the Act of 1984 were complied with;

(b)   the complainant gave such a notification as is mentioned in Regulation 3(2)(c); or

(c)   the Authority, under Regulation 3, dispensed with the requirements mentioned in paragraph (1) of that Regulation.

4.   For the purposes of Regulation 3 it shall not be reasonably practicable to complete the investigation of a complaint if, and only if, in the opinion of the appropriate authority or, as the case may be, of the Authority, either—

(a)   it is not reasonably practicable to communicate with the complainant or, as the case may be, the person who submitted the complaint, or any other injured person, notwithstanding that the complaint is not an anonymous one within the meaning of paragraph 2, or

(b)   it is not reasonably practicable to complete a satisfactory investigation in consequence of—

(i)   a refusal or failure, on the part of the complainant, to make a statement or afford other reasonable assistance for the purposes of the investigation, or

(ii)   a refusal or failure, on the part of an injured person other than the complainant, to support the complaint, evidenced either by a statement in writing (signed by him or by his solicitor or other authorised agent on his behalf) to the effect that he does not support it or by a refusal or failure, on his part, such as is mentioned in sub-paragraph (i) above, or

(iii)   the lapse of time since the event or events forming the subject matter of the complaint.

EXPLANATORY NOTE
(This Note is not part of the Regulations.)

These Regulations relate to complaints against members of a police force made on or after 29th April 1985 under Part IX of the Police and Criminal Evidence Act 1984.

They replace those provisions of the Police (Withdrawn, Anonymous Etc. Complaints) Regulations 1977 which relate to anonymous and repetitious complaints and complaints which are incapable of investigation, with amendments to take account of the replacement of the Police Complaints Board by the Police Complaints Authority established under section 83(1) of the Act of 1984 and of the arrangements for dealing with complaints against police officers of the rank of chief superintendent and above under Part IX of that Act.

Appendix 11   The Police Appeals
Tribunals Rules 1999 (SI 1999 No. 818)

The Secretary of State, in exercise of the powers conferred on him by section 85 of the Police Act 1996 and after consultation with the Council on Tribunals in accordance with section 8 of the Tribunals and Inquiries Act 1992, hereby makes the following Rules:

1.   Citation and commencement
These Rules may be cited as the Police Appeals Tribunals Rules 1999 and shall come into force on 1st April 1999.

2.   Revocations and transitional provisions
(1)   Subject to paragraph (2), the Police (Appeals) Rules 1985 (hereinafter called 'the 1985 Rules') are hereby revoked.
(2)   In relation to an appeal against a decision made in accordance with the Police (Discipline) Regulations 1985 or the Police (Discipline) (Senior Officers) Regulations 1985—
  (a)   nothing in these Rules shall apply, and
  (b)   the 1985 Rules shall continue to have effect.

3.   Interpretation
  (1)   In these Rules, unless the context otherwise requires—
    'the Act' means the Police Act 1996;
    'original hearing' means the conduct hearing or inefficiency hearing at the conclusion of which the appellant was found to have failed to meet the appropriate standard or, as the case may be, the appellant's performance was found to have been unsatisfactory;
    'tribunal' in relation to a case means the police appeals tribunal appointed to determine that case.
  (2)   In these Rules, any expression which appears also in the Police (Conduct) Regulations 1999 or the Police (Efficiency) Regulations 1999 shall, unless the contrary intention appears, have the same meaning as in those Regulations.

4.   The respondent
  (1)   The respondent on an appeal by a senior officer shall be a person designated for the purpose by the relevant police authority.

(2)   The respondent on an appeal by a member of a police force who is not a senior officer shall be the chief officer of that force.

5.   Notice of appeal

(1)   Subject to rule 7 and paragraph (2), the time within which notice of an appeal under section 85 of the Act shall be given is 21 days from the date on which the decision appealed against was notified to the appellant in pursuance of regulations made in accordance with section 50(3) of the Act.

(2)   In a case to which regulation 39 of the Police (Conduct) Regulations 1999 or regulation 25 of the Police (Conduct) (Senior Officers) Regulations 1999 applies where the decision appealed against was given in pursuance of those Regulations as modified by Part II of Schedule 2 or, as the case may be, by Part II of the Schedule to those Regulations, the time within which notice of an appeal under section 85 of the Act shall be given is 28 days from—

(a)   the conclusion of any criminal proceedings in which the appellant is charged with an offence in respect of the conduct to which the decision appealed against related; or

(b)   a decision that no such criminal proceedings will be instituted or taken over by the Director of Public Prosecutions has been communicated to the appellant.

(3)   The notice of appeal shall be given in writing to the relevant police authority and a copy of the notice shall be sent to the respondent.

6.   Procedure on notice of appeal

(1)   As soon as practicable after receipt of a copy of the notice of appeal, the respondent shall provide to the relevant police authority—

(a)   a copy of the report of the person who made the decision appealed against;

(b)   the transcript of the proceedings at the original hearing; and

(c)   any documents which were made available to the person conducting the original hearing.

(2)   A copy of the transcript mentioned in paragraph (1)(b) shall at the same time be sent to the appellant.

(3)   Subject to rule 7, the appellant shall, within 28 days of the date on which he receives a copy of the transcript mentioned in paragraph (1)(b), submit to the relevant police authority—

(a)   a statement of the grounds of appeal;

(b)   any supporting documents; and

(c)   either—

(i)   any written representations which the appellant wishes to make under paragraph 6 of Schedule 6 to the Act or, as the case may be, any request to make oral representations under that paragraph; or

(ii)   a statement that he does not wish to make any such representations as are mentioned in paragraph (i):

Provided that, in a case where the appellant submits a statement under sub-paragraph (c)(ii), nothing in this paragraph shall prevent representations under paragraph 6 of Schedule 6 to the Act being made by him to the chairman of the tribunal.

(4)   The documents submitted to the police authority under paragraph (3) shall, as soon as practicable, be copied to the members of the tribunal and to the respondent.

(5)   The respondent shall, not later than 21 days from the date on which he receives the copy documents sent to him under paragraph (4), submit to the relevant police authority—

(a)   a statement of his response to the appeal;

(b)   any supporting documents; and

(c)   either—

(i)   any written representations which the respondent wishes to make under paragraph 6 of Schedule 6 to the Act or, as the case may be, any request to make oral representations under that paragraph; or

(ii)   a statement that he does not wish to make any such representations as are mentioned in paragraph (i):

Provided that, in a case where the respondent submits a statement under sub-paragraph (c)(ii), nothing in this paragraph shall prevent representations under paragraph 6 of Schedule 6 to the Act being made by him to the chairman of the tribunal.

(6)   The respondent shall at the same time send a copy of the documents referred to in paragraph (5)(a) and (c) to the appellant, together with a list of the documents (if any) referred to in paragraph (5)(b).

(7)   The documents submitted to the police authority under paragraph (5) shall, as soon as practicable, be copied to the members of the tribunal.

(8)   So far as applicable, rules 8 and 9 shall apply in relation to the hearing of any oral representations under paragraph 6 of Schedule 6 to the Act as they apply in relation to the hearing of an appeal under section 85 of the Act; and the appellant and the respondent shall be entitled to be represented at the hearing of such oral representations as if it were the hearing of such an appeal.

7.   Extensions of time limits

(1)   The relevant police authority may extend the period referred to in rule 5(1) or (2) or 6(3) in any case where the authority is satisfied, on the application of the appellant, that by reason of the special circumstances of the case it is just to do so; and in such a case rules 5 and 6 shall have effect as if for that period there were substituted such extended period as the authority may specify.

(2)   Where the relevant police authority refuses an application by the appellant under paragraph (1), it shall give the appellant notice in writing of the reasons for the decision and of the right of appeal conferred by paragraph (3).

(3)   An appellant whose application under paragraph (1) is refused may, not later than 14 days after receiving notice under paragraph (2), appeal in writing to the chairman of the tribunal against the decision of the relevant police authority.

(4)   The chairman may, on such an appeal, make any decision which the relevant police authority had power to make under paragraph (1); and, where he extends the period referred to in rule 5(1) or (2) or 6(3), rules 5 and 6 shall have effect as if for that period there were substituted such extended period as the chairman may specify.

8.   Procedure at hearing

(1)   Where a case is to be determined at a hearing, the chairman of the tribunal shall cause the appellant and the respondent to be given notice of the date of the hearing not less than 28 days, or such shorter period as may with the agreement of both parties be determined, before the hearing begins.

(2)   Subsections (2) and (3) of section 250 of the Local Government Act 1972 (powers in relation to local inquiries) shall apply to the hearing as if—

(a)   references to a local inquiry were references to a hearing held under Schedule 6 to the Act;

(b)   references to the person appointed to hold the inquiry, or to the person holding the inquiry, were references to the chairman of the tribunal; and

(c)   references to that section were references to this rule.

(3)   The tribunal may proceed with the hearing in the absence of either party, whether represented or not, if it appears to be just and proper to do so, and may adjourn it from time to time as may appear necessary for the due hearing of the case.

(4)   Subject to these Rules, the procedure at a hearing shall be determined by the tribunal.

9.   Hearing to be in private

(1)   Subject to paragraph (3) and rule 12, the hearing shall be held in private:

Provided that it shall be within the discretion of the tribunal to allow such person or persons as it considers desirable to attend the whole or such part of the hearing as it may think fit.

(2)   Notwithstanding that the tribunal has allowed a person to attend the hearing, where it appears to the tribunal that a witness may in giving evidence disclose information which, in the public interest, ought not to be disclosed to a member of the public, the tribunal shall require any member of the public present to withdraw while that evidence is given.

(3)   A member of the Council on Tribunals shall be entitled to attend the hearing.

10.   Evidence at hearing

(1)   Unless the tribunal otherwise determines, the evidence adduced by the respondent shall be given first.

(2)   All oral evidence given at the hearing shall be given on oath.

(3)   All witnesses giving evidence at the hearing shall be subject to examination and cross-examination.

(4)   Any question as to whether any evidence is admissible, or whether any question should or should not be put to a witness, shall be determined by the tribunal.

(5)   A verbatim record of the evidence given at the hearing shall be taken and kept for a period of not less than seven years from the date of the end of the hearing unless the chairman of the tribunal requests that a transcription of the record be made.

11.   Statements in lieu of oral evidence

(1)   Subject to the provisions of this rule, the tribunal may admit evidence by way of a written statement made by a person, notwithstanding that he may not be called as a witness, so, however, that evidence shall not be admissible under this rule if it would not have been admissible had it been given orally.

(2)   For the purposes of this rule, a written statement purporting to be made and signed by a person and witnessed by another person shall be presumed to have been made by that person unless the contrary be shown.

(3)   Nothing in this rule shall prejudice the admission of written evidence which would be admissible apart from the provisions of this rule.

12.   Attendance of complainant at hearing

(1)   This rule shall apply in relation to a hearing where the decision appealed against arose from a complaint and the appeal is not against sanction only.

(2)   The chairman of the tribunal shall cause notice of the date of the hearing to be sent to the complainant, at the same time as such notice is sent to the appellant and the respondent in pursuance of rule 8(1).

(3)   Notwithstanding anything in rule 9(1) but subject to paragraph (5), the tribunal shall allow the complainant to attend the hearing while witnesses are being examined, or cross-examined, on the facts alleged and, if the tribunal considers it appropriate so to do on account of the age of the complainant, or otherwise, shall allow him to be accompanied by a personal friend or relative who is not to be called as a witness at the inquiry:

Provided that—

(a)   where the complainant is to be called as a witness at the hearing he and any person allowed to accompany him shall not be allowed to attend before he gives his evidence; and

(b)   where it appears to the tribunal that a witness may in giving evidence disclose information which, in the public interest, ought not to be disclosed to a member of the public, it shall require the complainant and any person allowed to accompany him to withdraw while that evidence is given.

(4)   Where the appellant gives evidence, then, after the person representing the respondent has had an opportunity of cross-examining him, the chairman of the tribunal shall put to him any questions which the complainant requests should be so put and might have been properly so put by way of cross-examination and, at his discretion, may allow the complainant himself to put such questions to the appellant.

(5)   Subject as aforesaid, the complainant and any person allowed to accompany him shall neither intervene in, nor interrupt the hearing; and if he or such a person should behave in a disorderly or abusive manner, or otherwise misconduct himself, the chairman of the tribunal may exclude him from the remainder of the hearing.

13.   Statement of tribunal's determination

(1)   The chairman of the tribunal shall prepare a written statement of the tribunal's determination of the appeal and of the reasons for the decision.

(2)   The statement prepared under paragraph (1) and a record of any order made under section 85(2) of the Act shall be submitted to the relevant police authority and, in the case of an appeal by a senior officer, to the Secretary of State within a reasonable period after the determination of the appeal.

(3)   The relevant police authority shall, as soon as practicable, copy the statement and any record of an order submitted to it under paragraph (2) to the appellant and the respondent.

(4)   In a case where the decision appealed against arose from a complaint, the relevant police authority shall notify the complainant of the outcome of the appeal.

EXPLANATORY NOTE

(This note is not part of the Rules)

These Rules make provision as to the procedure on appeals to police appeals tribunals under section 85 of the Police Act 1996 ('the Act').

Rule 2 revokes, with transitional provisions, the Police (Appeals) Rules 1985 and rule 3 provides for the interpretation of these Rules. Rule 4 prescribes who shall be the respondent to an appeal and rules 5 and 6 provide for the notice of appeal to be given in writing within the prescribed period and for the procedure on such notice being given. Rule 7 allows for the extension of prescribed time limits.

Rules 8 to 11 provide for the procedure to be followed, and for the evidence to be given, at a hearing held to determine an appeal and rule 12 makes provision for the attendance of the complainant in a case arising from a complaint by a member of the public. Rule 13 requires a written statement of the tribunal's determination to be prepared.

Appendix 12   The Police (Conduct) (Senior Officers) Regulations 1999 (SI 1999 No. 731)

ARRANGEMENT OF REGULATIONS

The Secretary of State, in exercise of the powers conferred on him by section 50 of the Police Act 1996, and after complying with the requirements of section 63(3) of that Act, hereby makes the following Regulations:

1. Citation and commencement
These Regulations may be cited as the Police (Conduct) (Senior Officers) Regulations 1999 and shall come into force on 1st April 1999.

2. Revocations and transitional provisions
(1)   Subject to the following provisions of this regulation, the Police (Discipline) (Senior Officers) Regulations 1985 ('1985 Regulations') are hereby revoked.

(2)   Subject to paragraph (3), where a report, complaint or allegation has been or is received in respect of conduct by a senior officer which occurred or commenced before 1st April 1999—

(a)   nothing in these Regulations shall apply, and

(b)   the 1985 Regulations shall, as far as applicable, continue to have effect.

(3)   In the case of a report, complaint or allegation which—

(a)   relates to conduct by a senior officer which occurred or commenced before 1st April 1999, but

(b)   is received on or after 1st April 2000,

the conduct shall be treated, for the purposes of this regulation, as having occurred or, as the case may be, commenced on 1st April 1999.

(4)   Subject to paragraph (5), where a report, complaint or allegation has been or is received in respect of conduct by a commander in the metropolitan police force which occurred or commenced before 3rd July 2000 these Regulations shall have effect as if the Greater London Authority Act 1999 (Consequential Amendments) (Police) Order 2000 had not been made.

(5)   In the case of a report, complaint or allegation which relates to conduct by a commander in the metropolitan police force which occurred or commenced before 3rd July 2000, but is received on or after 3rd July 2000 the conduct shall be treated for the purposes of this regulation as having occurred, or as the case may be, commenced on 3rd July 2000.

3. Regulations applicable only to senior officers
These Regulations shall only apply in relation to conduct by a senior officer, that is to say, by a chief constable or an assistant chief constable or, in the case of the City of London and metropolitan police forces, by a member of the force in question of or above the rank of commander.

4. Interpretation
(1)   In these Regulations, unless the context otherwise requires—

'the appropriate authority' means, in relation to a senior officer of any police force, the police authority for the force's area;

'appropriate standard' means the standard set out in the Code of Conduct;

'Authority' means the Police Complaints Authority;

'Code of Conduct' means the code of conduct contained in Schedule 1 to the Police (Conduct) Regulations 1999;

'complaint' has the meaning assigned to it by section 65 of the 1996 Act;

'investigating officer' means a person (whether a member of a police force or not) appointed under section 68(2B) or section 68(3) of the 1996 Act or under regulation 7, to investigate a complaint or other matter relating to the conduct of a senior officer;

'police force concerned' means, in relation to a senior officer whose conduct is the subject of a report, complaint or allegation, the police force of which he is a member; and any reference to the chief officer concerned is a reference to the chief officer of that force;

'representative' means, in relation to proceedings under these Regulations in respect of the conduct of a senior officer, counsel, a solicitor or a member of a police force selected by him for the purpose of those proceedings;

'senior officer' has the meaning assigned to it by regulation 3; and 'the senior officer concerned' means the senior officer in relation to whose conduct there has been a report, complaint or allegation;

'tribunal' means such a tribunal as is mentioned in regulation 14;

'the 1996 Act' means the Police Act 1996.

(2) (omitted)

(3) In these Regulations, unless the context otherwise requires, any reference to a regulation shall be construed as a reference to a regulation contained in these Regulations.

5. Suspension — ordinary procedure

(1) Where it appears to the appropriate authority, on receiving a report, complaint or allegation which indicates that the conduct of a senior officer does not meet the appropriate standard, that the senior officer concerned ought to be suspended from membership of the force and from his office as constable, the appropriate authority may, subject to the following provisions of this regulation, so suspend him.

(2) The appropriate authority shall not so suspend a senior officer unless it appears to them that either of the following conditions ('the suspension conditions') is satisfied:

(a) that the effective investigation of the matter may be prejudiced unless the senior officer concerned is so suspended;

(b) that the public interest, having regard to the nature of the report, complaint or allegation, and any other relevant considerations, requires that he should be so suspended.

(3) If the appropriate authority determine that a senior officer ought to be suspended under this regulation, they shall forthwith notify the Authority of their decision and of the suspension condition appearing to them to justify their decision.

(4) If, upon being so notified of the decision of the appropriate authority, the Authority are satisfied that the suspension condition in question is fulfilled, they shall as soon as practicable notify their approval of the suspension of the senior officer concerned to the appropriate authority; and the suspension of the officer shall not have effect unless the approval of the Authority is so given.

(5) Where the Authority give their approval to the suspension of a senior officer, his suspension shall take effect from the time he receives notice of that approval from the appropriate authority and he shall be suspended until—

(a) the Authority decide otherwise; or

(b) the appropriate authority decide otherwise; or

(c) it is decided that the conduct of the senior officer concerned shall not be the subject of proceedings under regulation 11; or

(d) the notification of a finding that the conduct of the senior officer concerned did not fail to meet the appropriate standard or notification that, in spite of a finding that his conduct did fail to meet the appropriate standard, no sanction should be imposed; or

(e) a sanction has been imposed, whichever first occurs.

6. Suspension — urgent cases

(1) Subject to paragraph (2), in cases of urgency, the like power of suspension as under regulation 5 may be exercised with immediate effect—

    (a) in relation to a chief officer, by the police authority; and

    (b) in any other case, by the chief officer concerned.

(2) Where a senior officer has been suspended under paragraph (1), the appropriate authority shall notify the Authority forthwith.

(3) Without prejudice to regulation 5(5), the suspension of a senior officer under this regulation shall cease to have effect at the expiry of 24 hours from its imposition unless within that period the Authority have notified the appropriate authority of their approval of it.

7. Investigating officers

(1) Where a report, complaint or allegation is received which indicates that the conduct of a senior officer did not meet the appropriate standard, the following provisions of this regulation shall have effect for the purpose of investigating the matter.

(2) The provisions of paragraphs (3) and (3A) or (4) shall have effect—

    (a) in relation to cases arising otherwise than from a complaint to which Chapter I of Part IV of the 1996 Act applies; and

    (b) in cases arising from such a complaint when the requirements of that chapter are dispensed with by or under regulations made under section 81 of the 1996 Act.

(3) Unless the appropriate authority decide, in the light of such preliminary enquiries as they may make, that no proceedings under regulation 11 need be taken, the matter shall be referred to an investigating officer who shall cause it to be investigated.

(3A) If the matter concerns the conduct of the Commissioner of Police of the Metropolis or the Deputy Commissioner of Police of the Metropolis—

    (a) the appropriate authority shall notify the Secretary of State; and

    (b) the Secretary of State shall appoint a person (whether a member of a police force or not) as the investigating officer.

(4) In any other case, the investigating officer shall be appointed by the appropriate authority and shall be—

    (a) a member of the police force concerned; or

    (b) if the chief officer of some other force is requested and agrees to provide an investigating officer, a member of that other force,

and of at least the rank of the senior officer concerned.

(5) Neither—

    (a) the chief officer concerned; nor

    (b) any member of the police force concerned serving in the same division as the senior officer concerned,

shall be appointed as the investigating officer for the purposes of paragraph (3A) or (4) or section 68(2B) of the 1996 Act.

(6) The provisions of this regulation are without prejudice to the powers of the Authority with regard to the approval of the investigating officer under section 72(3)(a) or (b) of the 1996 Act in a case where the Authority are required, or have determined, to supervise the investigation of a complaint or other matter under that section.

8. Initial personal explanation

The investigating officer shall, as soon as is practicable (without prejudicing his or any other investigation of the matter), cause the senior officer concerned to be given written notice—

    (a) that there is to be an investigation into the case;

(b)   of the nature of the report, complaint or allegation;

(c)   informing him that he is not obliged to say anything concerning the matter, but that he may, if he so desires, make a written or oral statement concerning the matter to the investigating officer or to the appropriate authority; and

(d)   informing him that if he makes such a statement it may be used in any subsequent proceedings under these Regulations.

9.   Personal explanation following investigation

(1)   Where, following or, where paragraph (2) applies, during the investigation of a report, complaint or allegation, it appears that the conduct of a senior officer may not have met the appropriate standard, the appropriate authority shall consider whether proceedings under regulation 11 need be taken.

(2)   This paragraph applies where, before the end of the investigation, it appears to the investigating officer that the case is one in respect of which the conditions specified in Part I of the Schedule to these Regulations are likely to be satisfied and informs the appropriate authority accordingly.

(3)   Unless the appropriate authority decide that no such proceedings need be taken, the appropriate authority shall inform the senior officer in writing of the report, allegation or complaint and give him a written notice—

(a)   asking him whether or not he accepts that his conduct did not meet the appropriate standard;

(b)   informing him that he is not obliged to say anything concerning the matter, but that he may, if he so desires, make a written or oral statement concerning the matter to the authority; and

(c)   informing him that if he makes such a statement it may be used in any subsequent proceedings under these Regulations.

(4)   If the appropriate authority decide that no proceedings under regulation 11 need be taken, they shall so inform the senior officer in writing forthwith.

(5)   In a case where paragraph (2) applies, the appropriate authority shall—

(a)   determine whether the case is one in respect of which the conditions specified in Part I of the Schedule to these Regulations are satisfied; and

(b)   if they determine that the case is one in respect of which those conditions are satisfied and unless they are of the opinion that the circumstances are such that it would be inappropriate to do so, certify the case as a special case;

and where the appropriate authority certify the case under sub-paragraph (b), the notice given under paragraph (3) shall inform the senior officer concerned that it has been so certified.

10.   Sanction without hearing

(1)   If the senior officer concerned accepts that his conduct did not meet the appropriate standard, the appropriate authority may impose a sanction under regulation 22 without the case being dealt with in accordance with regulations 11 to 21.

(2)   Notwithstanding that the senior officer concerned accepts that his conduct did not meet the appropriate standard, the appropriate authority may, after considering the report of the investigation, deal with the matter according to the appropriate authority's discretion if they are satisfied that it does not justify the imposition of any sanction under these Regulations.

11.   Notice of proceedings

(1)   This regulation shall apply where the senior officer concerned—

(a)   accepts that his conduct did not meet the appropriate standard but the appropriate authority do not proceed as mentioned in regulation 10(1) or (2); or

(b)   does not accept that his conduct failed to meet the appropriate standard but the appropriate authority, after taking into account any statement he may have made in pursuance of notice given under regulation 8 or 9, are not satisfied that his conduct did meet the appropriate standard.

(2)   Subject to paragraph (4), where this regulation applies the appropriate authority shall refer the case to a hearing and instruct an independent solicitor to give written notice to the senior officer concerned—

(a)   that the case is being referred to a hearing, and

(b)   specifying the conduct of that senior officer which it is alleged failed to meet the appropriate standard and the paragraph of the Code of Conduct in respect of which the appropriate standard is alleged not to have been met.

(3)   The reference in paragraph (2) to an independent solicitor is a reference to a solicitor who is not a member, officer or servant of the appropriate authority or of any local authority which appoints any member of the appropriate authority.

(4)   Notwithstanding that a case is one to which this regulation applies by virtue of paragraph (1)(b), if, after considering the report of the investigation, the appropriate authority are satisfied that the conduct in question, even if found to have failed to meet the appropriate standard, would not justify the imposition of any sanction under these Regulations, the steps mentioned in paragraph (2) need not be taken and the matter may be dealt with according to the appropriate authority's discretion.

(5)   Proceedings at or in connection with a hearing to which a case is referred under this regulation shall, for the purposes of section 65 of the 1996 Act (interpretation of Chapter I of Part IV) be disciplinary proceedings.

12.   Withdrawal of case

(1)   At any time before the beginning of the hearing referred to in a notice under regulation 11, the appropriate authority may direct that the case be withdrawn.

(2)   Where a direction is given under paragraph (1), the appropriate authority shall, as soon as possible, cause the senior officer concerned to be served with a written notice of the direction and the case shall be treated as if it had not been referred to a hearing.

13.   Documents to be supplied to the senior officer concerned

(1)   Where a senior officer is given notice under regulation 11, he shall, at least 21 days before the date of the hearing referred to in that notice, be notified of the time, date and place of the hearing and be supplied with copies of—

(a)   any statement he may have made under regulation 8 or 9;

(b)   any relevant statement, document or other material obtained during the course of the investigation.

(2)   In this regulation any reference to a copy of a statement shall, where it was not made in writing, be construed as a reference to a copy of an account thereof.

14.   Hearing by tribunal

(1)   Where a case is referred to a hearing it shall be heard by a tribunal consisting of a single person selected and appointed by the appropriate authority from a list of persons nominated by the Lord Chancellor.

(2)   To assist the tribunal on matters pertaining to the police there shall also be appointed by the appropriate authority one or more assessors selected by that authority with the approval of the tribunal one of whom is or has been a chief officer of police, so, however, that there shall not be so appointed—

(a)   a person who is one of Her Majesty's inspectors of constabulary;

(b)   the chief officer of the force of which the senior officer concerned is a member; or

(c) a member, officer or servant of the appropriate authority or of any local authority which appoints any member of the appropriate authority.

15. Procedure at hearing

(1) The hearing shall be in private.

(2) The case shall be presented—

    (a) by the independent solicitor mentioned in regulation 11(2); or

    (b) by some other independent solicitor.

(3) In paragraph (2)(b), 'independent solicitor' has the same meaning as in regulation 11.

(4) The senior officer concerned may conduct his case either in person or by a representative.

(5) Any question as to whether any evidence is admissible, or whether any question should or should not be put to a witness, shall be determined by the tribunal.

(6) A verbatim record of the proceedings before the tribunal shall be taken and a transcript of the record shall be made and sent to the appropriate authority; and, if a sanction is imposed by that authority and the senior officer concerned so requests within the time limit for any appeal and after he has lodged notice of appeal in accordance with rules made under section 85 of the 1996 Act, a copy of the transcript shall be supplied to him.

16. Statements in lieu of oral evidence

With the consent of the senior officer concerned the tribunal may allow any document to be adduced in evidence during the hearing notwithstanding that a copy thereof has not been supplied to the senior officer concerned in accordance with regulation 13(1).

17. Adjournment of hearing

The tribunal may from time to time adjourn the hearing if it appears to it to be necessary or expedient to do so for the due hearing of the case.

18. Hearing in absence of senior officer concerned

(1) It shall be within the discretion of the tribunal to proceed with the hearing of the case in the absence of the senior officer concerned if it appears just and proper to do so.

(2) Where, owing to the absence of the senior officer concerned, it is impossible to comply with any of the procedures set out in these Regulations, that procedure shall be dispensed with.

19. Attendance of complainant at hearing

(1) This regulation shall apply where there has been a complaint against the senior officer concerned.

(2) Notwithstanding anything in regulation 15(1) but subject to paragraphs (3), (4) and (6), the tribunal shall allow the complainant to attend the hearing while witnesses are being examined, or cross-examined, and the complainant may at the discretion of the tribunal be accompanied by a friend or relative.

(3) Where the complainant or any person allowed to accompany him is to be called as a witness at the hearing, he and any person allowed to accompany him shall not be allowed to attend before he gives his evidence.

(4) Where it appears to the tribunal that a witness may, in giving evidence, disclose information which, in the public interest, ought not to be disclosed to a member of the public, it shall require the complainant and any person allowed to accompany him to withdraw while the evidence is given.

(5) Where the senior officer concerned gives evidence, then after the person presenting the case has had an opportunity of cross-examining him, the tribunal shall put to him any questions which the complainant requests should be so put and might

have been properly so put by way of cross-examination and, at its discretion, may allow the complainant himself to put such questions to the senior officer concerned.

(6)   Subject as aforesaid, the complainant and any person allowed to accompany him shall neither intervene in, nor interrupt, the hearing; and if he or such a person should behave in a disorderly or abusive manner, or otherwise misconduct himself, the tribunal may exclude him from the remainder of the hearing.

(7)   In this regulation, a reference to the complainant is a reference to the originator of the complaint notwithstanding that it was transmitted to the appropriate authority by some other person or by the Authority or some other body.

20.   Tribunal's report

(1)   The tribunal shall review the facts of the case and decide whether or not the conduct of the senior officer concerned met the appropriate standard.

(2)   The tribunal shall not find that the conduct of the senior officer concerned failed to meet the appropriate standard unless the conduct is—

(a)   admitted by the senior officer concerned; or

(b)   proved by the person presenting the case on the balance of probabilities, to have failed to meet that standard.

(3)   The tribunal shall, as soon as possible after the hearing, submit a report to the appropriate authority setting out—

(a)   the finding of the tribunal under paragraph (1);

(b)   if that finding was that the conduct of the senior officer concerned failed to meet the appropriate standard, a recommendation as to any sanction which, subject to regulation 21, in its opinion should be imposed; and

(c)   any other matter arising out of the hearing which it desires to bring to the notice of the appropriate authority.

(4)   The tribunal shall send the senior officer concerned a copy of the report.

21.   Decision of appropriate authority

(1)   On receipt of the report of the tribunal the appropriate authority shall decide either to dismiss the case or—

(a)   to record a finding that the conduct of the senior officer concerned failed to meet the appropriate standard but to take no further action, or

(b)   to record such a finding and impose a sanction.

(2)   As soon as possible after the appropriate authority has taken its decision in the case that decision shall be notified in writing to the senior officer concerned.

22.   Sanctions

(1)   For the purposes of regulation 10, 20 or 21, the sanctions which may be recommended or imposed shall be—

(a)   dismissal from the force;

(b)   requirement to resign from the force as an alternative to dismissal taking effect forthwith or on such date as may be specified in the recommendation or decision;

(c)   reprimand.

(2)   Where the question of the sanction to be imposed is being considered by the appropriate authority under regulation 10 or 21—

(a)   they shall have regard to the record of police service of the senior officer concerned as shown on his personal record and may receive evidence from any witness whose evidence would, in their opinion, assist them in determining the question; and

(b)   the senior officer concerned, or his representative, shall be afforded an opportunity to make oral or, if appropriate, written representations as respects the question or to adduce evidence relevant thereto.

(3)   Regulation 15(5) shall apply to proceedings at which such evidence as is referred to in paragraph (2)(a) or (b) or such oral representations as are referred to in paragraph (2)(b) is given or are made as it applies to the proceedings before the tribunal.

23.   Copy of report and decision to be sent to the Secretary of State

A copy of the report of the tribunal together with the decision of the appropriate authority shall be sent by the appropriate authority to the Secretary of State.

24.   Expenses of hearing

(1)   All the expenses of a hearing under these Regulations, including the costs of the senior officer concerned, shall be defrayed out of the police fund.

(2)   Any costs payable under this regulation shall be subject to taxation in such manner as the Secretary of State may direct.

25.   Special cases

(1)   This regulation applies to any case in which a report, complaint or allegation is made which indicates that the conduct of a senior officer did not meet the appropriate standard and in respect of which the conditions specified in Part I of the Schedule to these Regulations are satisfied and a certificate has been issued under regulation 9(5)(b).

(2)   In the application of these Regulations to a case to which this regulation applies, regulations 11 to 22 shall, subject to paragraph (3), have effect subject to the modifications specified in Part II of the Schedule to these Regulations.

(3)   Where the appropriate authority have determined that the case is one to which this regulation applies but have directed that the case be returned to the investigating officer the provisions referred to in paragraph (2) shall have effect without modification.

(4)   In Part II of the Schedule to these Regulations, any reference to a provision of these Regulations shall, unless the contrary intention appears, be construed as a reference to that provision as modified by that Part.

Regulation 25   SCHEDULE
                                         SPECIAL CASES

PART I   CONDITIONS

1.—(1)   The conditions referred to in regulation 25(1) are—

(a)   the report, complaint or allegation indicates that the conduct of the senior officer concerned is of a serious nature and that an imprisonable offence may have been committed by the senior officer concerned; and

(b)   the conduct is such that, were his case to be referred to a hearing under regulation 11 and the tribunal hearing the case were to find that the conduct failed to meet the appropriate standard, it would in the opinion of the appropriate authority be reasonable to impose the sanction specified in regulation 22(1)(a) (dismissal from the force); and

(c)   the report, complaint or allegation is supported by written statements, documents or other material which is, in the opinion of the appropriate authority, sufficient without further evidence to establish on the balance of probabilities that the conduct of the senior officer concerned did not meet the appropriate standard; and

(d)   the appropriate authority are of the opinion that it is in the public interest for the senior officer concerned to cease to be a member of a police force without delay.

(2)   In this paragraph, an 'imprisonable offence' means an offence which is punishable with imprisonment in the case of a person aged 21 or over.

PART II   MODIFICATIONS

2.—(1) In regulation 11 (notice of proceedings) for paragraphs (1) and (2) there shall be substituted the following paragraphs:

'(1) This regulation shall apply where the appropriate authority certify the case as a special case under regulation 9(5)(b) and do not proceed as mentioned in regulation 10(1) or (2).

(2) The appropriate authority shall, as soon as is practicable—

(a) refer the case to a hearing and fix a date for that hearing; and

(b) instruct an independent solicitor to give written notice to the senior officer concerned—

(i) that the case has been certified as a special case and referred to a hearing to be held at a time, date and place specified in the notice; and

(ii) specifying the conduct of that senior officer which it is alleged failed to meet the appropriate standard and the paragraph of the Code of Conduct in respect of which the appropriate standard is alleged not to have been met.'.

(2) For paragraph (4) of regulation 11 there shall be substituted the following paragraph:

'(4) The hearing referred to in paragraph (2)(a) shall be fixed for a date not less than 21 and not more than 28 days from the date on which notice is given under paragraph (2)(b).'.

3.—For regulations 12 and 13 there shall be substituted the following regulations:

'12. At any time before the beginning of the hearing the appropriate authority may direct that the case be returned to the investigating officer.

13.—(1) The appropriate authority shall ensure that the notice referred to in regulation 11(2)(b) is—

(a) delivered to the senior officer concerned personally; or

(b) left with some person at, or sent by recorded delivery to, the address at which he is residing; and

(c) accompanied by copies of—

(i) the certificate under regulation 9(5)(b);

(ii) any statement he may have made under regulation 8 or 9; and

(iii) any relevant statement, document or other material obtained during the course of the investigation.

(2) In this regulation any reference to a copy of a statement shall, where it was not made in writing, be construed as a reference to a copy of an account thereof.'.

4.—In regulation 15 (procedure at hearing) in paragraph (5) the words ', or whether any question should or should not be put to a witness,' shall be omitted.

5.—In regulation 16 (statements in lieu of oral evidence), at the end there shall be added the following paragraph:

'(2) No witness shall be called by either party to the case.'.

6.—For regulation 17 (adjournment of hearing) there shall be substituted the following regulation:

'17. The tribunal may adjourn if it appears to it to be necessary or expedient to do so for the due hearing of the case; but

(a) shall not exercise the power to adjourn more than once; and

(b) shall not adjourn for longer than a period of one week or, on application by the senior officer concerned, 4 weeks.'.

7.—In regulation 19 (attendance of complainant at hearing)—

(a)   in paragraph (2) for the words 'paragraphs (3), (4) and (6)' there shall be substituted 'paragraph (6)' and the words 'while witnesses are being examined, or cross-examined,' shall be omitted; and

(b)   paragraphs (3) to (5) and, in paragraph (6), the words 'subject as aforesaid,' shall be omitted.

8.—In regulation 21 (decision of appropriate authority), in paragraph (1) after the words 'dismiss the case or' there shall be inserted 'direct that it be returned to the investigating officer or'.

9.—In regulation 22 (sanctions)—

(a)   in paragraph (2)(a), for the words 'receive evidence from any witness whose evidence would' there shall be substituted 'admit such documentary evidence as would'; and

(b)   in paragraph (2)(b), after the word 'adduce' there shall be inserted 'documentary'.

EXPLANATORY NOTE
(This note is not part of the Regulations)

These Regulations make provision, in pursuance of section 50 of the Police Act 1996, with respect to the conduct of members of police forces and the maintenance of discipline and establish procedures for cases in which a member of a police force may be dealt with by dismissal, requirement to resign or reprimand. These Regulations, by virtue of regulation 3, apply only to senior officers.

The Regulations revoke (with savings) the Police (Discipline) (Senior Officers) Regulations 1985 and provide new procedures for dealing with conduct by senior officers which fails to meet the standard set out in the Code of Conduct contained in Schedule 1 to the Police (Conduct) Regulations 1999 (SI 1999/730).

Regulations 5 and 6 enable the appropriate authority (as defined in regulation 4) to suspend a senior officer in respect of whose conduct a report, complaint or allegation has indicated failure to meet the appropriate standard.

Regulations 7 to 10 provide for investigation of such a report, complaint or allegation and for the appropriate authority to deal with the case without a hearing if the senior officer accepts that his conduct did not meet the appropriate standard. Regulations 11 to 14 deal with the preliminary stages prior to a hearing and regulations 15 to 19 with procedure, evidence and attendance at the hearing. Regulation 20 requires the tribunal to make a finding as to the conduct of the officer and report to the appropriate authority with a recommendation as to sanction, if appropriate. Regulation 21 requires the appropriate authority to dismiss the case or record a finding as to the conduct and either impose a sanction or take no further action. Regulation 22 deals with the imposition of sanctions and regulations 23 and 24 deal with reporting to the Secretary of State and providing for the expenses of the hearing.

Regulation 25 and the Schedule provide for the Regulations to be modified in the case of special cases of serious conduct of a criminal nature.

Appendix 13 Extracts from The Police Regulations 1995 (SI 1995 No. 215), as amended

ARRANGEMENT OF REGULATIONS

PART I

Commencement and interpretation

PART II

Government

PART III

Duty, overtime and leave

PART V

Allowances and other emoluments

PART VII

Revocations and savings

SCHEDULES

The Secretary of State in exercise of the powers conferred on him by section 33 of the Police Act 1964, and after satisfying the requirements of section 46 of that Act and section 2(1) of the Police Negotiating Board Act 1980 as to the furnishing of drafts of the Regulations to the Police Negotiating Board for the United Kingdom and to the Police Advisory Board for England and Wales, hereby makes the following Regulations:

PART I COMMENCEMENT AND INTERPRETATION

1. Citation and commencement

These Regulations may be cited as the Police Regulations 1995 and shall come into force on 8th March 1995, but—

(a)   the increase (from £1,290 to £1,315) in the maximum amount authorised by regulation 52(8) (removal allowance) shall have effect from 1st April 1994, and

(b)   the increase (from £1,344 to £1,365) in the amount authorised by paragraph 3(2) of Schedule 5 (university scholars) shall have effect from 1st July 1993.

2.   References to transfers

(1)   Except where the context otherwise requires, a reference in these Regulations to a member of a police force voluntarily transferring from one force to another shall be construed as a reference to such a member leaving a force for the purpose of joining another force and joining that other force, where—

(a)   he left the force first mentioned in this regulation on or after 1st January 1963 for the purposes aforesaid with, in the case of the chief officer of police, the consent of the police authority;

(b)   he left the force first mentioned in this regulation before 1st January 1963 for the purposes aforesaid with the written consent of the chief officer of police.

(2)   Except where the context otherwise requires, a reference in these Regulations to a member of a police force being statutorily transferred from one force to another shall be construed as a reference to such a member being transferred—

(a)   by or under the Local Government Act 1933, the Police Act 1946, the Local Government Act 1958, the London Government Act 1963, the Police Act 1964 (including that Act as amended by the Police and Magistrates' Courts Act 1994), the Local Government Act 1972 or the Local Government Act 1992;

(b)   in the case of a person who was a member of the River Tyne police force, under the Harbours Act 1964.

(3)   Except where the context otherwise requires, a reference in these Regulations to a member of a police force transferring from one force to another shall be construed as a reference to his either voluntarily so transferring or being statutorily so transferred.

3.   References to provisions of these Regulations

In these Regulations, unless the context otherwise requires, a reference to a regulation shall be construed as a reference to a regulation contained in these Regulations, a reference to a Schedule shall be construed as a reference to a Schedule to these Regulations, a reference to a paragraph shall be construed as a reference to a paragraph in the same regulation or, as the case may be, the same Part of the same Schedule and a reference to a sub-paragraph shall be construed as a reference to a sub-paragraph contained in the same paragraph.

4.   Meanings assigned to certain expressions, etc.

(1)   In these Regulations, unless the context otherwise requires—

'1964 Act' means the Police Act 1964;

'central police officer' has the same meaning as in the Police Pensions Regulations;

'chief officer' means chief officer of police;

'Discipline Regulations' means the regulations relating to discipline from time to time in force under section 33 of the Police Act 1964 and sections 94(5), 101 and 102 of the Police and Criminal Evidence Act 1984;

'joint branch board' means the joint branch board mentioned in regulation 7(3) of the Police Federation Regulations 1969;

'maternity leave' has the meaning assigned thereto by regulation 36A(1);

'member of a police force' includes such a member who is suspended under the Discipline Regulations;

'overseas policeman' has the same meaning as in the Police Pensions Regulations;
'pensionable service' has the same meaning as in the Police Pensions Regulations;
'Police Pensions Regulations' means the regulations from time to time in force
under the Police Pensions Act 1976;
'Promotion Regulations' means the regulations relating to qualification and
selection for promotion from time to time in force under section 33 of the Police
Act 1964;
'public holiday' means Christmas Day, the 26th December (if it falls on a
Saturday or a Sunday), the 1st January (if it so falls), Good Friday or a bank
holiday;
'the representative bodies' means the Police Federation for England and Wales
and all bodies for the time being recognised by the Secretary of State for the
purposes of Section 47 of the Police Act 1964;
'reversionary member of a home police force' has the same meaning as in the
Police Pensions Regulations;
'rostered rest day' has the meaning assigned thereto by regulation 27(1);
'university scholar' and, in relation to such a scholar, 'course' and 'study' have
the meanings respectively assigned to them in paragraph 1 of Schedule 5.

(2)   In these Regulations, unless the context otherwise requires, a reference to a
police force shall include a reference to the Royal Ulster Constabulary and a police
force maintained under the Police (Scotland) Act 1967, so however that nothing in
these Regulations shall be construed as relating to the government, administration or
conditions of service of the Royal Ulster Constabulary or such a force.

(3)   In these Regulations a reference to an aerodrome constabulary is a reference
to such a constabulary within the meaning of the Aviation Security Act 1982; and a
reference to a rank in such a constabulary corresponding to a rank in a police force is
a reference to a rank in that constabulary designated for the purposes hereof by the
Secretary of State as the rank corresponding to the rank in question.

(4)   Nothing in these Regulations shall be construed as authorising pay or allowances payable to any person to be reduced retrospectively.

5.   [Repealed by the Greater London Authority Act 1999 (Consequential Amendments) (Police) Order 2000 (SI 2000 No. 1549).]

5A.   Metropolitan police force: delegation of functions
Subject to regulation 10(11), the Commissioner of Police of the Metropolis may
delegate, to such extent and subject to such conditions as he may specify, any of his
functions under these Regulations as chief officer to the Assistant Commissioners of
Police of the Metropolis, or to one or more of them; and references in these
Regulations to the chief officer shall be construed accordingly.

PART II   GOVERNMENT

6.   Ranks
(1)   Subject to paragraphs (2) to (4), the ranks of a police force shall be known by
the following designations—
Chief Constable;
Assistant Chief Constable;
Superintendent;
Chief Inspector;
Inspector;
Sergeant;
Constable.

(2)   In its application to the metropolitan police force, paragraph (1) shall have effect as if—

(a)   the references to Chief Constable and Assistant Chief Constable were omitted; and

(b)   there were references to Commissioner, Deputy Commissioner and Assistant Commissioner of Police of the Metropolis and to Commander.

(3)   In its application to the City of London police force (in respect of which a Commissioner of the City of London Police is appointed under the Acts relating to that force) paragraph (1) shall have effect as if—

(a)   the references to Chief Constable and Assistant Chief Constable were omitted; and

(b)   there were references to Assistant Commissioner and Commander.

(4)   Until 1st April 1995, paragraph (1) shall have effect as if it included a reference to deputy chief constable and chief superintendent.

(5)   On 1st April 1995 the rank of chief superintendent shall cease to exist.

(6)   Any person who on 1st April 1995 would hold the rank of chief superintendent but for this regulation shall hold the rank of superintendent.

7.   Part-time appointments

(1)   A chief officer of police may, after consultation with local representatives of the representative bodies, appoint persons to perform part-time service in any rank.

(2)   A person serving as a full-time member of a police force may not be appointed to perform part-time service without his consent.

(3)   A person may be appointed under this regulation in the rank of constable only if he has, as a full-time member of a police force, completed the period of probation in that rank that was required by regulation 14.

(4)   Any appointment under this regulation in any rank above that of sergeant may only be made on terms that provide for the holder to share with one other person appointed under this regulation in the rank in question the performance of duties that would otherwise fall to be performed by a single person appointed in that rank as a full-time member of the force; if either of the persons sharing the duties ceases to hold his appointment and is not replaced, the other continues to hold the rank in which he was appointed under this regulation but is to be treated as having become a full-time member of the force.

(5)   In this regulation 'full-time member' means a member appointed otherwise than under this regulation.

(6)   In relation to persons appointed under this regulation to perform part-time service these Regulations have effect with the modifications set out in Schedule 1.

8.   Beats, sections, sub-divisions and divisions

The area to which a constable is assigned for duty either generally or for a particular period of hours shall be known as a beat; a number of beats grouped for supervision by a sergeant or an inspector shall be known as a section; a number of sections grouped for supervision by an inspector, chief inspector or superintendent shall be known as a sub-division; a number of sections or sub-divisions grouped for supervision by a superintendent shall be known as a division.

9.   Restrictions on the private life of members

The restrictions on private life contained in Schedule 2 shall apply to all members of a police force; and no restrictions other than those designed to secure the proper exercise of the functions of a constable shall be imposed by the police authority or the chief officer of police on the private life of members of a police force except such as may temporarily be necessary or such as may be approved by the Secretary of State after consultation with the Police Advisory Board for England and Wales, and any such restriction temporarily imposed shall be reported forthwith to the Secretary of State.

10.   Business interests incompatible with membership of a police force

(1)   If a member of a police force or a relative included in his family proposes to have, or has, a business interest within the meaning of this regulation, the member shall forthwith give written notice of that interest to the chief officer of police unless that business interest was disclosed at the time of his appointment as a member of the force.

(2)   On receipt of a notice given under paragraph (1), the chief officer of police shall determine whether or not the interest in question is compatible with the member concerned remaining a member of the force and, within 28 days of the receipt of that notice, shall notify the member in writing of his decision.

(3)   Within 10 days of being notified of the chief officer's decision as aforesaid, or within such longer period as the police authority may in all the circumstances allow, the member concerned may appeal to the police authority against that decision by sending written notice of his appeal to the police authority.

(4)   Upon receipt of such notice, the police authority shall forthwith require the chief officer of police to submit to them, within the next following 10 days, a notice setting out the reasons for his decision and copies of any documents on which he relies in support of that decision; and the police authority shall send to the member concerned copies of such notice and documents and shall afford him a reasonable opportunity, being in no case less than 14 days, to comment thereon.

(5)   Where a member of a police force has appealed to the police authority under paragraph (3) the police authority shall, within 28 days of receiving his comments on the notice and any other documents submitted by the chief officer of police under paragraph (4), or of the expiration of the period afforded for making comments if none have by then been received, give him written notice of their determination of the appeal but, where they have upheld the decision of the chief officer of police and, within 10 days of being so notified or within such longer period as the police authority may in all the circumstances allow, the member makes written request to the police authority for the reference of the matter to the Secretary of State, the matter shall be so referred and, unless and until the determination of the police authority is confirmed by the Secretary of State, it shall be of no effect and in particular, no action in pursuance thereof shall be taken under paragraph (6).

(6)   Where a member of a police force, or a relative included in his family, has a business interest within the meaning of this regulation which the chief officer of police has determined, under paragraph (2), to be incompatible with his remaining a member of the force and either the member has not appealed against that decision under paragraph (3) or, subject to paragraph (5), on such appeal, the police authority has upheld that decision, then, the chief officer of police may, subject to the approval of the police authority, dispense with the services of that member; and before giving such approval, the police authority shall give the member concerned an opportunity to make representations and shall consider any representations so made.

(7)   For the purposes of this regulation, a member of a police force or, as the case may be, a relative included in his family, shall have a business interest if—

(a)   the member holds any office or employment for hire or gain (otherwise than as a member of a police force) or carries on any business;

(b)   a shop is kept or a like business carried on by the member's spouse (not being separated from him) at any premises in the area of the police force in question or by any relative included in his family at the premises at which he resides; or

(c)   the member, his spouse (not being separated from him) or any relative included in his family living with him holds, or possesses a pecuniary interest in, any such licence or permit as is mentioned in paragraph (8);

and a reference to a relative included in a member's family shall include a reference to his spouse, parent, son, daughter, brother or sister.

(8)   The licence or permit referred to in paragraph (7)(c) is a licence or permit granted in pursuance of the law relating to liquor licensing, refreshment houses or betting and gaming or regulating places of entertainment in the area of the police force in question.

(9)   If a member of a police force or a relative included in his family has a business interest within the meaning of this regulation and, on that interest being notified or disclosed as mentioned in paragraph (1), the chief officer of police has, by written notice, required the member to furnish particulars of such changes in that interest, as respects its nature, extent or otherwise, as may be mentioned in the notice then, in the event of any such change in that interest being proposed or occurring, this regulation shall have effect as though the changed interest were a newly proposed, or newly acquired, interest which has not been notified or disclosed as aforesaid.

(10)   In its application to a chief constable or assistant chief constable, this regulation shall have effect as if—

(a)   for any reference therein to the chief officer of police there were substituted a reference to the police authority;

(b)   for any reference in paragraph (3), (5) or (6) to an appeal there were substituted a reference to a request for reconsideration; and

(c)   the references in paragraph (6) to the approval of the police authority were omitted; but a police authority shall not dispense with the services of a chief constable or assistant chief constable under this regulation without giving him an opportunity of making representations and shall consider any representations so made.

(11)   In its application to a member of the metropolitan police force, this regulation shall have effect as if—

(a)   for any reference to the chief officer of police there were substituted a reference to an assistant commissioner of police of the metropolis.

11.   Business interests precluding appointment to a police force

(1)   Save in so far as the chief officer of police may allow at the request of the candidate concerned, a person shall not be eligible for appointment to a police force if he or a relative included in his family has a business interest within the meaning of regulation 10, and paragraphs (7) and (8) thereof shall apply for the purposes of the interpretation of this regulation as they apply for the purposes of that regulation.

(2)   In its application to a candidate for appointment as chief officer of police or assistant chief constable, paragraph (1) shall have effect as if for any reference to the chief officer of police there were substituted a reference to the police authority.

12.   Qualifications for appointment to a police force

(1)   A candidate for appointment to a police force—

(a)   must produce satisfactory references as to character, and, if he has served in any police force, in the armed forces, in the civil service or as a seaman, produce satisfactory proof of his good conduct while so serving;

(b)   must have attained the age of 18 years 6 months;

(c)　must be certified by a registered medical practitioner approved by the police authority to be in good health, of sound constitution and fitted both physically and mentally to perform the duties on which he will be employed after appointment;

(d)　must, if a candidate for appointment in the rank of constable, satisfy the chief officer of police that he is sufficiently educated by passing a written or oral examination in reading, writing and simple arithmetic, or an examination of a higher standard, as may be prescribed by the chief officer of police;

(e)　must, if a candidate for appointment in the rank of sergeant, or inspector, be qualified for promotion to such rank in accordance with the provisions of the Promotion Regulations;

(f)　must give such information as may be required as to his previous history or employment or any other matter relating to his appointment to the police force;

(g)　shall be given a notice in terms approved by the Secretary of State drawing attention to the conditions of service contained therein.

(2)　For the purposes of this regulation—

(a)　'armed forces' means the naval, military or air forces of the Crown including any women's service administered by the Defence Council, and

(b)　'seaman' has the same meaning as in the Merchant Shipping Act 1894.

13.　Appointment of chief constable

(1)　Subject to section 5A(1) of the Police Act 1964 and regulations 11 and 12, no person shall be appointed as chief constable of a police force unless for a period of not less than two years he holds or has held the rank of assistant chief constable or above—

(a)　in some other police force;

(b)　whilst engaged on relevant service within the meaning of section 97(1) of the Police Act 1996; or

(c)　partly in one of the capacities described in paragraphs (a) and (b) above and partly in another.

(2)　In its application to the metropolitan police force and the City of London police force, paragraph (1) shall have effect as if the reference to assistant chief constable was to commander.

13A.　Fixed term appointments for certain ranks

(1)　This regulation applies to every appointment on or after 1st April 1995 of a person to the rank of—

(a)　chief constable or assistant chief constable of a police force maintained under section 2 of the Police Act 1964, and

(b)　commander in the metropolitan police force and the City of London police force or assistant commissioner in the City of London police force.

(1A)　This regulation applies to every appointment on or after 3rd July 2000 to the rank of commissioner, deputy commissioner or assistant commissioner in the metropolitan police force.

(2)　Where it is proposed to vary by agreement the conditions of service of a person who on 1st April 1995 holds one of the ranks specified in paragraph (1) above indefinitely so that he holds that rank instead for a fixed term—

(a)　that term shall be for a period authorised by paragraph (3) or, as the case may be, paragraph (4); and

(b)　this regulation shall apply to such a variation as it applies to an appointment and as if the variation was an appointment.

(2A)　Where it is proposed to vary by agreement the conditions of service of an assistant commissioner in the metropolitan police force who holds that rank indefinitely on 3rd July 2000 so that he holds that rank instead for a fixed term—

(a)   that term shall be for a period authorised by paragraph (3);

(b)   this regulation shall apply to such a variation as it applies to an appointment and as if the variation was an appointment;

(c)   in paragraph (3) after 'chief constable' there shall be inserted 'or to the rank of commissioner, deputy commissioner or assistant commissioner in the metropolitan police force;' and

(d)   in paragraph (4) for 'commander or assistant commissioner' there shall be substituted 'commander in the metropolitan police force and the City of London police force or assistant commissioner in the City of London police force'.

(3)   Subject to paragraphs (5) to (9), an appointment to the rank of chief constable shall be for a term of not less than four years and not more than seven years.

(4)   Subject to paragraphs (5) to (9), an appointment to the rank of assistant chief constable or commander or assistant commissioner shall be for a term of not less than four years and not more than either—

(a)   ten years, or

(b)   a period expiring with the date on which the person appointed reaches minimum retirement age or, if that period is less than four years, four years whichever of the periods in sub-paragraphs (a) and (b) is the shorter.

(5)   The term of an appointment to which this regulation applies may be for a period of less than four years with the consent of the Secretary of State.

(6)   The term of an appointment to which this regulation applies may, with the consent of the Secretary of State, be extended by agreement for a single period not exceeding one year where the extension cannot be made under paragraph (7) and, in the opinion of the Secretary of State, the particular circumstances in which such an extension is sought are such as to justify it.

(7)   The term of an appointment to which this regulation applies may be extended by agreement for a period or periods up to the time when the person appointed—

(a)   has completed 30 years' pensionable service for the purposes of the Police Pensions Regulations 1987, or

(b)   has completed 25 years' pensionable service for those purposes and has attained the age of 50, whichever is the earlier.

(8)   Subject to paragraph (10) where the term of appointment of a person who—

(a)   has been appointed under this regulation, and

(b)   is subsequently engaged on relevant service within the meaning of section 53C(1) of the Police Act 1964, would otherwise expire whilst he is so engaged, that term shall expire one day after the end of the period of relevant service.

(9)   This regulation is without prejudice to any provision whereby a term of appointment comes to an end on promotion, dismissal or transfer to another police force and to regulation 16(1) and (2) (retirement) and the provisions referred to in regulation 16(3).

(10)   Paragraph (8) shall not apply where the exception specified in section 53C(3) of the Police Act 1964 applies.

(11)   A person does not cease to be eligible for an appointment to which this regulation applies by reason only of the fact that he has completed an appointment for a term determined in accordance with this regulation.

(12)   In this regulation 'minimum retirement age' means—

(a)   in the case of a person who, on attaining the age of 55, will be entitled to reckon not less than 25 years' pensionable service for the purposes of the Police Pensions Regulations 1987, that age; or

(b)   in the case of a person who, on attaining that age, will not be entitled to reckon 25 years' pensionable service for the purposes of those Regulations, the age at which he will be so entitled or the age at which he will be required to retire under regulation A18(1) of those Regulations, whichever is the earlier.

(13)   For the purposes of determining an entitlement under paragraph (12), an election under regulation G4 of the Police Pensions Regulations 1987 (election not to pay pension contributions) shall be disregarded.

(14)   Paragraph (12) shall have effect as if regulation A18(1) of the Police Pensions Regulations 1987 provided that the compulsory retirement age of a commander in the City of London police force was 65 years.

13B.   Requirement to advertise vacancies in certain ranks

(1)   Subject to paragraph (4), where a vacancy exists in one of the ranks specified in regulation 13A(1)(a) and (b) or (1A), a notice of the vacancy which complies with paragraph (2) shall be published by the relevant authority.

(2)   The notice referred to in paragraph (1) must—
(a)   invite applications to fill the vacancy;
(b)   be published in—
(i)   not less than one newspaper, or
(ii)   not less than one journal which deals with police matters,
circulating throughout England and Wales; and
(c)   specify the date, which shall not be less than three weeks after the date of the publication of the notice, by which applications must be made.

(3)   Subject to paragraph (4), no appointment shall be made to fill a vacancy in one of the ranks specified in regulation 13A(1)(a) and (b) or (1A) until after the date specified in accordance with paragraph (2)(c) in a notice in respect of that vacancy.

(4)   Paragraphs (1) and (3) shall not apply where—
(a)   the term of appointment of the person who currently holds the rank in which the vacancy would otherwise occur is extended under regulation 13A(6) or (7), or
(b)   that person is appointed for a further term and the conditions set out in paragraph (5) below are satisfied.

(5)   The conditions referred to in paragraph (4) are that—
(a)   the person who currently holds the rank in which the vacancy would otherwise occur does so by virtue of an appointment under regulation 13A;
(b)   the relevant appointment of that person was for a term which was less than the maximum term authorised in respect of that person by paragraph (3) or, as the case may be, (4) of regulation 13A; and
(c)   the term for which it is proposed to appoint that person (and for which that person is subsequently appointed) is such that, when taken together with—
(i)   the term for which he was appointed by the relevant appointment, and
(ii)   the term for which he was appointed by any subsequent appointment,
the terms in total do not exceed the maximum term of appointment to which he could have been appointed at the time of the relevant appointment under paragraph (3) or, as the case may be, (4) of regulation 13A.

(6)   In paragraph (5) 'relevant appointment' means—
(a)   an appointment made under regulation 13A after the procedures required by paragraphs (1) and (3) of this regulation have been complied with; or
(b)   a variation in the conditions of service in accordance with regulation 13A(2) or (2A).

(7)   In this regulation 'the relevant authority' means—

(a)   in the case of the ranks specified in regulation 13A(1)(a) or (1A) and commanders in the metropolitan police force, the police authority for the force in question;

(b)   in the case of commanders and assistant commissioners in the City of London police force, the Commissioner of the City of London police.

14.   Probationary service in the rank of constable

(1)   This regulation applies to a member of a police force appointed in the rank of constable other than such a member who transferred to the force from another police force, having completed the required period of probation therein.

(2)   A member of a police force to whom this regulation applies shall, unless paragraph (3) applies to his case, be on probation for the first 2 years of his service as a constable in that police force following his last appointment thereto or for such longer period as the chief officer of police determines in the circumstances of a particular case:

(3)   A member of a police force to whom this regulation applies who has served on probation for a period of not less than a year following a previous appointment to that or any other police force shall be on probation for the first year of his service as a constable in the police force first mentioned in this paragraph following his last appointment thereto or for such longer period as the chief officer of police determines in the circumstances of a particular case:

Provided that the chief officer of police may at his discretion—

(a)   reduce the period of probation, so however that the reduced period, when aggregated with the previous period of probation, shall not be less than 2 years, or

(b)   dispense with the period of probation, if the member, following his previous appointment, completed the required period of probation in the force in question.

(4)   For the purposes of this regulation—

(a)   in reckoning service, any period of unpaid leave shall be disregarded;

(b)   in the case of a university scholar, in reckoning service his period of study shall be disregarded;

(c)   in the case of a member who has been statutorily transferred from one force to some other force, his service in those two forces shall be treated as if it were service in the same police force;

(d)   in the case of a member of a police force who has been transferred thereto from an aerodrome constabulary by an order under section 30 of the Aviation Security Act 1982, his service in that constabulary shall be treated as if it were service in that police force;

(e)   in reckoning service in the case of a female member of a police force who has taken one or more periods of maternity leave—

(i)   where that leave has been for more than fourteen weeks, the first fourteen weeks whilst on maternity leave shall be treated as if it were service in the police force;

(ii)   where that leave has been for less than fourteen weeks, any period spent on maternity leave shall be treated as if it were service in the police force.

15.   Discharge of probationer

(1)   Subject to the provisions of this regulation, during his period of probation in the force the services of a constable may be dispensed with at any time if the chief officer of police considers that he is not fitted, physically or mentally, to perform the duties of his office, or that he is not likely to become an efficient or well conducted constable.

(2)   A constable whose services are dispensed with under this regulation shall be entitled to receive a month's notice or a month's pay in lieu thereof.

(3)   A constable's services shall not be dispensed with in accordance with this regulation and any notice given for the purposes thereof shall cease to have effect if he gives written notice to the police authority of his intention to retire and retires in pursuance of the said notice on or before the date on which his services would otherwise be dispensed with; and such a notice taking effect on that date shall be accepted by the police authority notwithstanding that less than a month's notice is given.

(4)   Where a constable has received a notice under this regulation that his services are to be dispensed with and he gives written notice of his intention to retire and retires under paragraph (3), he shall nevertheless be entitled to receive pay up to and until the date on which the month's notice he has received would have expired or where he has received or is due to receive a month's pay in lieu of notice he shall remain entitled to that pay notwithstanding the notice he has given under paragraph (3).

16.   Retirement

(1)   Without prejudice to the provisions mentioned in paragraph (3) and subject to paragraph (2), a member of a police force may retire only if he has given to the police authority one month's written notice of his intention to retire or such shorter notice as may have been accepted by that authority:

Provided that, while suspended under the Discipline Regulations, a member may not, without the consent of the chief officer of police, give notice for the purposes of this regulation or retire in pursuance of a notice previously given.

(2)   In the case of a chief officer of police, Deputy Commissioner of Police of the Metropolis, Assistant Commissioner of Police of the Metropolis, commander in the City of London or metropolitan police force or assistant chief constable, paragraph (1) shall have effect as if—

(a)   for 'one month's' there were substituted 'three months',; and

(b)   for 'chief officer of police' there were substituted 'police authority'.

(3)   The provisions referred to in paragraph (1) are—

(a)   prior to 1st April 1995, the provisions of sections 5 and 6 of the 1964 Act relating to retirement in the interests of efficiency;

(b)   on or after 1st April 1995, the provisions of sections 5A(2) to (4) and 6(3) of the 1964 Act relating to retirement in the interests of efficiency and effectiveness;

(c)   the provisions of section 58(3) of the 1964 Act relating to the retirement of chief constables affected by amalgamations or local government reorganisation;

(d)   the provisions of the Police Pensions Regulations relating to compulsory retirement,

(e)   the provisions of the Discipline Regulations relating to resignation as an alternative to dismissal, and

(f)   the provisions of sections 9E(1) to (3) of the Police Act 1996 relating to retirement in the interests of efficiency or effectiveness.

17.   Contents of personal records

(1)   The chief officer of police shall cause a personal record of each member of the police force to be kept.

(2)   The personal record shall contain—

(a)   a personal description of the member;

(b)   particulars of the member's place and date of birth;

(c)   particulars of his marriage (if any) and of his children (if any);

(d)   a record of his service (if any) in any branch of Her Majesty's naval, military or air forces or in the civil service;

(e)   a record of his service (if any) in any other police force and of his transfers (if any) from one police force to another;

(f)   a record of whether he passed or failed to pass any qualifying examination at which he was a candidate;

(g)   a record of his service in the police force including particulars of all promotions, postings, removals, injuries received, periods of illness, commendations, rewards, punishments other than cautions, and the date of his ceasing to be a member of the police force with the reason, cause or manner thereof:

Provided that—

(i)   a punishment of a fine or of a reprimand shall be expunged after 3 years free from punishment other than a caution;

(ii)   any other punishment shall be expunged after 5 years free from punishment other than a caution,

but in the case of a period free from punishment other than a caution which expired before 1st January 1989 only if the member so requests.

(3)   A member of a police force shall, if he so requests, be entitled to inspect his personal record.

18.   Transfer of personal records

Where a member of a police force transfers to another police force his personal record shall be transferred to the chief officer of police of that other police force.

19.   Personal record of member leaving force

(1)   Where a member of a police force ceases to be a member of that police force the member shall, unless he transfers to another police force, be given a certificate showing his rank and setting out the period of his service in that police force and in any other police force.

(2)   The chief officer of police may append to the certificate any recommendation which he feels justified in giving, such as that—

his conduct was exemplary;

his conduct was very good;

his conduct was good.

(3)   Where a member of a police force ceases to be a member of that police force, otherwise than by transferring to another police force, his personal record shall be kept for such time as the chief officer of police may think fit and shall then be destroyed.

20.   Fingerprints

(1)   Every member of a police force shall in accordance with the directions of the chief officer of police have his fingerprints taken.

(2)   Fingerprints of members of a police force taken in accordance with paragraph (1) shall be kept separate from the fingerprints of persons whose fingerprints have been taken otherwise than in accordance with that paragraph.

(3)   The fingerprints of a member of a police force taken in accordance with paragraph (1) and all copies and records thereof shall be destroyed on his ceasing to be a member of that force, except that, where by reason of a statutory transfer he becomes a member of another force, his fingerprints and all copies and records thereof shall be transferred to the chief officer of police of that other police force.

PART III   DUTY, OVERTIME AND LEAVE

21.   Duty to carry out lawful orders

Every member of a police force shall carry out all lawful orders and shall at all times punctually and promptly perform all appointed duties and attend to all matters within the scope of his office as a constable.

22.   Limitations on duties to be assigned to members statutorily transferred

(1)   Where a member of a police force has previously served in a police force for an area comprised in whole or in part in the area for which his present force is maintained and he ceased to be a member of his former force and became a member of his present force by reason only of one or more such statutory transfers as are mentioned in paragraph (2), then, subject to paragraph (3), he shall not be assigned to duties which, in the opinion of the Secretary of State, make it necessary for him to move his home to a place which is outside the area for which his former force was maintained.

(2)   In paragraph (1) the reference to a statutory transfer is a reference to a statutory transfer being—

(a)   prior to 1st April 1995, a transfer in accordance with the provisions of an amalgamation scheme under the 1964 Act,

(b)   on or after 1st April 1995, a transfer in accordance with an order made under section 21 or 21A of the 1964 Act, or

(c)   a transfer taking effect on 1st April 1974,

except that where the former force was the police force for a borough, the said reference is to any statutory transfer.

(3)   Paragraph (1) shall not apply to a person by reason of his previous service in a particular police force if—

(a)   since he became a member of that police force he has been a chief officer of police, or

(b)   after he was statutorily transferred from that police force he has given written notice to the chief officer of the police force of which he was at the time a member that the protection accorded by paragraph (1) should cease to apply to him, or

(c)   that force was a county or combined police force and after he was statutorily transferred therefrom but before 1st February 1968 he was assigned to such duties as are mentioned in paragraph (1),

without prejudice, however, to the application of paragraph (1) to him by reason of service in another police force after his statutory transfer from the force first mentioned in this paragraph and before his statutory transfer to his present force.

(4)   Paragraph (1) shall apply in the case of a member of a police force who ceased to be such and became a serviceman, a reversionary member of a home police force or a central police officer—

(a)   where on ceasing to be such, he resumed service in, or, as the case may be, exercised his right of reversion to, his former force, as if he had not ceased to be a member of that force, or

(b)   where on ceasing to be such, he resumed service in, or, as the case may be, exercised his right of reversion to some other force to which members of his former force had been transferred as mentioned in paragraph (2), as if he had been so transferred from his former force to that other force.

(5)   In this regulation 'present force' and 'former force' mean, respectively, the force first mentioned and that secondly mentioned in paragraph (1).

23.   Work not required to be performed

A member of a police force shall not be required to perform—

(a)   the regular duty of cleaning or any part of the cleaning of a particular police station which the Secretary of State has directed is not a duty which the police may be required to perform;

(b)   any other work not connected with police duty which, in the opinion of the Secretary of State, the police may not properly be required to perform.

24. Normal daily period of duty

(1) This regulation applies to every member of a police force below the rank of inspector who is not assigned to duties which the Secretary of State has specially excepted from the provisions of this regulation.

(2) The normal daily period of duty (including the period for refreshment referred to in paragraph (3)) of a member of a police force to whom this regulation applies shall be 8 hours.

(3) As far as the exigencies of duty permit—

(a) the normal daily period of duty shall be performed in one tour of duty; and

(b) subject to paragraph 4 of Schedule 4, an interval of 45 minutes shall be allowed for refreshment.

(4) Where a member is required to perform his normal daily period of duty in more than one tour of duty and does not travel to and from his home between tours, an interval for refreshment and rest shall normally be included at the beginning or end of one of those tours.

25. Meaning of 'day' in Part III

(1) In this Part of these Regulations, 'day', in relation to members of a police force, means a period of 24 hours commencing at such time or times as the chief officer shall fix and the chief officer may fix different times in relation to different groups of members.

(2) In discharging his functions under paragraph (1), the chief officer shall have regard to the wishes of the joint branch board.

26. Variable shift arrangements

(1) This regulation applies to members of a police force below the rank of inspector appointed otherwise than under regulation 7 (part-time appointments).

(2) A chief officer of police may bring into operation variable shift arrangements agreed by him with the joint branch board for all members to whom this regulation applies or for any particular class of such members.

(3) Variable shift arrangements must provide, as respects members for whom they are in operation—

(a) for hours of duty equivalent to those resulting from the application of regulations 24(2) and 29(2), and

(b) for annual leave equivalent to that resulting from the application of regulation 34(1) and Schedule 4,
to other members of police forces.

(4) In relation to members of a police force for whom variable shift arrangements are in operation these Regulations have effect with the modifications set out in Schedule 3.

27. Rostering of duties

(1) A chief officer shall cause to be published, in accordance with this regulation, annual duty rosters for members of his force below the rank of inspector and in these Regulations—

(a) a reference to a rostered rest day is to be construed, in relation to a member of a police force who is required to do duty on that day, as a reference to a day which according to the duty roster was, immediately before he was so required to do duty, to have been a rest day for the member; and

(b) a day off granted in lieu of a rostered rest day shall be treated as a rostered rest day.

(2) Each such roster shall be published at intervals not exceeding 12 months and not later than one month before the date on which it is to come into force.

(3) Each such roster shall set out, for the 12 months following the date on which it comes into force, in relation to each member of the force to which it relates—

(a) his rest days;

(b) those days, being public holidays, on which he may be required to do duty; and

(c) the times at which his scheduled daily periods of duty are to begin and end.

(4) Subject to paragraph (5), a duty roster shall make provision for—

(a) an interval of not less than 8 hours between the ending of each of a member's daily periods of duty and the beginning of the next; and

(b) an interval between each of his rostered rest days not exceeding 7 days; unless the joint branch board agrees otherwise.

(5) Where, owing to the exigencies of duty, it is necessary to alter a duty roster, the officer responsible for making the alteration shall endeavour, so far as practicable, to avoid thereby requiring a member to do an additional daily period of duty such that the condition in paragraph (4)(a) would not be satisfied in relation thereto.

28. Overtime

(1) Subject to, and in accordance with, the provisions of this regulation a member of a police force below the rank of inspector shall be compensated in respect of time—

(a) for which he remains on duty after his tour of duty ends, or

(b) for which he is recalled between two tours of duty, or

(c) which forms part of a tour of duty which he is required to begin earlier than the rostered time without due notice and on a day when he has already completed his normal daily period of duty;

and such time is referred to hereafter in these Regulations as 'overtime'.

(2) Such a member shall not be compensated under this regulation for overtime for which he receives an allowance or time off under regulation 29 (public holidays and rest days for ranks below inspector) or regulation 61 (allowance for recurring escort duty, etc.).

(3) Subject to paragraphs (4) and (6), a member of a police force below the rank of inspector shall be granted an allowance in respect of each week at the rate of a twenty-fourth of a day's pay for each completed period of 15 minutes of overtime worked by him on any occasion during that week, except that on each of the first 4 occasions on which overtime in respect of which the member was not informed as mentioned in paragraph (6) is worked during a week 30 minutes of the overtime worked is to be disregarded.

(4) Where such a member, before the expiry of any pay period, elects in respect of specified overtime worked by him during the weeks ending within that period, to be granted in lieu of an allowance time off subject to and in accordance with paragraph (5), and in accordance therewith receives time off in respect of any overtime, no allowance in respect thereof shall be payable under paragraph (3).

(5) Subject to the exigencies of duty, where by virtue of an election under paragraph (4) time off falls to be granted to a member in respect of any overtime worked by him in any week then, within such time (not exceeding 3 months) after that week as the chief officer of police may fix, he shall grant to the member time off equal, subject to paragraph (6), to the period of that overtime worked by him during that week and, in addition, for each completed 45 minutes of such overtime, an additional 15 minutes off.

(6) For the purposes of paragraphs (3) and (5), no account shall be taken of any period of less than 30 minutes of overtime worked on any occasion other than a period of 15 minutes of overtime in respect of which the member was informed at the

commencement of his tour of duty that he would be required to remain on duty after his tour of duty ended.

(7)   In computing any period of overtime for the purposes of this regulation—

(a)   where the member is engaged in casual escort duty, account shall be taken only of—

(i)   time during which he is in charge of the person under escort,

(ii)   such other time as is necessarily spent in travelling to or from the place where the member is to take charge of, or hand over, the person under escort, as the case may be, and

(iii)   any other time that may be allowed by the chief officer of police, so however, that, if the member is so engaged overnight and has proper sleeping accommodation, whether in a train or otherwise, the chief officer of police may exclude such period not exceeding eight hours, during which the member is not in charge of the person under escort as he considers appropriate in the circumstances;

(b)   subject to sub-paragraph (d), where the tour or tours of duty does not or do not amount in the aggregate to more than the normal daily period of duty, no account shall be taken of any overtime except so much as together with the tour or tours of duty exceeds the normal daily period of duty;

(c)   where a member is recalled to duty between two rostered tours of duty and is entitled to reckon less than 4 hours of overtime in respect of any period for which he is recalled, disregarding any overtime reckonable by virtue of regulation 32 (travelling time treated as duty), he shall be deemed to have worked for such period 4 hours of overtime in addition to any overtime reckonable by virtue of regulation 32; and

(d)   where the time at which a member is required to begin a rostered tour of duty is brought forward without due notice so that he is required to begin that tour of duty on a day on which he has already completed his normal daily period of duty, the time for which he is on duty before the rostered commencement time—

(i)   shall be reckonable as overtime, and

(ii)   shall be taken into account as part of that tour of duty.

(8)   For the purposes of this regulation—

'a day's pay' means the member's pay for the week in question divided by 5;

'due notice' means notice given at least 8 hours before the revised starting time of the rostered tour of duty in question;

'member recalled to duty' does not include a member who is only warned to be in readiness for duty if required;

'normal daily period of duty' shall be construed in accordance with regulation 24;

'pay period' means the period for which, in pursuance of regulation 49, a member is paid;

'week' means the period of 7 days beginning with such day as is fixed by the chief officer of police.

29.   Public holidays and rest days for ranks below inspector

(1)   This regulation applies to every member of a police force below the rank of inspector.

(2)   Subject to the following provisions of this regulation, a member shall, so far as the exigencies of duty permit, be allowed a day's leave on each public holiday and be granted rest days at the rate of two rest days in respect of each week.

(3)   A member shall, if required to do duty on a day which is a rostered rest day, be granted—

(a)   where he receives less than 15 days' notice of the requirement, an allowance at the appropriate rest-day rate; or

(b)   in any other case, another rest day, which shall be notified to him within 4 days of notification of the requirement.

(4)   The appropriate rest-day rate is, for each completed 15 minutes of duty on a rostered rest day, the fraction of a day's pay specified in paragraph (5).

(5)   The fraction is—

(a)   where the member received less than 8 days' notice of the requirement, one sixteenth; and

(b)   in any other case, three sixty-fourths.

(6)   A member shall, if required to do duty on a day which is a public holiday, be granted—

(a)   where he receives less than 8 days' notice of the requirement—

(i)   an allowance at the appropriate rate and, in addition,

(ii)   another day off in lieu thereof, which shall be notified to him within 4 days of notification of the requirement, and which shall be treated for the purposes of this regulation as a public holiday;

(b)   in any other case, an allowance at the appropriate rate.

(7)   A member who is required to do duty on a day which is a public holiday or a rostered rest day may, within 28 days of the day in question, elect to receive, in lieu of an allowance as mentioned in paragraph (3)(a) or paragraph (6)(a) or (b), time off equal—

(a)   in the case of a day which is a public holiday, to double, and

(b)   in the case of a rostered rest day—

(i)   where the member received less than 8 days' notice of the requirement, to double, and

(ii)   in any other case, to one and a half times,

the period of completed quarters of an hour of duty on the day in question.

(8)   Where such a member who is required to do duty on a day which is a public holiday or a rostered rest day has elected to receive time off as mentioned in paragraph (7), the chief officer of police shall, subject to the exigencies of duty, grant such time off within such time (not exceeding 3 months) as he may fix, and subject to such time off being taken, no allowance in respect of the day in question shall be payable under paragraph (3)(a) or, as the case may be, paragraph (6)(a) or (b).

(9)   Subject to paragraph (10), for the purposes of this regulation—

(a)   a member of a police force who is paid a dog handler's allowance shall not be treated as required to do duty by reason only of his being required to care for the dog;

(b)   'a day's pay' means a week's pay at the rate at which the member was paid on the day in question divided by five;

(c)   'the appropriate rate' means a sixteenth of a day's pay for each completed 15 minutes of duty done on a public holiday;

(d)   a reference to a day which is a public holiday is to be construed, in relation to the member concerned, as a reference to a day within the meaning of regulation 25(1) commencing at any time on the calendar date of the public holiday in question;

(e)   'week' means a period of 7 days beginning with such day as is fixed by the chief officer of police;

(f)   where a member is required to do duty, or is recalled to duty, for a period of less than 4 completed hours on a day which is a public holiday or a rostered rest day, such period or, as the case may be, each such period, shall be treated as though it were a period of 4 completed hours, except that a period of not more than one hour of duty on a rostered rest day shall, if it immediately follows a period for which he was on duty as part of a normal daily period of duty, count as the number of periods of 15 minutes actually completed;

(g)   where a member is required to do duty on a day which is a public holiday or on a rostered rest day, his period of duty shall include (save for the purposes of sub-paragraph (f)) the time occupied by him in going to, and returning from, his place of duty, not exceeding such reasonable limit as may be fixed by the chief officer of police, save that, for the purposes of this sub-paragraph, there shall be disregarded any period of time so occupied—

     (i)   which together with the member's period of duty exceeds 6 hours, or

     (ii)   which is treated as a period of duty under regulation 32 (travelling time treated as duty).

(10)   Where it is at his own request that a member works on a day which is a public holiday or a rostered rest day he shall not be treated for the purposes of this regulation as having been required to do duty on that day but shall be granted another day off in lieu thereof, which shall be treated as a public holiday or a rostered rest day as the case may be.

30.   Public holidays and rest days for inspectors and chief inspectors

(1)   This regulation applies to every member of a police force of the rank of inspector or chief inspector.

(2)   Such a member shall, so far as the exigencies of duty permit, be allowed a day's leave on each public holiday and be granted rest days at the rate of two rest days in each week.

(3)   Where the exigencies of duty have precluded—

    (a)   the allowance of a day's leave on a public holiday, or (b) the grant in any week of two rest days,

to such a member, he shall, during the next following twelve months and so far as the exigencies of duty permit, be allowed or (as the case may be) granted a day's leave in lieu of any such day not allowed or granted.

31.   Public holidays and monthly leave days for ranks above chief inspector

(1)   This regulation applies to every member of a police force of, or above, the rank of superintendent.

(2)   Such a member shall, so far as the exigencies of duty permit, be allowed a day's leave on each public holiday and be granted in each month—

    (a)   in the case of a superintendent, 8 monthly leave days;

    (b)   in any other case $1\frac{1}{2}$ monthly leave days.

(3)   Where the exigencies of duty have precluded—

    (a)   the allowance of a day's leave on a public holiday, or

    (b)   the grant in any month of eight monthly leave days,

to a superintendent, he shall, during the next twelve months and so far as the exigencies of duty permit, be allowed or (as the case may be) granted a day's leave in lieu of any such day not allowed or granted.

(4)   Where the exigencies of duty have precluded the allowance of a day's leave on a public holiday to any such member other than a superintendent, he shall, during the next three months and so far as the exigencies of duty permit, be allowed a day's leave in lieu of any such day not allowed.

(5)   For the purposes of this regulation 'month' means that period of 28 days beginning with such day as is fixed by the chief officer of police.

32.   Travelling time treated as duty

(1)   This regulation applies where a member of a police force is—

    (a)   required to perform his normal daily period of duty in more than one tour of duty, or

(b)   recalled to duty between two tours of duty,
and travels to and from his home between tours or, as the case may be, in consequence of his recall (in this regulation referred to as 'relevant travelling').

(2)   In computing any period of overtime for the purposes of regulation 28 or any period of duty for the purposes of regulation 29 (save for the purposes of paragraph (9)(f) thereof) the time occupied by such a member in relevant travelling, not exceeding such reasonable limit as may be fixed by the chief officer of police, shall be treated as a period of duty.

(3)   For the purposes of regulation 57, the use of a motor vehicle for relevant travelling shall be treated as such use for the purpose of duties performed by the member concerned.

(4)   Relevant travelling expenses shall be treated as expenses incurred in the execution of duty and, unless they are expenses in respect of which an allowance is payable under these Regulations, the member concerned shall be reimbursed those expenses to the extent that they do not exceed such reasonable limit as the police authority may fix.

33.   Meetings of Police Federation treated as police duty

(1)   The attendance of a member of a police force at one of the following meetings of the Police Federation, that is to say, a quarterly meeting of a branch board, an ordinary meeting of a central committee, a meeting of the conferences arrangements committee, the annual meeting of the joint central committee with the joint central committee of the Scottish Police Federation and the central committee of the Police Federation for Northern Ireland, the annual meeting of a central conference or a women's regional conference shall be treated as an occasion of police duty.

(2)   Subject to the approval of the chief officer of police, the attendance of a member of a police force at an additional meeting of a branch board of the Police Federation or at a meeting of a committee of a branch board shall be treated as an occasion of police duty.

(3)   Subject to the approval of the Secretary of State, the attendance of a member of a police force at a meeting of the Police Federation, other than such a meeting as is mentioned in paragraph (1) or (2), shall be treated as an occasion of police duty.

34.   Annual leave

(1)   Every member of a police force shall, so far as the exigencies of duty permit, be granted annual leave in accordance with Schedule 4.

(2)   The annual leave of a member of a police force shall be additional to the days upon which he is not required to perform police duties in accordance with—
(a)   regulation 29, in the case of a member below the rank of inspector, or
(b)   regulation 30 or 31, in the case of a member of, or above, that rank;
and a member below the rank of superintendent shall, so far as the exigencies of duty permit, be allowed to take his annual leave in one period continuous with such days as aforesaid falling within the period in which he desires to take annual leave.

35.   Sick leave

(1)   A member of a police force shall not be entitled to be absent from duty on account of injury or illness unless a registered medical practitioner has certified him to be unfit for duty:
Provided that—
(a)   with the consent of the police authority, a member may be so absent without such certificate of unfitness where the period of unfitness for duty does not exceed 7 days, including any day on which, even if he were fit to do so, he would not have been required to perform police duty;

(b)   if, notwithstanding such certificate of unfitness for duty, a registered medical practitioner appointed or approved by the police authority has examined the member and considers him to be fit for duty, the police authority shall, if the medical practitioner who issued the certificate of unfitness for duty agrees, within 28 days of the difference of opinion coming to their attention arrange for a third registered medical practitioner to examine the member and to report in writing to the other two practitioners concerned; the third registered practitioner shall be acceptable to the practitioner who issued the certificate of unfitness for duty and to the practitioner who has examined the member on behalf of the police authority, except that in the event of a failure to agree, the police authority may appoint such third medical practitioner as it considers appropriate; and if the third registered medical practitioner certifies the member to be fit for duty, or if the medical practitioner who issued the certificate of unfitness for duty does not agree to such further examination, the member shall no longer be entitled to be absent from duty.

(2)   This regulation applies to a member who is in quarantine as it applies to a member who is ill and any reference to fitness or unfitness for duty shall be construed accordingly.

36.   Leave for ante-natal care

(1)   A female member of a police force who is pregnant and who, on the advice of a registered medical practitioner, registered midwife or registered health visitor, has made an appointment to attend at any place for the purpose of receiving ante-natal care shall, subject to the following provisions of this regulation, have the right not to be unreasonably refused special leave from duty to enable her to keep the appointment.

(2)   Subject to paragraph (3), a chief officer shall not be required by virtue of this regulation to permit a female member of a police force to take special leave from duty to keep an appointment unless, if he requests her to do so, she produces for his inspection—

(a)   a certificate from a registered medical practitioner, registered midwife or registered health visitor stating that she is pregnant, and

(b)   an appointment card or other document showing that the appointment has been made.

(3)   Paragraph (2) shall not apply where the female member of a police force's appointment is the first appointment during her pregnancy for which she seeks permission to take special leave from duty in accordance with paragraph (1).

(4)   A period of special leave from duty taken in accordance with paragraph (1) shall be treated as a period of duty.

36A.   Maternity leave

(1)   In this regulation—

'expected date of birth' means, subject to paragraph (4), the date given in accordance with paragraph (2)(b);

'maternity leave' means leave taken in accordance with the provisions of this regulation by a qualified member of a police force during the maternity period;

'maternity period', in relation to such a member, means the period beginning six months before the probable date of birth of the member's child, as given under paragraph (2)(b) or, as the case may be, paragraph (4), and ending nine months after the date so given; and

'qualified member' means a member of a police force who qualifies under paragraph (2).

(2)   Subject to the following provisions of this regulation, a female member of a police force qualifies for maternity leave when she has given to the chief officer of police notice stating—

   (a)   that she is pregnant;

   (b)   the probable date of the birth of her child; and

   (c)   the date on which she intends to commence maternity leave or, where she proposes to take more than one period of maternity leave before the probable date of the birth of her child, the proposed dates of those periods.

(3)   A female member of a police force does not qualify for maternity leave where the chief officer of police has requested a certificate from a registered medical practitioner, registered midwife or registered health visitor setting out the matters referred to in paragraph (2)(a) and (b) and she fails to produce such a certificate.

(4)   Where a certificate produced under paragraph (3) sets out a different date as the probable date of the birth of the child of the female member of a police force from the date given in accordance with paragraph (2)(b), the date given in the certificate shall have effect in place of the date given in the notice.

(5)   A female member of a police force who is pregnant shall give the notice required by paragraph (2) as soon as reasonably practicable after she becomes aware of the probable date of birth of her child.

(6)   The date or dates given in accordance with paragraph (2)(c) may be amended by a subsequent notice to the chief officer of police, provided that not less than 21 days' notice is given of the qualified member's intention to return to duty.

(7)   A qualified member shall commence maternity leave no later than the date given in accordance with paragraph (2)(b) and, subject to paragraphs (8) and (9), the leave shall continue until the last day of the maternity leave.

(8)   Where a qualified member intends to return to duty before the end of the maternity period after taking maternity leave, she shall give to the chief officer of police not less than 21 days' notice of her intention.

(9)   A notice under paragraph (8) may be subsequently revoked; and any such revocation shall be without prejudice to the giving of another notice under that paragraph of an intention to return to duty before the end of the maternity period.

(10)   During any period of maternity leave, a qualified member shall not be entitled to any sick leave under regulation 35.

(11)   In paragraph (10) 'period of maternity leave' means the period—

   (a)   beginning on—

      (i)   the date given in accordance with paragraph (2)(c) as the date on which the qualified member intends to commence maternity leave or, where she proposes to take more than one period of such leave, the first of those dates, or

      (ii)   where that date or, as the case may be, the first of those dates has been amended by a subsequent notice under paragraph (6), that date; and

   (b)   ending on—

      (i)   where a notice has been given under paragraph (8) and has not been subsequently revoked, the date so given; or

      (ii)   where no such notice has been given or remains in force, the last day of the maternity period.

37. Paternity leave

(1)   So far as the exigencies of duty permit, a male member of a police force shall be granted 2 days' paternity leave during the relevant part of a woman's maternity period.

(2)   A woman's maternity period is one beginning with the later of—

(a)   the date on which she is certified by a registered medical practitioner to be pregnant, and

(b)   the date 6 months before the one estimated by that practitioner as being the probable date of birth,

and ending 9 months after the birth of the child.

(3)   The relevant part of a woman's maternity period is any part during which—

(a)   the member is married to and not separated from her, or

(b)   they are not married to each other but are living together as husband and wife.

38.   University scholars

This Part of these Regulations shall have effect in relation to a university scholar subject to the provisions of paragraph 2 of Schedule 5.

. . .

PART V   ALLOWANCES AND OTHER EMOLUMENTS

50.   Restriction on payment of allowances

(1)   No allowances shall be paid to a member of a police force except as provided by these Regulations or approved by the Secretary of State, and the amounts and conditions of payment of such allowances shall be as so provided or approved.

(2)   Subject to paragraph (3), nothing in this regulation shall apply to the reimbursement of expenses incurred by a member of a police force in the execution of his duty, being expenses authorised either generally or specifically by the police authority in respect of which no allowance is payable under these Regulations.

(3)   A member of a police force of the rank of superintendent or above who is required to travel by train in the execution of his duty shall be entitled to travel in first-class accommodation and to be reimbursed his expenses accordingly.

51.   Restriction on payments for private employment of police

Without prejudice to the generality of regulation 50, a member of a police force who is engaged on duty at the request of any person who has agreed to pay the police authority for the member's services shall not be entitled to any payment for those services except as provided by these Regulations; and any payments made in pursuance of that agreement shall be made by that person to the police authority.

. . .

PART VII   REVOCATIONS AND SAVINGS

70.   Revocations and savings

(1)   The Regulations specified in Part I of Schedule 12 are revoked to the extent specified.

(2)   The revocations have effect subject to the savings in Part II of Schedule 12.

71.   Temporary provision about deputy chief constable

Until 1st April 1995 the following regulations, namely—

regulation 10(10) (business interests incompatible with membership of a police force);

regulation 11(2) (business interests precluding appointment to a police force); and regulation 16(2) (retirement),

shall have effect as if any reference to assistant chief constable (or, as the case may be, officer) included a reference to deputy chief constable (or officer).

Regulation 7   SCHEDULE 1
                    MODIFICATION FOR PART-TIME SERVICE

1. In regulation 4 (meanings assigned to certain expressions) after paragraph (4) insert—

'(5)   In relation to a member of a police force below the rank of inspector—

(a)   the determined hours are the number of hours which the chief officer of police has determined under regulation 24(2) or (4A)(a) as his normal period of duty in a relevant period,

(b)   a relevant period is a period for which a duty roster relating to him has effect for the time being under regulation 27, and

(c)   the appropriate factor is $\frac{A}{B}$,

where—

A is the number of the determined hours, and

B is 40 times the number of weeks in the relevant period.

(6)   In relation to a member of a police force above the rank of sergeant the appropriate factor is ½.'.

2. In regulation 14 (probationary service in the rank of constable)—

(a)   in paragraph (1) omit the words after 'constable';

(b)   in paragraph (2) for the words after 'this regulation applies' substitute 'may be required to serve on probation for such period, not exceeding 2 years and 6 months, as the chief officer of police determines in the circumstances of a particular case.'; and

(c)   omit paragraph (3) and paragraph (4)(c) and (d).

3. In regulation 15 (discharge of probationer)—

(a)   in paragraph (1) for the words 'his period' substitute 'any period'; and

(b)   after paragraph (4) insert—

'(4A)   For the purposes of this regulation a month's pay is to be calculated by multiplying one twelfth of the annual rate ascertained from Schedule 6 by the appropriate factor.'.

4. In regulation 24 (normal daily period of duty) for paragraphs (2) to (4) substitute—

'(2)   The normal period of duty in every relevant period of a member of a police force to whom this regulation applies, which is to be performed in accordance with general arrangements made by the chief officer of police after consulting the police authority and local representatives of the representative bodies, is, subject to paragraph (4A), the total number of hours determined by the chief officer with the agreement of the member at the time of his appointment.

(3)   For the purposes of paragraph (2) a day of annual leave counts as a period of duty of 8 hours multiplied by the appropriate factor.

(4)   The chief officer shall review a member's normal period of duty at intervals of not more than 52 weeks, and in doing so shall have regard to the number of hours actually spent on duty during the interval preceding the review.

(4A)   After a review under paragraph (4)—

(a)   any number of hours different from that determined under paragraph (2) which was determined by the chief officer and agreed to by the member becomes the member's normal period of duty, and

(b)   if no different number was agreed to by the member, his normal period of duty is the number of hours determined under paragraph (2).

(4B)   The number of hours determined under paragraph (2) or (4A)(a) must not be less than 16 times the number of weeks in the relevant period.

(4C)   As far as the exigencies of duty permit, a shift shall consist of one continuous period.

(4D)   Where in one day a member is on duty for a continuous period of 5 hours or more, an interval for refreshment shall, as far as the exigencies of duty permit, be allowed in accordance with the Table below.

Number of hours	*Refreshment interval*
Less than 6 hours	30 minutes
6 hours or more, but less than 7 hours	35 minutes
7 hours or more, but less than 8 hours	40 minutes
8 hours or more	45 minutes

(4E)   Where a shift consists of two periods amounting in total to 5 hours or more and the member does not travel to and from his home between those periods, an interval for refreshment and rest shall normally be included at the beginning or end of one of them.'.

5.   In regulation 27 (rostering of duties)—
    (a)   in paragraph (1)—
        (i)   omit the word 'annual', and
        (ii)   after sub-paragraph (b) insert—
        'and
            (c)   a reference to a free day is to be construed as a reference to a day which is not—
                (i)   a day on which a shift is, according to the duty roster, to begin or end, or
                (ii)   a rostered rest day, or
                (iii)   a public holiday.';
    (b)   in paragraph (2) after the word 'roster' insert '(except one relating to a member who has agreed with the chief officer on a different period) shall have effect for a period of 12 months, and';
    (c)   in paragraph (3)—
        (i)   for the words 'the 12 months following the date on which it comes into force' substitute 'the period for which it has effect',
        (ii)   after sub-paragraph (a) insert—
        '(aa)   his free days;', and
        (iii)   in sub-paragraph (c) for the words 'his scheduled daily periods of duty are' substitute 'each of his shifts is';
    (d)   in paragraph (4)—
        (i)   in sub-paragraph (a) for the words 'daily periods of duty' substitute 'shifts', and
        (ii)   in sub-paragraph (b) before the words 'an interval' insert 'unless he has agreed with the chief officer on a longer interval,'; and
    (e)   in paragraph (5) for the words 'daily period of duty' substitute 'shift'.

6.   For regulation 28 (overtime) substitute—
    '**28.**—(1)   This regulation applies to a member of a police force below the rank of inspector.

(2)   A member who has been on duty for more than 40 hours in any period of 7 days beginning with such day as is fixed for the purposes of this regulation by the chief officer of police (a "relevant week") is entitled in respect of any day during that period in which he has been on duty for more than 8 hours (a "long-duty day") to an allowance at the rate of one twelfth of an hour's pay for each completed 15 minutes in excess of 8 hours, except that on each of the first 4 occasions on which overtime which the member was not told at the beginning of the shift would be required is worked during a relevant week 30 minutes of the overtime worked is to be disregarded.

(3)   A member may, before the end of a pay period (that is to say, a period comprising one of the intervals between payments under regulation 49), elect to be granted time off, instead of an allowance under paragraph (2), in respect of any long-duty day that occurred during a relevant week ending within the pay period.

(4)   Subject to the exigencies of duty, where a member has elected as mentioned in paragraph (3) the chief officer of police shall, within 3 months after the end of the relevant week, grant him time off equal to the total of—

(a)   the time in excess of 8 hours spent on duty in the day, or as the case may be in each of the days, in respect of which the election was made, and

(b)   15 minutes in respect of each completed 45 minutes of that time.

(5)   Any time counting for the purposes of regulation 39(1) (pay) as time spent on duty, except—

(a)   time for which an allowance is received under paragraph (7) or under regulation 29 or 61, and

(b)   any period of less than 30 minutes worked during the first 30 minutes after the end of a rostered shift, except a period of 15 minutes which the member was told at the beginning of the shift would be required,

counts as time spent on duty for the purposes of paragraph (2).

(6)   For the purposes of paragraph (2) a period of duty—

(a)   which resulted from a member's being recalled and returning to duty between two rostered shifts, and

(b)   the length of which, after deducting any travelling time counting as a period of duty by virtue of regulation 32, was less than 4 hours,

counts as a period of duty lasting for the aggregate of 4 hours and any period counting by virtue of regulation 32.

(7)   Where the time at which a member is required to commence a rostered shift is brought forward—

(a)   without giving him notice 8 hours or more before the new commencement time, and

(b)   so that he is required to commence that shift on the day on which his previous shift ended,

he is entitled to an allowance at the rate of one twelfth of an hour's pay for each completed 15 minutes of the time for which he is on duty before the rostered commencement time.

(8)   A member who has become entitled to an allowance under paragraph (7) may, before the end of the pay period during which the day on which he was required to commence the shift occurred, elect to be granted time off instead of the allowance.

(9)   Subject to the exigencies of duty, where a member has elected as mentioned in paragraph (8) the chief officer of police shall, within 3 months after the date of the election, grant him time off equal to one and one third times the number of completed quarters of an hour for which he was on duty before the rostered commencement time.

(10) Where—

(a) on any day on which he has a rostered shift a member has been on duty for a period exceeding the length of that shift, and

(b) he is not entitled in respect of that day to any allowance under paragraph (2) or (7),

he may, not later than 4 days after the end of the relevant week in which the day in question occurred, elect to be granted time off in respect of the excess over the length of the shift ("the excess period").

(11) For the purposes of paragraphs (2) and (10) a continuous period of duty which began before and ended after the beginning of a day shall—

(a) if the day on which it ended was not—

(i) a public holiday,

(ii) a rostered rest day, or

(iii) a free day, in respect of which he became entitled to an allowance under regulation 29, be treated as having fallen wholly within, and

(b) in any other case, be treated as having consisted only of so much of the period as fell within, the day on which the period began.

(12) Subject to the exigencies of duty, where a member has elected as mentioned in paragraph (10) the chief officer of police shall, within 3 months after the date of the election, grant him time off equal to the excess period.

(13) For the purposes of regulation 39(1) (pay) any extra period of duty in respect of which time off is granted under paragraph (4) or (9) counts as one and one third times the number of completed quarters of an hour comprised in the extra period of duty, and a period falling within paragraph (6)(a) and (b) counts as one of 4 hours.'.

7. In regulation 29 (public holidays and rest days for ranks below inspector)—

(a) in paragraph (4) for the words 'a day's pay' substitute 'the member's hourly rate of pay calculated in accordance with regulation 39(1)';

(b) in paragraph (5)—

(i) for the words 'one sixteenth' substitute 'one quarter', and

(ii) for the words 'three sixty-fourths' substitute 'one eighth';

(c) after paragraph (5) insert—

'(5A) A member who—

(a) is required to do duty on a free day, and

(b) receives not less than 15 days' notice of the requirement,

shall be granted another free day in lieu, which shall be notified to him within 4 days of notification of the requirement.

(5B) This paragraph applies where—

(a) a member is required to do duty on a free day, and

(b) he receives less than 15 days' notice of the requirement, and

(c) the duty is of such a nature that it would not in the circumstances have been reasonably practicable for it to be done by any other member.

(5C) Where paragraph (5B) applies—

(a) if the member was on duty for more than 8 hours on the free day and for more than 40 hours (in addition to any hours on a rostered rest day or a public holiday for which an allowance fell to be granted under paragraph (3)(a) or (6)(a) or (b)) during the week in which the free day occurred, he is entitled to an allowance at the rate of one twelfth of an hour's pay for each completed period of 15 minutes of duty done on the free day, and

(b) in any other case, he is entitled to time off equal to the total length of those periods.

(5D)   Where—

(a)   a member is required to do duty on a free day, and

(b)   he receives less than 15 days' notice of the requirement,

but paragraph (5C) does not apply, he is entitled to an allowance at the appropriate rest-day rate.';

(d)   after paragraph (7) insert—

'(7A)   A member who is required to do duty on a free day may within 28 days of that day elect to receive—

(a)   in lieu of an allowance under paragraph (5C)(a), time off equal to one and one third times, and

(b)   in lieu of an allowance under paragraph (5D), time off equal to one and a half times,

the period of completed quarters of an hour of duty done on the free day.';

(e)   in paragraph (8)—

(i)   after the words 'rostered rest day' insert 'or on a free day',

(ii)   after the words 'paragraph (7)' insert 'or (7A)'.

(iii)   after the words 'as the case may be,' insert 'paragraph (5C) or (5D) or';

and

(f)   in paragraph (9)—

(i)   for sub-paragraph (b) substitute—

'(b)   "the appropriate rate" is, for each completed 15 minutes of duty done on a public holiday, one quarter of the member's hourly rate of pay calculated in accordance with regulation 39(1);';

(ii)   omit sub-paragraph (c), and

(iii)   in sub-paragraphs (f) and (g) after the words 'rostered rest day', wherever occurring, insert 'or a free day' and in sub-paragraph (f) for the words 'a normal daily period of duty' substitute 'a rostered shift';

(g)   in paragraph (10) after the words 'rostered rest day', wherever occurring, insert 'or a free day'; and

(h)   after paragraph (10) insert—

'(11)   For the purposes of regulation 39(1) (pay)—

(a)   a day's leave allowed under paragraph (2) and a day off granted under paragraph (4)(a) or under paragraph (10) in respect of a public holiday each count as a period of duty of 8 hours multiplied by the appropriate factor, and

(b)   so much of any time off granted under paragraph (7A) or (8) as exceeds the time spent on duty on the public holiday, rest day or free day counts as time spent on duty.'.

8.   In regulation 31 (public holidays and monthly leave days for ranks above chief inspector)—

(a)   in paragraph (2) after the words 'each month' insert 'the amount of leave arrived at by multiplying by the appropriate factor'; and

(b)   in paragraph (3)—

(i)   for the words 'eight monthly leave days' substitute 'the amount of leave arrived at by multiplying 8 days by the appropriate factor', and

(ii)   for the words after 'permit' substitute 'be allowed a day's leave in lieu of any day on a public holiday not allowed (or as the case may be) be granted the balance of monthly leave as additional monthly leave'.

9.   In regulation 32 (travelling time treated as duty)—

(a)   for paragraph (1) substitute—

'(1)   This regulation applies to a member of a police force where—
(a)   a shift consists of two separate periods, or
(b)   he is recalled to duty between two shifts,
and he travels to and from his home between those periods or, as the case may be, in consequence of his recall (in this regulation referred to as "relevant travelling").'; and

(b)   in paragraph (2) for the words from 'overtime' to 'thereof)' substitute 'duty for the purposes of regulation 28, regulation 29 (except paragraph (9)(f)) or regulation 39(1)'.

10.   In regulation 34 (annual leave)—
(a)   in paragraph (1) after the words 'Schedule 4' insert ', except that in the case of a member above the rank of chief inspector any period of leave calculated in accordance with Schedule 4 is to be multiplied by the appropriate factor'; and
(b)   after paragraph (1) insert—
'(1A)   In the case of a member below the rank of superintendent, each day of annual leave granted counts for the purposes of regulation 39(1) (pay) as a period of duty of 8 hours multiplied by the appropriate factor.'.

11.   In regulation 35 (sick leave) after paragraph (2) insert—
'(3)   While a member below the rank of inspector is entitled under this regulation to be absent from duty, any rostered shift counts for the purposes of regulation 39(1) (pay) as a period of duty of the same duration.'.

. . .

13.   In regulation 37 (paternity leave) after paragraph (3) insert—
'(4)   In the case of a member below the rank of superintendent, each day of paternity leave granted counts for the purposes of regulation 39(1) (pay) as a period of duty of 8 hours multiplied the appropriate factor.'.

. . .

Regulation 9   SCHEDULE 2
RESTRICTIONS ON THE PRIVATE LIFE OF MEMBERS OF POLICE
FORCES

1.   A member of a police force shall at all times abstain from any activity which is likely to interfere with the impartial discharge of his duties or which is likely to give rise to the impression amongst members of the public that it may so interfere; and in particular a member of a police force shall not take any active part in politics.

2.   A member of a police force shall not reside at premises which are not for the time being approved by the chief officer of police.

3.—(1)   A member of a police force shall not, without the previous consent of the chief officer of police, receive a lodger in a house or quarters with which he is provided by the police authority or sub-let any part of the house or quarters.
(2)   A member of a police force shall not, unless he has previously given written notice to the chief officer of police, receive a lodger in a house in which he resides and in respect of which he receives an allowance under Part II of Schedule 12 or sub-let any part of such a house.

4.   A member of a police force shall not wilfully refuse or neglect to discharge any lawful debt.

. . .

Regulation 70   SCHEDULE 12
                     REVOCATIONS AND SAVINGS

                       PART I   REVOCATIONS

Regulations revoked	References	Extent of revocation
The Police Regulations 1987	SI 1987/851	The whole Regulations
The Police (Amendment) Regulations 1987	SI 1987/1753	The whole Regulations
The Police (Amendment) Regulations 1988	SI 1988/727	The whole Regulations
The Police (Amendment) (No. 2) Regulations 1988	SI 1988/1821	The whole Regulations
The Police (Amendment) (No. 3) Regulations 1988	SI 1988/2162	The whole Regulations
The Police (Amendment) Regulations 1989	SI 1989/895	The whole Regulations
The Police (Amendment) (No. 2) Regulations 1989	SI 1989/1745	The whole Regulations
The Police (Amendment) Regulations 1990	SI 1990/401	The whole Regulations
The Police (Amendment) (No. 2) Regulations 1990	SI 1990/1127	The whole Regulations
The Police (Amendment) (No. 3) Regulations 1990	SI 1990/1573	The whole Regulations
The Police (Amendment) (No. 4) Regulations 1990	SI 1990/2619	The whole Regulations
The Police (Amendment) Regulations 1991	SI 1991/2484	The whole Regulations
The Police (Amendment) (No. 2) Regulations 1991	SI 1991/2650	The whole Regulations
The Police (Amendment) (No. 3) Regulations 1991	SI 1991/2869	The whole Regulations
The Police (Amendment) Regulations 1992	SI 1992/275	The whole Regulations
The Police (Amendment) (No. 2) Regulations 1992	SI 1992/1278	The whole Regulations
The Police (Amendment) Regulations 1993	SI 1993/313	The whole Regulations
The Police (Amendment) (No. 2) Regulations 1993	SI 1993/1198	The whole Regulations
The Police (Amendment) (No. 3) Regulations 1993	SI 1993/2047	The whole Regulations
The Police (Amendment) (No. 4) Regulations 1993	SI 1993/2527	The whole Regulations
The Police (Amendment) Regulations 1994	SI 1994/1308	The whole Regulations
The Police (Amendment) (No. 2) Regulations 1994	SI 1994/2195	The whole Regulations

Regulations revoked	References	Extent of revocation
The Police (Amendment) (No. 3) Regulations 1994	SI 1994/2331	The whole Regulations
The Police (Amendment) (No. 4) Regulations 1994	SI 1994/2993	The whole Regulations

PART II   SAVINGS

General interpretation

1.   In this Part 'the 1987 Regulations' means the Police Regulations 1987.

Part-time service

2.   In relation to a person performing part-time service in the rank of inspector or chief inspector pursuant to an appointment in the rank in question made under regulation 8A of the 1987 Regulations before 1st September 1994, these Regulations shall have effect as if for all purposes except that of determining pay the appointment had been in a rank lower than inspector.

Housing payments

3.   Interpretation
   (1)   This paragraph has effect for defining expressions used in paragraphs 4 to 9.
   (2)   'Qualifying member' means a member of a police force who—
      (a)   immediately before 1st September 1994 was a member of that or another police force,
      (b)   was not then on unpaid leave,
      (c)   has at all times after 31st August 1994 been a member of a police force, and
      (d)   has not after that date been on unpaid leave.
   (2A)   Where a member of a police force in Scotland or Northern Ireland in receipt of a replacement allowance under a corresponding regulation which has effect there transfers to a police force in England and Wales he shall be treated from the date of his transfer as if he were a qualifying member.
   (3)   'Re-joining member' means a member of a police force who by reason only of a relevant absence is not a qualifying member.
   (4)   'Relevant absence' means—
      (a)   a period of central service or overseas service, or
      (aa)   a period of relevant service within the meaning of paragraph (ca), (cb) or (cc) of section 97(1) of the Police Act 1996 or any corresponding provision for the time being in force in Scotland or Northern Ireland, or
      (b)   a period of unpaid leave,
ending after 31st August 1994.
   (5)   'Housing emoluments' means any one or more of the following kinds of payments under the revoked provisions as they had effect before 1st September 1994—
      (a)   a housing allowance under regulation 49,
      (b)   a transitional rent allowance and a transitional supplementary rent allowance under regulation 49B,
      (c)   a supplementary housing allowance under regulation 50,
      (d)   a compensatory grant under regulation 52, and
      (e)   a compensatory allowance under regulation 52B,

and in relation to a re-joining member includes a rent allowance under regulation 49 as it had effect before 1st April 1990; and 'housing allowance' and 'transitional rent allowance' mean respectively the allowances mentioned in (a) and (b) above.

(6)   'The revoked provisions' means the provisions of the 1987 Regulations relating to housing and housing payments that were revoked on 1st September 1994, that is to say regulations 49 to 52, 52B and 72, paragraphs 16 to 18 of Schedule 1A and paragraph 4(1) and (2) of Schedule 4.

Regulation 65A   SCHEDULE 13
                            REPLACEMENT ALLOWANCE

1. Interpretation

(1)   This paragraph has effect for defining expressions used in paragraphs 2 to 7.

(2)   'Qualifying member' means a member of a police force who—

(a)   immediately before 1st September 1994 was a member of that or another police force,

(b)   was not then on unpaid leave,

(c)   has at all times after 31st August 1994 been a member of a police force, and

(d)   has not after that date been on unpaid leave.

(3)   Where a member of a police force in Scotland or Northern Ireland in receipt of a replacement allowance under a corresponding regulation which has effect there transfers to a police force in England and Wales he shall be treated from the date of his transfer as if he were a qualifying member.

(4)   'Re-joining member' means a member of a police force who by reason only of a relevant absence is not a qualifying member.

(5)   'Relevant absence' means—

(a)   a period of central service or overseas service, or

(b)   a period of relevant service within the meaning of paragraph (ca), (cb) or (cc) of section 97(1) of the Police Act 1996 or any corresponding provision for the time being in force in Scotland or Northern Ireland, or

(c)   a period of unpaid leave,

ending after 31st August 1994.

(6)   'Housing emoluments' means any one or more of the following kinds of payments under the revoked provisions as they had effect before 1st September 1994—

(a)   a housing allowance under regulation 49,

(b)   a transitional rent allowance and a transitional supplementary rent allowance under regulation 49B,

(c)   a supplementary housing allowance under regulation 50,

(d)   a compensatory grant under regulation 52, and

(e)   a compensatory allowance under regulation 52B,

and in relation to a re-joining member includes a rent allowance under regulation 49 as it had effect before 1st April 1990; and 'housing allowance' and 'transitional rent allowance' mean respectively the allowances mentioned in (a) and (b) above.

(7)   'The revoked provisions' means the provisions of the 1987 Regulations relating to housing and housing payments that were revoked on 1st September 1994, that is to say regulations 49 to 52, 52B and 72, paragraphs 16 to 18 of Schedule 1A and paragraph 4(1) and (2) of Schedule 4.

(8)   'The 1987 Regulations' means the Police Regulations 1987.

2.   Qualifying member previously provided with accommodation

(1)   A qualifying member who ceases to occupy a house or quarters with which he was provided free of rent becomes entitled to a replacement allowance.

(2)   The replacement allowance is, subject to paragraph 7, an allowance at a rate equal to the total of—

(a)   the rate at which housing allowance, or as the case may be transitional rent allowance, was payable, or would have been payable if he had not been occupying the house or quarters,

immediately before 1st September 1994, and

(b)   the rate at which any allowance under regulation 49(11) or 50(3) was or would have been then payable.

3.   Qualifying member with housing emoluments

(1)   A qualifying member who immediately before 1st September 1994 was in receipt of housing emoluments is entitled to a replacement allowance unless he is provided with a house or quarters free of rent.

(2)   The replacement allowance is, subject to paragraph 7, an allowance at the rate at which the housing emoluments were payable immediately before 1st September 1994.

4.   Re-joining member previously provided with accommodation

(1)   A re-joining member who immediately before the relevant absence began was occupying a house or quarters with which he was provided free of rent becomes entitled to a replacement allowance unless he is again provided with a house or quarters free of rent.

(2)   The replacement allowance is, subject to paragraph 7, an allowance at the rate at which, if he had not been occupying the house or quarters, housing allowance, or as the case may be transitional rent allowance, would have been payable—

(a)   where the relevant absence began before 1st September 1994, immediately before it began, and

(b)   in any other case, immediately before 1st September 1994.

5.   Re-joining member previously in receipt of housing payments

(1)   A re-joining member who immediately before the relevant absence began was in receipt—

(a)   of housing emoluments, or

(b)   of a replacement allowance under paragraph 2 or 3,

becomes entitled to a replacement allowance unless he is provided with a house or quarters free of rent.

(2)   The replacement allowance is, subject to paragraph 7, an allowance—

(a)   where sub-paragraph (1)(a) applies, at the rate at which the housing emoluments were payable, and

(b)   where sub-paragraph (1)(b) applies, at the rate at which the previous replacement allowance was payable,

immediately before the relevant absence began.

6.   Members provided with house or quarters

A qualifying member or a re-joining member who—

(a)   is provided with a house or quarters free of rent, and

(b)   if the revoked provisions had continued in force would have been entitled to an allowance under regulation 49(11) or 50(3) of the 1987 Regulations,

is, subject to paragraph 7, entitled to an equivalent replacement allowance.

7. Variation and termination of replacement allowances

(1) Subject to sub-paragraph (2), in circumstances in which—

(a) a housing allowance or transitional rent allowance payable as mentioned in paragraph 2(2) or 4(2), or

(b) any of the housing emoluments mentioned in paragraphs 3(1), 5(1)(a) and 6,

would, if the revoked provisions had continued in force, have fallen to be reduced or discontinued, the replacement allowance in question is reduced accordingly or, if the effect of a discontinuance would have been that no housing emoluments remained payable, terminated.

(2) For the purposes of sub-paragraph (1) it is to be assumed that a housing allowance or transitional rent allowance would not have fallen to be reduced by reason of the member's being married to or sharing accommodation with another member of a police force appointed after 31st August 1994.

(3) In circumstances in which any allowance or housing emoluments mentioned in sub-paragraph (1) would, if the revoked provisions had continued in force, have fallen to be increased otherwise than under regulation 49A of the 1987 Regulations (which provided for biennial adjustment of housing allowances), or in which any new housing emoluments would in that case have become payable, the replacement allowance in question is increased accordingly.

[The amendments to sched 12 are made in accordance with SI 2000 No. 2013 except that the requirement to replace paras *3* to 10 have been shown here as a requirement to replace paras *4* to 10 in order to make sense of the amendment and to correct a suspected error in SI 2013.]

[These extracts have been amended in accordance with:
* The Police (Amendment) Regulations 1995 (SI 1995 No. 547);
* The Police (Amendment) Regulations 1995 (SI 1995 No. 2020);
* The Police (Amendment) Regulations 1996 (SI 1996 No. 699);
* The Police (Amendment) Regulations 1998 (SI 1998 No. 493);
* The Greater London Authority Act 1999 (Consequential Amendments) (Police) Order 2000 (SI 2000 No. 1549); and
* The Police (Amendment) Regulations 2000 (SI 2000 No. 2013).]

Appendix 14   Miscellaneous Statutory Materials

SEX DISCRIMINATION ACT 1975

PART I   DISCRIMINATION TO WHICH ACT APPLIES

1. Sex discrimination against women

(1)   A person discriminates against a woman in any circumstances relevant for the purposes of any provision of this Act if—

(a)   on the ground of her sex he treats her less favourably than he treats or would treat a man, or

(b)   he applies to her a requirement or condition which he applies or would apply equally to a man but—

(i)   which is such that the proportion of women who can comply with it is considerably smaller than the proportion of men who can comply with it, and

(ii)   which he cannot show to be justifiable irrespective of the sex of the person to whom it is applied, and

(iii)   which is to her detriment because she cannot comply with it.

(2)   If a person treats or would treat a man differently according to the man's marital status, his treatment of a woman is for the purposes of subsection (1)(a) to be compared to his treatment of a man having the like marital status.

2. Sex discrimination against men

(1)   Section 1, and the provisions of Parts II and III relating to sex discrimination against women, are to be read as applying equally to the treatment of men, and for that purpose shall have effect with such modifications as are requisite.

(2)   In the application of subsection (1) no account shall be taken of special treatment afforded to women in connection with pregnancy or childbirth.

2A. Discrimination on the grounds of gender reassignment

(1)   A person ('A') discriminates against another person ('B') in any circumstances relevant for the purposes of—

(a)   any provision of Part II,

(b)   section 35A or 35B, or

(c)   any other provision of Part III, so far as it applies to vocational training, if he treats B less favourably than he treats or would treat other persons, and does so on the grounds that B intends to undergo, is undergoing or has undergone gender reassignment.

(2) Subsection (3) applies to arrangements made by any person in relation to another's absence from work or from vocational training.

(3) For the purposes of subsection (1), B is treated less favourably than others under such arrangements if, in the application of the arrangements to any absence due to B undergoing gender reassignment—

(a) he is treated less favourably than he would be if the absence was due to sickness or injury, or

(b) he is treated less favourably than he would be if the absence was due to some other cause and, having regard to the circumstances of the case, it is reasonable for him to be treated no less favourably.

(4) In subsections (2) and (3) 'arrangements' includes terms, conditions or arrangements on which employment, a pupillage or tenancy or vocational training is offered.

(5) For the purposes of subsection (1), a provision mentioned in that subsection framed with reference to discrimination against women shall be treated as applying equally to the treatment of men with such modifications as are requisite.

3. Discrimination against married persons in employment field

(1) A person discriminates against a married person of either sex in any circumstances relevant for the purposes of any provision of Part II if—

(a) on the ground of his or her marital status he treats that person less favourably than he treats or would treat an unmarried person of the same sex, or

(b) he applies to that person a requirement or condition which he applies or would apply equally to an unmarried person but—

(i) which is such that the proportion of married persons who can comply with it is considerably smaller than the proportion of unmarried persons of the same sex who can comply with it, and

(ii) which he cannot show to be justifiable irrespective of the marital status of the person to whom it is applied, and

(iii) which is to that person's detriment because he cannot comply with it.

(2) For the purposes of subsection (1), a provision of Part II framed with reference to discrimination against women shall be treated as applying equally to the treatment of men, and for that purpose shall have effect with such modifications as are requisite.

4. Discrimination by way of victimisation

(1) A person ('the discriminator') discriminates against another person ('the person victimised') in any circumstances relevant for the purposes of any provision of this Act if he treats the person victimised less favourably than in those circumstances he treats or would treat other persons, and does so by reason that the person victimised has—

(a) brought proceedings against the discriminator or any other person under this Act or the Equal Pay Act 1970 or sections 62 to 65 of the Pensions Act 1995, or

(b) given evidence or information in connection with proceedings brought by any person against the discriminator or any other person under this Act or the Equal Pay Act 1970 or sections 62 to 65 of the Pensions Act 1995, or

(c) otherwise done anything under or by reference to this Act or the Equal Pay Act 1970 or sections 62 to 65 of the Pensions Act 1995 in relation to the discriminator or any other person, or

(d) alleged that the discriminator or any other person has committed an act which (whether or not the allegation so states) would amount to a contravention of

this Act or give rise to a claim under the Equal Pay Act 1970 or under sections 62 to 65 of the Pensions Act 1995,
or by reason that the discriminator knows the person victimised intends to do any of those things, or suspects the person victimised has done, or intends to do, any of them.

(2)   Subsection (1) does not apply to treatment of a person by reason of any allegation made by him if the allegation was false and not made in good faith.

(3)   For the purposes of subsection (1), a provision of Part II or III framed with reference to discrimination against women shall be treated as applying equally to the treatment of men and for that purpose shall have effect with such modifications as are requisite.

5. Interpretation

(1)   In this Act—

(a)   references to discrimination refer to any discrimination falling within sections 1 to 4; and

(b)   references to sex discrimination refer to any discrimination falling within section 1 or 2,
and related expressions shall be construed accordingly.

(2)   In this Act—

'woman' includes a female of any age, and

'man' includes a male of any age.

(3)   A comparison of the cases of persons of different sex or marital status under section 1(1) or 3(1), or a comparison of the cases of persons required for the purposes of section 2A, must be such that the relevant circumstances in the one case are the same, or not materially different, in the other.

PART II   DISCRIMINATION IN THE EMPLOYMENT FIELD

6. Discrimination against applicants and employees

(1)   It is unlawful for a person, in relation to employment by him at an establishment in Great Britain, to discriminate against a woman—

(a)   in the arrangements he makes for the purpose of determining who should be offered that employment, or

(b)   in the terms on which he offers her that employment, or

(c)   by refusing or deliberately omitting to offer her that employment.

(2)   It is unlawful for a person, in the case of a woman employed by him at an establishment in Great Britain, to discriminate against her—

(a)   in the way he affords her access to opportunities for promotion, transfer or training, or any other benefits, facilities or services, or by refusing or deliberately omitting to afford her access to them, or

(b)   by dismissing her, or subjecting her to any other detriment.

(3)   (repealed)

(4)   Subsections (1)(b) and (2) do not render it unlawful for a person to discriminate against a woman in relation to her membership of, or rights under, an occupational pension scheme in such a way that, were any term of the scheme to provide for discrimination in that way, then, by reason only of any provision made by or under sections 62 to 64 of the Pensions Act 1995 (equal treatment), an equal treatment rule would not operate in relation to that term.

(4A)   In subsection (4), 'occupational pension scheme' has the same meaning as in the Pension Schemes Act 1993 and 'equal treatment rule' has the meaning given by section 62 of the Pensions Act 1995.

(5)   Subject to section 8(3), subsection (1)(b) does not apply to any provision for the payment of money which, if the woman in question were given the employment, would be included (directly or otherwise) in the contract under which she was employed.

(6)   Subsection (2) does not apply to benefits consisting of the payment of money when the provision of those benefits is regulated by the woman's contract of employment.

(7)   Subsection (2) does not apply to benefits, facilities or services of any description if the employer is concerned with the provision (for payment or not) of benefits, facilities or services of that description to the public, or to a section of the public comprising the woman in question, unless—

(a)   that provision differs in a material respect from the provision of the benefits, facilities or services by the employer to his employees, or

(b)   the provision of the benefits, facilities or services to the woman in question is regulated by her contract of employment, or

(c)   the benefits, facilities or services relate to training.

(8)   In its application to any discrimination falling within section 2A, this section shall have effect with the omission of subsections (4) to (6).

. . .

17. Police

(1)   For the purposes of this Part, the holding of the office of constable shall be treated as employment—

(a)   by the chief officer of police as respects any act done by him in relation to a constable or that office;

(b)   by the police authority as respects any act done by them in relation to a constable or that office.

(2)   Regulations made under section 50, 51 or 52 of the Police Act 1996 shall not treat men and women differently except—

(a)   as to requirements relating to height, uniform or equipment, or allowances in lieu of uniform or equipment, or

(b)   so far as special treatment is accorded to women in connection with pregnancy or childbirth, or

(c)   in relation to pensions to or in respect of special constables or police cadets.

(3)   Nothing in this Part renders unlawful any discrimination between male and female constables as to matters such as are mentioned in subsection (2)(a).

(4)   There shall be paid out of the police fund—

(a)   any compensation, costs or expenses awarded against a chief officer of police in any proceedings brought against him under this Act, and any costs or expenses incurred by him in any such proceedings so far as not recovered by him in the proceedings; and

(b)   any sum required by a chief officer of police for the settlement of any claim made against him under this Act if the settlement is approved by the police authority.

(5)   Any proceedings under this Act which, by virtue of subsection (1), would lie against a chief officer of police shall be brought against the chief officer of police for the time being or, in the case of a vacancy in that office, against the person for the time being performing the functions of that office; and references in subsection (4) to the chief officer of police shall be construed accordingly.

(6)   Subsections (1) and (3) apply to a police cadet and appointment as a police cadet as they apply to a constable and the office of constable.

(7)   In this section—

'chief officer of police'—

(a)   in relation to a person appointed, or an appointment falling to be made, under a specified Act, has the same meaning as in the Police Act 1996,

(b)   in relation to any other person or appointment means the officer who has the direction and control of the body of constables or cadets in question;

'policy authority'—

(a)   in relation to a person appointed, or an appointment falling to be made, under a specified Act, has the same meaning as in the Police Act 1996,

(b)   in relation to any other person or appointment, means the authority by whom the person in question is or on appointment would be paid;

'police cadet' means any person appointed to undergo training with a view to becoming a constable;

'police fund' in relation to a chief officer of police within paragraph (a) of the above definition of that term has the same meaning as in the Police Act 1996, and in any other case means money provided by the police authority;

'specified Act' means the Metropolitan Police Act 1829, the City of London Police Act 1839 or the Police Act 1996.

(8)   In the application of this section to Scotland, in subsection (7) for any reference to the Police Act 1996 there shall be substituted a reference to the Police (Scotland) Act 1967, and for the reference to sections 50, 51 and 52 of the former Act in subsection (2) there shall be substituted a reference to sections 26 and 27 of the latter Act.

PART IV   OTHER UNLAWFUL ACTS

. . .

41.   Liability of employers and principals

(1)   Anything done by a person in the course of his employment shall be treated for the purposes of this Act as done by his employer as well as by him, whether or not it was done with the employer's knowledge or approval.

(2)   Anything done by a person as agent for another person with the authority (whether express or implied, and whether precedent or subsequent) of that other person shall be treated for the purposes of this Act as done by that other person as well as by him.

(3)   In proceedings brought under this Act against any person in respect of an act alleged to have been done by an employee of his it shall be a defence for that person to prove that he took such steps as were reasonably practicable to prevent the employee from doing that act, or from doing in the course of his employment acts of that description.

RACE RELATIONS ACT 1976

PART I   DISCRIMINATION TO WHICH ACT APPLIES

1.   Racial discrimination

(1)   A person discriminates against another in any circumstances relevant for the purposes of any provision of this Act if—

(a)   on racial grounds he treats that other less favourably than he treats or would treat other persons; or

(b)   he applies to that other a requirement or condition which he applies or would apply equally to persons not of the same racial group as that other but—

(i)   which is such that the proportions of persons of the same racial group as that other who can comply with it is considerably smaller than the proportion of persons not of that racial group who can comply with it; and

(ii)   which he cannot show to be justifiable irrespective of the colour, race, nationality or ethnic or national origins of the person to whom it is applied; and

(iii)   which is to the detriment of that other because he cannot comply with it.

(2)   It is hereby declared that, for the purposes of this Act, segregating a person from other persons on racial grounds is treating him less favourably than they are treated.

2.   Discrimination by way of victimisation

(1)   A person ('the discriminator') discriminates against another person ('the person victimised') in any circumstances relevant for the purposes of any provision of this Act if he treats the person victimised less favourably than in those circumstances he treats or would treat other persons, and does so by reason that the person victimised has—

(a)   brought proceedings against the discriminator or any other person under this Act; or

(b)   given evidence or information in connection with proceedings brought by any person against the discriminator or any other person under this Act; or

(c)   otherwise done anything under or by reference to this Act in relation to the discriminator or any other person; or

(d)   alleged that the discriminator or any other person has committed an act which (whether or not the allegation so states) would amount to a contravention of this Act,

or by reason that the discriminator knows that the person victimised intends to do any of those things, or suspects that the person victimised has done, or intends to do, any of them.

(2)   Subsection (1) does not apply to treatment of a person by reason of any allegation made by him if the allegation was false and not made in good faith.

3.   Meaning of 'racial grounds', 'racial group' etc.

(1)   In this Act, unless the context otherwise requires—

'racial grounds' means any of the following grounds, namely colour, race, nationality or ethnic or national origins;

'racial group' means a group of persons defined by reference to colour, race, nationality or ethnic or national origins, and references to person's racial group refer to any racial group into which he falls.

(2)   The fact that a racial group comprises two or more distinct racial groups does not prevent it from constituting a particular racial group for the purposes of this Act.

(3)   In this Act—

(a)   references to discrimination refer to any discrimination falling within section 1 or 2; and

(b)   references to racial discrimination refer to any discrimination falling within section 1,

and related expressions shall be construed accordingly.

(4)   A comparison of the case of a person of a particular racial group with that of a person not of that group under section 1(1) must be such that the relevant circumstances in the one case are the same, or not materially different, in the other.

PART II   DISCRIMINATION IN THE EMPLOYMENT FIELD

4.   Discrimination against applicants and employees

(1)   It is unlawful for a person, in relation to employment by him at an establishment in Great Britain, to discriminate against another—

(a)   in the arrangements he makes for the purpose of determining who should be offered that employment; or

(b)   in the terms on which he offers him that employment; or

(c)   by refusing or deliberately omitting to offer him that employment.

(2)   It is unlawful for a person, in the case of a person employed by him at an establishment in Great Britain, to discriminate against that employee—

(a)   in the terms of employment which he affords him; or

(b)   in the way he affords him access to opportunities for promotion, transfer or training, or to any other benefits, facilities or services, or by refusing or deliberately omitting to afford him access to them; or

(c)   by dismissing him, or subjecting him to any other detriment.

(3)   Except in relation to discrimination falling within section 2, subsections (1) and (2) do not apply to employment for the purposes of a private household.

(4)   Subsection (2) does not apply to benefits, facilities or services of any description if the employer is concerned with the provision (for payment or not) of benefits, facilities or services of that description to the public, or to a section of the public comprising the employee in question, unless—

(a)   that provision differs in a material respect from the provision of the benefits, facilities or services by the employer to his employees; or

(b)   the provision of the benefits, facilities or services to the employee in question is regulated by his contract of employment; or

(c)   the benefits, facilities or services relate to training.

. . .

32.   Liability of employers and principals

(1)   Anything done by a person in the course of his employment shall be treated for the purposes of this Act (except as regards offences thereunder) as done by his employer as well as by him, whether or not it was done with the employer's knowledge or approval.

(2)   Anything done by a person as agent for another person with the authority (whether express or implied, and whether precedent or subsequent) of that other person shall be treated for the purposes of this Act (except as regards offences thereunder) as done by that other person as well as by him.

(3)   In proceedings brought under this Act any person in respect of an act alleged to have been done by an employee of his it shall be a defence for that person to prove that he took such steps as were reasonably practicable to prevent the employee from doing that act, or from doing in the course of his employment acts of that description.

RACE RELATIONS (AMENDMENT) ACT 2000

Further extension of 1976 Act to police and other public authorities

1. Discrimination by police and other public authorities

After section 19A of the Race Relations Act 1976 (in this Act referred to as 'the 1976 Act') there is inserted—

'*Public authorities*

19B. Discrimination by public authorities

(1)   It is unlawful for a public authority in carrying out any functions of the authority to do any act which constitutes discrimination.

(2)   In this section "public authority"—

(a)   includes any person certain of whose functions are functions of a public nature; but

(b)   does not include any person mentioned in subsection (3).

(3)   The persons mentioned in this subsection are—

(a)   either House of Parliament;

(b)   a person exercising functions in connection with proceedings in Parliament;

(c)   the Security Service;

(d)   the Secret Intelligence Service;

(e)   the Government Communications Headquarters; and

(f)   any unit or part of a unit of any of the naval, military or air forces of the Crown which is for the time being required by the Secretary of State to assist the Government Communications Headquarters in carrying out its functions.

(4)   In relation to a particular act, a person is not a public authority by virtue only of subsection (2)(a) if the nature of the act is private.

(5)   This section is subject to sections 19C to 19F.

(6)   Nothing in this section makes unlawful any act of discrimination which—

(a)   is made unlawful by virtue of any other provision of this Act; or

(b)   would be so made but for any provision made by or under this Act.
. . .'

2. Specified authorities: general statutory duty

(1)   For section 71 of the 1976 Act (local authorities: general statutory duty) there is substituted—

'71. Specified authorities: general statutory duty

(1)   Every body or other person specified in Schedule 1A or of a description falling within that Schedule shall, in carrying out its functions, have due regard to the need—

(a)   to eliminate unlawful racial discrimination; and

(b)   to promote equality of opportunity and good relations between persons of different racial groups.

(2)   The Secretary of State may by order impose, on such persons falling within Schedule 1A as he considers appropriate, such duties as he considers appropriate for the purpose of ensuring the better performance by those persons of their duties under subsection (1).

(3)   An order under subsection (2)—

(a)   may be made in relation to a particular person falling within Schedule 1A, any description of persons falling within that Schedule or every person falling within that Schedule;

(b)   may make different provision for different purposes.

(4)   Before making an order under subsection (2), the Secretary of State shall consult the Commission.

(5)   The Secretary of State may by order amend Schedule 1A; but no such order may extend the application of this section unless the Secretary of State considers that the extension relates to a person who exercises functions of a public nature.

(6)   An order under subsection (2) or (5) may contain such incidental, supplementary or consequential provision as the Secretary of State considers appropriate (including provision amending or repealing provision made by or under this Act or any other enactment).

(7)   This section is subject to section 71A and 71B and is without prejudice to the obligation of any person to comply with any other provision of this Act.

. . .

71C.   General statutory duty: codes of practice

(1)   The Commission may issue codes of practice containing such practical guidance as the Commission think fit in relation to the performance by persons of duties imposed on them by virtue of subsections (1) and (2) of section 71.

. . .

71D.   General statutory duty: compliance notices

(1)   If the Commission are satisfied that a person has failed to comply with, or is failing to comply with, any duty imposed by an order under section 71(2), the Commission may serve on that person a notice ("a compliance notice").

(2)   A compliance notice shall require the person concerned—

(a)   to comply with the duty concerned; and

(b)   to inform the Commission, within 28 days of the date on which the notice is served, of the steps that the person has taken, or is taking, to comply with the duty.

(3)   A compliance notice may also require the person concerned to furnish the Commission with such other written information as may be reasonably required by the notice in order to verify that the duty has been complied with.

(4)   The notice may specify—

(a)   the time (no later than three months from the date on which the notice is served) at which any information is to be furnished to the Commission;

(b)   the manner and form in which any such information is to be so furnished.

(5)   A compliance notice shall not require a person to furnish information which the person could not be compelled to furnish in evidence in civil proceedings before the High Court or the Court of Session.

71E.   Enforcement of compliance notices

(1)   The Commission may apply to a designated county court or, in Scotland, a sheriff court for an order requiring a person falling within Schedule 1A to furnish any information required by a compliance notice if—

(a)   the person fails to furnish the information to the Commission in accordance with the notice; or

(b)   the Commission have reasonable cause to believe that the person does not intend to furnish the information.

(2)   If the Commission consider that a person has not, within three months of the date on which a compliance notice was served on that person, complied with

any requirement of the notice for that person to comply with a duty imposed by an order under section 71(2), the Commission may apply to a designated county court or, in Scotland, a sheriff court for an order requiring the person to comply with the requirement of the notice.

(3)   If the court is satisfied that the application is well-founded, it may grant the order in the terms applied for or in more limited terms.

(4)   The sanctions in section 71D and this section shall be the only sanctions for breach of any duty imposed by an order under section 71(2), but without prejudice to the enforcement under section 57 or otherwise of any other provision of this Act (where the breach is also a contravention of that provision).'

. . .

4.   Police: extension of liability of chief offciers etc.

After section 76 of the 1976 Act there is inserted—

'*Police*

76A.   Police forces

(1)   In this section, "relevant police office" means—

(a)   the office of constable held—

(i)   as a member of a police force; or

(ii)   on appointment as a special constable for a police area; or

(b)   an appointment as police cadet to undergo training with a view to becoming a member of a police force.

(2)   For the purposes of Part II, the holding of a relevant police office shall be treated as employment—

(a)   by the chief officer of police as respects any act done by him in relation to that office or a holder of it;

(b)   by the police authority as respects any act done by it in relation to that office or a holder of it.

(3)   For the purposes of section 32—

(a)   the holding of a relevant police office shall be treated as employment by the chief officer of police (and as not being employment by any other person); and

(b)   anything done by a person holding such an office in the performance, or purported performance, of his functions shall be treated as done in the course of that employment.

(4)   There shall be paid out of the police fund—

(a)   any compensation, costs or expenses awarded against a chief officer of police in any proceedings brought against him under this Act, and any costs or expenses incurred by him in any such proceedings so far as not recovered by him in the proceedings; and

(b)   any sum required by a chief officer of police for the settlement of any claim made against him under this Act if the settlement is approved by the police authority.

(5)   Any proceedings under this Act which, by virtue of this section, would lie against a chief officer of police shall be brought against—

(a)   the chief officer of police for the time being; or

(b)   in the case of a vacancy in that office, against the person for the time being performing the functions of that office;

and references in subsection (4) to the chief officer of police shall be construed accordingly.

(6)   A police authority may, in such cases and to such extent as appear to it to be appropriate, pay out of the police fund—

(a) any damages or costs awarded in proceedings under this Act against a person under the direction and control of the chief officer of police;

(b) any costs incurred and not recovered by such a person in such proceedings; and

(c) any sum required in connection with the settlement of a claim that has or might have given rise to such proceedings.

76B. Other police bodies etc.

(1) Section 76A applies in relation to the National Criminal Intelligence Service ("NCIS") and the National Crime Squad ("the NCS") as it applies in relation to a police force but as if any reference—

(a) to the chief officer of police were to the Director General of NCIS or of the NCS, as the case may be;

(b) to the police authority were to the Service Authority for the National Criminal Intelligence Service or the Service Authority for the National Crime Squad, as the case may be;

(c) to the police fund were to the service fund established under section 16 of the Police Act 1997 (NCIS service fund) or section 61 of that Act (the NCS service fund), as the case may be.

(2) Section 76A also applies in relation to any other body of constables or cadets as it applies in relation to a police force, but as if any reference—

(a) to the chief officer of police were to the officer or other person who has the direction and control of the body in question;

(b) to the police authority were to the authority by whom the members of the body are paid;

(c) to the police fund were to money provided by that authority.

(3) In relation to a member of a police force or a special constable who is not under the direction and control of the chief officer of police for that police force or, as the case may be, for the police area to which he is appointed, references in section 76A to the chief officer of police are references to the chief officer under whose direction and control he is.'

Special cases: procedural and other consequences

5. Criminal investigations and proceedings

(1) After section 57(4) of the 1976 Act (enforcement of Part III of that Act) there is inserted—

'(4A) As respects an act which is done, or by virtue of section 32 or 33 is treated as done, by a person in carrying out public investigator functions or functions as a public prosecutor and which is unlawful by virtue of section 19B, no remedy other than—

(a) damages; or

(b) a declaration or, in Scotland, a declarator;

shall be obtainable unless the court is satisfied that the remedy concerned would not prejudice a criminal investigation, a decision to institute criminal proceedings or any criminal proceedings.

(4B) In this section—

"criminal investigation" means—

(a) any investigation which a person in carrying out functions to which section 19B applies has a duty to conduct with a view to it being ascertained whether a person should be charged with, or in Scotland prosecuted for, an offence, or whether a person charged with or prosecuted for an offence is guilty of it;

(b)   any investigation which is conducted by a person in carrying out functions to which section 19B applies and which in the circumstances may lead to a decision by that person to institute criminal proceedings which the person has power to conduct; or

(c)   any investigation which is conducted by a person in carrying out functions to which section 19B applies and which in the circumstances may lead to a decision by that person to make a report to the procurator fiscal for the purpose of enabling him to determine whether criminal proceedings should be instituted; and

"public investigator functions" means functions of conducting criminal investigations or charging offenders;

and in this subsection "offence" includes any offence under the Army Act 1955, the Air Force Act 1955 or the Naval Discipline Act 1957 (and "offender" shall be construed accordingly).

(4C)   Subsection (4D) applies where a party to proceedings under subsection (1) which have arisen by virtue of section 19B has applied for a stay or sist of those proceedings on the grounds of prejudice to—

(a)   particular criminal proceedings;

(b)   a criminal investigation; or

(c)   a decision to institute criminal proceedings.

(4D)   The court shall grant the stay or sist unless it is satisfied that the continuance of the proceedings under subsection (1) would not result in the prejudice alleged.'

(2)   After section 65(4) of the 1976 Act (help for aggrieved persons in obtaining information etc.) there is inserted—

'(4A)   In section 19B proceedings, subsection (2)(b) does not apply in relation to a failure to reply, or a particular reply, if the conditions specified in subsection (4B) are satisfied.

(4B)   Those conditions are that—

(a)   at the time of doing any relevant act, the respondent was carrying out public investigator functions or was a public prosecutor; and

(b)   he reasonably believes that a reply or (as the case may be) a different reply would be likely to prejudice any criminal investigation, any decision to institute criminal proceedings or any criminal proceedings or would reveal the reasons behind a decision not to institute, or a decision not to continue, criminal proceedings.

(4C)   For the purposes of subsections (4A) and (4B)—

"public investigator functions" has the same meaning as in section 57;

"section 19B proceedings" means proceedings in respect of a claim under section 57 which has arisen by virtue of section 19B.'

. . .

EMPLOYMENT RIGHTS ACT 1996

200. Police Officers

(1)   Sections 8 to 10, Part III, Part IVA, sections 45, 45A, 47, 47B, 47C, 50 to 57B and 61 to 63, Parts VII and VIII, sections 92 and 93, and Part X (except sections 100 and 134A and the other provisions of that Part so far as relating to the right not to be unfairly dismissed in a case where the dismissal is unfair by virtue of section 100) do not apply to employment under a contract of employment in police service or to persons engaged in such employment.

(2)   In subsection (1) 'police service' means—

(a)   service as a member of a constabulary maintained by virtue of an enactment, or

(b)   subject to section 126 of the Criminal Justice and Public Order Act 1994 (prison staff not to be regarded as in police service), service in any other capacity by virtue of which a person has the powers or privileges of a constable.

POLICE (HEALTH AND SAFETY) ACT 1997

1.   Application of Part I of Health and Safety at Work etc. Act 1974 to police

After section 51 of the Health and Safety at Work etc. Act 1974 there is inserted—

'51A.   Application of Part to police

(1)   For the purposes of this Part, a person who, otherwise than under a contract of employment, holds the office of constable or an appointment as police cadet shall be treated as an employee of the relevant officer.

(2)   In this section "the relevant officer"—

(a)   in relation to a member of a police force or a special constable or police cadet appointed for a police area, means the chief officer of police,

(b)   in relation to a person holding office under section 9(1)(b) or 55(1)(b) of the Police Act 1997 (police members of the National Criminal Intelligence Service and the National Crime Squad) means the Director General of the National Criminal Intelligence Service or, as the case may be, the Director General of the National Crime Squad, and

(c)   in relation to any other person holding the office of constable or an appointment as police cadet, means the person who has the direction and control of the body of constables or cadets in question.

(3)   For the purposes of regulations under section 2(4) above—

(a)   the Police Federation for England and Wales shall be treated as a recognised trade union recognised by each chief officer of police in England and Wales,

(b)   the Police Federation for Scotland shall be treated as a recognised trade union recognised by each chief officer of police in Scotland, and

(c)   any body recognised by the Secretary of State for the purposes of section 64 of the Police Act 1996 shall be treated as a recognised trade union recognised by each chief officer of police in England, Wales and Scotland.

(4)   Regulations under section 2(4) above may provide, in relation to persons falling within subsection (2)(b) or (c) above, that a body specified in the regulations is to be treated as a recognised trade union recognised by such person as may be specified.'

. . .

4.   Rights of police not to be dismissed on certain grounds relating to health and safety

In Chapter III of Part X of the Employment Rights Act 1996 (right not to be unfairly dismissed) after section 134 there is inserted—

'134A.   Application to police

(1)   For the purposes of section 100, and of the other provisions of this Part so far as relating to the right not to be unfairly dismissed in a case where the dismissal is unfair by virtue of section 100, the holding, otherwise than under a contract of employment, of the office of constable or an appointment as police cadet shall be treated as employment by the relevant officer under a contract of employment.

(2)   In this section "the relevant officer"—

(a)   in relation to a member of a police force or a special constable or police cadet appointed for a police area, means the chief officer of police,

(b)   in relation to a person holding office under section 9(1)(b) or 55(1)(b) of the Police Act 1997 (police members of the National Criminal Intelligence Service and the National Crime Squad) means the Director General of the National

Criminal Intelligence Service or, as the case may be, the Director General of the National Crime Squad, and

(c)   in relation to any other person holding the office of constable or an appointment as police cadet, means the person who has the direction and control of the body of constables or cadets in question.'

INDEX